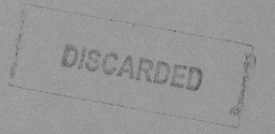

The
ENCYCLOPEDIA
of AQUARIUM
FISH

The
ENCYCLOPEDIA
of AQUARIUM
FISH

DICK MILLS

Consultant Editor: JOHN TULLOCK

BARRON'S

A QUARTO BOOK

First edition for the United States, its territories and dependencies
and Canada published in 2000 by Barron's Educational Series, Inc.

All inquiries should be addressed to
Barron's Educational Series, Inc.
250 Wireless Boulevard
Hauppauge, NY 11788
http://www.barronseduc.com

Library of Congress Cataloging-in-Publication
Data No. 99-69841

ISBN 0-7641-5300-5

QUAR.AQF

Conceived, designed, and produced by
Quarto Publishing plc
The Old Brewery
6 Blundell Street
London
N7 9BH

Editor: Clare Hubbard
Indexer: Pamela Ellis
Art Editor: Elizabeth Healey
Designer: Sheila Volpe
Photographers: Paul Forrester, Colin Bowling
Art Director: Moira Clinch
Publisher: Piers Spence

Manufactured in China by Regent Publishing Services Limited
Printed in China by Midas Printing Limited

9 8 7 6 5 4 3 2 1

PUBLISHER'S NOTE

Some photographs of individual fish may not correspond exactly with
the accompanying textual description. This may be due to the stress of
photographic conditions or because they have not yet acquired their
mature coloration.

CONTENTS

22 FRESHWATER FISH

Visitors to Monterey Bay aquarium marvel at the grandeur of the marine world.

Fishkeeping
is an incredible opportunity
to enter an entirely different world—
one can keep fishes from almost any area of the
world—from jungle streams to coral reefs, from fishes that
have been cultivated by man for thousands of years to the latest
"discovery." Because fish are from an environment quite different from our
own, the risk of them causing any disruption to the human way of life is minimal.
They will bring a host of benefits into the household—vivid colors, soothing scenes—
and most species need only a small amount of regular care. The total time spent on
maintaining the aquarium and caring for the fishes is far less than the time you will spend
gazing at it for enjoyment. With today's reliable and readily-available equipment there is no
need to fear the technical complexities. The variety of fishes that is available to the aquarist
is also larger than ever before. This supply tends to arrive at the dealer's outlet in good
condition, as modern air transport systems make the journey quicker and dealers understand
more about how to avoid stressing the fish during transit. Conservationists want to ensure
that fish species do not become extinct in the wild, and for this reason some species may
cease to be available until methods for rearing them on a commercial scale are
developed. Aquarists should be patient, support fish conservation efforts, and
focus their attention upon the hundreds of species already being
bred. Keeping an aquarium is a rewarding hobby. You will
learn how fishes live and feed, how they react to each
other, and how they reproduce. You could be
the person to unlock the secret of a
species that has proved impossible to
breed in captivity and thereby help
save it from extinction.

*Freshwater cichlids
often use overturned
flower pots as
breeding sites.*

HISTORY OF FISHKEEPING

Fishkeeping is an integral part of the modern age with many people keeping an aquarium as a form of decoration or for the soothing properties of the sound of water and the sight of beautiful fish gently swimming. However, fish have played a part in human culture for thousands of years, particularly in the Far East where the carp has been venerated as a symbol of masculinity. The Egyptians too held fish in high esteem, even considering them sacred. However, in the past, the purpose of keeping fish was for food rather than decoration.

The earliest known instances of "caring" for fish as living creatures for decoration are in China. Many historical documents have been discovered, illustrating families and young children admiring goldfish swimming in ceramic bowls. The Romans also displayed fish in aquariums, with freshwater species being kept as a food source, while the more unusual marine species perhaps lent an air of mystery and wonderment to their living quarters.

The increase in travel and exploration naturally led to more fish being "discovered" and many were brought back as souvenirs, either in the form of illustrations or as live specimens by travelers. The best-known reference to fishkeeping is probably that by Samuel Pepys, the seventeenth century diarist, who reported fishes being kept in a bowl and spoke of them as *"…being exceedingly fine."*

On a parallel course, scientists and those interested in natural flora and fauna were also investigating the relationships between living ecosystems. Soon an understanding of the "balance" of underwater life began to emerge and the prospect of actually being able to keep a collection of aquatic animals was soon to become reality. The Victorian age was full of both the curious and those willing to satisfy curiosities and the first public aquarium was opened in London in 1853. In the years following

this, many exhibitions were held and public aquariums with their displays of wonders of the deep proliferated. Of course, being on the grand scale, these did not immediately find counterparts of domestic proportions and so it was not until the early 1900s that the beginning of home aquarium-keeping may be noted. Out of necessity, many of the early aquariums were stocked with coldwater fishes—goldfish, together with fish caught from local streams and rivers.

Regular and reliable supplies of fishes from warmer waters had to wait for another important development to occur—rapid transportation systems—

Rustic Anglers; *a nineteenth century painting by Charles E. Wilson.*

although that was only part of the story. Even when tentative supplies of tropical fishes were established the means to maintain them reliably was not entirely in place. Accurate control of water temperature was still to come and much experimenting was undertaken to heat an aquarium so that the heat losses were counteracted by the heat supply in order to achieve some sort of constant warmth. Tales of naked flames playing on the underside of slate-bottom tanks were no exaggeration. The advent of electricity and the introduction of faster air transportation meant two things; heating water became controllable through the use of thermostatic devices and, having spent less time in transit, fishes arrived in much better physical condition and were therefore more likely to survive in captivity. While these major developments were taking place, every piece of practical information about fishkeeping was being collected and passed on to aquarists with similar aspirations. Local fishkeeping societies were formed and the key factor for success— knowledge—made the increase in interest more than just wishful thinking.

There are still many people alive today whose pioneering works have left a wonderful legacy for anyone contemplating keeping an aquarium.

Today's equipment is both reliable and foolproof. The ubiquitous microchip has ensured that temperature control need no longer depend on bulky, electro-mechanical devices; lighting systems can now imitate the exact spectrum of light that pours down on the coral reef; you can mix your own sea water to simulate that of anywhere in the world. As for the fish themselves, hardly a month goes by without a new species making its first appearance, and the very latest information about its care is quickly posted on the Internet.

Modern aquariums are built from the latest materials—not just from glass and silicone adhesives but also, new, one-piece extruded acrylic aquariums are now being made, not only for the home-sized aquarium but also for large public aquariums, which are fast approaching theme park status. The public's exposure to fishes and other aquatic animals is sure to sustain future interest. However, the emphasis is on responsible collection and maintaining natural stocks wherever possible. Public aquariums are taking great pains to ensure that the message gets across that fish are not status symbols but living creatures with particular requirements that you need to be aware of if you are going to care for them properly in a home aquarium. Allowing the fish to stay in their natural habitat until we discover how to care for them correctly is a small price to pay for having a living picture in our living rooms. The aquarist, with the time to research and monitor the daily lives of his fishes, their routine behavior, and breeding habits, has an important part to play in keeping fish alive in a healthy condition and swimming freely, whether it be on the reef, in a jungle stream, or in the home aquarium.

Swimming with marine fish in warm coral seas can also encourage marine fishkeeping when the vacation is over.

FISH PHYSIOLOGY

Throughout this work, continual reference has been made to the visual attraction of fishes in all their shapes, sizes, and colors. While all these collectively may be of fascinating interest to us, to the fish they have a much more important purpose, for each, in its turn, provides the fish with its way of existence. Through our appreciation of these diverse purposes, we can assess and provide for the fish's needs while it is in our care.

With aquarium fish there are physiological factors that are necessarily different to those found in terrestrial animals due entirely to the difference in the living environment —water instead of air. The most important differences allow the fish to breathe, control its bodily fluid levels, and maintain its position; other abilities such as coloration for species identification, camouflage, or defense ploys may also be found in terrestrial animals.

The Guppy's upturned mouth finds food at the surface.

The Corydoras' downturned mouth makes bottom-feeding easy.

GILLS AND OTHER OXYGEN-EXTRACTING ORGANS

Fish require oxygen and to get it into their bloodstream they must extract it from its dissolved state in the surrounding water. Water is drawn in through the mouth and passed over a set of gill membranes, before being expelled past the gill cover (operculum) at the sides of the head. As the passing water comes into contact with the gill membranes, oxygen is transfused into the tiny blood vessels and is then conducted around the fish's body by the heart. At the same time, some waste products (including ammonia) are excreted from the gills as the now oxygen-deficient water is expelled.

Where the natural waters of a species are likely to be oxygen-deficient, the fishes native to that habitat have developed an auxiliary breathing organ. This consists of a labyrinth-like construction of tissue, located just behind the gills, in which atmospheric air can be stored and oxygen extracted from it. This organ is basically exclusive to fishes such as gouramies, in the anabantid family.

OSMOTIC REGULATION

Wherever two fluids of differing strengths are separated by a membrane there is an automatic tendency for the water from the weaker fluid to pass through the membrane to dilute the stronger. In a fish, this can be quite a problem. For example, in a freshwater species the internal body fluids are stronger than the water surrounding the fish; water then passes through the fish's skin (the membrane) and would cause the fish's body to swell up. To counteract this, the freshwater fish has to excrete as much water as possible. For marine fishes, the problem is reversed with water constantly being lost from the fish's body into the surrounding water. In order to maintain correct body fluid levels, the marine fish has to literally "drink like a fish" excreting little water but ensuring it does excrete salts.

OSMOTIC REGULATION
The freshwater Siamese Fighter must excrete copious amounts of water that continuously passes into its body. The marine clownfish replaces lost water from its body by literally "drinking like a fish."

There are only a few examples of fishes that can move comfortably between both fresh and salt waters on a regular seasonal basis and these include the salmon and the eel. Other species, inhabiting estuaries, are also able to tolerate changing conditions as the tides move in and out.

POSITIONING

In most species a special organ, the swim bladder, automatically regulates the fish to give it "neutral buoyancy" at any level in the water. The swim bladder also acts as an amplifier in those fishes that emit sounds.

Some bottom-dwelling fishes that live in fast moving or turbulent waters have other adaptations that help keep them in their chosen position and not be swept away. Apart from having flattened bodies which reduces the aerofoil effect, which would tend to lift them off the bottom, they have their pelvic fins fused together to form a suction disc by which means they can stick to any surface. The development of a "sucker mouth" in some fishes also helps in this respect, with the subsequent supposed hindrance to breathing being literally by-passed by a special spiracle arrangement in the head, that allows breathing to continue despite having to cling on to a surface (or even eat algae) with the mouth.

FINS

Usually there are seven fins on a fish (some may have eight, others only five)—the dorsal, anal, caudal, pectoral, and pelvic fins. Some fins are singular and are arranged in the vertical plane, while other fins are paired, allowing for more flexible movement.

Two of the single fins, the dorsal and anal, help to stabilize the fish from rolling from side to side when moving. The third, the caudal fin, is generally used to supply propulsion, although some marine species, such as triggerfishes and seahorses, use their dorsal fins instead.

The anal fin has a further function during spawning in many species—notably the livebearing group of fishes. In the male fish, the usual fan-shaped anal fin is folded into a rod-like structure called the "gonopodium," through which sperm is injected into the female's vent. This physical feature is clearly visible in livebearing species such as guppies, swordtails, platies, and mollies, but is less obvious in other male livebearers. Other fishes in the egg-laying groups, such as male characins, may have tiny hooks on the anal fin which help hold the female fish alongside the male during the spawning embrace.

The paired fins can be used for abrupt changes of movement and direction, acting as brakes or hydroplanes. In some particular instances, the pelvic fins may be developed into bony processes, as in freshwater angelfish for example, or long filaments equipped with taste cells, as in gouramies. There are examples of fishes whose fins do not comply with these general rules. For example catfishes have an extra fin behind the dorsal fin, rainbowfishes have two distinct dorsal fins, and triggerfishes have no pelvic fins.

BODY

The body shape of any fish provides an indication of the lifestyle it leads. Slender, torpedo-shaped bodies with crescent-shaped caudal fins are just right for speedy swimming either in short sharp dashes or more prolonged periods. A disc shape, usually compressed laterally, makes it easy for the fish to slip in among aquatic plant stems or reed beds; because of the larger surface area presented to the water by their bodies, these fish are generally found in slow moving or stationary waters. Vertically compressed fish such as marine rays are naturally best-suited to the bottom area where their body color patterns blend into the substrate.

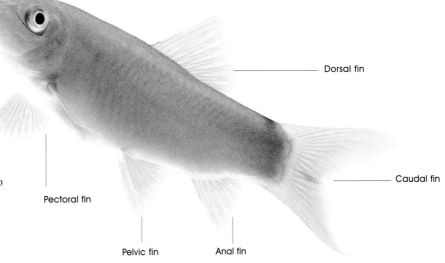

Dorsal fin

Caudal fin

Pectoral fin

Pelvic fin

Anal fin

SCALES

As water is such a dense medium, anything that makes moving through it easier is to be welcomed. Apart from their streamlined shape, fish also rely on their skin covering to help them effortlessly slip through the water. Scales are thin bonelike plates that cover the skin of most fishes and are laid in an overlapping fashion from the snout to the tail. There are two main types of scales—ctenoid, which have tiny teeth along their rear edge, and cycloid, which are smooth-edged. The purpose of scales is two-fold; they give the body a very smooth exterior and they also protect the vital internal organs from physical damage and, to some extent, deter parasites from burrowing into the skin. The scales, together with any other skin covering the fish may have (some have overlapping bony plates called "scutes"), are covered with a thin layer of mucus which gives the fish even more "slipperiness" and which, in times of physical damage, can be thickened to afford some protection over a healing wound.

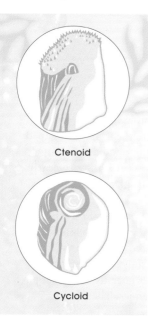

Ctenoid

Cycloid

Where scales or bony scutes are entirely missing from the fish, the skin itself forms the body covering. With such "naked" species, the use of some medications may not be tolerated.

SENSES

Like human beings, fish have the five senses of sight, hearing, taste, touch, and smell, although their senses of taste and smell are far superior to ours. Because of their permanent immersion in water, fishes do not need eyelids to protect their eyes. One exception to this is the Mudskipper (*Periophthalmus sp.*) which, while on its regular excursions on to dry land, has to periodically rotate its eyes in their sockets to re-moisten them. Another exception to the norm is found in Foureyes (*Anableps sp.*) which, as its name implies, appears to have four eyes—one pair looking above the water's surface and one pair looking below. There is really only one pair of eyes, but each is divided horizontally, by a membrane, into two halves.

Generally, nocturnal species have larger eyes, (for efficient light-gathering) than daytime-active species. The Archerfish (*Toxotes sp.*) uses its eyes to spectacular effect. Although it can see any perching insect on a branch above the water's surface, it has to compensate for refraction and "offset" its aim as it spits a jet of water to knock its prey from the safety of its perch. Although sight is important, it is of little use where the water is dark and muddy, so the fish has to use other methods for both navigation and location of food. The Blind Cave Fish (*Astyanax sp.*) is a prime example of how

The Squirrelfish has large eyes, indicative of a nocturnal feeder.

nature has compensated for this. Over the years, living in underground caves, the fish has lost the use, or rather the need for, eyes and these have become atrophied, the fish navigating its way around the water and finding food by other means.

Taste buds, for want of a better description, are often found at the ends of pelvic fins or in pits over the body (especially the head) and in the barbels surrounding the mouth. Unlike human beings, in fish the nostrils are exclusively used for smelling and play no part in the breathing process.

Because water is such a dense medium, the tiniest vibration is rapidly transmitted through it and herein lies the secret of how fish navigate safely and accurately through the murkiest waters. Along the flanks of the fish you may be able to see a line of pierced scales (generally along the middle of the body, although this "lateral line" as it is termed, may not be complete). These openings are the outer end of a nervous system that receives and translates vibrations and changes in water pressure to enable the fish to sense the structure of its surroundings.

It may be difficult to assess exactly how a fish hears as, strictly speaking, the perception of sound is basically translating received vibrations. While some fish perceive sound through a set of bones (the "Weberian ossicles") connected to the swim bladder, it is also likely that the fish "hears" via the lateral line system too.

Some fish are extremely sophisticated navigators, whether it is just cruising around the aquarium in the dark or crossing oceans to reach their original freshwater spawning grounds. The use of electro-magnetic force fields is employed by the African Elephant-nose to build up a map of its surroundings. It creates a magnetic field around itself and detects alterations in its strength (influenced by obstacles, other fish, etc.)

COLOR

The color of a fish serves several purposes—species recognition, camouflage as a means of defense, and as a warning deterrent. The typical "metallic" luster of a fish is created by deposits of guanin, a waste product, immediately beneath the scales. Depending upon the angle at which these scales are laid down, different reflected colors can be seen. Denser colors are made up of pigmentation in chromatophores, "color cells," over which some fish species have great control, enabling them to change their color to suit their environment and mood—to fade when frightened, or intensify when excited or in breeding condition.

DEFENSE

One popular defense that many fishes have at their disposal is an arsenal of prickly spines, either on the body or on the tips of the fins. The Stickleback is a good example. Triggerfish use these spines to lock themselves into a small crevice to prevent capture. Some marine species have other methods of defense—pufferfishes inflate their bodies, lionfishes have venom in the hollow spines of their fins, and stingrays have one or more large, sharp dorsal spines.

Color patterns are another widely used means of defense. Any number of cryptic patterns will disguise the fish's true body shape. Many fish and invertebrates are "over-colored" to advertise that their flesh is poisonous and, therefore, not good to eat. False "eyes" are positioned at the wrong end of the body to draw any predator's attention away from the real vital organ, which is often hidden in a dark patch too.

REPRODUCTION

In general terms, fish reproduction in the aquarium may be considered to comprise two distinct methods—egg laying and livebearing. In either case an egg needs to be fertilized by male sperm, but it is how this procedure is accomplished that categorizes fish reproduction for the hobbyist.

EGG SCATTERING Eggs are expelled into the water by the female and are fertilized by the male fish's milt (sperm), which is released into the water at approximately the same time. The fertilized eggs are

The Pufferfish (right) inflates to deter predators while the Stonefish (below) relies on camouflage to hide its presence.

then left to hang in plants or to be swept away by water currents to hatch, being totally disregarded (except perhaps as a meal) by the parents. The fishkeeper may be required to take steps to prevent egg eating during spawning.

EGG DEPOSITING Much more attention is given to the fertilized eggs and subsequent fry by egg depositing species. Some marine species deposit eggs in protective "egg cases" which become attached to submerged obstacles by tendrils, but no further parental attention is given. Others are care-givers much like the freshwater cichlids.

NESTING In freshwater anabantids, the male fish creates a bubble nest, made of saliva bubbles and sometimes pieces of plant material. In most cases, this nest floats on the water's surface and the male tries to coax a willing female beneath the nest into which the fertilized eggs are placed (or naturally float) following a spawning embrace. Some catfishes also build bubble nests, but these are usually placed under an aquatic plant below the water's surface. Among marine fishes, the Royal Gramma constructs a nest of algae and debris, into which he coaxes one or several females in turn. After spawning, the female is driven away and he guards the nest.

MOUTHBROODING After the eggs are fertilized on the substrate spawning site, the female takes the whole batch of eggs into her throat cavity to hatch. This procedure takes some time (10 days or so) during which time the mother does not feed. After the fry leave the mother's throat they will continue to treat her as a safe retreat and will dash back into her mouth at the first sign of danger. Mouthbrooding is found among freshwater cichlids and in marine groups such as jawfishes and cardinalfishes.

LIVEBEARING Livebearing female fishes have their eggs fertilized internally by means of the male's gonopodium. The gonopodium is the term given to the male's modified anal fin which can be swung in an arc to perform the sperm transfer when the female fish is alongside. There are two methods of fry development—ovoviviparous and viviparous. The former is the development of the young in individual yolk sacs within the female's body. In the latter case fry actually take nourishment from the female by means of a placenta-like connection known as the "trophotaenia." Both types of gestation take about 30 days, before the tiny fish are released as fully functional miniatures.

A further distinction between the two groups of livebearers is that females of the first group can store sperm within their bodies and can, therefore, produce successive batches of young fish without the need to be re-mated with a male fish. Females of the second group do not share this capability. As a guide, all fish that are recognized as "cultivated livebearers" (i.e., guppies, swordtails, platies, and mollies) belong to the first group. Male fish whose anal fin is merely notched after the first few front rays belong to the Goodeidae family whose female's lack the ability to store sperm.

A female angelfish cleans a selecting spawning site.

A male angelfish fertilizes eggs previously laid by the female

BASIC AQUARIUM NEEDS

No matter where fishes come from—fresh or saltwater, tropical or temperate climates, they all have the same basic need for space, suitable water conditions, warmth, lighting, decoration, feeding, and maintenance.

SPACE

Fish need living space. Depending upon the species, this may mean room to swim in a constantly active manner, an area in which to stake out a territory, or simply room to get away from other fish. Space, when translated into aquarium dimensions, is also another way of looking at providing adequate oxygenated water for the fish, and here the beginner should understand that a certain size "space" is not suitable for every type of fish, even if each of these individual fishes is the same physical size.

A rough guide as to how many fish any aquarium will hold is to allocate a set water surface area to a set "length" of fish (don't include the caudal fin in this measurement). Below are some useful guidelines:

TROPICAL FRESHWATER: 1 in (2.5 cm) body length of fish per 12 sq. in (75 sq. cm) of water surface

COLDWATER FRESHWATER: 1 in (2.5 cm) body length of fish per 30 sq. in (190 sq. cm) of water surface

TROPICAL MARINE: 1 inch (2.5 cm) body length of fish per 48 sq. in (300 sq. cm) of water surface

Taking a "standard" size aquarium, 36 x 12 inches (90 x 30 cm), which offers a water surface area of 432 sq. in (2,700 sq. cm) the following total "body length" of fish can be kept:

TROPICAL	COLDWATER	MARINE

$\dfrac{432}{12}$ = 36 in (90 cm) of fish

$\dfrac{432}{30}$ = 14 in (36 cm) of fish

$\dfrac{432}{48}$ = 9 in (22.5cm) of fish

WATER CONDITIONS

All species should be given excellent and well-maintained water conditions. Generally, freshwater fish, whether tropical or coldwater, can be maintained in correctly treated municipal tap water but will do best, especially when breeding is attempted, when given those water conditions that approximate their place of origination—this may be conditions in the wild or those at their commercial hatching station.

Obviously, marine fishes will need to be kept in saltwater. While some fishkeepers may be lucky enough to live near to the sea (and can guarantee a source of clean sea water), most hobbyists keep their marine species in synthetic salt water made up from commercially available "salt mixes." The degree of "saltiness" is monitored by checking the specific gravity (S.G.) of the aquarium water. It should be maintained at the correct level and water of the same S.G. used to "top up" the aquarium after water changes. "Topping up" evaporation losses is done using "fresh" water as no salts will have been lost and adding more saltwater will upset the S.G.

The problem with keeping fish in static water is that it is not exposed to the self-cleaning procedures as in a river or the sea, and even in these natural areas the fish has the ability to swim away to cleaner areas. The main problem is ammonia-based compounds that build up in the water as a result of the fishes' excretions, and the decay of food and plant debris. However, an efficient filtration system, which should embody mechanical (straining out visible suspended matter), chemical (adsorbing organics from the water), and biological (converting ammonia-based compounds into less harmful nitrate) functions will ensure water deterioration is kept to a minimum. Regular partial water changes (about 15–20% per month) will also keep the level of dissolved toxins down to a manageable level by simple replacement with new water and siphoning out sediment in the same process.

INSTALLING A BIOLOGICAL FILTER
Fit the base plate of the biological filter into the bare tank.

Attach an up-lift tube to the base plate (a powerhead can be connected later.)

A good depth of substrate (at least 2 in/ 5 cm), provides a home for nitrifying bacteria.

When breeding is to be attempted, the question of water quality is often of prime importance and sometimes changes have to be made to trigger spawning activity. Fish may have to be subjected to temperature changes (up or down, depending on the species) or more specific water conditions may have to be created. This requires measurement of the water's acidity or alkalinity (pH), and its softness or hardness. All necessary adjustments, especially to temperature and pH, must be made gradually, over a period of time and in small increments.

Modern filtration units generally encompass mechanical and chemical methods, although they will eventually act "biologically," to a degree, once they become established. They are available in units conveniently designed by the manufacturers to suit standard tank sizes. Marine aquariums will require more sophisticated filtration equipment than freshwater, as they need biological filtration with the added provision for removing excessive organic material from the water by protein skimming. Aeration—once a mandatory addition to any aquarium—is no longer quite as necessary (the rising bubbles of air from an airpump via a diffuser or airstone, can be added for visual effect, if so desired) but sufficient agitation of the water surface to assist gas exchanges, is generally provided automatically by the action of the filtration equipment.

HEATING
Both freshwater and marine tropical species will require the water to be maintained at a steady temperature, usually around 75°F (24°C). Heating is not necessary in coldwater fishkeeping except in special circumstances—for instance, to increase the rate of growth in young goldfish or, with garden ponds, to maintain an opening in any ice which would otherwise cover the pond.

Heating the aquarium is achieved by using submersible, thermostatically controlled heating elements. Also available are microchip controlled devices that provide audible and visual alarms should the set temperatures be exceeded and can keep a log of maximum and minimum temperatures.

The size of the aquarium heater should be chosen to suit the size of the aquarium. Roughly 10 watts of electricity per 1.3 gallons (5 liters) of water should be adequate for an aquarium in the average living room. In large

Mount heating units clear of the substrate to allow good water circulation.

aquariums (over 35.4 inches/90 cms in length) the wattage required can be shared between two heating units, one placed at either end of the aquarium, to ensure an even distribution of heat. Using an oversize heater in a small aquarium means that it will operate in frequent short bursts, but the real danger is of rapidly overheating the aquarium should the thermostat fall into the permanently "on" position.

External liquid crystal thermometers provide at-a-glance monitoring.

Many beginners worry about power failures, thinking that the resulting temperature drop will have fatal consequences for their fish. A point worth remembering is that the aquarium is quite an effective "heat store" and, as it is usually situated in a warm room, it will take several hours for the temperature to drop to harmful levels. Furthermore, as the temperature will fall slowly, there is even less chance of the fish becoming stressed. Perhaps the real threat is from the failure of aerating and filtration equipment which will lead to losses, especially if the aquarium is overcrowded.

LIGHTING
Light enables freshwater aquatic plants to photosynthesize, and in the process to remove carbon dioxide from the water and add a little surplus oxygen. Algae fulfill the same role in marine systems. Also, many corals have symbiotic algae living within them that also require light.

The tropical "day" is typically around 12 hours of daylight and most aquariums function well when provided with between 12 to 14 hours of light. You may need to experiment with the strength of the light (as opposed to the time period) in order to produce luxuriant plant growth. Doubling the amount of light (achieved either by fitting another lamp or an additional reflector to the existing lamp) will improve matters but you must ensure that you then have enough plants to make use of the extra light energy and not simply encourage the growth of unsightly, and often unwanted, algae. A further doubling of the light may be needed in a marine "reef style" aquarium in which large amounts of invertebrate life is kept.

It is the norm for fluorescent lamps to be used for aquarium lighting. These give an even light and they operate at a cooler temperature than tungsten lamps, which have a shortened life in the enclosed space of the aquarium hood. There are several types of fluorescent lamps available to provide the exact "hue" of lighting required; some tubes emit extra energy at certain points of the lighting spectrum to encourage plant growth or to give special effects—moonlight for instance—or to bring out the colors of the fish.

If an aquarium has a water depth greater than the usual 15 to 17.5 inches (38 to 45 cm), the use of pendant metal halide or mercury vapor lamps may be preferred. In this instance, the regular aquarium hood has to be dispensed with and the lamp fitting hung immediately above the water's surface, taking care to protect the very hot lamps from splashes by fitting a cover glass.

SHELTER AND DECORATION

Despite the fact that we want to be able to see our fishes clearly, a bare aquarium is not a particularly aesthetic sight and the fish will not display their true colors or feel at ease within it. Generally, freshwater aquariums are furnished with a layer of substrate material in which aquatic plants can root. (The substrate can also function as a biological filter if so desired). The presence of plants serves several purposes in the aquarium—as decoration, as natural water cleansers, as shelter, as spawning sites for the fish, and, in some cases, as food. If the tank contains herbivorous fish live aquatic plants can be replaced with realistic plastic replicas.

Stones and rocks

Marine aquariums can be decorated with the skeletons of dead corals or with living rock and living corals, too. The choice of fish may have to be modified to exclude species that would prey on live invertebrates in this instance.

Many species of fish appreciate the opportunity to "get away from it all" at some time of the day or night. Rocky retreats form an important part of their needs. Make sure that all rock work is firmly anchored and that it does not form a trap behind which a fish could become imprisoned. It is best to use rocks that are impervious

Pebbles

and that will not dissolve so that the water quality is not affected. Realistic looking rock work is available made from synthetic materials that will not affect the water.

FEEDING

All fish require food, but not all fish eat the same foods or feed in the same way. Most tropical freshwater fishes are omnivores, although there are some that are more herbivorous. Coldwater freshwater fish are also omnivores. Tropical marine fish can be more selective in their eating habits, some preferring algae and green materials, others preying on smaller fish and invertebrates.

By looking at the position of the mouth, a fish's method of feeding becomes clear: an upward tilting mouth indicates a fish that takes its food from the water's surface (insect life and floating foods); a terminally-situated mouth at the tip of the snout on a horizontal line through the center of the body usually belongs to a mid-water swimmer that catches its food as it falls through the water or, if equipped with teeth, bites at any passing meal. A downturned mouth, accompanied by a flat-bottomed profile, often has barbels (fleshy "whiskers") associated with it: this is an ideal arrangement for locating and collecting food from the riverbed and shows that its owner is a bottom-dwelling species. Many species of bottom-dwelling fish may be nocturnal by nature and require feeding at night.

All the dietary needs of an aquarium fish have been carefully researched by aquarium food manufacturers and, apart from some marine species, there isn't a fish in captivity whose nutrional needs cannot be met. Foods can be in various forms—flake, pellet, granular, tablet, powder, or liquid—and made in different formulae according to a fish's natural preferences and age.

Naturally, fish in the wild do not receive the same diet but catch their own foods, much of which is available in freeze-dried or frozen forms. Some live foods can be cultured or collected by the hobbyist and fed to aquarium fish. The occupants of the rain-barrel—mosquito, midge, and gnat larvae—are all relished by aquarium fish. Garden worms may be collected and other types—whiteworm, grindalworm, microworm, etc.—maybe cultured for feeding to young fry. Another excellent cultured food is brine shrimp, *Artemia salina*, whose eggs may be dry-stored for years before being hatched in warm salt water to produce minute shrimps, ideal for feeding to baby fishes.

Sand and gravel

Plants

Novorift

Freeze-dried *Tubifex*

Flake food

Bloodworm

Freeze-dried *Daphnia*

Ant eggs

A catfish's downturned mouth and flat-bottomed profile enables it to locate food on the aquarium floor.

MAINTENANCE

One of the attractions of fishkeeping is that it can be considered a "low maintenance" interest. A daily check would obviously include a "fish count"—do this at feeding times when all the fish should gather together. Investigate any missing fishes, however, bear in mind that nocturnal species usually hide away during "tank light." Once the aquarium is established there is no need to check water temperatures—an occasional touch on the glass with the hand is usually enough to confirm that everything is fine.

Weekly tasks may involve siphoning off any accumulated mulm or detritus that has collected on the substrate. If an undergravel biological filter is used, an occasional raking over of the substrate (and the use of a gravel washer) will ensure that the oxygenating water flow through the substrate is unimpeded. Remove algae from the front glass but leave any growth on the side and rear walls of the aquarium for the benefit of any herbivores. Prune back any excessive plant growth and use by re-rooting any cuttings to provide new plants. Keep cover glasses scrupulously clean so that all the available light energy reaches the aquarium.

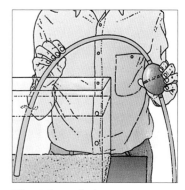

This siphon tube has a "squeeze to start" bulb.

Regular partial water changes, coupled with filtration, keep the levels of dissolved (possibly toxic) material to a minimum. When siphoning out the desired proportion of old aquarium water, take it from the substrate level to remove detritus at the same time. Keep some of the old water to use when rinsing out foam blocks from the filter; this way you will not kill off any beneficial bacteria that might be living in the foam. For marine aquariums, it is best to prepare replacement synthetic saltwater ahead of water changes. Make sure that the specific gravity and temperature of the new water matches that of the water removed.

Waterborne crustacea such as *Daphnia* and *Cyclops* can provide extra food for fish but there is a risk that if these are collected from the wild they may introduce disease into the aquarium. There is a similar risk with *Tubifex* worms, which come from polluted muddy riverbanks. As frozen or freeze-dried forms of these foods are available, it is not worth risking the health of your fishes to use suspect "live" forms.

Overfeeding kills more fish than anything else: not from producing overweight fishes but from polluting the water with uneaten food. It is best to feed "little and often," making sure that the fish eat what is given within a few minutes at most. It is often the case, especially when the whole family may be taking a turn at looking after the aquarium, that fish always seem to be on the look out for food, with the result that everyone gives them food whenever convenient, usually without telling the other members of the family that they have done so. The result? Chronic overfeeding.

The annual vacation often brings worries as to how the fish will cope during the owner's absence. Leaving a box of food with a non-fishkeeping neighbor is risky as they can be tempted to feed the fish the whole box. Either leave daily, prepacked mini-food parcels or just leave the fish to their own devices. Provided they have been regularly fed with quality foods prior to the vacation, they will come to no harm if left unfed—they may even clean up the aquarium in your absence.

Young angelfish feed from a tablet stuck to the front glass.

An angle-mounted razor blade makes for easy removal of algae from the aquarium glass.

AVAILABILITY AND CHOICE

The next time you are kept waiting for a flight at an overcrowded airport, think about the fact that at any one time there are probably more fish flying around the skies than people, such is the volume of trade. It follows, therefore, that there is an enormous selection available at your local dealers, just waiting for you to choose from. The basic guidelines are that fish should be chosen for their compatibility to each other, their foods, and the aquarium set-up.

SIZE

It should be fairly obvious, for economic reasons, that all imported fish (of whatever species) destined for the aquarium will be juveniles—you get more to a transportation bag per box that way. However, it might not be so obvious to the beginner that fishes, depending upon the species, grow at different rates. So, from a selection of young specimens that are all the same size, in a few months time there could be an enormous variation in size. When selecting a fish, always try to find out its adult size or the size that it is likely to attain under captive conditions.

COMPATIBILITY

The largest and fastest developing fish from a group of mixed juvenile specimens could become aggressive and look upon some of the remainder as potential food. Work on the principle that big fish always eat little ones. The sheer bulk of a large fish can upset smaller fishes; for example the larger fishes will get to the food first and eat most of it. Small fish may also be intimidated about showing themselves when there is a large, dominant species in the tank. Sometimes it's not just size but natural instinct that turns a fish into a social liability. It is not always confined to specific fishes; some fish, particularly some varieties of marines, simply cannot tolerate another fish that might have the same body shape or coloration as their own. Part of the problem has to be lack of "space" in captivity when compared to the areas that the same fish would enjoy in nature.

Conversely, while some fish are definite loners, there are those that are gregarious and do best when kept in small schools. In nature, this is a defensive ploy of safety in numbers, but if you keep just one of these type of fish as a solitary specimen in the comparative safety of the home aquarium, it will pine for company of its own kind.

Vibrant colors and interesting breeding behavior are but two of fishkeepings many attractions.

You will learn how the physical features of the fish, particularly the position of the mouth, dictates at what water depths the fish normally swims, i.e., where food is most plentiful. Use this information to select a cross section of fish from the three strata of water levels—top, middle, and bottom—so that your aquarium represents the whole underwater scene. Once you become a more experienced aquarist, you can specialize in single level fishes.

If you have a particular preference for a certain type of fish then make sure that the aquarium suits them. For instance, "tall" fish such as freshwater angelfish and discus look their best (and feel more comfortable) in a deep aquarium; fishes with streamlined, torpedo-shaped bodies, which are constantly on the move, require a long tank.

CHOOSING YOUR FISH

Always buy carefully and, if possible, do some research on your intended purchases beforehand. Reject any fish you cannot care for in terms of space or food; never buy a fish that is showing signs of stress (folded down fins is a good guide in freshwater fishes), or that has spots, pimples, cuts, sores, wounds, split (or missing) fins, is bloated or too thin, cannot swim effortlessly, or maintain its position in the water. With marine fish it is also prudent to ask to see the fish feeding.

Never buy fish the first time you see them in a dealer's tanks. Buying the newest arrival may keep you ahead of your fishkeeping friends but it is better to wait until the dealer has quarantined the fish and it has settled down first; after all, it may suddenly show signs of disease or exhibit some antisocial behavior in the first few days in your care. Find out what water conditions the fish is used to—you may have to set up a special acclimatization tank for it until you can change it over gradually to the water conditions prevailing in your system.

Try to shop at a local dealer. He will most certainly be keeping fish in the same water conditions as you are, and should know all the pitfalls about doing so. Buying fish from suppliers outside your locale is a bit of a gamble unless you know about the water conditions. By regularly using a local dealer, he will get to know your previous purchases and be in a better position to advise you.

Place the "travel home" bag in the aquarium for 15 to 20 minutes to equalize the water temperatures...

...before opening the bag and letting the fish...

...swim out into their new home. By doing this the fish will not be subjected to stress through thermal shock.

A colorful freshwater collection.

In addition to researching your fish in books and seeing them at your dealers, a good place to see fish in more or less their adult form is at a public aquarium or at a local fishkeeping society's annual show. With the latter, you can reap vital words of wisdom from local people about fish—how to care for them, how to breed them, and so on. You may even be able to buy some of their surplus stock, safe in the knowledge that they are likely to be free from disease and are already acclimatized to your local water conditions.

Don't be in a hurry to get your new fish into your aquarium. Take your time to acclimatize it properly and not give it more stress. Float the transportation bag in the aquarium until the temperature of the water in each is the same. To acclimatize the fish to the quality of the water, add some of the aquarium water to the bag during this temperature equalization period.

To avoid adding potentially contaminated water to your aquarium, gently transfer the fish by net to the main aquarium and discard the water in the plastic bag. Some hobbyists try to divert the attention of fish already in the aquarium away from the newcomer by giving them a light feed at the time of release. In the event of adding a fish with known territorial tendencies, another trick is to slightly rearrange all the rock work in the aquarium before release, so that every fish has to look for a new home at once and the newcomer will not then be "shut out." When adding new fish to the marine aquarium, you may like to do so with the tank lights switched off.

HEALTH PROBLEMS

The last thing any would be fishkeeper wants to think about is health risks to the fish—surely in a well cared for aquarium environment, where everything is under strict control, nothing untoward can possibly happen. Unfortunately fish are susceptible to outbreaks of disease and, just like humans, disease can be the result of stress. Remember, being trapped in a small room with complete strangers is hardly a stress-free situation and this is what some fish must feel like in the aquarium. Disease can be unwittingly introduced into the aquarium through new additions of fish and plants, contaminated transportation water, and all manner of other causes.

PREVENTING DISEASE

The first (and best) defense against disease is to obtain healthy fish right from the start and then try to keep them that way. Never buy fish from a dealer's tank in which other fish are obviously sick, dying, or dead. If you have the facilities, try to quarantine new stock for two to three weeks before adding them to your main collection. Even the apparently simple act of introducing the fish into your tank can be traumatic unless the water temperatures (and quality) have been equalized as far as possible before releasing the fish into its new home.

The second most important defense against disease is to know your fishes and what constitutes their normal behavior. Observing the fishes as they go about their daily routine should provide you with useful information, so that anything out of the ordinary should be obvious right away. There is always a reason for unnatural behavior and these signs are the earliest warning you will get about the possible onset of disease.

If you do spot any irregularities check up on the fishes' environment first. If you've been lazy about water changes, overfed the fish, or generally neglected the aquarium, correct these things before investigating further. There is an adage in fishkeeping that states "Look after the water and the fish will look after themselves." Indeed, many health problems can be prevented through better aquarium management.

RECOGNIZING DISEASE

It would be unfortunate if all of your newly-acquired fish succumb to disease at once and, barring equipment failure, this hardly ever happens. It is not always easy to diagnose correctly, particularly where the problem may be internal with few external, visible symptoms. In these cases, once external symptoms do become visible it may be too late to effect a remedy.

Sometimes the disease may be a secondary effect with the real reason for the problem hard to find or unsuspected. Fish seen gasping at the surface might give the impression that oxygen in the water is in short supply, when, in fact, there is plenty of it available but they cannot make good use of it as a result of the parasites coating their gills. It may be taken as a general guide that the more common ailments seen on the fish can be treated successfully, with only a few requiring expert attention or the use of antibiotics supplied by your veterinarian. However, the first step is to recognize the symptoms of the disease positively before treatment begins.

This fish's deformed back is due to vitamin deficiency.

Visible spots, an increased breathing rate, and "flicking" against firm objects in the aquarium are all signs of a parasitic attack. Viruses (or rather the effect of) are much more difficult to diagnose but may cause a bloated body, inability to swim or position properly, and the feces trailing from the vent may be white. Most viral infections, particularly in marine fish, may be regarded as secondary infections which can often be traced back to poor aquarium conditions.

Healthy angelfishes and gouramies in an established aquarium.

DISEASES

WHITE SPOT (*Ichthyophthiriasis*) This illness is easy to identify as the fish's body and fins are covered with tiny white spots. There is a theory held by many hobbyists that this disease is always present in the aquarium and is just waiting to strike should the fish become stressed. The responsible parasite has a three-part cyclic life cycle, living on the fish, encysting at the substrate, and free-swimming as it searches for a new host. It is only during its free-swimming phase that it can be treated. Treating the whole aquarium with a remedy is reliably effective. The marine fish equivalent is called *Cryptocaryon*.

VELVET If you can imagine the visible symptoms of White Spot but with much smaller spots, you will have a good idea of what Velvet looks like. The tiny spots give a dusty covering effect. Both freshwater and marine fish are affected and the parasites are similar species of *Oodinium* and *Amyloodimium*. Both respond to treatments available at aquatic dealers.

FUNGUS (*Saprolegnia*) The body of the fish may break out into tufts of "cotton wool-like" growths. Remedies are effective, although a basic salt bath (for freshwater species only) may also bring about a cure.

MOUTH "FUNGUS" This particular ailment requires different treatment than fungus and usually only reacts favorably to antibiotics available from your veterinarian.

SKIN AND GILL FLUKES Affected fish scratch themselves against rocks or the bottom substrate as though to dislodge the parasite of skin flukes (*Gyrodactylus*); excess mucus may be produced. Fishes with gill flukes (*Dactylogyrus*) have difficulty breathing and will hang at the water's surface, panting, with wide, inflamed gills. Remedies are effective but the fish should be removed to a hospital tank while their main home is disinfected and re-set up.

FIN ROT The tissues between the fin rays degenerate. This ailment is not a disease in itself but often sets in as a secondary effect, when a fin gets torn or as a result of dirty aquarium water conditions. The real remedy (or prevention) is to maintain clean water conditions at all times.

DROPSY The scales stand out from the body due to a build up of fluid within the body. There is no reliable cure and the fish is best euthanized.

LYMPHOCYSTIS This is a seasonal ailment often striking when coldwater fish (especially those kept outside in a pond) are emerging from winter conditions into spring and are at their weakest before their natural immune systems kick in for the summer. The cauliflower-like growths may look unpleasant but very often, when left

White spot

Velvet

Fungus

Fin rot

Carcinoma

untreated, will fade away of their own accord. A similar condition occurs in marine fishes, and is thought to be associated with dietary deficiencies.

TUBERCULOSIS The fish loses color and gradually gets thinner due to an internal ailment that is usually too far advanced once the external signs are noticed. The victim is best euthanized.

CARCINOMA A tumor whose accelerated growth impinges on the vital organs of a fish, causing deformity and eventually, death.

TREATING DISEASE

Usually, the contagious diseases are best treated in the tank, with the whole population of the tank being treated. For freshwater collections (tropical and coldwater) this is usually unproblematic, but with marine fishes you must only treat the fishes. The reason for this is that many remedies are lethal to certain invertebrates. You may also want to check that any remedy used will not severely disrupt any beneficial nitrifying bacteria in the filtration system. It is vital to use any remedy in strict accordance with the manufacturer's instructions. Dosing the aquarium correctly relies on one vital piece of information—how much water your aquarium holds.

If you continue running the filtration system that includes activated carbon as one of the filter media you might as well not bother to use the remedy, for the carbon will extract it from the water before it has a chance to do its job. Additionally, many remedies put an extra burden on the oxygen consumption of the aquarium, so extra aeration during treatment is recommended. Once the remedy has done its job, the water must be cleared of it. A few partial water changes should restore the tank to normality.

If the treatment does not appear to be working, don't just add a dose of a different remedy. This could be disastrous should the ingredients in each remedy interact to produce a toxic substance. Always return the water to normal conditions before trying a new remedy.

The use of antibiotics is a difficult area as regulations differ on a country by country basis. All are only obtainable through a veterinarian and can either be administered by him or, where the antibiotic is contained within a medicated fish food, by the fishkeeper.

Sometimes a single fish may be struck down, or maybe you spot the disease at its earliest appearance on one particular fish. Often with parasitic attacks, a short term bath in saltwater (for freshwater species) and freshwater (for saltwater species) may effect a rapid cure, but always remove the fish from the bath as soon as it appears to become distressed.

FRESHWATER FISH

While the major groups of popular freshwater aquarium fishes are represented, the experienced fishkeeper will be aware that some species are conspicuous by their absence, for example killifishes. They are spectacularly beautiful and have a most interesting method of breeding. Unfortunately, they are not available worldwide, their care is somewhat specialized, and the majority of aquatic dealers do not stock them. However, thanks to the growth of specialist societies, obtaining stocks is becoming easier. Monthly aquarium journals will be able to direct you to a source of these fishes. It is for these reasons that killifishes have been omitted. Another consideration is whether or not to encourage the keeping of endangered species; those whose "in-captivity" care is known to be problematical or species that have been "color-injected." Where such conflicts occur, information is provided.

EXPLANATORY NOTES FOR CARE SYMBOLS

FEEDING
HERBIVORE prefers mainly vegetable matter in diet.

OMNIVORE all foods taken, any preferences are noted in the text.

PREDATOR mainly a carnivorous diet, which often includes other fish.

COMPATIBILITY
SINGLE SPECIMEN to be kept as a solitary specimen within a community collection, or, alternatively, in a separate species tank with its own kind.

COMMUNITY FISH may be kept in a mixed collection with due regard to any extremes of physical size between species being kept together.

SAFE WITH SMALL FISH large fish with a peaceful disposition toward smaller tank mates.

SAFE WITH INVERTEBRATES relevant to marine species only.

EASE OF KEEPING
Indicated on a scale of 1 to 10, with 1 being the easiest.

1 to 3—the easiest species to care for.
5 to 8—extra care needed.
9 to 10—most difficult.

5 to 8—intermediate numbers indicate that the species requires special care (diet, water conditions, temperature adjustments, incompatibility with other fish, etc.) beyond those required for normal community collections.
9 to 10—you should consider most carefully your reasons for wanting to keep any species with this high rating.

SIZE
IN THE WILD indicates adult size (in inches and centimeters), of species in nature.

IN CAPTIVITY indicates size species may attain in captivity under ideal conditions, i.e., plenty of room, correct feeding, and optimum water conditions.

NOTE
Within each aquarium group the fish species are ordered alphabetically, first according to their biological family affiliation, then by species within each family.

CYPRINIDS

Fishes within the Cyprinidae family make excellent aquarium subjects for three main reasons. First, there are over 1,500 species to choose from; second, they are very adaptable; and third they range in size from around 1 inch (2.5 cm) up to 1 foot (30 cm), meaning that there is a family member to suit any fishkeeper.

Rasbora pauciperforata
RED-STRIPED RASBORA

Unlike some other fish species, cyprinids do not have teeth in their mouth, but this is balanced by the presence of pharyngeal teeth in the throat, which help grind up food as it passes to the stomach. Close examination of the arrangement of these teeth enables ichthyologists to identify, or distinguish between, the various species.

Within aquarium circles, three main tropical groups stand out in the family: these are the barbs, danios, and rasboras. While cyprinids are obviously members of the Cyprinidae family, this family is but one within the larger Order, Cypriniformes. Another family within this Order is the Family Cobitidae, the popular group of fishes known as loaches. They are included in this chapter for ease of reference.

The popularity of cyprinids is not limited to tropical species. The family also boasts several genera that are classed as coldwater fishes—in the context of this book

this means those fishes that do not require heated aquarium water. The favorite among coldwater cyprinids is, of course, the goldfish, *Carassius auratus*, together with its many aquarium-developed varieties. Cyprinids are called "opportunistic spawners"—ripe adults that come together to spawn using egg scattering methods and for the most part do not exercise any parental care—although the spawning method of *Rasbora heteromorpha* differs from the family norm as it deposits its eggs beneath plant leaves.

Cyprinids are generally easy to keep, being hardy, resistant to disease, and very accommodating in their housing and feeding needs. Apart from a varied diet, all they require is a clean, suitably furnished aquarium (usually with plants, although some species do have vegetarian tendencies). For breeding, it is normal practice to use a separate breeding aquarium, set up with spawn-saving precautions as cyprinids have a taste for their own eggs.

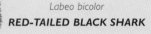

Labeo bicolor
RED-TAILED BLACK SHARK

TIGER BARB
Tiger Barbs are best kept as a shoal to deter "fin-nipping" by otherwise isolated specimens.

FEATURED IN THIS SECTION

BARBS

The name "barb" is derived from the scientific name *Barbus* which is Latin for "bearded," a reference to the small barbels, or fleshy whiskers, found around the mouth area. The popularity of barbs is quite justifiable as they offer the fishkeeper a range of fishes suitable for all sizes of aquarium. In physical terms, most barbs are deep-bodied, almost rhomboid- or diamond-shaped, although there are some more sleekly-built species found in related groups other than *Barbus*. The majority of barbs suitable for the aquarium are modest in size. All are omnivorous, accepting a range of foods, have a hardy constitution, are active aquarium subjects, and have a compatible disposition toward other tank inhabitants.

BARBUS ARULIUS

FAMILY: *CYPRINIDAE*
COMMON NAME: *ARULIUS BARB*

This active shoaling fish, a native of southern India, has three ill-defined vertical black bands that reach halfway down the flanks of its blue-gray body; the beginnings of a fourth band appear at the base of its dorsal fin. The top-half of the body is green-yellow, accentuated with attractive iridescences when the fish is viewed under light coming from the side. The dorsal fin is black, and the male has long extensions to its first few rays; the female's dorsal fin is not as pronounced. Reddish-yellow anal caudal fins appear in both sexes, and the gill cover features a shiny area. The scales are marked by tiny, reflecting dots with dark edges; a pair of barbels are present on the upper lips.

SPECIAL CARE: The Arulius Barb cruises all levels of water and is happy in an aquarium with normal-sized planting, where it may nibble soft-leaved plants. Although it accepts most types of water, it breeds better in soft water, which mimics its natural habitat. Caution must be exercised when breeding, since it tends to eat its own eggs; a small brood of around 100 fry can be expected. Smaller fishes may not feel comfortable in its presence, due to Arulius Barb's constant movement around the tank.

FEEDING

COMPATIBILITY

EASE OF KEEPING

SIZE

5 in (12 cm) 4 in (10 cm)

BARBUS CONCHONIUS

FAMILY: *CYPRINIDAE*
COMMON NAME: *ROSY BARB*

From the Assam and Bengal areas of north-eastern India, this long-established favorite takes its popular name from the copper-red metallic sheen on the flanks of the male. The dorsal, anal, and pelvic fins of the male are black; these markings are less pronounced on the female, and she can be further identified by a plumper body shape when viewed from above. In recent years, a new long-finned strain has been developed.

FEEDING

COMPATIBILITY

EASE OF KEEPING

SIZE

6 in (15 cm) 3 in (7.5 cm)

SPECIAL CARE: It is most content in a well-planted tank with some top shading from floating plants. Ideal for fishkeepers attempting aquarium breeding for the first time, this species is very prolific, although precautions must be taken to prevent parents from eating the eggs.

BARBUS EUGRAMMUS

FAMILY: *CYPRINIDAE*
COMMON NAME: *ZEBRA BARB; STRIPED BARB*

An active, fast-swimming fish found in Malaysia, Sumatra, and Borneo. It has an elongated body with a high dorsal fin and a deep, boat-shaped belly. Its pale golden yellow body is crossed horizontally by a number of even, dark stripes. The male is differentiated from the female by its slimmer body with more pronounced stripes; the plumper female has a higher arched back.

SPECIAL CARE: A middle- and lower-level swimmer, the Zebra Barb is peaceful and coexists well with a community of fishes mixed in size. It is omnivorous and will thrive in most types of water.

FEEDING

COMPATIBILITY

EASE OF KEEPING

SIZE

6 in (15 cm) 4.1 in (10.5 cm)

BARBUS FASCIATUS

FAMILY: *CYPRINIDAE*
COMMON NAME: *EMBER OR "MELON BARB"*

Native to Malaysia and parts of Indonesia, the Ember or "Melon Barb" has an elongated body and a pronounced convex curve to the ventral contour. The body color is pale golden brown, which shades down to silver in females and to a pink hue in males. The male's dorsal fin is black with a red edge, while the pelvic fins are reddish, and the anal fin is black with a dark edge. Characteristically, the female's fins are much less intensely colored, with only a hint of a dark edge showing on the dorsal and anal fins. When mature, the male fish shows intense pink-red coloration with the black bars almost becoming merged together by an overall dusting of black. The earlier specific name of *B. melanympyx* gave rise to the popular name of Melon Barb.
SPECIAL CARE: This is a peaceful fish, and is suitable for a community collection of mixed-sized fishes. It requires a well-planted aquarium and will accept most types of water. Note that if trying to breed this species, precautions need to be taken against egg eating.

FEEDING

COMPATIBILITY

EASE OF KEEPING

SIZE
6 in (15 cm) 4 in (10 cm)

BARBUS FILAMENTOSUS

FAMILY: *CYPRINIDAE*
COMMON NAME: *FILAMENT BARB; BLACK-SPOT BARB*

Found in the waters of southern India and Sri Lanka, the body shape of the Filament Barb is equally contoured and fairly elongated, especially in juveniles. Juvenile coloration is more striking than adult, with three bars running down the yellowish-brown flanks, beginning at the front of the dorsal fin and ending at the caudal peduncle. The dorsal fin shows some red but it is the caudal fin that has the most attractive coloration, with a red patch in each fin lobe, together with a darker outer area and a white tip. With adulthood, the body of this fish undergoes a marked change. The dark bars disappear (with the exception of a patch just above the anal fin) and the body deepens considerably, taking on a silvery greenish-yellow color. The most obvious feature is found at the tip of the male's dorsal fin where filaments extend from the first few rays, hence the popular name. The plumper females do not have the dorsal fin extensions.
SPECIAL CARE: This fish is a prolific breeder, but care does need to be taken to prevent egg eating. It can tolerate lower than normal aquarium temperatures.

FEEDING

COMPATIBILITY

EASE OF KEEPING

SIZE
6 in (15 cm) 6 in (15 cm)

BARBUS GELIUS

FAMILY: *CYPRINIDAE*
COMMON NAME: *GELIUS BARB; GOLDEN DWARF BARB*

Native to northeastern India and Bengal, this fish has a high back and a deep belly, coupled with a slender caudal peduncle. The basic body color is golden brown on the upper parts, shading to silver below. Look out for extra coloration in the caudal peduncle of males, although this may not be visible unless the fish feels really at home in its surroundings. A few irregular smudged black patches appear on the body, and the general effect is of a sparkling, alert little fish.
SPECIAL CARE: This species is an active, gregarious fish and should be kept in a small shoal. It is not intimidated by larger fishes and is determined to get its own share of food. It makes an excellent subject for a species tank or a community of small fishes. It does not need high temperatures for general upkeep or for breeding. It will tolerate waters as warm as 72°F (22°C) and can survive in temperatures as low as 65°F (18°C). Only mature adults should be used for breeding.

FEEDING

COMPATIBILITY

EASE OF KEEPING

SIZE
1.5 in (4 cm) 1.5 in (4 cm)

SYMBOL KEY

FEEDING
Herbivore
Omnivore
Predator

COMPATIBILITY
single specimen
community fish
safe with small fish
safe with invertebrates

EASE OF KEEPING
scale of 1 to 10
(with 1 being easiest to keep)

SIZE
in the wild
in captivity

BARBUS LATERISTRIGA

FAMILY: *CYPRINIDAE*
COMMON NAME: *SPANNER BARB; "T" BARB*

The Spanner Barb is native to Southeast Asia: Thailand, Indonesia, and Malaysia. In juvenile fish, the body shape is slightly elongated. The basic body color is a light golden brown with silvery-metallic iridescences caused by the lighter rear edge on the scales. The head may be dark with a silvery lower-half and two impressive black vertical bars cross the body. A broadening black line runs horizontally to connect the two bars, running across the caudal peduncle into the central rays of the caudal fin itself. The top and bottom edges at the front of the caudal fin are black, as are the leading areas of the dorsal and pelvic fins. With the onset of maturity, the body color deepens and the dramatic patterning become less distinct. The fish takes on a blackish-pink hue and looks much coarser.
SPECIAL CARE: This middle- and lower-level swimmer should be kept in a normally-planted aquarium. It will tolerate most types of water. A peaceful fish, it can be kept with a community of fishes of varying sizes. Care should be taken that parents do not eat the eggs.

FEEDING

COMPATIBILITY

EASE OF KEEPING

SIZE

7 in (18 cm) 6.3 in (16 cm)

BARBUS NIGROFASCIATUS

FAMILY: *CYPRINIDAE*
COMMON NAME: *BLACK RUBY BARB; PURPLE-HEADED BARB*

This fish inhabits the hilly streams of Sri Lanka. It is a stocky fish with a high back, deep belly, and a tapering caudal peduncle. Its basic body color is pale golden yellow and it has some iridescences. Three broad but faint black bars cross the body vertically, the foremost not quite reaching the pectoral fins. A short, often indistinct black bar crosses the head between the eyes. The scales have dark forward edges and silver rear edges. The dorsal, pelvic, and anal fins are cloudy black, with the caudal fin less so. When it is in breeding condition, males take on a spectacular change of color; the whole body turns deep red, with the head region turning to deep purple. The fins become jet black and are constantly held erect during proud displays to the female. Females can be further distinguished by their plumper bodies.
SPECIAL CARE: Although hardy, this easy-to-spawn fish may be among the first to contract White Spot Disease, should the responsible parasite be present in the tank. It is an ailment from which it recovers easily, however, using readily available remedies.

FEEDING

COMPATIBILITY

EASE OF KEEPING

SIZE

2.5 in (6.5 cm) 2.4 in (6 cm)

BARBUS "ODESSA"

FAMILY: *CYPRINIDAE*
COMMON NAME: *ODESSA BARB*

This fish has an elongated body but its body depth falls between that of the deeper-bellied barbs and the slimmer species. Its body coloration is a pale greenish-brown with clearly defined scales. It is notable for the two dark blotches on the flanks, one just behind the gill cover, and the other just ahead of the caudal peduncle. The difference between the sexes is easy to recognize, especially at breeding times. The male develops a broad red band along the body and some dark speckling in the dorsal fin. Like most egg-laying species, the female is generally duller in coloration and plumper through the body. This fish is not found in the wild. It takes its name from the town in the Ukraine where it was first reported to have entered Russia and come to the notice of hobbyists. Close examination of the species brings some clues as to its possible ancestry.
SPECIAL CARE: A fish that is easy to keep in a well-planted aquarium. Tolerant of most types of water, this fish swims in the middle- and lower-levels of the tank and can be kept in a community of fishes. This fish breeds well in captivity, but take care that parents do not eat the eggs.

FEEDING

COMPATIBILITY

EASE OF KEEPING

SIZE

N/A 2.5 in (6 cm)

BARBUS OLIGOLEPIS

FAMILY: *CYPRINIDAE*
COMMON NAME: *CHECKER BARB*

The common name of this brilliant colored fish derives from the checkerboard pattern of its scales: each one has a dark edge and a dark front area. A native of the streams and rivers of Indonesia and Sumatra, the Checker Barb has a golden yellow-brown hue. Its body is more elongated compared to body depth, although the dorsal and ventral contours are relatively arched. The area beneath the dark line along the flanks is sometimes less checkered, especially in the male. Generally, the fins are reddish-orange, veering toward a more yellowish hue on the female, and edged with black on the male.
SPECIAL CARE: This fish looks best in a well-planted aquarium with open swimming spaces, where it will cruise the middle and lower levels in shoals. Although males often display to each other, they are not violent. During spawning, the Checker Barb's coloring intensifies, and as with many species, parents must be prevented from eating their eggs.

FEEDING

COMPATIBILITY

EASE OF KEEPING
1

SIZE
2 in (5 cm) 2 in (5 cm)

BARBUS PENTAZONA

FAMILY: *CYPRINIDAE*
COMMON NAME: *FIVE-BANDED BARB*

FEEDING

COMPATIBILITY

EASE OF KEEPING
5

SIZE
2 in (5 cm) 2 in (5 cm)

Originating in the streams of Borneo, Malaysia, and Sumatra, this peaceful fish has a slightly more elongated shape than other vertically-striped barbs. Its body color is a yellowy, golden brown. Five prominent dark bands cross the body, with the first band passing through the eye, but none reaching completely around the ventral surface. Most of the fins have some reddish tinting at the base, less so with the caudal fins, and two pairs of barbels appear at the mouth. The female is plumper with a paler color than the male. The Five-Banded Barb has a number of subspecies; identification involves studying the differences around the front bar, with some species carrying an extra, very thin bar at the rear of the caudal peduncle.

SPECIAL CARE: A middle- and lower-level swimmer, this fish mixes well with a community of different species. It tends to be less bold in captivity than its close relatives, and so prefers plenty of lush plants for use as hiding places in the aquarium. Content in most types of water, its eggs must be protected during breeding.

BARBUS SACHSI

FAMILY: *CYPRINIDAE*
COMMON NAME: *GOLDEN BARB*

FEEDING

COMPATIBILITY

EASE OF KEEPING
4

SIZE
4 in (10 cm) 3 in (7.5 cm)

Commonly found in the streams of Singapore, the Golden Barb may also be a native of similar waterways in south Vietnam. Its overall yellowish hue contrasts with a subtle silvery sheen on the ventral surface. Some fishes—especially juveniles—have dark vertical streaks distributed randomly, but these tend to fade with age. The female is plumper than the male. Golden Barb's similarity to B. *"schuberti"* makes the two species difficult to differentiate.

SPECIAL CARE: Content in most types of water, with an average level of planting. Take the usual precautions during breeding to keep parents from eating the eggs.

BARBUS "SCHUBERTI"

FAMILY: *CYPRINIDAE*
COMMON NAME: *SCHUBERTI BARB*

The mystery surrounding the origin of this fish—not found in the wild—revolves around a Mr. Thomas Schubert in the United States. The name B. *"schuberti"* was given to the species in his honor, but has yet to be confirmed. Some suggest that this elongated, plump-sided fish is an unusual (and unnatural) color strain of B. *semifasciolatus*. Yellow in hue, with dark green metallic areas around the top-half of the body, it has a number of dark speckles on the dorsal surface. Larger blotches run along the top lateral line, and a dark vertical blotch crosses the tip of the narrow caudal peduncle. The eyes are reddish, and the fins are red streaked with yellow; the base of the caudal fin and the two lobes also have bright red areas. Females are more plump than males.

SPECIAL CARE: Despite arguments over its true origin, the Schuberti Barb breeds very readily in captivity, which accounts for the constant replenishment of the species. A middle- to lower-level swimmer, it can be kept easily in a mixed community of fishes.

FEEDING

COMPATIBILITY

EASE OF KEEPING

SIZE

N/A   3 in (7.5 cm)

BARBUS SCHWANENFELDI

FAMILY: *CYPRINIDAE*
COMMON NAME: *TINFOIL BARB*

Native to the rivers and lakes in Borneo, Sumatra, and Thailand, where it is a food fish, the Tinfoil Barb is also known by the Malay names *Lampam Sungai* and *Kepiat*. An active fish, its diamond-shaped body has a high dorsal profile and a moderately deep belly. The greenish-brown tinge of the dorsal surface shades down to silver flanks with well-defined scales. The head is small, with dark, gold-rimmed eyes. The triangular dorsal fin has a concave rear edge and is black with a red base; the pelvic and anal fins are bright red-orange. The large, deeply forked caudal is a softer red and has black edges at the top and bottom lobes.

FEEDING

COMPATIBILITY

EASE OF KEEPING

SIZE

17.7 in (45 cm) 12 in (30 cm)

SPECIAL CARE: The Tinfoil prefers soft water in a spacious aquarium where it has plenty of room to eat undisturbed. It has a great liking for green vegetation: aquarium plants are not suitable, but surface plants such as duckweed (*Lemna*), *Riccia*, etc. make a perfect meal. Although peaceful, this barb may be a little too active for smaller fishes in its tank. The adults make excellent exhibition specimens.

BARBUS TETRAZONA

FAMILY: *CYPRINIDAE*
COMMON NAME: *TIGER BARB*

From the fresh waterways of Sumatra, Indonesia, and Borneo, the body of this fish is crossed by four vertical dark bands, suggesting tiger stripes: one band through the eyes; one on each side of the dorsal fin, and one at the extreme rear end of the caudal peduncle. The snout of the male is bright red. The female is less intensely marked. The scales have dark edges, and these markings can be exaggerated by feeding the fish proprietary color-enhancing foods.

FEEDING

COMPATIBILITY

EASE OF KEEPING

SIZE

2.8 in (7 cm) 2.5 in (6.5 cm)

SPECIAL CARE: When kept with slower-moving, long-finned fishes it may develop a tendency toward fin nipping. This can be avoided by keeping the barb in sufficient numbers so that it does not annoy other species.

BARBUS TETRAZONA

FAMILY: *CYPRINIDAE*
COMMON NAME: *RED TIGER BARB*

FEEDING

COMPATIBILITY

EASE OF KEEPING

SIZE

2.8 in (7 cm) 2.5 in (6.5 cm)

Developed using selective aquarium-breeding techniques, its body has a red hue, with very few of the original bands showing. Breeders have produced "albino" variants; the dark vertical bands are replaced with white. However, in most cases, the albino claim cannot be justified because the eyes remain pigmented.

SPECIAL CARE: See Tiger Barb.

BARBUS TETRAZONA

FAMILY: *CYPRINIDAE*
COMMON NAME: *GREEN TIGER BARB*

FEEDING

COMPATIBILITY

EASE OF KEEPING

SIZE
2.8 in (7 cm) 2.5 in (6.5 cm)

An aquarium-developed strain of *B. tetrazona*, the Green Tiger Barb is sometimes known as the Moss-Banded Barb. The coloring of the fins remains the same but the overall coloring and pattern do not remain constant from fish to fish. The female is distinguished by her plumper profile when she is in breeding condition. **SPECIAL CARE:** See Tiger Barb.

BARBUS TICTO

FAMILY: *CYPRINIDAE*
COMMON NAME: *TICTO BARB; TWO SPOT BARB; TIC TAC TOE BARB*

FEEDING

COMPATIBILITY

EASE OF KEEPING

SIZE
4 in (10 cm) 3 in (7.5 cm)

There is some confusion between the peaceful *B. ticto* and *B. stoliczkae* (*stoliczkanus*) as visually they are almost identical. To tell them apart, some experts measure the differences in lateral line length (*B. ticto* has an incomplete lateral line), or body depth (*B. ticto* has a shallower body). The Ticto Barb, from the hill streams of Sri Lanka and India, has a pale silver-brown body with well-defined scales outlined by dark edges. Two small black patches appear on the flanks: one behind the gill cover and another at the front of the caudal peduncle. The main distinguishing features, particularly in the male, are the red dorsal fin flecked with black, and the reddish tinge of the pelvic fins; the other fins are colorless. The female's fins are paler in color, and she has a plumper body. The upper part of the eyes is red, and barbels are absent.
SPECIAL CARE: This fish prefers a water temperature that is slightly less than tropical. Care must be taken to prevent parents from eating eggs.

BARBUS TITTEYA

FAMILY: *CYPRINIDAE*
COMMON NAME: *CHERRY BARB*

FEEDING

COMPATIBILITY

EASE OF KEEPING

SIZE
2 in (5 cm) 2 in (5 cm)

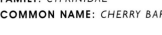

Originating in the streams of Sri Lanka, the Cherry Barb has a shape that is slimmer than the typical carp. The body is a reddish-brown color, and in the male the red is intensified, particularly during breeding. A longitudinal band is present, stretching from the snout to the end of the caudal peduncle; this may be repeated partially on the row of scales directly underneath. Fins match the body color of both sexes, but the female may lack color.
SPECIAL CARE: Due to its tendency toward shyness, the Cherry Barb is suitable for the smaller aquarium and prefers being kept with fishes of similar size. This fish can be bred in a domestic tank, but it does not produce many fry.

DANIOS AND MINNOWS

The fishes in this popular group have two things to offer the fishkeeper—active movement in the aquarium and a willingness to breed. Their slim body, flattened dorsal surface, and slightly upturned mouth indicate that they inhabit the upper levels of the water. Like all cyprinids they do have a tendency to eat their own eggs immediately after spawning. There are several methods of preventing this from happening in the aquarium. You can use physical barriers, such as a layer of marbles on the tank base, or a suspended netting cage which separates the parents from their eggs. Many danios can be spawned as a group, rather than just one pair at a time.

BRACHYDANIO ALBOLINEATUS

FAMILY: *CYPRINIDAE*
COMMON NAME: *PEARL DANIO*

FEEDING

COMPATIBILITY

EASE OF KEEPING

SIZE

2.2 in (5.5 cm) 2 in (5 cm)

From the fast-running streams of Burma, Thailand, and Sumatra, the very active Pearl Danio has an elongated body with dorsal and ventral contours of an equally shallow curvature. The body coloring is usually gray-green with some iridescences, but can vary depending on lighting conditions. Under side-lighting, and especially when spawning, the fish takes on a beautiful pearl blue-violet hue, with a red-gold line running along the rear-half of the body; the caudal peduncle shows shades of violet, and the gill cover shimmers with patches of metallic blue. Some red coloring occurs along the ventral surface of the male; the female can be distinguished by her deeper body. Two pairs of barbels are present and can be quite long. The fins are mostly translucent green, but some—including the caudal fin—may show a red tinge at the base.

SPECIAL CARE: This constantly moving fish enjoys a tank that simulates its natural environment: it is very fond of direct sunlight, and a power filter can be used to mimic the currents of its native waters. The Pearl Danio prefers a long aquarium with plenty of swimming space, but be sure to fit a secure lid, since these fish are excellent jumpers!

BRACHYDANIO FRANKEI

FAMILY: *CYPRINIDAE*
COMMON NAME: *LEOPARD DANIO*

FEEDING

COMPATIBILITY

EASE OF KEEPING

SIZE

N/A 1.8 in (4.5 cm)

This fish is a captive hybrid of *B. albolineatus* and *B. rerio*. As a cross-breed it is particularly streamlined with the dorsal surface being only slightly convex. The body color is a strong gold shade, covered in the darker spots which give the fish its name. The female body turns much deeper in front of the anal fin and may lose much of the spotty patterning. The female's girth also increases as she accumulates eggs. Even out of the breeding season, the female is always larger than the male, with a more curvaceous figure.

SPECIAL CARE: Although a good breeder in captivity, take care against egg-eating and always allow a generous amount of swimming space.

BRACHYDANIO KERRI

FAMILY: *CYPRINIDAE*
COMMON NAME: *BLUE DANIO*

Blue Danios enjoy the glistening streams of the islands in the Bay of Bengal and western Thailand. It usually appears an iridescent gray-blue, but turns to a lighter pastel-blue shade when spawning and when placed in side-lit conditions. It is distinguished by the two gold lines running rearward from the gold-rimmed eyes all the way to the caudal peduncle. Males usually show an increased depth of color compared to the female.

SPECIAL CARE: This fish will live peacefully with a community of modestly-sized fishes.

FEEDING

COMPATIBILITY

EASE OF KEEPING

SIZE

2 in (5 cm) 2 in (5 cm)

BRACHYDANIO RERIO

FAMILY: *CYPRINIDAE*
COMMON NAME: *ZEBRA DANIO*

Eastern India is the natural habitat of this distinctive danio. With a torpedo-shaped body, it sports a silver or gold body color covered in bright blue lines. The anal and caudal fins are also striped to highlight the zebra effect. The dorsal fin is set relatively far back on the body, and the mouth sports two sets of barbels. Sexual differences are easy to spot—the male is slimmer and smaller than the female. The background color also differs slightly between the sexes, with the female's stripes fading toward the ventral area. A long-finned and veil-tailed strain is also available.
SPECIAL CARE: As this fish is so active, it is happiest kept in a shoal. An ideal breeding fish for a beginner, it appreciates dense clumps of plants in which to lodge eggs. Although this fish can be spawned collectively, this can lead to increased egg eating while the adults are netted out at the end of the spawning period.

FEEDING

COMPATIBILITY

EASE OF KEEPING

SIZE

2 in (5 cm) 1.8 in (4.5 cm)

DANIO AEQUIPINNATUS

FAMILY: *CYPRINIDAE*
COMMON NAME: *GIANT DANIO*

FEEDING

COMPATIBILITY

EASE OF KEEPING

SIZE

4 in (10 cm) 4 in (10 cm)

Originating in southwestern India and Sri Lanka, the Giant Danio really is the "big boy" of the danio group. Measuring up to 4 in (10 cm) in the wild, in the right conditions it can also reach this size in captivity. Over a pale blue body color lies an attractive selection of yellow lines and dots, while the ventral area is a delicate shade of pink. As well as being rounder in body, females are distinguished by the fact that their yellow lines turn upward at the front of the caudal fin.
SPECIAL CARE: Previously known as "*Danio malabraricus*," this fish is highly active and needs plenty of swimming space. It looks best when kept in a shoal, although its energy will upset quieter tank members and smaller fish, who will be pushed aside in the rush for food.

TANICHTHYS ALBONUBES

FAMILY: *CYPRINIDAE*
COMMON NAME: *WHITE CLOUD MOUNTAIN MINNOW*

With such a poetic name, it is not surprising that this fish originates in the Oriental streams and lakes of China. Its name literally translates as "Tan's Fish," after an explorer named Tan. From an even brown shade on the top areas, the coloration gently blends down into white near the underside. The body color is offset by faint blue, red, and gold lines, which run from the eyes to the caudal peduncle, terminating in a red-edged dark patch. The dorsal, pelvic, and anal fins are shaded red, yellow, or white.
SPECIAL CARE: With its dark-edged scales, this fish looks particularly stunning under side-lighting and when placed in direct sunlight. Its hardiness means it can tolerate cooler temperatures, and can be kept outside in ponds during hot weather.

FEEDING

COMPATIBILITY

EASE OF KEEPING

SIZE

1.5 in (4 cm) 1.5 in (4 cm)

SYMBOL KEY

FEEDING
Herbivore

Omnivore

Predator

COMPATIBILITY
single specimen

community fish

safe with small fish

safe with invertebrates

EASE OF KEEPING
scale of 1 to 10
(with 1 being easiest to keep)

SIZE
in the wild

in captivity

RASBORAS

The species now known as *Rasbora* only became a member of its modern day genus after re-classifications by Pieter Bleeker in 1859, after he first altered it to *Leuciscus* (in 1839). As a companion group of slimmer cyprinids, rasboras offer a little extra in the way of color to the silvery danios and, although they can be speedy swimmers (especially when you try to catch them), they are usually a little more sedate in their movements around the aquarium. Although many of the body shapes may be toward the slim side, there are several deeper-bodied fish, and most of the genera occupy the middle- and upper-levels of the aquarium. Most reproduce in the familiar egg scattering manner but the Harlequin (*R. heteromorpha*) actually deposits eggs on the underside of a broad-leaved aquarium plant. Like the family as a whole, the size of fish within the *Rasbora* genus varies widely, from less than 1 inch (2.5 cm) to over three feet (90 cm). They may be distinguished from apparent near-related cyprinids by the absence of barbels.

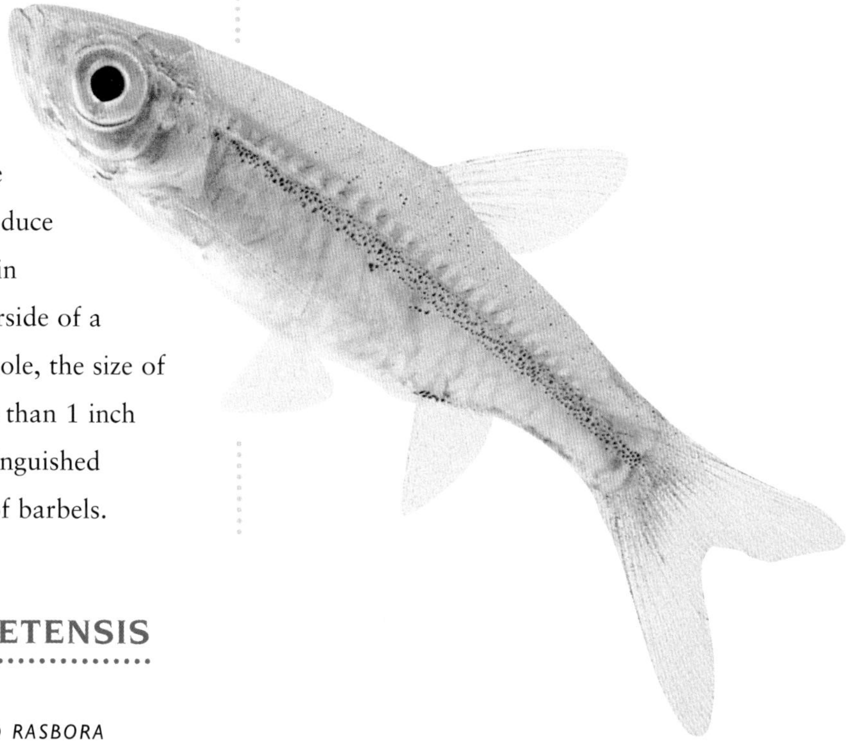

RASBORA BORAPETENSIS

FAMILY: *CYPRINIDAE*
COMMON NAME: *RED-TAILED RASBORA*

Plentiful in the swift-running waters of Thailand, the Red-Tailed Rasbora has an overall pale greenish-yellow hue. Its body is very slim, with a distinctive dark band running from gill cover to the end of the caudal peduncle; this band is accentuated by a thin gold band just above it. A further dark line is present along the bottom of the body at the base of the anal fin. The base of the caudal fin is red, inspiring the species' common name; the dorsal fin may have some reddish tinge, but otherwise the remaining fins are colorless. The mouth is slightly upturned and barbels are absent. As with many cyprinids, the male is slimmer than the female.
SPECIAL CARE: Swimming the upper- and middle-levels of a tank, this fish requires a medium-sized tank with well-aerated water. Although it mixes well with other fishes, a separate species tank for the Red-Tailed Rasbora can be very striking. The fish is very prolific, as long as the usual precautions against egg eating are observed.

FEEDING

COMPATIBILITY

EASE OF KEEPING

SIZE

2.2 in (5.5 cm) 2 in (5 cm)

RASBORA HETEROMORPHA

FAMILY: *CYPRINIDAE*
COMMON NAME: *HARLEQUIN*

Found in the waters of Thailand, Malaysia, and Sumatra, the distinguishing feature of this species is a blue-black triangular patch on its flanks, positioned immediately below the dorsal fin and tapering to reach the end of the caudal peduncle. An interesting note is that its lateral line is incomplete. It has a deep body that tapers rapidly after the anal fin to a narrow caudal peduncle. The head is slightly "snouty" with a pronounced notch in the outline just above the eyes. The body is an olive green on the dorsal surface shading down through pinkish-violet to silver. The dorsal fin is red-orange, the caudal fin has similarly colored top and bottom edges, and the other fins are transparent. The easiest way to tell the difference between the sexes is to look at the triangular patch. The triangular marking on the male has a straighter front edge and a more pointed lower corner than on the female. This may be due to the fact that the female's plumper body distorts her markings. A similar-looking species, *R. hengeli*, is a slightly smaller, slimmer fish with a narrower triangular marking.
SPECIAL CARE: A shoaling fish that looks effective in a well-planted aquarium with a dark substrate. Its method of spawning is unusual for a member of the cyprinid family. After a courtship dancing display by the males, the eggs are laid and fertilized on the underside of a broad-leaved plant (both fishes swim upside down to achieve this).

FEEDING

COMPATIBILITY

EASE OF KEEPING

SIZE

1.8 in (4.5 cm) 1.8 in (4.5 cm)

RASBORA ELEGANS

FAMILY: *CYPRINIDAE*
COMMON NAME: *ELEGANT RASBORA*

From the flowing and stationary waters of Borneo, Malaysia, and Sumatra, this streamlined fish lives up to its "elegant" common name: its elongated body is interrupted only by a slight curvature to the dorsal and ventral profiles. The body coloration begins with a greenish-brown hue on the dorsal surface, shading down to silvery flanks—when viewed under side-lighting conditions, a slight violet sheen appears. Each of its large, well-defined scales has a dark front area and dark edges. Two dark blue-black blotches appear on the body: one below the dorsal fin and one at the end of the caudal peduncle; a blue-black line also runs along the ventral surface at the base of the anal fin. Most fins are yellow, and the tips of the caudal fins are dark. As a general guideline, the female can be distinguished by her plumpness.
SPECIAL CARE: The Elegant Rasbora needs a tank with plenty of swimming space where it cruises the middle levels, displaying its graceful form. It is a peaceful species and coexists contentedly with fishes of mixed size.

FEEDING

COMPATIBILITY

EASE OF KEEPING

SIZE

6 in (15 cm) 5 in (12.5 cm)

SYMBOL KEY

FEEDING
Herbivore

Omnivore

Predator

COMPATIBILITY
single specimen

community fish

safe with small fish

safe with invertebrates

EASE OF KEEPING
scale of 1 to 10
(with 1 being easiest to keep)

SIZE
in the wild

in captivity

RASBORA KALACHROMA

FAMILY: *CYPRINIDAE*
COMMON NAME: *CLOWN RASBORA;*
IRIDESCENT RASBORA

The Clown Rasbora—a delicate fish found in parts of Borneo and Sumatra—is an unusual choice for aquariums. Its basic pink-violet hue, with well-defined iridescent scales, provides the inspiration for its second popular name. The body is quite stocky for an elongated species, and has a large blue-black blotch between the rear part of the dorsal fin and the anal fin; a smaller blue-black spot marks the body midway between the dorsal fin and the rear edge of the gill cover. In some cases, dark dots are scattered on individual scales where random pigmentation occurs. The fins are yellowish and tinged with red, and the tips of the anal and pelvic fins are black with white extremities. With its fairly small head, the large red and gold eyes can give the impression of a third "spot."

FEEDING

COMPATIBILITY

EASE OF KEEPING

8

SIZE

3.3 ft (1 m) 3.5 in (9 cm)

SPECIAL CARE: The Clown Rasbora is probably best suited for experienced fishkeepers: it has a reputation for being a fragile and hard-to-keep species. Experts suggest adding a little salt to the tank water or even keeping the fish in medium-hard water, although this advice seems contrary to the quality of water in the fish's natural habitat.

RASBORA MACULATA

FAMILY: *CYPRINIDAE*
COMMON NAME: *SPOTTED RASBORA; PYGMY RASBORA; DWARF RASBORA*

It would be easy to mistake this fish—as some do—for a miniature version of the Clown Rasbora, but the tiny Spotted Rasbora is definitely a true species in its own right. Native to Southeast Asia, close examination reveals that its body is not so uniform in shape as the Clown, with the caudal peduncle being longer and narrower in relation to the rest of the body. The body is a brown pinkish-red hue, with three dark spots marking the flanks: one to the rear of the glistening gill cover; one at the base of the anal fin; and one at the rear of the caudal peduncle, highlighted by a golden red area just in front. The fins may be slightly reddish; the first few rays of the dorsal are marked with black and pink, colors also seen on the anal fin. The eyes are large against its small head, and the ventral profile of the male is much flatter than that of the female.

SPECIAL CARE: One of the smallest cyprinids, the Spotted Rasbora is suitable only for a community tank with fishes that match its diminutive size. Alternatively, a separate species tank can be an effective way to house the fish.

FEEDING

COMPATIBILITY

EASE OF KEEPING

1

SIZE

1 in (2.5 cm) 1 in (2.5 cm)

RASBORA PAUCIPERFORATA

FAMILY: *CYPRINIDAE*
COMMON NAME: *RED-STRIPED RASBORA*

Its very slim and elongated body, with only the slightest convex curves, forms the Red-Striped Rasbora's striking outline. The dorsal surface of this Malaysian and Sumatran native is a medium-brown color, shading down to silver. The fish takes its name, of course, from the long red stripe running from the snout to the rear edge of the caudal peduncle, further emphasized by a narrow blue-black line just below it (this is more apparent to the rear of the dorsal fin). The caudal peduncle is only slightly tapered, and the fins are a very pale yellow color. Their large eyes are red at the top, continuing the red of the body line, and the lower part of the eyes is gold. The scales have clearly-defined dark edges, and a silvery sac containing the internal organs is easy to spot. Sexual differences are exemplified by the flatness of the ventral surface on the male, and the more rounded shape of the female.

SPECIAL CARE: This active fish appreciates a well-planted aquarium with areas of open water where it will shoal in the upper and middle levels. Although it can be timid, the Red-Striped Rasbora will live in a tank with other fishes of a similar size. Spawning is aided by keeping large enough numbers in the shoal; it may take time for compatible pairs to meet, so try different combinations and watch for fishes that pair off naturally.

FEEDING

COMPATIBILITY

EASE OF KEEPING

SIZE

2.5 in (6.5 cm) 2.2 in (5.5 cm)

RASBORA TRILINEATA

FAMILY: *CYPRINIDAE*
COMMON NAME: *SCISSORTAIL; SPOT-TAIL RASBORA*

Constantly on the move, the Scissortail can be an amusing sight: it takes its name from the characteristic scissor action of its deeply forked caudal fin, even twitching it when at rest. Like its near relative, *R. caudimaculata*, the caudal fin is strikingly colored, with black and white areas on each lobe. At home in the streams of Borneo, Malaysia, and Sumatra, the fish's body is elongated with dorsal and ventral contours equally convex. The body is a greenish-gray color with a silver belly; the scales are dark-edged and well-defined. A thin dark band begins midway between the gill cover and the dorsal fin, continuing along the flanks to the end of the caudal peduncle where it is bordered in yellow. The other fins are colorless. The male intensifies in color when it is ripe for breeding, and the female is plumper than the male.

SPECIAL CARE: A spacious aquarium is appreciated by this lively fish, which needs plenty of swimming space to perform its calisthenics. Cruising the upper and middle levels, the Scissortail is compatible with a mixed community of fishes.

FEEDING

COMPATIBILITY

EASE OF KEEPING

SIZE

3.5 in (9 cm) 3 in (8 cm)

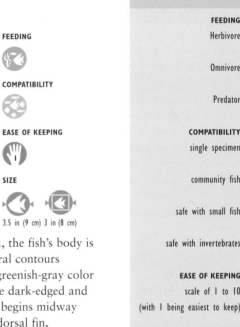

SYMBOL KEY

FEEDING

Herbivore

Omnivore

Predator

COMPATIBILITY

single specimen

community fish

safe with small fish

safe with invertebrates

EASE OF KEEPING

scale of 1 to 10
(with 1 being easiest to keep)

SIZE

in the wild

in captivity

FLYING FOXES

Here is a contrast in styles—the Flying Fox is a very smart fish, with its white, yellow, and black horizontal stripes. It is often seen perching on horizontal surfaces in mid-water before darting off to grab a snack. The lesser-colored Siamese Flying Fox is a less exciting specimen, spending much of its time on the floor of the aquarium. Flying Foxes will sometimes harass other species considered to be intruders into their swimming space.

EPALZEORHYNCHUS KALLOPTERUS

FAMILY: *CYPRINIDAE*
COMMON NAME: *FLYING FOX*

Running waters as far away as Java, Sumatra, Malaysia, and Thailand are home to the smart-looking Flying Fox. Its body is torpedo-shaped and divided into three distinct colors. The top is brown-green, separated by a bright yellow band from the dark main band, which runs the length of the body; below this, the ventral region is white. All the fins have white tips, the dorsal fin having a black base. The downturned mouth has two pairs of barbels. The male develops head tubercles when breeding in the wild, although the fish will not breed in an aquarium environment. A paler version of this fish, *Crossocheilus oblongus*, is also seen.

SPECIAL CARE: The Flying Fox is happy to browse upon algae-covered rocks, but is not strictly a vegetarian—live foods, such as worms, are eagerly consumed. Cruising in middle- to lower-level waters, it is often found at rest perched on flat horizontal surfaces, propped up by its ventral fins. Caution should be taken as to the number of fish that are kept together, since this fish tends to quarrel with members of its own species.

FEEDING

COMPATIBILITY

EASE OF KEEPING

SIZE

6 in (1.5 cm)   5.5 in (14 cm)

EPALZEORHYNCHUS SIAMENSIS

FAMILY: *CYPRINIDAE*
COMMON NAME: *SIAMESE FLYING FOX*

Originating in the streambeds of Malaysia, where it is called *Selimang Siam*, and Thailand, where it is known as *Pla Lab Mue Nang* (Lady's Fingernail Fish), the Siamese Flying Fox has exactly the same body shape as the Flying Fox. However, its coloring differs: the vivid yellow topping the broad dark band is absent and, consequently, the band is more vague; the band is also shorter, beginning behind the eyes rather than at the tip of the snout, and does not extend into the caudal fin. The dorsal fin is quite long-based, and all the fins are colorless. One pair of barbels appears at the downturned mouth.

SPECIAL CARE: This mainly bottom-dwelling fish forages for food among the detritus at the bottom of the tank, but also browses on algae—although it may not extend its vacuuming activities to clean the tank completely! Known to be quarrelsome with its own species, it is more amenable to other fishes and can be placed in a mixed tank. Some authorities refer to it as another genus, *Crossocheilus*.

FEEDING

COMPATIBILITY

EASE OF KEEPING

SIZE

5.5 in (14 cm)   5.5 in (14 cm)

SHARKS

It may come as a disappointment to those expecting some bloodthirsty behavior in the aquarium that the species in this section are not related to the marine *Jaws* either scientifically or behaviorally. The reason for the popular name "shark" is based on the fact that the species has a triangular dorsal fin reminiscent of the marine fish. The most colorful has to be the Red-Tailed Black Shark, whose name says it all. The other species—especially the Red-Finned and Ruby Sharks—have their own appeal. The large Black Shark is quite peaceful, content to rummage around the aquarium browsing on algae but, like the larger "barbs," it stirs up the water currents with its movements. The Silver and Apollo Sharks are active shoaling fishes and will grow to splendid proportions if you give them the room to do so.

BALANTIOCHEILUS MELANOPTERUS

FAMILY: *CYPRINIDAE*
COMMON NAME: *SILVER SHARK; BALA SHARK*

At home in the streams of Thailand, Borneo, and Sumatra, the Silver Shark is a very active, yet peaceful species. The fish takes its name from the metallic silver coloration of its body, with gleaming, well-defined scales. The body is an elongated shape with only moderately convex dorsal and ventral surfaces. The triangular dorsal fin is stiffly held and, like the anal and caudal fins, has a bright yellow area with a thick black margin. The caudal fin is large and deeply forked, and the pointed head has large eyes set well forward. No sexual differences are known, but the female probably gets plumper when spawning time approaches.

SPECIAL CARE: Although the Silver Shark is neither aggressive nor territorial, it is wise to choose tank mates of substantial size who won't be harassed by its constant movement up and down the middle levels of the aquarium. A tight-fitting lid is also required because the fish is not only a powerful swimmer but an excellent jumper as well.

FEEDING

COMPATIBILITY

EASE OF KEEPING

SIZE

13.8 in (35 cm)   12 in (30 cm)

SYMBOL KEY

FEEDING

Herbivore

Omnivore

Predator

COMPATIBILITY

single specimen

community fish

safe with small fish

safe with invertebrates

EASE OF KEEPING

scale of 1 to 10
(with 1 being easiest to keep)

SIZE

in the wild

in captivity

LABEO BICOLOR

FAMILY: *CYPRINIDAE*
COMMON NAME: *RED-TAILED BLACK SHARK*

Its sleek jet-black body and bright red caudal fin inspire this fish's common name. Naturally found in the streambeds of Thailand, the Red-Tailed Black Shark (and others in its genus) is not related to the "real thing" at all, although its highly triangular dorsal fin and flattened ventral contour, coupled with its constant patrolling tendency, are very reminiscent of the true marine shark. The dorsal, pelvic, and anal fins are all black, but the pectoral fins may be yellowish-orange; the overall black coloration is only seen at its best in healthy specimens—in less robust fish, the black may fade to gray. The downturned mouth has a fringed top lip and a horny bottom lip, ideal for rasping algae, and two pairs of barbels are present. Females tend toward a deeper body depth and become very rounded if they are well fed.

FEEDING

COMPATIBILITY

EASE OF KEEPING

SIZE

6 in (1.5 cm) 6 in (15 cm)

SPECIAL CARE: This middle- to lower-level swimmer is usually peaceful but requires plenty of hiding places into which it can retreat. Keep as part of a community tank so that it does not quarrel with other fishes. It often becomes increasingly territorial with age, displaying a marked intolerance toward members of its own species. No information is available on breeding, although it has been known to breed occasionally in the aquarium.

LABEO ERYTHRURUS

FAMILY: *CYPRINIDAE*
COMMON NAME: *RED-FINNED SHARK*

This species, found in the streambeds of Thailand, has a pale brown elongated body and, as you would expect from its name, its fins are red. A small dark patch is carried at the rear end of the caudal peduncle. Its mouth is fringe-lipped and downturned with two pairs of barbels. Although found in nature with the above coloration, there are other very similarly colored fishes available for sale which have all the appearances of albinism—red eyes for example. These may have been developed in the aquarium or bred by commercial fish farms.

SPECIAL CARE: Outwardly this fish appears peaceful, but it may demonstrate antisocial behavior as detailed for the other species in this family. It can be put in a community aquarium with a collection of fishes of mixed sizes, but it would be wise to choose tank mates who can look after themselves. No breeding information is available.

FEEDING

COMPATIBILITY

EASE OF KEEPING

SIZE

6 in (15 cm) 6 in (15 cm)

LABEO FRENATUS

FAMILY: *CYPRINIDAE*
COMMON NAME: *RUBY SHARK*

This species often suffers from mistaken identity: it is sometimes confused with the Red-Tailed Black Shark, but actually has a slimmer gray body, with dark-edged scales. Another inhabitant of the streambeds of Thailand, the Ruby Shark is sometimes called the rather cumbersome Green Fringed-Lipped Shark, a name possibly coined under unusual lighting conditions. A dark stripe runs from the snout to the center of the eyes, and if viewed closely, a dark patch can be seen at the rear extremity of the caudal peduncle. The fins are red overall, with the outer edges of the dorsal, pelvic, and anal fins showing black and white markings. The deeply forked caudal fin is plain red, as are the pectoral fins. Two pairs of barbels appear on the downturned mouth. Males are slimmer than females and have a black-streaked anal fin.
SPECIAL CARE: The Ruby Shark may appear in wide color variations due to age and origin, another factor in its confusion with other species. It cruises the middle and lower levels of the aquarium, and there is no information on its breeding habits.

LEPTOBARBUS HOEVENI

FEEDING

COMPATIBILITY

EASE OF KEEPING

SIZE

20 in (50 cm) 16 in (40 cm)

FAMILY: *CYPRINIDAE*
COMMON NAME: *MAROON SHARK*

Ikan Jelawat, Sultan Fish, and Red-Finned Shark are all alternative names for this fish native to the rivers of Borneo, Laos, Sumatra, and Thailand. It has an elongated body with a moderately arched dorsal surface and only a slightly curved ventral surface. The Maroon has silvery flanks with a greenish tinge to the area above the lateral line; the fairly large and well-defined scales each have a dark front area. In young fishes a black band runs from the head to the end of the caudal peduncle but this fades with age. Extra coloration comes from the fins; the pelvic fins are bright red, as is the anal fin. The green caudal fin has red tips, only the dorsal fin is plainer, being yellowish in color. There are two pairs of small barbels around the moderately large mouth. Little information is available on spotting the differences between the sexes. Considering the adult size of this species, it is not surprising to learn that it is a popular food in Malaysia. Further observation in nature reveals that it behaves erratically at times, usually after eating a certain tree fruit or seeds, and its flesh is then said to be poisonous. Its local name in Thailand is *pla ba* (*ba* meaning mad).
SPECIAL CARE: This fish is peaceful and very active but requires a large spacious aquarium. This middle- and lower-level swimmer should only be kept with a collection of other large fishes. No breeding information is available.

FEEDING

COMPATIBILITY

EASE OF KEEPING

SIZE

6 in (15 cm) 6 in (15 cm)

SYMBOL KEY

FEEDING

Herbivore

Omnivore'

Predator

COMPATIBILITY

single specimen

community fish

safe with small fish

safe with invertebrates

EASE OF KEEPING

scale of 1 to 10
(with 1 being easiest to keep)

SIZE

in the wild

in captivity

LOACHES

Loaches fall into two distinct body shapes: from a slightly modified orthodox "fish shape" to other species that might almost be described as "swimming worms." Loaches spend most of their time on the bottom of the aquarium and are often better kept in numbers rather than as solitary specimens. Many are nocturnal by nature, preferring to hide away among plants and rocks by day, only emerging as darkness falls or when a tempting piece of food drops within reach.

They prefer subdued lighting and this can be achieved by having a covering of floating plants on the water's surface. The substrate can be of a soft, sandy composition as it is not uncommon for these fish to burrow into the substrate. Loaches often make loud clicking noises particularly when feeding; this is produced by violently expelling water through the gills which are then snapped shut.

Little is know of their reproductive processes but artifical means are reported to have been used to condition some loaches into spawning in an egg-scattering manner.

ACANTHOPSIS CHOIRORHYNCHUS

FAMILY: *COBITIDAE*
COMMON NAME: *HORSEFACED LOACH*

This fish is found in the running streams of Southeast Asia, Burma, Java, Sumatra, and Thailand. It has other alternative popular names—Longfaced Loach, Ikan pasir, and Tali—the latter two being Malay. This spindly fish has a long, tapering head (the snout itself makes up about two-thirds of the head) with small eyes that are very high-set. The body coloration is a pale yellow-brown; a number of equally-spaced dark spots mark the flanks from behind the gill cover to the end of the caudal peduncle along the center line of the body. These are matched by a series of small dark blotches along the length of the dorsal surface and are separated from them by a row of very small dark speckles. Some variation in coloration is likely between specimens. There are no known differences between the sexes.

SPECIAL CARE: Since this is an active fish that likes burrowing in the substrate with just its snout protruding, provide soft sandy materials so the fish does not damage itself. It is perhaps looking for its favorite food, worms. It may uproot plants occasionally but this effect can be guarded against by placing specimen plants in individual pots. The water should be well-aerated, possibly with water currents. Currently, no information is available on captive breeding.

FEEDING

COMPATIBILITY

EASE OF KEEPING

SIZE

8.7 in (22 cm)   8 in (20 cm)

BOTIA LOHACHATA

FAMILY: *COBITIDAE*
COMMON NAME: *PAKISTANI LOACH; RETICULATED LOACH*

The body shape of this fish is elongated with an arched dorsal contour and a flat ventral surface. The body does not taper very much once its widest depth has been reached because it has a broad caudal peduncle. Its body coloration is light yellow covered with numerous dark "Y-shaped" markings each separated by a light centered dark blotch. The dark markings extend over the head, through the eyes, and down to the tip of the snout. Four pairs of barbels are present. The fairly colorless fins all have dark markings, particularly on the dorsal and caudal fin; the latter is deeply forked. This fish, native to the streams and rivers of northeastern India, Bangladesh, and Pakistan, often makes a clicking noise by sharply snapping its gills open and shut.

SPECIAL CARE: This fish may lie on its side on the substrate "playing dead," especially after a meal. Feeding at the surface presents no problems since it simply swims upside down to take any floating foods. It is usually quite active during the day and sometimes pesters other fishes. This loach swims at the middle and lower levels of a well-planted aquarium and likes to spend time among tangled roots. No information is available about captive breeding.

FEEDING

COMPATIBILITY

EASE OF KEEPING

SIZE

5 in (13 cm)   3 in (7.5 cm)

BOTIA MACRACANTHA

FEEDING

COMPATIBILITY

EASE OF KEEPING

SIZE

12 in (30 cm) 10 in (25 cm)

FAMILY: *COBITIDAE*
COMMON NAME: *CLOWN LOACH; TIGER BOTIA*

The scales on this particular species are very small which gives the fish an almost "naked" appearance. It has an elongated body with an arched dorsal surface and a flattened ventral surface. Three black bands of increasing size cross its body—the first, and narrowest, crosses the eyes, the second just ahead of the dorsal fin, and the third crosses immediately behind the dorsal fin and extends into the anal fin. The head is tapered and has a downturned mouth carrying four pairs of barbels. There is an erectile spine in front of each eye. In the wild the Clown Loach inhabits the slow-moving streams of Borneo, Indonesia, and Sumatra.
SPECIAL CARE: This species is both active and gregarious. It spends most of its time in the lower level of the aquarium and needs plenty of plants and tangled roots. A number should be kept together if its best aspects are to be observed—solitary specimens often hide away and refuse to thrive, almost in protest. It rarely reaches its full adult size in captivity.

BOTIA MODESTA

FAMILY: *COBITIDAE*
COMMON NAME: *ORANGE-FINNED LOACH*

This fish has an elongated body with an arched dorsal surface and a very slightly convex but generally flattened ventral surface. The body coloration is a plain dark bluish-gray and its small scales provide only a slight metallic sheen, but it is an attractive species thanks to its bright red-orange fins, hence its common name. (A similar-looking species, *B. lecontei*, has a yellow caudal fin and is slightly slimmer.) The spine just ahead of the apparently small eyes is difficult to see. The snout is tapered and the downturned mouth has four pairs of barbels. Its natural habitat is the streams of Malaysia, Thailand, and Vietnam.
SPECIAL CARE: As with many species in this family group, this fish can be quite timid and will hide away during the day at the lower level of the aquarium, only venturing out after dark. It can be kept in a community collection, but it only likes to keep company with fishes of a similar temperament. A feeding of live foods, however, usually tempts them out of their retreats in the plants or rocks.
A characteristic of the genus is the emission of clicking noises from time to time.

FEEDING

COMPATIBILITY

EASE OF KEEPING

SIZE

6 in (15 cm) 4 in (10 cm)

BOTIA MORLETI

FAMILY: *COBITIDAE*
COMMON NAME: *SKUNK LOACH; HORA'S LOACH*

This fish has an elongated body with a moderately arched dorsal contour, and a flat ventral surface. Generally it is golden gray in color with a silvery ventral surface, although there are exceptions to this rule. A dark stripe runs from the tip of the snout along the dorsal ridge and passes down the rear end of the fairly deep caudal peduncle. Some faint dark vertical streakings may be visible on the flanks. The scales are very small and the skin has a dull finish. The eyes appear to be deceptively small because they have a dark center in a silvery, almost body-colored surround. Three pairs of barbels are present. The fins are only slightly greenish-yellow, and are otherwise almost transparent. It originates from the streams and rivers of northern India and Thailand.
SPECIAL CARE: This fish is not an accomplished swimmer—until you try to catch it. It swims with a jerky movement and prefers to rest during the day among plants or in other retreats around the aquarium. No information is available on captive breeding.

FEEDING

COMPATIBILITY

EASE OF KEEPING

SIZE

8 in (20 cm) 4 in (10 cm)

SYMBOL KEY

FEEDING
Herbivore
Omnivore
Predator

COMPATIBILITY
single specimen
community fish
safe with small fish
safe with invertebrates

EASE OF KEEPING
scale of 1 to 10
(with 1 being easiest to keep)

SIZE
in the wild
in captivity

BOTIA SIDTHIMUNKI

FAMILY: *COBITIDAE*
COMMON NAME: *DWARF CHAINED LOACH*

This peaceful, shoaling fish can be found in the streams of Thailand. Its body shape is more cylindrical compared with other members of the genus, with a very slightly arched dorsal surface and a flattened ventral surface. Its body is light metallic-gold in color, over which is a dark "chain-link" pattern. This is seen mostly over the top-half of the body, although in mature specimens the dark pattern may reach further down the flanks. The ventral surface is silvery-white below the bottom edge of the chain marking, appproximately midway down the flanks. The head is small and the eyes have a gold rim. There are three pairs of barbels. The fins are clear with the exception of the caudal fin, which may have a dark patterning in each lobe.

SPECIAL CARE: An active, gregarious species by day (as well as being nocturnal) it ventures into midwater areas more regularly than other members of the genus. It should be kept in a generously-planted aquarium as it often likes to perch on broad leaves in a similar fashion to the Flying Fox, *Epalzeorhynchus kallopterus*. No information is available on breeding in captivity.

FEEDING

COMPATIBILITY

EASE OF KEEPING

SIZE

2.4 in (6 cm) 2.4 in (6 cm)

BOTIA ROSTRATA

FAMILY: *COBITIDAE*
COMMON NAME: *LADDER LOACH*

The cream-colored body is crossed by a number of slightly-oblique, dark bands some of which are connected by a horizontal bar. The two lobes of the caudal fin are marked with three to four dark stripes that continue the body patterning. The dorsal fin has a dark band along the edge nearest to the body surface and another toward its tip. A dark central band runs from the snout rearward, over the head. Absolute identification of some *Botia* species is not always possible, especially with those exhibiting similar body patterning which may (or may not) extend into adult life from the juvenile stage. This species, from Asia, Burma, and India, has attracted several synonyms according to much aquatic literature.

SPECIAL CARE: Like all other members of the genus, the Ladder Loach appreciates a well-planted aquarium with some areas of open substrate over which it can browse for food. It is especially fond of worm-type live foods and does not hesitate to come out of hiding in order to make a meal of them.

FEEDING

COMPATIBILITY

EASE OF KEEPING

SIZE

2.4 in (6 cm) 2.4 in (6 cm)

COBITIS TAENIATA

FAMILY: *COBITIDAE*
COMMON NAME: *SPINY LOACH*

The long laterally-compressed body of this fish has a spotted dorsal surface that continues down to the midline of the body, where the pattern is separated from the silvery-white ventral area by a row of dark oblong blotches. The dorsal and caudal fins are patterned with dark dots. The eyes, set up high on the small head, have a double erectile spine beneath them. Six barbels are present around the mouth. The Spiny Loach is found in waters throughout Europe.

SPECIAL CARE: This fish does best in very clean water. It is more active at night and often buries itself in substrate during the day. Their eggs stick to roots and rocks, so the aquarium should be planted and contain some rocky furnishing. Its preferred foods are crustaceans and small worms.

FEEDING

COMPATIBILITY

EASE OF KEEPING

SIZE

4 in (10 cm) 3.5 in (9 cm)

MISGURNUS ANGUILLICAUDATUS

FAMILY: *COBITIDAE*
COMMON NAME: *JAPANESE WEATHERLOACH; DOJO*

The body shape of this fish resembles that of an eel. This unusual fish is found in the streams of northeastern Asia, including those of central China. The brownish-yellow body is covered with dark specklings that extend into the rounded fins. The dorsal fin and pelvic fins are set halfway back on the body. The head is small and the eyes are set well forward. The downturned mouth has five pairs of barbels.

SPECIAL CARE: This fish has several interesting characteristics. It becomes very active during periods of bad weather or immediately before a storm when there is low barometric pressure. It has the ability to utilize atmospheric air breathed at the water's surface. In the wild, it will burrow in the mud of the streambed during the winter or excessively dry periods, therefore in an aquarium it needs plenty of places to hide. It tolerates cooler than normal tropical water temperatures— temperatures above 70°F (21°C) are not particularly required. If the species conforms to the generic pattern, its eggs are laid among plants and roots on the aquarium floor. This peaceful, often nocturnal, fish is suitable for a community collection of mixed-size fishes.

FEEDING

COMPATIBILITY

EASE OF KEEPING

SIZE

10 in (25 cm) 8 in (20 cm)

PANGIO KUHLI

FAMILY: *COBITIDAE*
COMMON NAME: *COOLIE LOACH*

The old generic name of the Coolie Loach, *Acanthophthalmus*, means "Thorn-eye" or "Prickle-eye" because it has a sharp spine above each eye. This fish's natural habitat is the streams of Southeast Asia, Borneo, Java, Malaysia, and Thailand. It has a wormlike body shape that is yellowish, light brown in color and it has a pink ventral surface. A number of dark brown-black bands cross the body vertically but stop short of the actual ventral surface. Most of the dark bands are partially interrupted by a yellow line or small area. The eyes are very small and are hidden in a dark band; four pairs of barbels are present. The dorsal fin is set about two-thirds of the way back along the body, just behind the pelvic fins. The rounded caudal fin has a dark area at its base.

FEEDING

COMPATIBILITY

EASE OF KEEPING

SIZE

4.3 in (11 cm) 3.2 in (8 cm)

SPECIAL CARE: This peaceful, gregarious fish spends most of its time at the lower level of the aquarium swimming among tangled plant roots; this habit makes it very difficult to catch. Although not regularly bred in captivity, isolated reports suggest eggs are expelled and fertilized near the water surface and may lodge in plants.

SYMBOL KEY

FEEDING
Herbivore

Omnivore

Predator

COMPATIBILITY
single specimen

community fish

safe with small fish

safe with invertebrates

EASE OF KEEPING
scale of 1 to 10
(with 1 being easiest to keep)

SIZE
in the wild

in captivity

COLDWATER CYPRINIDS

Keeping coldwater species is not considerably different from caring for tropicals, but there are a few things to keep in mind. Note that the size of your tank will determine the amount of fish you will be able to keep, so don't expect to crowd your tank. Also, while the coldwater aquarium does not require heating, it may well become overheated during summer months. It is important to situate the aquarium in a shady location. If temperatures do become high during the summer it is likely that some form of cooling will be necessary. Aeration and efficient filtration systems are almost mandatory to provide well-oxygenated, moving water and to remove the dangers from decomposing waste products.

Carassius auratus have been kept in captivity longer than any other fishes. This coldwater cyprinid retains an enormous following due to the wide range of new varieties being bred. Generally, development is centered around exaggerating finnage or producing new color strains. Differences in color are achieved by breeding specific scale types. Nacreous and matte forms let more of the natural pigmentation show through instead of the usual metallic-gold finish.

In addition to being kept in aquariums, goldfish can rightly be regarded as successful pond fish. However, not all varieties are suitable for outdoor cultivation where frost damage and/or other adverse pond water qualities can affect them. Due to their changed physical forms, away from their natural shape in the original wild form, many of the more "exotically-designed" fishes are simply not physically able to cope with pond life. As bodies become more truncated and egg-shaped, their ability to swim is progressively impaired. Because of this, such fishes are not suited to outdoor ponds where they are uncompetitive in the race for food or away from predators. Their delicate fins may also get congested through contact with water conditions that are less-than-ideal. Water conditions can be kept under much closer control in the aquarium and, here too, the wonderful flowing fins and specially-bred body shapes can be seen more easily through the glass.

CARASSIUS AURATUS

FAMILY: *CYPRINIDAE*
COMMON NAME: *GOLDFISH*

This popular fish is bred worldwide in captivity. The goldfish is an egg scatterer by nature, but the fish can be hand-stripped to release sperm and eggs independently during selective breeding programs. The various varieties are discussed in more detail on pages 46 to 49.

VARIETY: *BUBBLE-EYE*
This twin-tailed variety is instantly recognizable. Each eye is almost surrounded by a fluid-filled sac and these wobble as the fish swims. The body is egg-shaped and it does not have a dorsal fin. Body coloration can be variable, but it is usually the familiar metallic red-orange.
SPECIAL CARE: Because of the vulnerability of the eye-sacs to physical damage, it is best to keep this strain in its own aquarium with no rocky furnishings or boisterous fishes. Its environment needs to be controlled. It is not hardy enough to survive winters in outdoor ponds.

FEEDING

COMPATIBILITY

EASE OF KEEPING

5

SIZE

N/A

Varies according to space given and whether kept in pond or aquarium

VARIETY: *CALICO MOOR*
Combines the calico pigments—red-gold, white, and black, with the fantail—flowing fins, and the "pop" eyes of the moor. The caudal, dorsal, and anal fins are long and flowing, and the paired fins well-formed. Unlike some other "fancy" goldfish varieties, this one is equally happy in an outdoor pond as in the aquarium.
SPECIAL CARE: Feed a pelleted or flake food made especially for fancy goldfish. Specimens kept in outdoor ponds must be brought in for the winter if there is a danger that the pond will freeze solid. Feed outdoor fish only once or twice a week, aquarium fish daily.

FEEDING

COMPATIBILITY

EASE OF KEEPING
4

SIZE
N/A

Varies according to space given and whether kept in pond or aquarium

VARIETY: *COMET*
The Comet has an elongated body, with equally curved dorsal and ventral contours. It is not as deep or as heavily-built as the Common Goldfish. The color of this fish depends on the strain, but red-orange and lemon yellow tend to be the most common. The main, deliberately-created, feature of this variety is the deeply-forked caudal fin which can be almost as long as the body itself.
SPECIAL CARE: The Comet requires plenty of swimming room and can swim exceptionally fast for short periods of time. It is a hardy variety and can benefit by being kept outdoors in a pond all year round, rather than in the close confines of the indoor aquarium.

FEEDING

COMPATIBILITY

EASE OF KEEPING
1

SIZE

N/A

Varies according to space given and whether kept in pond or aquarium

VARIETY: *COMMON GOLDFISH*
This popular aquarium favorite has a stocky body with equally convex dorsal and ventral contours. The body is a brilliant metallic orange-red, and this vivid color extends into the fins. The dorsal fin has a long base, the anal and caudal fins are not divided, and the caudal fin is moderately forked. No barbels appear on the mouth. Young fish are dark in color when hatched, changing to adult coloration at around 1 year of age, although not every fish changes color. Spotting the difference between the sexes is fairly straightforward: females usually have much plumper bodies when seen from above and at spawning time the male fish develops small white spots, knows as tubercles, on the gill covers and pectoral fins.
SPECIAL CARE: The Common Goldfish is one of the easiest fish to keep successfully if you follow the general guidelines of keeping the aquarium out of direct sunlight and monitor the water temperature to ensure that it is not too high.

FEEDING

COMPATIBILITY

EASE OF KEEPING
1

SIZE
N/A

Varies according to space given and whether kept in pond or aquarium

SYMBOL KEY

FEEDING
Herbivore
Omnivore
Predator

COMPATIBILITY
single specimen
community fish
safe with small fish
safe with invertebrates

EASE OF KEEPING
scale of 1 to 10 (with 1 being easiest to keep)

SIZE
in the wild
in captivity

FEEDING

COMPATIBILITY

EASE OF KEEPING

3

SIZE

N/A

Varies according to space
given and whether kept
in pond or aquarium

FEEDING

COMPATIBILITY

EASE OF KEEPING

4

SIZE

N/A

Varies according to space
given and whether kept
in pond or aquarium

VARIETY: *LIONHEAD*

The short, egg-shaped body of the
Lionhead does not have a dorsal fin. In
some respects the Lionhead is similar to
the Red-Cap Oranda, as both varieties
have a raspberry-like growth on the
head. The caudal fin should be held
stiffly and not allowed to drop.
SPECIAL CARE: The Lionhead is best
kept in the indoor aquarium where its
colorful features can be easily seen.

VARIETY: *MOOR*

At one time purists insisted that the Moor was always completely black,
without any hint of color showing through. However, today other colors are
becoming more acceptable. One unusual feature about this particular variety
is its eyes; they may be normal, but in some strains they are developed as
"telescopic" eyes that protrude from the head. This fish has a similar body
shape to the Veiltail.

SPECIAL CARE: When trying to maintain any kind
of color strain it is imperative to use only the very
best adult fish from which to breed and to select
only the young fish showing the desired qualities to
grow up to adulthood and thus form the future
ongoing breeding stock.

VARIETY: *FANTAIL*

The Fantail has a relatively short body with a
deep, short caudal peduncle. Body coloration is
variable, depending on the scale formation and
pigmentation. The dorsal fin is held high and in
healthy specimens it should be around half the
body depth. It has double anal and caudal fins.
Something to look out for when buying one of
these fish is to make sure that the caudal fin is
held above the horizontal line. If it is, you know
that it is a prime specimen.
SPECIAL CARE: The Fantail can be kept in an
outdoor pond all year round providing the water
is deep enough to ensure a warm layer at the
bottom where the fish can lie dormant.

FEEDING

COMPATIBILITY

EASE OF KEEPING

4

SIZE

N/A

Varies according to space
given and whether kept
in pond or aquarium

VARIETY: *RED-CAP ORANDA*

The Red-Cap Oranda has a short, deep body, with a short, slightly downturned caudal peduncle. The strain shown has a white body with a red coloration restricted to the raspberry-like growth on the head, known as the "wen." This particular physical characteristic is peculiar to the Oranda and Lionhead strains. The dorsal fin is held high and the anal and caudal fins are double, much in the manner of the Veiltail.

SPECIAL CARE: Like many of the goldfish strains with more fully developed fins, the Oranda needs very clean water conditions if fin damage and deterioration are not to occur. The company of any active fishes should be avoided to prevent damage to the wen.

FEEDING

COMPATIBILITY

EASE OF KEEPING

4

SIZE

N/A

Varies according to space given and whether kept in pond or aquarium

VARIETY: *PEARLSCALE*

The emphasis of interest in this particular variety has shifted from coloration and finnage toward a further development of the scales. As the name suggests, the scales on this fish have a pearl-like appearance; this is due to each scale having a domed, or raised center. These fishes are usually metallic or calico in color and, in most other respects, the strain appears to conform to the usual rounded body shape and "double" anal and caudal fins of the twin-tailed group of goldfishes. In more mature specimens, the body can appear almost completely spherical and the swimming action is decidedly awkward. In some instances cramping of the internal organs (by virtue of the egg-shaped body) may result in problems with the swim bladder .

SPECIAL CARE: This fish should be kept in a well-planted aquarium with a central swimming area that is devoid of sharp rocky decorations on which the scales might become damaged. It is not suitable for year-round, outdoor pond cultivation and is also said to dislike cold temperatures.

FEEDING

COMPATIBILITY

EASE OF KEEPING

4

SIZE

N/A

Varies according to space given and whether kept in pond or aquarium

VARIETY:

SHUBUNKIN

Shubunkins may be considered as the next color-stage development beyond the Common Goldfish as the body shape is almost identical in one of the two recognized varieties of Shubunkin. Generally, coloration depends very much on the strain and the scale formation; the most popular are where black, red, purple, blue, and brown all appear beneath the nacreous or matte scales. The London Shubunkin has the same body shape and finnage as the Common Goldfish; it does not have the highly reflective scales but does have multi-coloration instead; it does not have any special fin development. The Bristol Shubunkin is often quite stockily-built, but the main feature of this variety is the specially developed large caudal fin with its rounded lobes that should be carried without any drooping.

SPECIAL CARE:

The Shubunkin is the ideal fish for both the outdoor pond and indoor aquarium. Specimens living outside usually take on better color due to exposure to sunshine and the availability of natural aquatic live foods. However, keeping the fish indoors enables the fishkeeper to monitor water conditions more closely and organize breeding programs more efficiently.

FEEDING

COMPATIBILITY

EASE OF KEEPING

1

SIZE

N/A

Varies according to space given and whether kept in pond or aquarium

CHARACINS

With almost 1,200 species, characins rival the cyprinid family in numbers. In the wild, characins are split between Central and South America and Africa. The number of fish is truly astounding, with millions being exported each year—mostly from the Amazon region. The family contains many popular fishes. Among the tetras, for example, are found the brilliant neons and cardinals—distant relatives of the notorious piranha, which brings us to one of the main characteristics of this family—teeth. They have extremely sharp teeth, even though not all characins are meat-eaters or predatory. For instance, in the wild, the pacu is a fruit-eater, devouring the juicy berries which fall into the water. Another feature of this family is the presence of an extra fin known as the adipose, between the dorsal fin and the tail. Males have tiny hooks on the anal fin to assist spawning; they also sport more intense coloration, slimmer bodies, and more exaggerated finnage.

Body sizes vary in the wild, from 1 inch (2.5 cm) of the South American Neon Tetra to the 12 inches (30 cm) of the African Longnosed Distichodus. Shapes are

Hyphessobrycon flammeus
FLAME TETRA

equally diverse: hatchetfish are flat-backed and deep-bodied, while pencilfish are as slim as their name suggests. Piranhas are muscular, producing good speed, with teeth positioned forward in the jaw to facilitate flesh tearing. Other characins are not as carnivorous, but enthusiastically eat aquarium plants.

All characins are natural schoolers, but differences in mouth position affect feeding habits: hatchetfish have upturned mouths, well suited to catching insects that alight on the water surface. Most of the popular tetras have mouths suited for midwater feeding while Distichodus has a flattened body, with a downturned mouth suited to low levels.

Most characins spawn in an egg scattering fashion—the eggs are adhesive and usually lodge among plants. An exception is the Splashing Tetra, which lays its eggs out of water to protect them from water-living predators. Although the eggs remain safe, they must be kept moist until they hatch—constant splashing is required by the male swimming below.

NEON TETRA

A shoal of Neon Tetras is all you need to bring brilliant color and movement to the aquarium.

Gasteropelecus sternicla
SILVER HATCHETFISH

ANOSTOMUS ANOSTOMUS

FAMILY: *ANOSTOMIDAE*
COMMON NAME: *STRIPED* ANOSTOMUS

This hardy native of the Orinoco and Amazon river systems, Guyana, and Suriname loves to lurk among the tank's underwater roots, where its camouflaging lines mimic the lines of the roots. The dorsal and ventral profiles of this torpedo-shaped fish curve only slightly. The head is flat with a very upturned mouth and a protruding lower jaw at the end of a long, tapered snout. Three dark, broad, jagged-edged bands run along the yellow-gold body. The dorsal and caudal fins have red blotches; the pelvic, adipose, and anal fins are only slightly tinged with red. Larger, plumper fish are likely to be female.
SPECIAL CARE: Provide this all-level swimmer with a spacious aquarium, well-planted with tough-leaved (or plastic) plants, and keep in small shoals to avoid quarreling between individual fish. Occasionally it may harass slower-moving fishes, such as angels or discus, whose slime-covered skin appears to hold some attraction. This fish needs plenty of green matter in its diet. There is no information available on breeding.

FEEDING

COMPATIBILITY

EASE OF KEEPING

SIZE

7 in (18 cm) 5.5 in (14 cm)

ANOSTOMUS TERNETZI

FAMILY: *ANOSTOMIDAE*
COMMON NAME: *TERNETZ'S* ANOSTOMUS

This fish from the Orinoco and Amazon river systems is understandably often confused with the previous species, *A. anostomus*, with whom it shares the same aquarium requirements. The dorsal and ventral profiles of this torpedo-shaped fish curve only slightly. The body coloration is yellow-gold with three broad, dark bands running along the body. The upturned mouth has a distinct degree of red. The fins are colorless, with the exception of the caudal fin. This has two small yellow areas at its base, which match the body color. The small adipose fin is marked with red. Larger, plumper fish are likely to be female.
SPECIAL CARE: This fish is best suited to an aquarium generously planted with tough-leaved vegetation. It is less likely than the previous species to harass other slower-moving species as it swims through all levels of the tank. Breeding information is not available.

FEEDING

COMPATIBILITY

EASE OF KEEPING

SIZE

6.3 in (16 cm) 4.1 in (10.5 cm)

LEPORINUS OCTOFASCIATUM

FAMILY: *ANOSTOMIDAE*
COMMON NAME: *EIGHT-BANDED* LEPORINUS

Found in the slow-moving streams of *Amazonia*, from Guyana to the Plate River, this species is easy to confuse with similar-looking species—the problem being that the genus contains over 50 species, not every one of which has been completely classified. The body shape of the Eight-Banded Leporinus is elongated and cylindrical, with the dorsal and ventral contours having an equal, moderate curve. The body coloration is a very pale blend of white and yellow. Eight dark bands encircle the body, although the actual number may vary, since some can give the appearance of being split to form double bandings. The head is small, the mouth is terminally situated, and the red-rimmed eyes are relatively large. The pelvic, adipose, and anal fins have some black color. As with many members of the genus, the color patterns may become less intense or distinct with maturity.
SPECIAL CARE: Occupying the middle and lower levels of the tank, this fish requires a spacious aquarium provided with large plastic replica plants or tough-leaved natural plants. There is no information available on breeding.

FEEDING

COMPATIBILITY

EASE OF KEEPING

SIZE

8.5 in (22 cm) 6 in (15 cm)

APHYOCHARAX ANISITSI

FAMILY: *CHARACIDAE*
COMMON NAME: *BLOODFIN; ARGENTINE BLOODFIN;*
RED-FINNED CHARACIN; RED-FINNED TETRA

Coming from Argentina and Paraguay, this fish was formerly described as
A. rubripinnis. Its body has equally curved dorsal and ventral profiles.
However, it is not as deep in the body as the more traditionally kept characins,
like the tetras. The body coloration consists of an olive green dorsal surface
and silvery flanks. As the common name suggests, the main coloration is
present in the fins. The pelvic, anal, and lower-half of the caudal fins are blood
red, with only a little red in the dorsal fin. When capturing the fish for
transportation try herding them into a plastic container as the tiny hooks on
the anal fin of the male can often become entangled in a net.
SPECIAL CARE: Keep this species in a shoal in a well-planted aquarium. It
breeds freely, but precautions should be taken to prevent egg eating.

FEEDING

COMPATIBILITY

EASE OF KEEPING

SIZE

2.5 in (6 cm)   2.5 in (6 cm)

SYMBOL KEY

FEEDING
Herbivore

Omnivore

Predator

COMPATIBILITY
single specimen

community fish

safe with small fish

safe with invertebrates

EASE OF KEEPING
scale of 1 to 10
(with 1 being easiest to keep)

SIZE
in the wild

in captivity

ASTYANAX FASCIATUS MEXICANUS

FAMILY: *CHARACIDAE*
COMMON NAME: *BLIND CAVE FISH*

The natural habitat of this
peaceful fish, formerly
known as *Anoptichthys
jordani*, is the underwater
caves of Mexico. The
outstanding physical characteristic is the
absence of eyes, and it is this "blindness" that
is the obvious attraction for aquarists. In the wild this
fish navigates around its totally dark waters using its
lateral line system to avoid bumping into obstacles. In
an aquarium, this system helps it avoid crashing into
other fish, with whom it is quite at ease. The body
shape follows the usual tetra pattern, although the
dorsal profile has a slightly higher arch. The body
coloration is plain pink with a silvery sheen. The fins
resemble the body color.
SPECIAL CARE: The Blind Cave Fish swims at all levels
of the aquarium. The requirement for light is
optional, and is only necessary to view the fish
and to make the aquarium plants grow. Visual
decoration of the tank is also unimportant, but
normal aquarium conditions must otherwise be
maintained. Despite their "blind" parents, fry are
born with eyes, which
degenerate, if, as in
nature, the fish are kept
in complete darkness.

FEEDING

COMPATIBILITY

EASE OF KEEPING

SIZE

3.5 in (9 cm)   3.5 in (9 cm)

BRACHYCHALCINUS ORBICULARIS

FAMILY: *CHARACIDAE*
COMMON NAME: *SILVER
DOLLAR TETRA; DISK TETRA*

Found over a vast area from
Guyana down to the *Rio
Paraguay*, this shoaling fish
was formerly classified as
Echippicharax. In Europe it is
also known as the Salmon
Discus and Disc Tetra. The
body shape is not typical of
the characin, but could be
described as a cross between
the more heavily built piranha
and the smaller, more orthodox tetra.
SPECIAL CARE: This active species needs room
to swim at mid-tank level. Plastic or tough-
leaved plants are appropriate, as it will eat
soft-leaved plants. Provide some
vegetable matter in its normal diet. It
needs areas of bushy plants or, more
suitably, inedible spawning mops, in
which to lay eggs.

FEEDING

COMPATIBILITY

EASE OF KEEPING

SIZE

4.7 in (12 cm)   4 in (10 cm)

CHALCEUS MACROLEPIDOTUS

FAMILY: *CHALCEIDAE*
COMMON NAME: *PINK-TAILED* CHALCEUS

FEEDING

COMPATIBILITY

EASE OF KEEPING

4

SIZE

10 in (25 cm) 8 in (20 cm)

Except for the caudal fin, this predatory fish, from the rivers of *Amazonia* and Guyana, is very similar in appearance to the much smaller African species *Arnoldichthys spilopterus*, and even more like a much nearer relative, *C. erythrurus*. The elongated body shape is stocky and somewhat cylindrical. The body coloration features an olive green dorsal surface with silver-green flanks. There may be an indistinct blotch just behind the gill cover. The scales are very large and well-defined. The mouth has a longer upper lip, and the eyes have a red top section. All fins, with the exception of the pectoral, can be pinkish with some yellow. The deeply forked caudal fin, as the popular name implies, is colored bright pink.

SPECIAL CARE: This large, active, hungry species needs plenty of room. Although it is suitable for a community of larger-sized fishes, its tankmates should be chosen carefully for their ability to fend for themselves. The aquarium, where it swims at the upper and middle levels, should be well-planted around the edges. No information is available on breeding.

GYMNOCORYMBUS TERNETZI

FAMILY: *CHARACIDAE*
COMMON NAME: *BLACK WIDOW*

FEEDING

COMPATIBILITY

EASE OF KEEPING

1

SIZE

2.2 in (5.5 cm) 2 in (5 cm)

A peaceful native of the *Mato Grosso* area of central South America, the Black Widow is an ideal fish for beginners. Its body shape is oval, the front two-thirds colored silver and the rear one-third a sooty black with occasional iridescences. Three vertical dark bars cross the body—through the eye, behind the gill cover, and in front of the dorsal fin. The anal fin runs half the length of the body, from below the dorsal fin to the front of the caudal peduncle. The dorsal and anal fins are black, the adipose fin is black-edged, and the remaining fins are colorless. Its black coloration fades with age. The male's caudal fin may have white tips, which are set off nicely against generous planting. The male is otherwise distinguished by a more pointed dorsal fin and a broader front part of the anal fin. The body of the female is plumper. An aquarium-bred, long-finned strain has been developed; wild fish have less exaggerated finnage.

SPECIAL CARE: This fish, which swims at the upper and middle levels of the aquarium, should be kept in shoals. It prefers floating foods and needs a well-planted aquarium with tall grassy types of plants. This fish is easy to breed.

HASEMANIA NANA

FAMILY: *CHARACIDAE*
COMMON NAME: *SILVERTIP TETRA*

FEEDING

COMPATIBILITY

EASE OF KEEPING

1

SIZE

2 in (5 cm) 2 in (5 cm)

This peaceful shoaling species, from the *Rio San Francisco* area of Brazil, has suffered an identity crisis over the years: it is virtually identical to fishes classified as *Hemigrammus nanus*, has also been known as *Hasemania marginata* (itself a possible synonym for *Hasemania melanura*), and appears to be inconsistent in sometimes having an adipose fin and sometimes not! Various sources have wrestled with the problem; the most recent decided on *Hasemania nana* for fishes without an adipose fin and *Hemigrammus nanus* for those with. The outline of this fish is slimmer than is usually expected for a tetra. The basic body color is golden brown, but varies from pale silver in females to a rich coppery brown in sexually mature males. A broadening black line, topped by a lighter gold area, begins just behind the dorsal fin and runs into the caudal fin. As its common name suggests, all of its fins are tipped with white. The females are plumper than the males, particularly at spawning times.

SPECIAL CARE: This upper- and middle-level swimmer requires a well-planted aquarium that includes some bushy plants. This fish is hardy and easily spawned. The young fry are very small and take some days to become readily visible.

HEMIGRAMMUS CAUDOVITTATUS

FAMILY: *CHARACIDAE*
COMMON NAME: *BUENOS AIRES TETRA*

FEEDING

COMPATIBILITY

EASE OF KEEPING

SIZE

3 in (7.5 cm)   3 in (7.5 cm)

This popular aquarium fish, from the Plate River region of Argentina, Paraguay, and Brazil, is best kept in a shoal. Its slim body has a silvery coloration. A vertical dark bar partially crosses the body just behind the gill cover, and there is another small dark blotch to the rear of this. A thin blue line runs horizontally along the body, ending in the central section of the bright red caudal fin; at the caudal peduncle it is obscured by a black line that broadens out before diminishing rapidly. The pelvic and anal fins are red, the latter edged with black and tipped with white. The dorsal fin is yellowish. The top-half of the eye is red. Males have the typical intensification of colors at spawning times, when the females can be more easily recognized by their swollen bodies.

SPECIAL CARE: This all-level swimmer may nibble soft-leaved plants, so provide tougher-leaved vegetation in a generally well-planted aquarium. This fish is easy to breed.

HEMIGRAMMUS ERYTHROZONUS

FAMILY: *CHARACIDAE*
COMMON NAME: *GLOWLIGHT TETRA*

The delicately colored Glowlight Tetra is found in the northern areas of South America. Its elongated oval body is strikingly divided by a glowing red-gold line. This starts on the snout, takes in the red top-half of the eye, and continues along the almost transparent body to end in a small red area on the base of the colorless caudal fin. The dorsal and anal fins have some red at their bases and, like the pelvic fins, have milky-white tips.

SPECIAL CARE: These small peaceful fish look best in a shoal and are suitable for a modest-sized species aquarium. They prefer a well-planted aquarium, where they cruise the middle and lower levels. Although they can be bred, the best successes take place in soft, acidic water. Take the usual precautions to prevent parents from eating the eggs, or remove the adult fishes immediately after spawning is over.

FEEDING

COMPATIBILITY

EASE OF KEEPING

SIZE

1.5 in (4 cm)   1.5 in (4 cm)

HEMIGRAMMUS OCELLIFER

FAMILY: *CHARACIDAE*
COMMON NAME: *BEACON FISH; HEAD AND TAILLIGHT FISH; MOTORIST FISH*

The Beacon Fish, found in the northern areas of South America, is representative of the decorative tetra group of fishes and has been an aquarium favorite for a long time. The body outline is fairly deep, following the general tetra pattern. The main color is silvery gray, which forms the background to contrasting areas of coloration. There is a small gold-green spot just behind the gill cover, the top-half of the eye is bright red, and there is a gold spot above a red-bordered black blotch at the base of the caudal fin. The caudal fin has a hint of red in its upper section, and the anal and pelvic fins are white-tipped. The remaining fins, however, are colorless.

SPECIAL CARE: This fish needs a well-planted aquarium. It is easy to breed.

FEEDING

COMPATIBILITY

EASE OF KEEPING

SIZE

1.8 in (4.5 cm)   1.8 in (4.5 cm)

SYMBOL KEY

FEEDING

Herbivore

Omnivore

Predator

COMPATIBILITY

single specimen

community fish

safe with small fish

safe with invertebrates

EASE OF KEEPING

scale of 1 to 10
(with 1 being easiest to keep)

SIZE

in the wild

in captivity

HEMMIGRAMMUS PULCHER

FAMILY: *CHARACIDAE*
COMMON NAME: *PRETTY TETRA*

The Peruvian area of the Amazon River is home to this popular shoaling species. The body outline is deeper than normal. The back, including the head, is a dark gray-green color shading down through a brief purple-copper phase to the silver lower-half. Iridescences may be seen depending on lighting conditions. The scales are dark-edged and show up particularly well in the darker areas. The eyes are bicolored, reddish-purple above with a bluish-green bottom-half. Directly behind the gill cover there is a purplish-red mark; the lower area of the caudal peduncle, forward above the anal fin, is dark colored and accentuated by a thin gold line. All of the fins are pinkish-purple.

SPECIAL CARE: The Pretty Tetra needs a generally well-planted aquarium, where it keeps to the middle and lower levels. It can be difficult to find a compatible pair of fishes that are willing to spawn. Be sure that the female is ready for spawning (filled with eggs, as indicated by the swollen body), otherwise the male might reject her. The breeding tank should be fairly large since the fishes require plenty of swimming space during pre-spawning courtship diving. Replacing an unwilling male often results in success.

FEEDING

COMPATIBILITY

EASE OF KEEPING

SIZE

1.8 in (4.5 cm)   1.8 in (4.5 cm)

HEMIGRAMMUS RHODOSTOMUS

FAMILY: *CHARACIDAE*
COMMON NAME: *RUMMY-NOSED TETRA*

FEEDING

COMPATIBILITY

EASE OF KEEPING

SIZE

2 in (5 cm)   2 in (5 cm)

The most obvious features of this slim-bodied, beautiful lower Amazon fish are, of course, its red head and its strikingly patterned caudal fin. (The red area on the very similar False Rummy-Nose, *Petitella georgiae*, extends past the gill covers toward the dorsal fin, a useful distinguishing characteristic between the two species.) With several similar-looking species available (*H. bleheri* and the above-mentioned *P. georgiae*), the task of making a positive identification is problematical; some authorities feel that most species kept by aquarists are, in fact, either of the stated alternatives.

SPECIAL CARE: A well-planted aquarium is required. Whichever species is kept, it may be difficult to maintain, being both shy and sensitive to changes in water conditions. For this reason, details on breeding are sparse. It is only suitable for a community of small, nonboisterous fishes and is probably best kept in a separate species aquarium.

HYPHESSOBRYCON CALLISTUS

FAMILY: *CHARACIDAE*
COMMON NAME: *BLACKFIN FLAME TETRA*

FEEDING

COMPATIBILITY

EASE OF KEEPING

SIZE

1.5 in (4 cm)   1 in (2.5 cm)

Although commonly bred in hatcheries, this beautiful tetra is native to the streams of the southern Amazon Basin in Brazil and Paraguay. The body is red-orange, with this coloration extending to the caudal fin. The dorsal fin is black, edged in white at the rear. The pelvic and anal fins are reddish, with white on their distal edges, and the anal fin is smudged with black posteriorly. A black patch lies behind the gill cover at about the level of the lateral line. It schools along the shaded edges of blackwater streams and appreciates plant cover and a dark-colored aquarium substrate.

SPECIAL CARE: This is a good choice for a community tank; a shoal of five to seven fishes is recommended. It adapts to all commonly available aquarium foods. For a species tank or breeding purposes, provide moderately soft, slightly acidic water, and maintain a temperature of around 80°F (27°C). It is among the easier tetras to spawn. Caution: if not well fed, this species may attack weaker members of its own school.

HYPHESSOBRYCON ERYTHROSTIGMA

FAMILY: *CHARACIDAE*
COMMON NAME: *BLEEDING HEART TETRA*

Previously known as *H. rubrostigma*, this is a very
beautiful species that comes from Colombia and
northern South America. A similar-looking species,
H. socolofi, has more rounded fins and perhaps lacks the
exaggerated finnage. The body is both high-backed and deep. The
general coloration is pinkish-silver, but the most striking feature is
the glowing pink spot located on the flanks. A vertical black bar
crosses the red-topped eyes. There is no problem in distinguishing the
sexes. The male has a large sickle-shaped dorsal fin, which is white at
the base and red on the remainder and streaked with dark blue-black.
The female's dorsal fin, though a similar color, is much shorter and rounded.
The anal fin of the male, like that of the female, is long-based and tinged blue-
white with a black edge, but far more concave. The caudal fin is bluish-pink.
SPECIAL CARE: The Bleeding Heart is quite nervous and tends to dart around
when introduced to new surroundings. A spacious aquarium, well-planted,
provides a sense of security for this middle- and lower-level swimmer. Breeding
is not a regular occurrence.

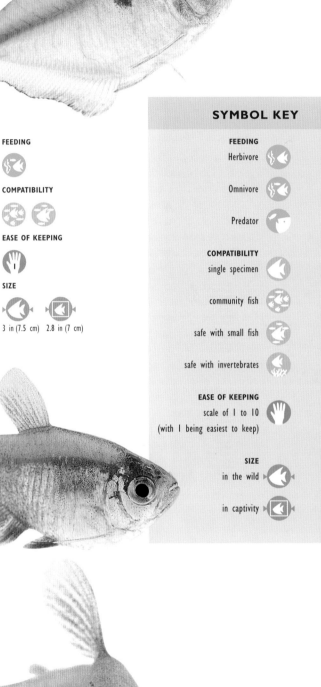

FEEDING

COMPATIBILITY

EASE OF KEEPING

SIZE

3 in (7.5 cm) 2.8 in (7 cm)

HYPHESSOBRYCON FLAMMEUS

FAMILY: *CHARACIDAE*
COMMON NAME: *FLAME TETRA*

FEEDING

COMPATIBILITY

EASE OF KEEPING

SIZE

1.5 in (4 cm) 1.6 in (4 cm)

Although long-established among
hobbyists, this native of the *Rio de
Janeiro* area drifts in and out of
favor. A similar, though paler,
species is *H. griemi*. The body
shape of this fish is typical of the
tetra group, though it is slightly
more elongated. The coloration of the body is pinkish-
brown with a silvery area, crossed by two dark bars,
just behind the gill cover and extending down to the
belly. The lower rear-half of the body is much more
reddish. The eyes are blue. The pelvic, anal, and caudal
fins are red-edged with black; the dorsal fin may be
black with some white streaks, and an adipose fin is
present. Spawning
males have intensified coloration, and the
female shows an increasing girth.
SPECIAL CARE: A normally-planted aquarium
suits the Flame Tetra, which swims at all levels of
the aquarium. This fish is easily bred.

SYMBOL KEY

FEEDING

Herbivore

Omnivore

Predator

COMPATIBILITY

single specimen

community fish

safe with small fish

safe with invertebrates

EASE OF KEEPING

scale of 1 to 10
(with 1 being easiest to keep)

SIZE

in the wild

in captivity

HYPHESSOBRYCON HERBERTAXELRODI

FAMILY: *CHARACIDAE*
COMMON NAME: *BLACK NEON*

Like the Black Widow, a native of the *Mato Grosso* area in Brazil, this fish is not as deep-bodied as most tetras. A bright, light greenish-blue line along the flanks, from the top of the red-topped eyes to the top of the caudal peduncle, separates the olive green dorsal surface from a black area, which gradually pales to a silvery belly. The black area extends into the center rays of the caudal fin, where it is bordered by two light patches. Females have generally deeper bodies and become plump when they are in spawning condition.

SPECIAL CARE: Provide a dark substrate in a well-planted aquarium, where the Black Neon will swim at all levels. Like all tetras, this fish prefers soft, acidic water, which will bring out its colors, though it will tolerate water of medium hardness. Feeding live foods will induce the onset of spawning.

FEEDING

COMPATIBILITY

EASE OF KEEPING

SIZE

1.5 in (4 cm)   1.5 in (4 cm)

HYPHESSOBRYCON PULCHRIPINNIS

FAMILY: *CHARACIDAE*
COMMON NAME: *LEMON TETRA*

FEEDING

COMPATIBILITY

EASE OF KEEPING

SIZE

2 in (5 cm) 2 in (5 cm)

This is a very attractive, subtly colored tetra from the *Rio Tocantins* in the lower Amazon. The body shape is typical of the group, with a high profile tapering evenly down to the caudal peduncle. The body coloration is a translucent greenish-yellow, and its silvery internal organs and backbone are fairly visible. The top-half of the eye is bright red. All fins have an element of black with strong yellow in them, particularly the front of the dorsal and anal fins. Males have the greater coloration. Females, being much deeper in the body, are easy to recognize. It seems rather pointless to produce an albino form, but that is exactly what has been done.

SPECIAL CARE: Swimming at all levels, a shoal of Lemon Tetras looks very impressive when kept in a well-planted aquarium with a dark substrate. They require space for spawning among bushy plants.

HYPHESSOBRYCON ROSACEUS

FAMILY: *CHARACIDAE*
COMMON NAME: *ROSY TETRA*

The natural distribution of this peaceful fish is in Guyana in the lower Amazon. At first sight, and to an unkindly eye, this species could be nicknamed the "Poor Man's Bleeding Heart Tetra," since the coloring is fairly similar. However, the shape of its smaller-proportioned body is not as deep and it lacks the glowing spot. The dorsal fin is marked with red, streaked with black, and has a white tip. That of the male is a well-developed sickle or pennant shape and can reach back over the adipose fin in mature specimens. This species forms part of a fairly large group of similarly colored fishes, which also includes *H. bentosi, H. erythrostigma, H. ornatus,* and possibly *H. robertsi.* Of these, *H. erythrostigma*, with its decorative body spot, is the one most easily identified. The confusion over the exact classification of the other species, and whether they are all related subspecies within a common genus, has yet to be resolved.

SPECIAL CARE: Provide a dark substrate and a generously planted aquarium, where it will cruise the middle and lower levels. Breeding is possible in soft, acidic water conditions.

FEEDING

COMPATIBILITY

EASE OF KEEPING

SIZE

2 in (5 cm) 2 in (5 cm)

HYPHESSOBRYCON SERPAE

FAMILY: *CHARACIDAE*
COMMON NAME: SERPAE *TETRA*

From Guyana and the Amazon area, this is yet another member of a group of similarly colored fishes (*H. callistus, H. minor*, and possibly *H. haraldschultzei* and *H. hasemani*). Many classification wrangles revolve around the existence, shape, and color of the shoulder spot, and an early resolution of such problems would be welcomed. The body outline of this fish follows the typical tetra shape. The overall coloration is blood red with a dark shoulder spot. The lower part of the body is a paler shade on the belly. Pectoral, pelvic, and caudal fins are red, and the anal fin is red with a black margin. The dorsal fin, only slightly exaggerated in the male fish, is mostly black, with some red at its base and front and a whitish tip. The females are generally plumper and a shade lighter overall.
SPECIAL CARE: This fish thrives in a well-planted aquarium with a dark substrate. It swims peacefully at the middle and lower levels, though like the Yellow Tetra (*H. bifasciatus*) it is likely to nip the fins of other fishes. It follows the standard egg-scattering procedure among bushy plants.

FEEDING

COMPATIBILITY

EASE OF KEEPING
1

SIZE
2 in (5 cm)   2 in (5 cm)

INPAICHTHYS KERRI

FAMILY: *CHARACIDAE*
COMMON NAME: *BLUE EMPEROR*

FEEDING

COMPATIBILITY

EASE OF KEEPING
5

SIZE
1.5 in (4 cm) 1.5 in (4 cm)

Males and females are distinctive, with the former being pale blue above, with a less distinct dark mid-lateral stripe from the tip of the snout to the caudal peduncle. Although the female's stripe is darker, the upper portion of her body is pale yellowish-green. The fins of both sexes are colorless. Found in the upper Amazon region, this species is sometimes confused with the Emperor Tetra, *Nematobrycon palmeri*.
SPECIAL CARE: The lovely blue coloration of the male tends to fade if conditions are less than perfect. It needs soft, acidic water, with plenty of vegetation in a large tank that affords swimming space. It is best exhibited in a tank devoted only to a school of its own kind.

MEGALAMPHODUS MEGALOPTERUS

FAMILY: *CHARACIDAE*
COMMON NAME: *BLACK PHANTOM TETRA*

The body shape of this fish, from the Bolivian and Brazilian borders, is typical of the family. Its coloration is a transparent silvery gray. A black teardrop-shaped mark appears on the fish's shoulder and is outlined by a surrounding bright area. This is one species where the female has an edge over the male as far as coloration is concerned: the adipose, pelvic, and anal fins contain some red in their overall blackness, while the male's fins are less brightly marked. The dorsal fin of the male may become larger with age.
SPECIAL CARE: This middle- and lower-level swimmer likes a generously planted aquarium. A separate species tank where all the fish's requirements can be met is advisable, although it can share a quiet tank with smaller nonboisterous fishes quite happily. It needs soft, acidic water for its well-being in general and especially if breeding is to be attempted. The fish are more than likely to eat their eggs, and the eggs themselves are said to be light-sensitive.

FEEDING

COMPATIBILITY

EASE OF KEEPING
5

SIZE
2 in (5 cm)   2 in (5 cm)

SYMBOL KEY

FEEDING

Herbivore

Omnivore

Predator

COMPATIBILITY

single specimen

community fish

safe with small fish

safe with invertebrates

EASE OF KEEPING

scale of 1 to 10
(with 1 being easiest to keep)

SIZE

in the wild

in captivity

MEGALAMPHODUS SWEGLESI

FAMILY: *CHARACIDAE*
COMMON NAME: *RED PHANTOM TETRA*

FEEDING

COMPATIBILITY

EASE OF KEEPING

5

SIZE

2 in (5 cm)   2 in (5 cm)

At first sight this fish, from the *Orinoco* region of northern South America, is a color twin of the previous species, *M. megalopterus*. In fact, the two fishes come from completely separate rivers. The general color of this species transposes red for the black of the previous species: the body is a transparent crimson, with all fins having a matching denser shade of the same color; the dorsal fin also has some black markings, with a white tip seen on the female. The dark shoulder blotch is again present. The predominantly red dorsal fin in the male fish is often well-produced but may be narrower than that of the Black Phantom. The pelvic and anal fins are often tipped with white. Due to the transparency of the body, the silvery sac containing the internal organs is often easily seen.

SPECIAL CARE: Cruising the middle and lower levels, the somewhat sensitive Red Phantom, like the previous species, can be kept with nonboisterous small fishes or in a separate well-planted species aquarium where its particular requirements can be met. It needs soft, acidic water for its well-being in general and especially if breeding is to be attempted. This can be difficult: the fish tend to eat their eggs, and the light-sensitive eggs themselves may be prone to disintegration unless shielded from direct light.

MOENKHAUSIA OLIGOLEPIS

FAMILY: *CHARACIDAE*
COMMON NAME: *GLASS TETRA*

FEEDING

COMPATIBILITY

EASE OF KEEPING

1

SIZE

4.7 in (12 cm)   4 in (10 cm)

The peaceful Glass Tetra is found in the slow-moving or stationary waters of the Amazonian river system and Guyana. A very similar but smaller species is *M. sanctaefilomenae*. The body shape is an elongated ellipse, with the ventral contour slightly more deeply curved than the dorsal. Its body coloration is a silvery but dull gray. When young, it displays quite distinct color patterns, but these may fade with increasing age. The scales are especially well-defined, but become less so toward the silvery belly. The lower-half of the iris of the eye is yellow, and the top is red. A dark patch crosses the base of the caudal fin, highlighted by yellow on the caudal peduncle. The fins are faintly reddish-yellow, with the anal and pelvic fins having light-colored front edges. Females are built much more heavily than males.

SPECIAL CARE: Suitable for a species aquarium, the Glass Tetra swims at the middle and lower levels of the aquarium, which should be generously planted. Although not a total herbivore, it may nibble at plants unless it is given sufficient green matter in its diet, so provide tough-leaved vegetation. It follows standard egg-scattering procedure among bushy plants.

MOENKHAUSIA PITTIERI

FAMILY: *CHARACIDAE*
COMMON NAME: *DIAMOND TETRA*

FEEDING

COMPATIBILITY

EASE OF KEEPING

SIZE

2.6 in (6.5 cm)   2.4 in (6 cm)

Found in the waters of Lake Valencia, Venezuela, this fish has a body shape typical of the tetra group, with the dorsal and ventral profiles curving equally. When caught in side-lighting, its dark gray-blue body coloration reveals an iridescent sparkling on the flanks. These sparkles are formed by the metallic-looking yellowy-silver scales, some of which encroach on the caudal fin base. In juveniles a dark line may run along the body to end on the caudal peduncle, but this line fades with age. The top part of the gold-rimmed eyes is bright red. The dorsal fin is sickle-shaped, especially in mature males. The pelvic fins are rather long, and the caudal fin is deeply forked. All of the fins are bluish and have white edges.

SPECIAL CARE: With its delicate fin coloring, this middle-swimming, shoaling species looks best in a spacious, well-planted aquarium with dark substrate and decorated with bogwood. Under these conditions, it will probably feel right at home, though it may take some time to reach mature adulthood and fully develop its physical characteristics. It follows the standard egg-scattering procedure among bushy plants.

MOENKHAUSIA SANCTAEFILOMENAE

FAMILY: *CHARACIDAE*
COMMON NAME: *YELLOW-BANDED TETRA*

This peaceful, easily accommodated tetra comes from the rivers and streams of Paraguay, western Brazil, eastern Peru, and eastern Bolivia. Most of the specimens encountered in aquarium shops, however, are captive bred, as this is an easy species to spawn. Silver-colored scales cover the body surface, reflecting light and producing an attractive diamond pattern. The upper-halves of the eyes are bright red. Their fins are colorless. The caudal peduncle is bright yellow at its narrowest point, black posteriorly with some dark pigment spreading on to the caudal fin.

SPECIAL CARE: Sexing the adults can be difficult. The only outer indication of gender is the more fully rounded belly of the female. Eggs are attached to spawning mops or to the roots of floating plants by either schools or pairs of fish. Soft water acidified with peat is recommended for the spawning tank, and the eggs must be protected from the parents after spawning is complete.

FEEDING

COMPATIBILITY

EASE OF KEEPING

SIZE

2.7 in (7 cm)   2.7 in (7 cm)

NEMATOBRYCON PALMERI

FAMILY: *CHARACIDAE*
COMMON NAME: *EMPEROR TETRA*

This elongated fish from Colombia has a highly arched back and a slightly convex ventral surface. The dorsal surface is a light brownish-green with a violet sheen; a broad blue-black (or very deep violet) band runs along the whole body, tapering to a thin line through the center of the caudal fin; the ventral surface is silvery. Male fish may have a row of red-brown scales just above the dark band from midway along the body to the end of the caudal peduncle. The eyes of the male are blue-turquoise; those of the female are less blue. The male's dorsal fin is sickle-shaped with a dark leading edge, extending well back over the body; its caudal fin has a dark edge on the top and bottom, and extended rays from the tip of each lobe and also from the center. The long-based anal fin is yellow with a dark line running just inside its outer edge.

SPECIAL CARE: A peaceful fish, this all-level swimmer looks best in a well-planted aquarium with a dark substrate and subdued lighting. It follows a protracted spawning sequence of egg scattering among bushy plants, producing a small number of eggs at a time.

FEEDING

COMPATIBILITY

EASE OF KEEPING

SIZE

2.5 in (6 cm)   2.5 in (6 cm)

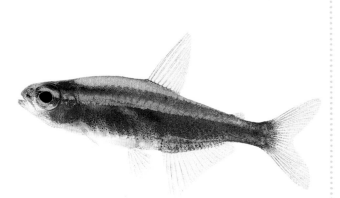

PARACHEIRODON AXELRODI

FAMILY: *CHARACIDAE*
COMMON NAME: *CARDINAL TETRA*

The majority of Cardinal Tetras are caught in the wilderness, in the slow-flowing or stationary waters of Venezuela, Brazil, and Colombia, since large-scale commercial breeding has not been established. The dorsal surface of its slim body is dark greenish-brown underlined by an electric blue stripe running from its snout through the top-halves of the eyes and on the base of the adipose fin. The females are noticeably deeper in the body than the males.
SPECIAL CARE: A shoaling, all-level swimmer, this species appreciates a shady aquarium with clear areas of water into which it can venture. Avoid excessive water currents and bright lighting. Although it can tolerate most water conditions satisfactorily, soft, acidic water encourages the best colors and enhances breeding conditions. Both the eggs and fry may be susceptible to damage from bright light.

FEEDING

COMPATIBILITY

EASE OF KEEPING

SIZE

1.8 in (4.5 cm) 1.8 in (4.5 cm)

PARACHEIRODON INNESI

FAMILY: *CHARACIDAE*
COMMON NAME: *NEON TETRA*

A long established aquarium favorite from Peru, this slim, shoaling fish looks its best under subdued lighting. Its coloration is unmistakable. The dorsal surface is a dark green-brown surmounting an electric blue-green stripe running from the snout through the top-halves of the eyes to the base of the adipose fin. Below this line the rear-half of the body is bright red and the forward part is silver.

FEEDING

COMPATIBILITY

EASE OF KEEPING

SIZE

1.5 in (4 cm) 1.5 in (4 cm)

The females are deeper in the body, and the blue-green line often appears bent due to their plumper shape.
SPECIAL CARE: The Neon Tetra likes a well-planted aquarium with a dark substrate. Although hardy, it may fall victim to neon disease (*pleistophora*), an attack by parasites that is not completely curable. The symptoms are a cloudiness and general dullness of the red coloration. Don't be tempted to keep this species with larger fish like cichlids. Angelfish, though theoretically coming from the same waters in nature, will eventually eat them. They are not difficult to breed, and follow the standard egg scattering procedure among plants.

PRIONOBRAMA FILIGERA

FAMILY: *CHARACIDAE*
COMMON NAME: *GLASS BLOODFIN; TRANSLUCENT BLOODFIN*

A native of Brazil's *Rio Madeira* area in the Amazon Basin, this elongated fish is fairly streamlined and very similar to the genuine Bloodfin (see *Aphyocharax anisitsi*). Its body coloration is blue-gray, but it often appears semi-transparent. The long-based anal fin has a much longer first ray that is often white, as is the first ray of the pelvic fin. The coloration of the fins is generally scant, but the male has a dark line immediately behind the first ray of the anal fin, and its caudal fin is deep red. The female only has red at the base of the caudal fin.
SPECIAL CARE: This active fish prefers a well-planted aquarium, with some water currents and floating plants under which a shoal may gather. For general upkeep, the degree of water hardness is not critical, but soft water brings excellent results for breeding purposes.

FEEDING

COMPATIBILITY

EASE OF KEEPING

SIZE

2.5 in (6 cm) 2.5 in (6 cm)

PRISTELLA MAXILLARIS

FAMILY: *CHARACIDAE*
COMMON NAME: *X-RAY FISH*

FEEDING

COMPATIBILITY

EASE OF KEEPING

SIZE

1.8 in (4.5 cm)   1.8 in (4.5 cm)

Most specimens are now bred in captivity rather than collected from the wilds of Venezuela, Guyana, or Amazonian Brazil. Hardy, peaceful, and very decorative in a shoal, it has been popular with hobbyists for some 70 years. The body shape of this fish follows the common tetra pattern, with equal curvature to both the dorsal and ventral surfaces. The fish is apparently translucent, perhaps pale greenish-yellow at best, with the backbone and the internal organs in their silver sac clearly visible. A dark spot lies on the shoulder just behind the gill cover. The dorsal and anal fins are tri-colored, with yellow, black, and white bands progressing away from the body. The pelvic fins are similarly marked. The females are plump and the males have brighter colors. The shape of the silvery sac containing the body organs is pointed in the male and round in the female.
SPECIAL CARE: This fish uses all levels of a well-planted aquarium. You may need to try several different male/female pairings before a successful spawning is achieved.

THAYERIA OBLIQUUA

FAMILY: *CHARACIDAE*
COMMON NAME: *PENGUIN FISH*

This species, imported from the streams of Brazil, is less commonly seen than the previous species. The body shape of this fish is elongated, and the dorsal and ventral contours are only slightly convex. Olive green on the dorsal ridge shades down through a brassy light yellow to silver on the belly; a gold line runs from just behind the gill cover rearward along the rest of the body and continues to the end of the caudal peduncle. From the rear of the dorsal fin, a blurred dark band runs across the body and continues down into the lower lobe of the caudal fin, where it is bordered by white. Females are noticeably fatter at spawning times.
SPECIAL CARE: This fish needs a well-planted aquarium with some water currents provided. There is no information available on breeding.

FEEDING

COMPATIBILITY

EASE OF KEEPING

SIZE

3 in (7.5 cm) 3 in (7.5 cm)

THAYERIA BOEHLKEI

FAMILY: *CHARACIDAE*
COMMON NAME: *PENGUIN FISH*

A native of Brazil and Peru, this fish displays a distinctive behavior trait: its swimming attitude, which is opposite to that of head-standing fishes. It assumes a "tail-standing" posture, remaining at the same oblique angle even when resting. The body shape is elongated, with only slightly convex dorsal and ventral contours. The coloration is olive green on the dorsal ridge, shading down through light yellow to silver on the belly. A fairly wide dark band runs from the gill cover rearward along the rest of the body and continues down into the lower lobe of the caudal fin. The bright yellow areas immediately above and below this dark band accentuate it even more. Fins are yellowish with a hint of red in the dorsal and caudal fins; the anal fin has a white front edge. Females are similarly marked but are noticeably fatter at spawning times.
SPECIAL CARE: Provide generous vegetation and some water currents in the aquarium. It is a prolific breeder that lays large numbers of eggs.

FEEDING

COMPATIBILITY

EASE OF KEEPING

SIZE

2.4 in (6 cm) 2.4 in (6 cm)

SYMBOL KEY

FEEDING
Herbivore

Omnivore

Predator

COMPATIBILITY
single specimen

community fish

safe with small fish

safe with invertebrates

EASE OF KEEPING
scale of 1 to 10
(with 1 being easiest to keep)

SIZE
in the wild

in captivity

DISTICHODUS LUSSOSO

FAMILY: *CITHARINIDAE*
COMMON NAME: *LONGNOSED* DISTICHODUS

FEEDING

COMPATIBILITY

EASE OF KEEPING
6

SIZE
16 in (40 cm) 13 in (33 cm)

This peaceful fish, a native of equatorial Africa, has a heavily built, elongated body that is laterally-compressed and a low, slowly rising dorsal profile. The body coloration is a greenish golden brown. Several equally spaced dark bands run transversely across the body but do not quite reach the ventral surface. The head is relatively small compared to the rest of the body, with a noticeably pointed snout and a silver lower jaw.
SPECIAL CARE: Despite its good looks, this species is impractical for a typical domestic aquarium. It is only suitable for those who can offer a very spacious aquarium, where it swims at the middle- and lower- levels, and plenty of vegetable matter. It will eat aquarium plants, so a rock-furnished aquarium is best, with tough-leaved or plastic plants. There is no information available on breeding.

DISTICHODUS SEXFASCIATUS

FAMILY: *CITHARINIDAE*
COMMON NAME: *SIX-BARRED* DISTICHODUS

Equatorial Africa is the home of this fish, which is elongated, laterally compressed, and heavily built. The dorsal contour is more curved than the rather flattened ventral surface. In juveniles the body coloration consists of reddish-gold flanks, down which six transverse dark bands extend just to the ventral surface. The scales are well-defined. The head has large eyes, and the lower jaw is silver. All of the fins are bright reddish-yellow except for the black adipose fin, which also has a red outer edge. In adults this coloration changes to plain gray.
SPECIAL CARE: Smaller and more colorful than
D. lussoso, this middle- and lower-level swimmer can be kept in a proportionately smaller, though still very spacious, aquarium. It retains the family appetite for plants, and needs a rocky environment; any other furnishings should be nibbleproof (plastic or tough-leaved plants). No information is available on breeding.

FEEDING

COMPATIBILITY

EASE OF KEEPING
6

SIZE
12 in (30 cm) 10 in (25 cm)

CARNEGIELLA STRIGATA

FAMILY: *GASTEROPELECIDAE*
COMMON NAME: *MARBLED HATCHETFISH*

Coming from the Amazon region and Guyana, this species is also described as *C. strigata strigata*, and there is a look-alike species, *C. strigata vesca*. The body shape is typical of the family. Its coloration is light greenish-yellow above a gold-topped dark line running from the eyes to the caudal peduncle. Several dark,

FEEDING

COMPATIBILITY

EASE OF KEEPING
1

SIZE
2.5 in (6.5 cm) 1.8 in (4.5 cm)

irregularly shaped bands run downward and forward across the lower body, almost parallel with the anal edge. Another dark line follows the ventral edge, ending beneath the eyes. The head is very small, the mouth upturned, and the eyes set well forward. The dorsal fin is set well back and the anal fin is long-based. It has a relatively large caudal fin and no adipose fin. The pectoral fins are exceptionally well-developed and almost reach back to the dorsal fin. The pelvic fins are hardly noticeable. The fins are generally clear, but the dorsal fin occasionally has a small dark mark.
SPECIAL CARE: Swimming at the upper levels, the Hatchetfish prefers a well-planted, spacious aquarium with a firmly secured lid and some shade, which floating plants can provide (its patterns appear to fade under bright lights). They also prefer their own company even in the presence of other nonboisterous species. Reports suggest that healthy parents and subdued lighting will assist a successful spawning.

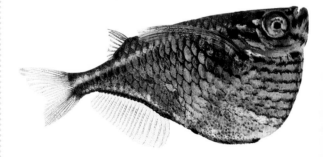

GASTEROPELECUS STERNICLA

FAMILY: *GASTEROPELECIDAE*
COMMON NAME: *SILVER HATCHETFISH*

Native to the Amazonian region and Guyana, this fish has an extra-deep body whose powerful muscles enable the pectoral fins to be flapped like wings—an action that gives them sufficient impetus to leap out of the water and fly across the surface, either to catch insects or to escape from predators. The body shape follows the family pattern. Its body coloration is plain silver with a thin dark line on the flanks along the rear-half of the body. The head is very small, the eyes are set well forward, and the mouth is upturned. The dorsal fin is set well back on the body, and the anal fin is fairly long-based. The pectoral fins are large and winglike, in contrast to the rudimentary pelvic fins. An adipose fin is present in this genus. The caudal fin is deeply forked.

SPECIAL CARE: Though mainly feeding on insects in nature, the Silver Hatchetfish readily accepts floating foods of all types in the aquarium, where it swims at the upper levels. As for all hatchetfishes, the aquarium should have some floating plants to offer shade to these surface swimmers and a tight-fitting hood to deter escape attempts by these jumping fishes. Soft, slightly acidic water with little current or disturbance suit it best.

FEEDING

COMPATIBILITY

EASE OF KEEPING

SIZE

2.5 in (6.5 cm)   2.5 in (6.5 cm)

HEMIODOPSIS GRACILIS

FAMILY: *HEMIODONTIDAE*
COMMON NAME: *SLENDER HEMIODOPSIS*

The body is very streamlined, cylindrical in shape, and equipped with a deeply forked caudal fin; this combination adds up to a very efficient use of energy and results in the fish being a very fast swimmer. Like the majority of the fishes in this genus, the body coloration is silver, marked with a dark spot midway along each flank which extends as a dark line into the lower lobe of the caudal fin. In mature specimens the lower edge of the caudal fin may be red. Sexing may be difficult but females should be plumper. There are several variations on this silver body/dark spot/dark lines into the caudal fin color scheme and exact identification between juvenile specimens is often hard. There is no information regarding breeding in captivity.

SPECIAL CARE: With such an active fish, a large spacious aquarium with plenty of swimming space is required, together with very well-oxygenated water. Because it is so energetic, it is also an expert jumper and the aquarium should have a tight-fitting hood.

FEEDING

COMPATIBILITY

EASE OF KEEPING

SIZE

6 in (15 cm) 1 in (10 cm)

SYMBOL KEY

FEEDING
Herbivore
Omnivore
Predator

COMPATIBILITY
single specimen
community fish
safe with small fish
safe with invertebrates

EASE OF KEEPING
scale of 1 to 10
(with 1 being easiest to keep)

SIZE
in the wild
in captivity

COPEINA GUTTATA

FAMILY: *LEBIASINIDAE*
COMMON NAME: *RED-SPOTTED* COPEINA

The central Amazon region is the natural habitat of this elongated fish. It dorsal surface is only very slightly convex. The ventral profile is deeper, and there is a thick caudal peduncle. The body coloration features a somewhat iridescent green-brown dorsal surface with purple-violet blue flanks and a pinkish-white ventral surface. Each large scale has a red dot, which gives the fish the red-spotted appearance of its popular name. The head is small with large eyes set well forward, quite near the upturned mouth. The fins are yellowish, and the anal and pelvic fins often have reddish-orange edges. The dorsal fin may be marked with black, especially in the female. The lower lobe of the male's caudal fin is smaller than the top lobe.

SPECIAL CARE: The Red-Spotted Copeina needs a well-planted tank, where it cruises the upper and middle levels. Despite being a fish from naturally soft waters, this species breeds readily even in hard water. The male guards and fans the fertilized eggs, usually laid in a depression in the substrate, until they hatch.

FEEDING

COMPATIBILITY

EASE OF KEEPING
3

SIZE
6 in (15 cm) 4.7 in (12 cm)

HEMIODOPSIS THAYERIA

FAMILY: *HEMIODONTIDAE*
COMMON NAME: *SLENDER* HEMIODOPSIS

This species is very similar to *H. gracilis* in body shape and coloration, but this fish's body has a continuous thin black line along its entire length which splits into two at the end of the caudal peduncle to extend into both upper and lower lobes of the caudal fin. This South American genus can be distinguished from the related *Hemiodus* genus by looking at the fishes' scales. *Hemiodus* species have larger scales on the lower-half of the body.

SPECIAL CARE: With fish of this size, its continuous activity may cause more sedate fishes some disturbance; it is probably best to keep this genus in a shoal of its own kind and give it all the room it clearly needs and deserves. See *H. gracilis* on page 65 for aquarium requirements.

FEEDING

COMPATIBILITY

EASE OF KEEPING
4

SIZE
6 in (15 cm) 4 in (10 cm)

COPELLA ARNOLDI

FAMILY: *LEBIASINIDAE*
COMMON NAME: *JUMPING TETRA*

Its tan to olive body bears only a horizontal black bar through the eyes. In the male, the outer margins of the two elements of the caudal fin are tinted red-orange, the color sometimes extending to the caudal peduncle. Although not as spectacularly colored as others of its family, its remarkable spawning behavior makes it worth keeping. Eggs are laid on a leaf above the waterline. The pair will jump together to accomplish this. The male then keeps the eggs dampened by splashing them with his fins.

SPECIAL CARE: Provide a tank of about 20 gallons (76 liters) or more, with emergent plants and an air space above the water level. Make certain the tank is covered to prevent the fish from jumping out. Provide good filtration, soft, acidic water at a temperature of 80°F (27°C), and live foods for best results. The eggs remain on the leaf 2 to 3 days before hatching. The fry need small live foods from the beginning.

FEEDING

COMPATIBILITY

EASE OF KEEPING
5

SIZE
4 in (10 cm) 3.2 in (8 cm)

NANNOSTOMUS BECKFORDI

FAMILY: *LEBIASINIDAE*
COMMON NAME: *GOLDEN PENCILFISH; RED PENCILFISH*

There are several color strains of this species found in the lower Amazon region and Guyana, so identification has proved to be a little difficult. As its common name suggests, the body is shaped like a pencil, with only a slight curvature to the dorsal and ventral profiles. It has a light green-brown dorsal surface and a silver ventral surface, often with some red coloration between the pelvic and anal fins. A wide dark band runs the length of the body, ending at the base of the caudal fin between two red patches. There is a gold line above the dark band with possibly a hint of red above that. The general area along the flanks and dark band may be violet-hued under certain lighting conditions. At spawning times the male fish may show more intense red coloration on the rear of the body.

SPECIAL CARE: This middle-level swimmer, happy in the company of nonboisterous fishes, prefers a well-planted aquarium. Breeding is possible, but plenty of live food, soft water, and subdued lighting will increase the chance of success. Eggs may not develop if the water conditions are incorrect.

FEEDING

COMPATIBILITY

EASE OF KEEPING

SIZE

2.5 in (6.5 cm)   2.5 in (6.5 cm)

NANNOSTOMUS HARRISONI

FAMILY: *LEBIASINIDAE*
COMMON NAME: *HARRISON'S PENCILFISH*

FEEDING

COMPATIBILITY

EASE OF KEEPING

SIZE

2.4 in (6 cm) 2.4 in (6 cm)

This peaceful shoaling species is distributed among the streams of Guyana. Like most species in the genus, male fish like to show off in front of each other as well as in front of the females. Pre-spawning activity is quite lively, with the eventual pair of fishes enjoying a courtship dance. Its pencil-shaped body has only a slight curvature to the dorsal and ventral profiles. The body coloration is a light greenish-brown on the dorsal surface, shading through greenish-gold to a dark horizontal band running from the snout to the base of the caudal fin, where it terminates as a dark blotch bordered by gold-edged red areas.

SPECIAL CARE: Comfortable with other nonboisterous fishes, the Harrison's Pencilfish cruises at mid-tank level and likes a generously planted aquarium. Plenty of live food, soft water, and subdued lighting are recommended to assist in breeding success. Eggs may not develop if conditions are incorrect.

NANNOSTOMUS MARGINATUS

FAMILY: *LEBIASINIDAE*
COMMON NAME: *DWARF PENCILFISH*

The body is yellowish-green, paling to white in the mid-lateral region. A bold black stripe runs from the snout, through the eyes, to the end of the caudal fin. A less distinct line parallels it above, also extending to the caudal fin. There is a third stippled black line from the belly to the insertion of the anal fin. The dorsal fin bears a brilliant red splotch and black edging. The pelvic and anal fins are bright red, but the pectoral fins are colorless.

SPECIAL CARE: This is the smallest member of its genus, and needs a well-planted aquarium with some floating vegetation. It is an ideal choice for a small species tank. Soft, acidic water, and a temperature of 75–79°F (24–26°C) are necessary to preserve the lovely coloration. Feeding should consist of both small live foods and flakes, or frozen foods. Usually a stream dweller, it appreciates a moderate current.

FEEDING

COMPATIBILITY

EASE OF KEEPING

5

SIZE

1.2 in (3 cm) 1 in (2.5 cm)

SYMBOL KEY	
FEEDING Herbivore	
Omnivore	
Predator	
COMPATIBILITY single specimen	
community fish	
safe with small fish	
safe with invertebrates	
EASE OF KEEPING scale of 1 to 10 (with 1 being easiest to keep)	
SIZE in the wild	
in captivity	

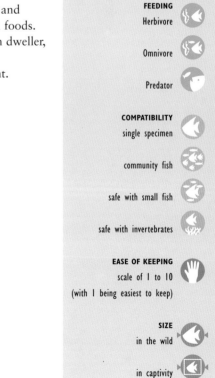

NANNOSTOMUS UNIFASCIATUS

FAMILY: *LEBIASINIDAE*
COMMON NAME: *ONE-LINED PENCILFISH*

The Amazon region and Guyana are home to this shoaling species, more correctly known as *N. unifasciatus ocellatus*, which unfortunately is not always in regular supply. There is a companion subspecies, *N. unifasciatus unifasciatus*, but it lacks the spot in the upper part of the caudal fin. Some authors suggest the correct genus classification is *Nannobrycon*. The body of this fish is shaped liked a pencil, with only a slight curvature to the dorsal and ventral profiles. The small, flattened head has a pointed snout. The light greenish-brown dorsal surface is edged by a single dark band that runs the length of the body, terminating in the first part of the caudal fin. The lower lobe of the caudal fin may be dark with some red coloration; the upper lobe often has a dark spot. The anal fin is often dark with a bluish-white front edge. The remaining fins are colorless, though the pelvic fins may have a hint of bluish-white on the tips. The entire ventral surface is silvery white, including underneath the jaw.
SPECIAL CARE: Swimming at the upper and middle levels, this species is compatible with other nonboisterous fishes and needs a generously planted aquarium. Breeding is possible, but plenty of live food, soft water, and subdued lighting are recommended for success. Incorrect water conditions can stop eggs from developing.

FEEDING

COMPATIBILITY

EASE OF KEEPING

1

SIZE

2.8 in (7 cm) 2.8 in (7 cm)

NANNOSTOMUS MARYLINAE

FAMILY: *LEBIASINIDAE*
COMMON NAME: *MARYLIN'S PENCILFISH*

A South American species with approximately the same range as the Cardinal Tetra, *Paracheirodon axelrodi*. It should be given a well-planted aquarium with peaceful tankmates. Olive green along the dorsal surface, a black stripe runs from the eyes to the caudal peduncle, flanked above and below by white stripes; the fins are colorless. It does not tolerate variations in water quality, and therefore is probably a better choice for the aquarist with some experience.
SPECIAL CARE: This species does best in a small shoal, where individual males will establish small territories. It requires soft, acidic water and subdued lighting. For breeding purposes, keep a single pair in a species tank, and take the usual precautions to prevent the parents from eating the eggs, which are produced almost continuously if the pair is healthy. However, eggs are only produced in small numbers making the breeding of this species less attractive as a commercial venture.

FEEDING

COMPATIBILITY

EASE OF KEEPING

3

SIZE

2 in (5 cm) 1.5 in (3.8 cm)

SEMAPROCHILODUS TAENIURUS

FAMILY: *PROCHILODONTIDAE*
COMMON NAME: *NONE*

This large vegetarian characin can be found from Brazil to eastern Colombia. The posterior two-thirds of the silvery body is marked with a pattern of black dots extending to the dorsal fin, and can be seen faintly on the anal fin. The caudal fin is transparent, with a series of horizontal black stripes extending across it from tip to tip; the pelvic fins are bright red. It schools in fast-flowing water, and needs a current in the aquarium. At spawning time, adults migrate upstream (much like salmon), even ascending strong rapids and small waterfalls. Specimens imported for the aquarium trade may actually represent more than one species, but more research will be needed to determine if this is, in fact, the case.
SPECIAL CARE: Feed large amounts of vegetable foods, such as flake foods, spinach, or duckweed. Breeding this species in the home aquarium is unlikely. It may grow to 1 foot (30 cm) in length, and requires a large, shallow, preferably well-planted, aquarium with ample filtration to offset its hearty appetite.

FEEDING

COMPATIBILITY

EASE OF KEEPING

3

SIZE

12 in (30 cm) 6 in (15 cm)

METYNNIS ARGENTEUS

FAMILY: *SERRASALMIDAE*
COMMON NAME: *SILVER DOLLAR*

The Silver Dollar is distributed through the southern Amazon region, Paraguay, and the Plate River, and is sometimes confused with *Mylossoma argenteum*, itself a synonym of *M. duriventre*. Although from the same family as the piranha, this species does not share its taste for

FEEDING

COMPATIBILITY

EASE OF KEEPING

4

SIZE

8 in (20 cm) 5.1 in (13 cm)

flesh. The body shape is very deep, with a ventral region that resembles a keel. The dorsal profile, however, is not quite as convex. The body coloration is silvery and it has small scales. There is a small black blotch on the rear of the gill cover. There may be dark vertical bands across the body and a dark blotch midway along the flanks, but these fade with maturity. The dorsal fin has dark speckles and, along with the broad anal fin and paddle-shaped caudal fin, it has a red edge. The caudal fin has an almost straight rear edge. An adipose fin is present.
SPECIAL CARE: Although it needs a well-planted aquarium, living aquarium plants, especially softer-leaved types, are at risk from this middle-level swimmer, so provide plastic or tough-leaved plants. It has been bred in captivity but appreciates slightly higher temperatures than normal. The eggs are laid among floating plants but drop to the bottom of the aquarium, where they are ignored by the parents.

MYLEUS RUBRIPINNIS

FAMILY: *SERRASALMIDAE*
COMMON NAME: *NONE*

This is a large, vegetarian relative of the piranha, found in the larger streams of Guyana to the Amazon. It has a rounded, silvery body and colorless fins, except for the anal, which is bordered in black on the lower-third, and tinged with red. Similar to *Metynnis argenteus*, this fish benefits from plenty of water movement and aeration, as it comes from well-oxygenated waters.

SPECIAL CARE: Feed large amounts of vegetable foods, such as flake foods, spinach, or duckweed. An occasional feeding of live *daphnia* or mosquito larvae is beneficial. Breeding behavior for this species is unknown, but it is likely to be similar to that reported for closely related species. As many as several thousand eggs may be produced. The eggs fall to the bottom and are ignored by the parents. As with many larger species imported for aquariums, achieving a successful spawn may be largely dependent upon obtaining a mated pair. This fish is sometimes imported with an unidentified disease condition that produces tiny, transparent blisters on the body. The condition apparently does not harm the fish.

FEEDING

COMPATIBILITY

EASE OF KEEPING

3

SIZE

14 in (35 cm) 5 in (13 cm)

SERRASALMUS NATTERERI

FAMILY: *SERRASALMIDAE*
COMMON NAME: *RED BELLY PIRANHA*

FEEDING

COMPATIBILITY

EASE OF KEEPING

6

SIZE

11 in (28 cm) 9.4 in (24 cm)

Famous for its habit of travelling in schools that can reduce an animal the size of a small pig to shreds in a few seconds, it is rather timid in the aquarium, though inclined to bite the hand that feeds it. Its body is silvery with some darker areas on the caudal fin. From the underside of the lower jaw to the belly, the skin is tinted bright red.

SPECIAL CARE: This fish should be handled with extreme care. Larger specimens are capable of delivering a nasty bite. Provide a roomy tank with clear, clean, well-oxygenated water and a noticeable current. Small bait fish are the preferred live food. The fish's messy feeding habits necessitate regular cleaning of the tank. This species is not a suitable choice for every aquarist.

SYMBOL KEY

FEEDING
Herbivore

Omnivore

Predator

COMPATIBILITY
single specimen

community fish

safe with small fish

safe with invertebrates

EASE OF KEEPING
scale of 1 to 10
(with 1 being easiest to keep)

SIZE
in the wild

in captivity

CICHLIDS

Native to Central and South America, Africa, and Asia, the cichlid family, with over 1,000

Pseudotropheus tropheops
TROPHEOPS

species, contains something for everyone. Many of these fishes are territorial, particularly at spawning time, and often tear up aquarium plants when selecting a spawning site. Some are too large to be kept in a community tank, while others will happily raise young in a modest size aquarium.

Cichlids are hearty eaters producing quantities of waste products, so their aquarium should be fitted with an efficient filtration system and subjected to regular partial water changes. Some species, such as those from the Rift Valley Lakes of Africa, are herbivorous by nature and need a high content of vegetable matter in their diet. For good breeding results the South American species require water of a particular composition, usually soft and acidic; some such as the discus (*Symphysodon* spp.), need to have their water conditions constantly maintained, making these fantastic fishes very much for the experienced fishkeeper wishing to specialize.

The brilliantly colored African species from the Rift Valley Lakes prefer hard water and require rocky outcrops as furnishings among which they can claim

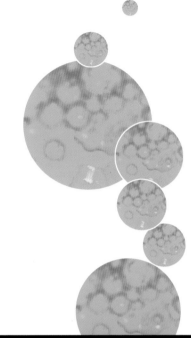

territories. A bright light over the tank will encourage algal growth on the rocks on which the fish will graze.

Generally, sexual differentiation (and mate selection) is best left to the fishes. In some cases sex determination is difficult; males may have longer, more pointed fins. Close examination of the breeding tubes extended at spawning times by males and females may prove to be a reliable guideline.

Egg depositors in general, cichlids are prolific breeders. The smaller species tend to be secretive spawners. Although the females of such species become pugnacious when guarding their young, large aquariums are not always needed in which to set up a nuclear family group. Larger species are happy to select a spawning site out in the open and defend the surrounding area.

Many of the African species are mouthbrooders. The male fish has imitation egg spots on his anal fin; as the female attempts to collect these she takes his fertilizing milt into her mouth at the same time.

Julidochromis regani
REGAN'S JULIE

ORANGE CHROMIDE
The Orange Chromide is one of the very few cichlids naturally occurring in Asia.

FEATURED IN THIS SECTION

AMPHILOPHUS OCTOFASCIATUM

FAMILY: *CICHLIDAE*
COMMON NAME: *JACK DEMPSEY*

Although this is a colorful species, this fish has a reputation as a disruptive influence on the aquarium. Its popular name pays homage to the famous boxing idol, giving a good indication as to its pugnacious nature. Its heavily-built body is darkish brown (normally turning to a darker blue-black when mature or spawning) with some darker barring across the dorsal surface and an often indistinct dark band along the flanks. This rather uninteresting background color is much relieved by the scalation which, because of having iridescent light metallic greeny-blue centers, makes the fish very attractive. Some iridescent speckling occurs around the eyes and on the gill covers and there are blue lines around the mouth, which become more apparent as the main body color becomes darker. The female is generally paler and her dorsal and anal fins are rounded.

SPECIAL CARE: This territorial fish is likely to uproot plants, harass small fishes, and generally makes life intolerable for other tank mates. It is best to give it a large aquarium to itself. Its living space should be well-planted with tough-leaved or plastic plants. It is a reliable breeder and is usually a good parent.

FEEDING

COMPATIBILITY

EASE OF KEEPING

4

SIZE

8 in (20 cm) 8 in (20 cm)

AEQUIDENS PULCHER

FAMILY: *CICHLIDAE*
COMMON NAME: *BLUE ACARA*

Formerly known as *"A. latifrons,"* this fish can be found in the waters of Panama, Colombia, and the Caribbean island of Trinidad and Tobago. This long-established aquarium favorite has an elongated body but is stockily-built. It has a light gray body with several dark bars crossing it vertically. These bars may be interconnected by a further dark line running from behind the eyes, arching along the body, to the caudal peduncle. The light metallic blue center to each scale gives the fish a sparkling effect and further blue lines can be seen on the head, particularly below the eyes, on the lower jaw, and the gill covers. All the fins are dark gray with further light blue speckling. The dorsal fin has a faint red and yellow edge and the anal and pelvic fins a dark edge. One obvious difference between the sexes is that the dorsal and anal fins of the male are

FEEDING

COMPATIBILITY

EASE OF KEEPING

1

SIZE

8 in (20 cm) 6.3 in (16 cm)

pointed, often reaching back around the caudal fin.

SPECIAL CARE: It swims at the middle and lower levels of the aquarium, and will thrive in a well-planted environment. It is a very prolific breeder that spawns in the open on flat stones. While this is a generally peaceful fish it may find small fishes, such as Neon Tetras, too tempting to ignore and it does become territorial at spawning time.

APISTOGRAMMA AGASSIZI

FAMILY: *CICHLIDAE*
COMMON NAME: *AGASSIZ'S DWARF CICHLID*

A native of the Amazonian basin, this dwarf cichlid has an elongated, yet stocky body. Its dorsal surface has a golden brown hue, and a dark stripe runs from snout to caudal peduncle along its greenish-blue iridescent flanks. The face is very well-marked with green-blue streaks and a dark diagonal bar through the eyes. With its reddish-yellow-orange hue, the dorsal fin has a very long, dark base; the spade-shaped caudal fin, coming to a central point, has a green-blue line around its margin. The smaller female is mostly light brown, with contrasting colors only on the dark horizontal stripe and the eye bar. Her fins are more rounded than the male's, whose dorsal fin and anal, spade-shaped fins are particularly pointed.

SPECIAL CARE: Often unavailable commercially, this fish spawns in a cave. Try using a flowerpot turned on its side to simulate the fish's natural environment, where the eggs may be laid on its interior "ceiling." Like all fishes in its genus, Agassiz's Dwarf Cichlid prefers live foods. It enjoys a well-planted aquarium with plenty of retreats.

FEEDING

COMPATIBILITY

EASE OF KEEPING

1

SIZE

3.2 in (8 cm) 3 in (7.5 cm)

APISTOGRAMMA CACATUOIDES

FAMILY: *CICHLIDAE*
COMMON NAME: *COCKATOO DWARF CICHLID; CRESTED DWARF CICHLID*

FEEDING

COMPATIBILITY

EASE OF KEEPING

SIZE

3.5 in (9 cm) 3 in (7.5 cm)

The most obvious feature of this colorful Peruvian Amazonian fish is its dorsal fin, of which the first few rays are very extended—much like a cockatoo's crest. The pelvic fins also have extended first rays. The fish's elongated body is slightly stocky, with a greenish-brown surface hue shading down to a yellowish color in the ventral area. A dark band runs horizontally along the flanks, and there may be repeated, often incomplete lines beneath this. The caudal fin is vividly marked with red and black at its base. Although the female has less well-endowed finnage, she has a dark band through the eyes (as do all females in the genus), an attractive feature that contrasts with her golden brown body color.
SPECIAL CARE: The Cockatoo spawns in secret. It is best to keep one male with several females in a medium size aquarium, but where space allows, additional males can be kept. Males are very competitive, but providing that their territories do not encroach on each other, it is possible for them to live peacefully together.

APISTOGRAMMA MACMASTERI

FAMILY: *CICHLIDAE*
COMMON NAME: *AFRICAN BUTTERFLY CICHLID*

The delightful African Butterfly Cichlid—as its name suggests—is native to the African continent, specifically Liberia and Sierre Leone. It has a stocky, deep body shape, and its golden brown flanks are spotted with rows of iridescent scales that take on a flush of violet when natural light shines through the front of the aquarium. Three or four incomplete bars pass through the body vertically, appearing and disappearing according to the fish's mood. A dark bar runs diagonally from the corner of the mouth through the red-rimmed eyes, and a dark spot appears on the rear of the gill cover. The long-based dorsal and caudal fins have red and blue top edges. The female of this amazingly colorful species may show dark markings more often; she is smaller than the male and, of course, plumper during spawning.
SPECIAL CARE: Cruising the middle and lower waters, this cichlid enjoys a well-planted aquarium with plenty of retreats. It spawns on a flat rock in open water, but exercise caution during hatching—reports of cannibalism with consecutive spawnings means that the youngest fry are vulnerable to parental consumption. The fish also becomes territorial during spawning.

FEEDING

COMPATIBILITY

EASE OF KEEPING

SIZE

3.15 in (8 cm) 2.8 in (7 cm)

APISTOGRAMMA NIJSSENI

FAMILY: *CICHLIDAE*
COMMON NAME: *NIJSSEN'S DWARF CICHLID*

This fish is found in the streams and rivers of central and northern South America. The elongated body of this fish is laterally-compressed and slightly stocky. It has a greenish-brown dorsal surface with bluish flanks and a number of dark bands cross the body vertically. These bands may vary in intensity depending on the fish's mood, sometimes only a few dark bars can be seen across the dorsal surface; it also has a dark diagonal band that runs from the eyes across to the gill cover. The dorsal fin is blue with a red and yellow margin and a few of the first rays are slightly black. The female of this species is less intensely colored than the male.
SPECIAL CARE: This fish likes to have sufficient space and may resent sharing it in a small aquarium. The tank should be well-planted and areas should be created where the fish can retreat. This fish does become territorial during breeding time, and is suitable for a community collection of modest-sized fishes or a single species aquarium.

FEEDING

COMPATIBILITY

EASE OF KEEPING

SIZE

2.5 in (6.5 cm) 2 in (5 cm)

SYMBOL KEY

FEEDING

Herbivore

Omnivore

Predator

COMPATIBILITY

single specimen

community fish

safe with small fish

safe with invertebrates

EASE OF KEEPING

scale of 1 to 10
(with 1 being easiest to keep)

SIZE

in the wild

in captivity

APISTOGRAMMA TRIFASCIATUM

FAMILY: *CICHLIDAE*
COMMON NAME: *THREE-STRIPED DWARF CICHLID; BLUE APISTOGRAMMA*

FEEDING

COMPATIBILITY

EASE OF KEEPING

SIZE

2.4 in (6 cm) 2 in (5 cm)

This secretive spawner is found in the *Rio Paraguay* and *Rio Guapore* in Paraguay and in the waters of western Brazil. Very similar in shape to the *A. nijsseni*, it has a greenish-brown dorsal surface shading down to cream on its flanks. This fish is marked with three dark bands; one runs along the dorsal ridge just beneath the dorsal fin, another from the tip of the snout to the caudal peduncle, with a third from the base of the pectoral fin to the start of the anal fin. These three bands are referred to in the specific name but appear more accentuated (or even visible) during breeding. The head is yellowish with some blue facial markings. The dorsal fin is bluish with a red edge, the anal fin is fairly long, and the long blue pelvic fins have white edges. The first few rays are much extended in the male and the female is usually smaller and less colored than the male.

SPECIAL CARE: The brooding instinct is very strong in the female who is quite likely to guard a ball of *Tubifex* worms when not actually spawning. This fish will thrive in a well-planted aquarium with plenty of places for it to hide and retreat.

APISTOGRAMMA VIEJITA

FEEDING

COMPATIBILITY

EASE OF KEEPING

SIZE

3 in (7.5 cm) 2.8 in (7 cm)

FAMILY: *CICHLIDAE*
COMMON NAME: *VIEJITA DWARF CICHLID*

This is another relatively modern species and has also been confused (thanks to several color variations in the males) with *A. macmasteri*. It comes from the *Rio Meta* in Colombia. Its golden brown body may have some dark flecking and there may be red margins to the caudal fin and/or a red edge to all or part of the dorsal fin. The female intensifies her coloration from the usual drab brown into yellow with black markings when spawning and caring for the subsequent fry.
SPECIAL CARE: This fish prefers the middle and lower levels of the aquarium and it tends to spawn in a very secretive manner. This species requires live foods and slightly warmer conditions (up to 85°F/30°C). It requires a well-planted aquarium with retreats.

ASTRONOTUS OCELLATUS

FAMILY: *CICHLIDAE*
COMMON NAME: *OSCAR; MARBLED, OR VELVET CICHLID*

FEEDING

COMPATIBILITY

EASE OF KEEPING

SIZE

13 in (33 cm) 11 in (28 cm)

This very large cichlid is extremely attractive when young and the unsuspecting purchaser is often surprised at its rapid rate of growth and enormous appetite. However, if enough space and food can be provided, it can become a popular pet. It has a very robust, thick body and a "rounding-off" of its features. Its matte body is dark gray in color with some irregular dark blotches and rust-colored markings. An "eye spot" on the caudal peduncle can be seen on wild specimens found in their natural habitat of the rivers of *Amazonia*. The head, generally gray with less red marking, is massive with a very large, fleshy-lipped mouth. Its fins are functional-looking rather than ornate or decorative; the dorsal and anal fins are wider at the rear than at the front; the caudal fin is well-rounded and paddle-shaped, and the pelvic fins are slightly elongated. Sexing this species is difficult. One thing to look for is that the breeding tube sizes may be dissimilar. A popular aquarium-developed variety of this species is the Red or Tiger Oscar. In this variety much of the original coloration has been replaced by a reddish-orange color over most of the body.

SPECIAL CARE: Aside from their sheer bulk, Oscars are generally peaceful (they can even become hand-tame) and are suitable for a community collection of larger fishes. This fish may well rearrange the aquarium furnishings when spawning, an activity likely to produce upward of 3,000 fry. The aquarium should have an efficient filtration system and regular partial water changes because of the amount of waste produced.

AULONACARA NYASSAE

FAMILY: *CICHLIDAE*
COMMON NAME: *PEACOCK CICHLID*

The Peacock Cichlid's gray body is covered with a number of vertical dark stripes. The ventral area is colored silver and gold. Coloration of the female (and lesser-ranking males) is more subdued. In young fishes, male coloration occurs after six months. The pelvic fins contain some yellow and the first few rays are pale blue. The anal fin of the male carries several yellow egg spots. The significance of these egg spot markings becomes important during spawning. The female assumes the egg spots are more eggs to pick up to incubate in her mouth and by nuzzling at the spots she stimulates the male into releasing sperm which fertilizes the already-collected eggs. The species has many color variations as well as equally numerous subspecies. This species is native to Lake Malawi and the fish seems to take on a different shade or color pattern depending upon the area it makes its home. **SPECIAL CARE**: A large, spacious aquarium is necessary for these fishes, who like to command fairly large territories. The water should be alkaline and special Malawi salt mixes have found their way onto the market to cater for these needs. This fish follows a typical mouthbrooding pattern—the female incubates the eggs in her throat, eating no food for a month or so, until the fry have hatched. It is territorial but peaceful and is suitable for a community collection of mixed-size fishes that tolerate similar water conditions.

FEEDING

COMPATIBILITY

EASE OF KEEPING
1

SIZE
4 in (10 cm)   4 in (10 cm)

CICHLA OCELLARIS

FAMILY: *CICHLIDAE*
COMMON NAME: *OCELLATED CICHLID*

FEEDING

COMPATIBILITY

EASE OF KEEPING
3

SIZE
12 in (30 cm) 12 in (30 cm)

This species shape resembles that of the perches and centrarchids of temperate climates. The body is olive, fading to golden yellow on the belly and throat. The eyes are bright red, as are the pelvic fins. The mid-lateral region is marked with three bold eye spots, stippled black, surrounded by a lemon yellow ring. A similar eye spot is located on the caudal peduncle. The dorsal and caudal fins are dark olive, with some reddish pigment on the lower element of the latter. **SPECIAL CARE**: Although not a fussy species, this one should be given a large, well-aerated tank, decorated with rocks and driftwood rather than plants. The latter will be rapidly uprooted and destroyed by the activities of the fish. Aggressive behavior is likely so it is probably best to exhibit a single specimen. Feeding is no problem, with virtually anything remotely edible being greedily consumed. Filtration should be adequate to compensate for its hearty appetite and messy habits.

CICHLASOMA CITRINELLUM

FAMILY: *CICHLIDAE*
COMMON NAME: *MIDAS CICHLID; LEMON CICHLID*

FEEDING

COMPATIBILITY

EASE OF KEEPING
6

SIZE
12 in (30 cm) 12 in (30 cm)

This cichlid is found in the waters of Central America, from southern Mexico to Nicaragua. Its body coloration, including all fins, is a lemon yellow-gold, the fish's popular name obviously being inspired more from the "golden" connection whereas the scientific name refers to the paler yellow shade. Mature males often develop a pronounced "forehead" (the nuchal hump) and their dorsal and anal fins are more pointed than those of the female. This species has recently been re-classified as *Amphilophus citrinellum*. **SPECIAL CARE**: This often aggressive fish needs a spacious aquarium with plastic plants and rocky decor. When breeding is attempted, take care to remove the female should the male attack her. Some "trials of strength" such as jaw-locking may occur before compatible pairings are achieved.

CICHLASOMA DOVII

FAMILY: *CICHLIDAE*
COMMON NAME: *DOW'S CICHLID*

FEEDING

COMPATIBILITY

EASE OF KEEPING
7

SIZE
27.5 in (70 cm)   16 in (40 cm)

Dow's Cichlid has an elongated but very heavily built body. Silvery-blue in color with a darker dorsal surface, it has equally-spaced dark dots covering its whole body. This gives a multi-lined appearance particularly on the lower flanks. A dark horizontal band made up of broken blotches runs from the gill cover to the end of the caudal peduncle terminating in a dark blotch at the root of the caudal fin. Depending upon the mood of the fish numerous dark narrow vertical bands can be seen crossing the sides. The mouth is wide and the forehead contour is markedly uneven. The fins may carry dark specklings and those of the male, particularly the dorsal and anal fins, are more pointed than those of the female. The female also lacks the small dark dotted patterning of the male and the horizontal dark line may be broader. Recent speculation over taxonomic matters has tentatively placed this, and other related species, in the genus *Heros*.
SPECIAL CARE: As might be expected by their appearance these fish have hearty appetites that result in large amounts of waste; an efficient filtration system coupled with frequent partial water changes will keep their environment clean. The aquarium should contain plastic plants and some flat rocky surfaces on which the fish can lay their eggs. This fish can be aggressive, but it is suitable to be kept with a community collection of larger fishes.

CICHLASOMA HARTWEGI

FAMILY: *CICHLIDAE*
COMMON NAME: *HARTWEG'S CICHLID*

FEEDING

COMPATIBILITY

EASE OF KEEPING
7

SIZE
12 in (30 cm)   12 in (30 cm)

This colorful cichlid made its first appearance in the 1980s and proved to be instantly popular, especially with hobbyists wanting something large to exhibit. The body coloration depends upon lighting conditions as the pinkish-turquoise sheen is best seen when light comes from the side rather than from directly overhead. The whole body is covered with small red-brown spots and, according to temperament, a number of dark, vertical crossbands may be seen, but generally a thin dark band along the flanks is the usual patterning. The rear edge of the caudal fin is red while the rest of the fins share the body colors. Females are generally smaller but tend to show more variation in color, again this is dependent on mood. Re-classifications have also affected this fish with *Herichthys*, *Paratheraps*, and most recently, *Vieja* being offered as generic names.
SPECIAL CARE: Coming from Central America, this species is highly adaptable to aquarium life as it not only tolerates a wide temperature range, 68–84°F (20–29°C) but is also quite happy with hard water. However, it is not tolerant of its own kind. For a large fish, it may seem surprising that it appreciates some hideaways among rocks and underwater roots, although it may eat aquarium plants. Should only be kept with other large fishes.

CRENICARA FILAMENTOSA

FAMILY: *CICHLIDAE*
COMMON NAME: *CHECKERBOARD CICHLID*

FEEDING

COMPATIBILITY

EASE OF KEEPING
1

SIZE
3.5 in (9 cm)   3 in (7.5 cm)

The Checkerboard Cichlid, native to the *Orinoco* region of South America, has an elongated, cylindrical body. It takes its name from its distinct body markings. Its body is greenish-yellow with a darker dorsal surface and silvery-white belly. A dark band runs from the snout through the eyes to the end of the gill cover, then becomes a number of equally-spaced blotches forming a horizontal pattern along the flanks ending on the caudal peduncle. Above and below these blotches are greenish-blue lines which are more apparent when viewed under side-lighting. A red line runs under the eyes and there may be red speckles on the flanks and fins. The long-based dorsal fin and lyre-shaped caudal fin are both edged with light blue, have reddish speckles, and terminate in extended filaments. The pelvic fins are also fairly well-produced. Males have much more color than females.
SPECIAL CARE: This shy species spends most of the time in and around the bottom of the aquarium among the plants and rocks, where it spawns in the open on flat surfaces. It prefers live foods. This fish may do better in a separate species aquarium in soft, acidic water.

CRENICICHLA LEPIDOTA

FAMILY: *CICHLIDAE*
COMMON NAME: *TWO-SPOT PIKE CICHLID*

FEEDING

COMPATIBILITY

EASE OF KEEPING
7

SIZE
10 in (25 cm) 8 in (20 cm)

The Two-Spot Pike Cichlid has an elongated, almost "torpedo-shaped" body but it is still quite heavily-built. It is interesting to note that the color of this fish's body can vary from silvery blue-gray, to pearly-green, to slightly yellowish, with a darker dorsal surface. A dark band runs from the snout, through the eyes, to the base of the caudal fin. Immediately behind the gill cover this line may be broken by a bright-ringed dark blotch and there is another similar "eye spot" on the base of the caudal fin.

A number of iridescent speckles cover the upper-half of the body and there may be some narrow dark bands visible from time to time above the dark line. The head is flattened with a wide mouth. The dorsal fin is long-based, the anal fin is short, and the caudal fin is rounded or it could even be described as spade-shaped. Females tend to develop a fatter mid-section and their ventral area becomes wine red in color. Males have more pointed dorsal and anal fins. This carnivore is native to the Amazon region, as far south as the waters of northern Argentina.

SPECIAL CARE: Like the coldwater pike, in the wild this species is a predator, lying in wait among plants for any passing prey. Therefore, when in captivity it appreciates live foods. The aquarium should be large and well planted. It spawns in pits excavated in the substrate. This fish can be aggressive and should only be kept with other large fish.

CYPRICHROMIS LEPTOSOMA

FAMILY: *CICHLIDAE*
COMMON NAME: *SLENDER CICHLID*

As its popular name suggests, this fish has an elongated body. The body is creamy-gray with certain iridescences visible under advantageous lighting conditions. The lower part of the head is pale yellow and there is a small yellow saddle-shaped area on the upper part of the caudal peduncle. The dorsal fin is long-based and rounded, the greater depth appearing to be at the rear of the fin. The anal fin is only half as long but also shares the same configuration. In their natural habitat of Lake Tanganyika in eastern Africa, spawning takes place in the open water rather than in pits and the female collects the eggs and incubates them in her mouth.

SPECIAL CARE: The males of this species are very intolerant of each other and, therefore, need a large aquarium with rocky retreats if a number are to be kept. Generally these fish are peaceful, if a little territorial, and can be kept with a collection of mixed-size fishes.

FEEDING

COMPATIBILITY

EASE OF KEEPING
4

SIZE
5 in (13 cm) 5 in (13 cm)

ETROPLUS MACULATUS

FAMILY: *CICHLIDAE*
COMMON NAME: *ORANGE CHROMIDE*

This species is found in the waters of southern India and Sri Lanka. Occasionally (and depending on the mood of the fish) a central black blotch may appear on the flanks and the anal and pelvic fins become darker. Their eggs are laid on sloping firm surfaces and secured with sticky threads. The fry feed from the mucus on their parents' bodies in the first few days.

SPECIAL CARE: This fish requires a well-planted aquarium with retreats; it may also be beneficial to put in a couple of small flowerpots in which they can lay their eggs. Although this fish is not too sensitive to water type, medium hardness suits it well and a small addition of sea salt may be conducive to its well-being.

FEEDING

COMPATIBILITY

EASE OF KEEPING
1

SIZE
3.5 in (9 cm) 3.2 in (8 cm)

SYMBOL KEY

FEEDING
Herbivore

Omnivore

Predator

COMPATIBILITY
single specimen

community fish

safe with small fish

safe with invertebrates

EASE OF KEEPING
scale of 1 to 10
(with 1 being easiest to keep)

SIZE
in the wild

in captivity

ETROPLUS SURATENSIS

FAMILY: *CICHLIDAE*
COMMON NAME: *GREEN CHROMIDE*

FEEDING

COMPATIBILITY

EASE OF KEEPING

3

SIZE

17.7 in (45 cm) 12 in (30 cm)

This fish inhabits fresh, brackish, and seawater habitats in coastal India and Sri Lanka. The dark olive body is paler behind the gill cover, and camouflaged with a series of dark green vertical bars. Its fins are light olive green to colorless. Bright dots cover the body from behind the gill cover to the caudal peduncle. No discernible differences in appearance exist between males and females.

SPECIAL CARE: Although it can be acclimated to freshwater exclusively, this fish does best in brackish water with fluctuating salinity. Combined with the fact that few plants will survive in brackish water is the predilection of this species to feed on them. Therefore, only plastic plants or other inedible decorations are recommended. Aquarium spawning is possible, and the fish exhibit the parental care typical of their family; however, the species must be at least 6 in (15 cm) in length to be sexually mature, and must be given an opportunity to self-select a partner.

GEOPHAGUS ACUTICEPS

FAMILY: *CICHLIDAE*
COMMON NAME: *SPARKLING GEOPHAGUS*

Found throughout the Amazon basin in low gradient streams with sandy bottoms, this "earth eater" feeds by taking in a mouthful of sand and expelling it through the gill covers to extract small invertebrates. In the aquarium, it adapts well to a variety of small, meaty foods, such as *Daphnia* or other crustaceans. The body is light olive green with a series of dark blotches mid-laterally, beginning just behind the gill cover and ending at the caudal peduncle. Pale lines extend from the snout through the eyes, and continue beyond the gill cover as horizontal rows of bright dots that give the species its common name.

SPECIAL CARE: Like other cichlids, this species attaches its eggs to a solid substrate such as a flat rock. Both parents participate in the care of the eggs and offspring, and are likely to become territorial during the breeding season. Otherwise, this is a peaceful species that is not interested in feeding upon smaller tank mates, unless they are invertebrates.

FEEDING

COMPATIBILITY

EASE OF KEEPING

1

SIZE

10 in (25 cm) 6 in (15 cm)

GEOPHAGUS DAEMON

FAMILY: *CICHLIDAE*
COMMON NAME: *SLENDER GEOPHAGUS*

This fish has an elongated body with a moderately-arched dorsal profile and a flattened ventral surface, although it is much less so than other members of the genus. Its body is blue-gray with a yellowish tinge to the lower flanks and the scales have dark edges. Two diamond-shaped

FEEDING

COMPATIBILITY

EASE OF KEEPING

1

SIZE

12 in (30 cm) 8 in (20 cm)

dark blotches appear on the flanks, the forwardmost being exactly midway along the body, the second between the rear parts of the dorsal and anal fin. A bright-ringed dark blotch appears on the base of the caudal fin, slightly above the horizontal line. The eyes have two red sections divided by a near-vertical dark mark; a light brown band bordered in yellow runs from the large mouth with its protruding lower lip, up to the eyes. The pelvic, anal, and lower regions of the caudal fins are golden red; the pelvic fins have long filamentous extensions. In the male the dorsal and anal fins have longer rays than those of the female. This fish is a mouthbrooder.

SPECIAL CARE: The generic name *Geophagus* means "earth eater" and refers to the fish's habit of sifting through the substrate for food, expelling unwanted material through its gills. Occasionally plants suffer from being uprooted during this constant food-searching process, so the aquarium should contain plastic plants and well-anchored rocks. This peaceful fish is suitable for a community collection of mixed-size fishes.

HEMICHROMIS BIMACULATUS

FAMILY: *CICHLIDAE*
COMMON NAME: *JEWEL CICHLID*

This elongated yet stockily-built cichlid, native to the waters of Ghana and Togoland, is among the most brilliantly colored of all freshwater species. It is golden brown with metallic blue iridescent speckling. Two bright-ringed dark spots appear on the flanks, one on the extreme rear edge of the gill covers and another midway along the body. The head is fairly small and the golden eyes have dark centers and are crossed by a dark bar. The long-based dorsal fin, the shorter anal fin and the rounded caudal fin carry the iridescent speckling. At spawning time the fish turns brilliant red, with the male often darkening further taking on an additional deep brown overcast.
SPECIAL CARE: This is a rather belligerent species that has a habit of digging among the substrate, which tends to spoil the tank set-up. Furnish the tank with a rocky decor (on which spawning can occur) and plastic plants. They are excellent parents but can be aggressive in carrying out this responsibility, so they should only be kept in a community tank with other large fishes. A single species tank of Jewel Cichlids is very effective.

FEEDING

COMPATIBILITY

EASE OF KEEPING
5

SIZE
6 in (15 cm) 4 in (10 cm)

HERICHTHYS CYANOGUTTATUS

FAMILY: *CICHLIDAE*
COMMON NAME: *TEXAS CICHLID*

FEEDING

COMPATIBILITY

EASE OF KEEPING
1

SIZE
12 in (30 cm) 10 in (25 cm)

As its name suggests, this fish is found in the waters of Texas and Central America. The Texas Cichlid has an elongated, yet fairly deep and heavily-built body. It is bluish-green in color and healthy specimens have many iridescences that spread onto all the fins. There are two dark blotches—one midway along the flanks and the other on the caudal peduncle. The former is much more apparent in juvenile specimens but the latter survives into adulthood and may be accompanied by additional smaller isolated blotches on the rear of the fish. The head is large and the eyes dark. Males often develop a pronounced hump on the forehead with maturity. Additional evidence to sexual differences is that the dorsal and anal fins may be more pointed in the male and the female may be less brightly colored and slightly smaller. Colors intensify during spawning and a number of vertical dark bars may appear on the body at this time.

For many years the species accepted by fishkeepers as the Texas Cichlid was in fact *"Cichlasoma carpinte,"* a species that is slightly more blue in color. The re-classification of *Cichlasoma* to *Hericthys* (and even *Heros*) is a relatively recent occurrence.
SPECIAL CARE: This territorial, sometimes aggressive fish should be kept in a spacious aquarium with plastic plants. This species should only be kept with other large fish.

HEROS LABIATUS

FAMILY: *CICHLIDAE*
COMMON NAME: *RED DEVIL*

For hobbyists who want a large, predatory fish that is easy to care for, this might be your first choice. Found in Central American lakes, these fish are notorious for aggressive behavior toward tankmates, including others of its own species. They are also diggers, making short work of tank decorations and plants.
SPECIAL CARE: Definitely not for the community tank, the Red Devil should be provided with a tank of at least 100 gallons (378 liters). Anything and everything that is edible is accepted. Water quality is of little importance, as long as the tank remains clean and biological filtration is ample. Mated pairs are tender parents, their behavior in sharp contrast to that shown to any other fish that might intrude.

FEEDING

COMPATIBILITY

EASE OF KEEPING
1

SIZE
10 in (25 cm) 8 in (20 cm)

HEROS LABIATUS X H. SEVERUS

FAMILY: *CICHLIDAE*
COMMON NAME: *BLOOD PARROT CICHLID*

FEEDING

COMPATIBILITY

EASE OF KEEPING

1

SIZE

N/A   6 in (15 cm)

This fish is an artificially created hybrid between *Heros labiatus*, the Red Devil cichlid, and *Heros severus*, the Severum Cichlid. The strangely shaped head with its narrow "beak" has given rise to the name "parrot cichlid," and the bright, red-orange coloration suggested the name "blood parrot." For the hobbyist interested in artificial creations, this one is readily available and adapts to any reasonable water conditions.

SPECIAL CARE: Spawning is not possible between individual hybrid fish, as a general rule, so producing offspring is best left to the professionals. Provide the fish with a roomy tank, sturdy robust plantings that will stand up to its occasional digging, and a varied diet of common aquarium foods. It seems to prefer well-oxygenated water, so a strong current from the filtration pump is beneficial. As with many larger cichlids, this one has messy eating habits, another reason to provide adequate filtration.

HEROS MANAGUENSIS

FEEDING

COMPATIBILITY

EASE OF KEEPING

7

SIZE

12 in (30 cm)   12 in (30 cm)

FAMILY: *CICHLIDAE*
COMMON NAME: *MANAGUA CICHLID; JAGUAR CICHLID*

The two common names for this particular species are inspired by its native habitat, Lake Managua in Nicaragua, and its coloration, similar to that of a jaguar. This fish can also be found in the wild in Costa Rica, Honduras, and Lake Nicaragua. It has an elongated, stocky, silvery blue-gray body that is covered with numerous dark irregular-shaped specklings which spread into all the fins. Depending upon the mood of the fish a dark band, made up of almost-connected blotches, may be seen along the flanks. The head is slightly flattened and the eyes are dark. The area around the wide mouth may take on a golden brown coloration. Sex differentiation is not easy but the usual guidelines such as pointed dorsal and anal fins in the often larger male are farily reliable indicators. This fish has recently been re-classified as *Parachromis managuensis*.

SPECIAL CARE: A large aquarium is needed and plastic rather than real plants should be used. Any rocky decorations should be firmly fixed as this fish's persistent digging actions may well disturb them. This middle- and lower-level swimmer can be territorial and aggressive.

HEROS NIGROFASCIATUM

FAMILY: *CICHLIDAE*
COMMON NAME: *CONVICT CICHLID; ZEBRA CICHLID*

FEEDING

COMPATIBILITY

EASE OF KEEPING

1

SIZE

6 in (15 cm) 4 in (10 cm)

The common names for this fish native to the streams, rivers, and lakes of Central America need no explanation. Its stocky body, including the fins, is gray with numerous vertical dark bands crossing it, although they only encroach into the dorsal and anal fins slightly. Coloration patterns vary with the mood of the fish. Some yellow coloring and iridescent scaling may be seen in the lower body of females. The dorsal and anal fins have filamentous extensions in male specimens. A pinkish, near-albino form has been developed by selective aquarium breeding. This species has recently been re-classified as *Archocentrus nigrofasciatum*.

SPECIAL CARE: This fish is a ready-spawner, but unfortunately it comes with a bad reputation as a plant-eater and for other antisocial disruptive tendencies. Keep in a well-planted (use plastic plants) aquarium and create retreats.

Above: The pinkish,
near-albino form of the Convict Cichlid.

HEROS SALVINI

FAMILY: *CICHLIDAE*
COMMON NAME: *SALVIN'S CICHLID*

FEEDING

COMPATIBILITY

EASE OF KEEPING

SIZE

6 in (15 cm) 4 in (10 cm)

An inhabitant of lakes and rivers in Mexico and Central America, this attractive member of the large, complex cichlid clan is regularly available from hatchery production. The body is golden yellow, with prominent dark bands running along the dorsal surface and over the lateral line from the eye to the caudal peduncle. The face bears a series of dark bands beginning just anterior to the dorsal fin and ending at the level of the eye. Below the mid-line, the body is marked in light blue and red, with the same colors being repeated in the fins. With such vivid coloration, it is no surprise that the fish has attracted alternative common names in addition to the simple translation of the specific name; European aquarists often referred to this fish as the Rainbow Cichlid, and American fishkeepers may be more familiar with the name of Tricolor Cichlid. The sexes are readily distinguished by the more pointed fins and brighter colors of the male.

SPECIAL CARE: Pairs become extremely aggressive, and even unpaired juveniles are likely to harass their tank mates. It spawns in typical cichlid fashion, attaching up to 500 eggs to a carefully cleaned rock, and extensive care is provided by both parents.

HEROS SEVERUS

FAMILY: *CICHLIDAE*
COMMON NAME: *SEVERUM; BANDED CICHLID*

This middle- and lower-level swimmer has an oblong rather than elongated body shape, with a relatively steep head profile, red-rimmed eyes, and a fairly short caudal peduncle. The body is greenish golden brown but there is a difference in patterning between juvenile and adult specimens. Juveniles have a number of vertical dark stripes crossing the body (not unlike those of the discus) whereas the adult has only remnants of the stripes showing as a series of dark blotches along the lower flanks. One dark stripe runs down from the rear of the dorsal fin across the caudal peduncle and only just reaches into the anal fin; the rest of the body is covered with small red-brown dots The fins are body-colored with only a slight reddish-brown coloring in the pelvic

FEEDING

COMPATIBILITY

EASE OF KEEPING

SIZE

8 in (20 cm) 8 in (20 cm)

and anal fins. A "gold" or xanthic strain has been introduced. The female lacks spots on the head and also has shorter dorsal and anal fins. This prolific breeder is native to the waters of northern South America and *Amazonia*.

SPECIAL CARE: A long-established aquarium favorite due to its gentle and peaceful disposition, this fish will become tame and take food from the hand. It will thrive in a well-planted, roomy aquarium with retreats. The Severum will breed in great numbers once compatible partners are established.

SYMBOL KEY

FEEDING
Herbivore
Omnivore
Predator

COMPATIBILITY
single specimen
community fish
safe with small fish
safe with invertebrates

EASE OF KEEPING
scale of 1 to 10
(with 1 being easiest to keep)

SIZE
in the wild
in captivity

JULIDOCHROMIS MARLIERI

FAMILY: *CICHLIDAE*
COMMON NAME: *MARLIER'S JULIE*

This species, together with *J. ornatus*, is probably the most colorful of the genus. Its cylindrical-shaped body is very light golden brown and is crossed with three dark bands, the lowest of which is on the center line. These lines are crossed vertically at regular intervals by indistinct dark bars that reach almost to the ventral surface. A further short dark bar runs from the corner of the mouth to the base of the pectoral fin. The eyes have a golden inner ring and are surrounded by a dark rim. The fins of this fish all have slightly different coloration; the dark dorsal fin is long-based with a gold stripe running along its middle and a light blue edge; the anal fin is dark with a few gold speckles and a light blue edge; the caudal fin has some dark blotches with a black margin inside the light blue outer edge; and the pelvic fins are fairly long with blue front edges. This fish is also similar to *J. transcriptus* from which it can be distinguished by its third row of blotches along the flanks; *J. transcriptus* has only two. It is found in the wild in the rocky shores of Lake Tanganyika, eastern Africa.

SPECIAL CARE: This peaceful fish is a secretive spawner that spends most of its time at the bottom of the aquarium. Its ideal environment in captivity is a well-planted aquarium with retreats.

FEEDING

COMPATIBILITY

EASE OF KEEPING

SIZE

4.7 in (12 cm) 4.7 in (12 cm)

JULIDOCHROMIS DICKFELDI

FAMILY: *CICHLIDAE*
COMMON NAME: *DICKFELD'S JULIE*

FEEDING

COMPATIBILITY

EASE OF KEEPING

SIZE

4 in (10 cm) 3.2 in (8 cm)

This distinctive fish has a cylindrical, pale white-brown body with three equally spaced longitudinal dark bands, the lowest of which occupies the center line of the fish and runs from the snout to the end of the caudal peduncle. A few dark lines also cross the forehead. It is worth noting that the scales are particularly well-defined in this species, which is found in Lake Tanganyika, Africa. The dorsal and anal fins are both long-based, with the dorsal being twice the length of the anal. The fins have dark rays with the intermediate tissues being pale blue, a color that runs along the edges of most of the fins. In terms of shape, the pelvic fins are very pointed and the caudal fin is rounded. There are no visible sexual differences except, perhaps, that the female tends to be larger. This fish is a secretive breeder and in the wild deposits its eggs in caves, where the female takes her share in defending the eggs.

SPECIAL CARE: One very welcome benefit with this species, also known as the Brown Julie, is that it can be kept in relatively small aquariums. Because of its slender body the fish has no difficulty in getting between crevices in the rockwork, and the aquarium should be furnished with many such retreats.

JULIDOCHROMIS ORNATUS

FAMILY: *CICHLIDAE*
COMMON NAME: *JULIE CICHLID*

Found only along the rocky coastline of Africa's Lake Tanganyika, this is among the most popular of that lake's many species. Males are a little larger than females, but otherwise both sexes are similar. The body is golden yellow, overlaid with horizontal dark bands, the first running from the bottom edge of the eyes to the caudal peduncle, the next beginning at the top of the eyes and extending to the rear margin of the dorsal fin, and the uppermost running from the snout across the top of the head and down the back. The uppermost band extends to the bottom third of the dorsal fin. Juvenile specimens lack yellow coloration but are otherwise similar.

SPECIAL CARE: Requires hard, alkaline water and good filtration. Numerous rocks arranged to provide caves will mimic its native habitat. Feeding is usually not a problem, although a varied diet must be supplied. Nitrate accumulation is harmful to this and other African cichlids.

FEEDING

COMPATIBILITY

EASE OF KEEPING

SIZE

3.2 in (8 cm) 3 in (7.5 cm)

JULIDOCHROMIS REGANI

FAMILY: *CICHLIDAE*
COMMON NAME: *REGAN'S JULIE; STRIPED JULIE*

This species has the characteristic cylindrical body shape of the Julies. This heavily-marked fish has a light yellow/gold body with four to five dark bands that run its whole length, covering the face and terminating at the end of the caudal peduncle. Some light blue lines may appear around the mouth and the lower head area. The long-based dorsal fin has a yellow/gold base followed by a black inner margin and light blue edging; the rounded caudal fin is similarly marked. The anal fin is dark with a little gold speckling, the pelvic fins dark, but the pectoral fin is particularly distinctive, being a bright, brilliant yellow.

SPECIAL CARE: While it is important to keep the water pure, Julies do not take too kindly to large water changes; a well-maintained filter and frequent, but small, water replacements is the best combination. Its ideal habitat is identical to that of the other *Julidochromis* species.

FEEDING

COMPATIBILITY

EASE OF KEEPING

1

SIZE

6 in (15 cm) 5 in (12 cm)

JULIDOCHROMIS TRANSCRIPTUS KISSI

FAMILY: *CICHLIDAE*
COMMON NAME: *BLACK AND WHITE JULIE*

Another charming member of its genus, this one is yellow below the level of the eye, dark brown above, and with a double row of lighter yellow spots forming a line from the tip of the snout, through the eyes, along the flanks and ending at the caudal peduncle. The dark brown coloration extends to the dorsal fin, which is edged in white. The caudal fin has a white margin with a thin, black edge, a second concentric inner white line, and an innermost series of white dots. The anal fin is similarly edged in white and marked with lines. The paired fins are yellow.

SPECIAL CARE: As this is a Lake Tanganyika native, it requires hard, alkaline water at a temperature of about 75°F (24°C). The tank should be furnished with numerous rocks, arranged to form caves. One of these will be used for spawning, with the eggs being attached to the roof. It is the smallest species in the genus, and a pair can be accommodated in a 20-gallon (76-liter) tank. Feed a varied diet incorporating live foods.

FEEDING

COMPATIBILITY

EASE OF KEEPING

5

SIZE

2.8 in (7 cm) 2.8 in (7 cm)

LABEOTROPHEUS FUELLEBORNI

FAMILY: *CICHLIDAE*
COMMON NAME: *FUELLEBORN'S CICHLID*

The fish is found in the shallow waters of the shores of Lake Malawi. This species often adds confusion to its own identification by having many different color variations, known as morphs. Although almost identical in body shape, the coloration of the two sexes is very distinct. The Red Top male is blue-gray with numerous vertical dark bars covering the body and forehead. The dorsal fin can be varying shades of red with some dark rays and a lighter edge in the rear portion. The anal fin is red with a few yellowish egg spots. The Orange Blotch female is light golden brown with some random specklings. Her fins are plain with no egg spots.

SPECIAL CARE: This aggressive fish is intolerant of its own kind and even of similarly colored fishes. Keep with other large fishes or in a separate species aquarium that is spacious with a rocky décor and algal growth.

FEEDING

COMPATIBILITY

EASE OF KEEPING

4

SIZE

6.3 in (16 cm) 4.7 in (12 cm)

SYMBOL KEY

FEEDING

Herbivore

Omnivore

Predator

COMPATIBILITY

single specimen

community fish

safe with small fish

safe with invertebrates

EASE OF KEEPING

scale of 1 to 10
(with 1 being easiest to keep)

SIZE

in the wild

in captivity

LABEOTROPHEUS TREVAWASAE

FAMILY: *CICHLIDAE*
COMMON NAME: *TREVAWAS' CICHLID; RED TOP TREVAWASAE*

This fish is found near rocky shores in the relatively shallow waters of Lake Malawi, Africa. Whatever the color morph of this species (various geographical locations result in their own local variants), sexual differentiation presents no problems as every male has the false "egg spot" patterning on the anal fin. The body colors of this species range from almost pure white to a black-mottled variation to blue/mauve with regular dark vertical bandings to orange. Add to these basics the presence of an orange-red long-based dorsal fin and you have a whole color spectrum to choose from. This fish prefers the middle and lower levels of the aquarium and follows a typical mouthbrooding pattern.

SPECIAL CARE: Observation of the turned-down top lip identifies this species as an algae grazer. The male will be content with a harem of females but this does not temper his aggressiveness in any way. Keep in a spacious aquarium furnished with rocks and algal growth.

FEEDING

COMPATIBILITY

EASE OF KEEPING

4

SIZE

4.7 in (12 cm) 4 in (10 cm)

LABIDOCHROMIS CAERULEUS

FAMILY: *CICHLIDAE*
COMMON NAME: *LABIDOCHROMIS SP 'GOLD'; 'YELLOW'*

Most cichlids native to Lake Malawi are blue; the specific name of this fish bears this out, yet it is yellow in color. The original species is known as the Blue-White Labido, which suggests that the blue coloration is not as dominant as expected. The yellow morph is more than likely found in a slightly different geographic

FEEDING

COMPATIBILITY

EASE OF KEEPING

2

SIZE

4 in (10 cm) 4 in (10 cm)

location than its relatives and, once collected, has formed the basic stock for future yellow offspring. This cichlid with its bright yellow body and black-edged fins rivals some marine fish for coloration.

SPECIAL CARE: This is a peaceful cichlid, quite happy in a community collection of similarly sized fishes. Adult males may quarrel but juvenile fish can be kept in shoals. The female incubates the eggs in her mouth for just over a month before the young fry are hatched.

MELANOCHROMIS AURATUS

FAMILY: *CICHLIDAE*
COMMON NAME: *AURATUS*

The coloration of juveniles of both sexes is bright yellow with two white-edged black bars on the upper-half of the body running from the snout to the end of the caudal fin. Some black lines also cross the forehead and run along the top lip. A third white-bordered dark line runs along the middle of the yellow dorsal fin. The caudal fin has a yellow lower-half and dark speckles on the upper. The anal fin is yellow with a single spot at its rear and the pelvic fins are edged with black. When males mature their color changes to dark blue-black, with a silvery-light blue streak along the center line and a yellow dorsal surface separated from the rest by another light blue line. The dorsal fin is pale blue with a yellow edge and the pelvic and anal fins are dark with light blue edges. The anal fin also carries a few egg spots. The caudal fin is dark with a yellow top and rear edge and a light blue bottom edge. Females retain the bright yellow juvenile coloration and the white-bordered black bands along the body.

SPECIAL CARE: This fish is intolerant of others and the male should be provided with a harem of females.

It should be cared for in the same way as the other species native to Lake Malawi, a spacious aquarium with plenty of rocky retreats and algal growth.

FEEDING

COMPATIBILITY

EASE OF KEEPING

4

SIZE

5 in (13 cm) 4.3 in (11 cm)

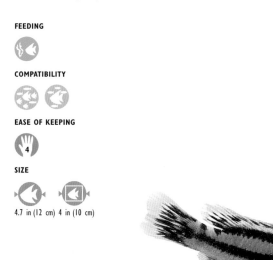

MELANOCHROMIS CHIPOKAE

FAMILY: *CICHLIDAE*
COMMON NAME: *CHIPOKAE*

This mouthbrooder is very similar in appearance to the previous species native to Lake Malawi. The only slight difference in physical shape is that the snout is slightly more elongated. Similarly to the Auratus, mature males lose the yellow coloring of juvenility and develop dark blue-black bodies with a broad silvery-light blue band along the center-line that ends just inside the base of the caudal fin. There is a second fainter band above it nearer the base of the dorsal fin. The long-based dorsal fin is pale blue with a yellow edge; the pelvic and anal fins also are dark with light blue. The anal fin also carries a few egg spots. The dark caudal fin has light blue top and bottom edges and a yellow rear edge. Females retain their juvenile coloration of bright yellow body with white-bordered black bands There is a dark crescent shape across the caudal fin surrounding a yellow patch and the termination of the lower black band along the body. Her pelvic and anal fins are yellow although the first few rays are dark.

SPECIAL CARE: This fish should be cared for in the same way as the other African lake cichlids (see *Melanochromis auratus*).

FEEDING

COMPATIBILITY

EASE OF KEEPING
4

SIZE
6 in (15 cm) 5 in (13 cm)

SYMBOL KEY

FEEDING
Herbivore
Omnivore
Predator

COMPATIBILITY
single specimen
community fish
safe with small fish
safe with invertebrates

EASE OF KEEPING
scale of 1 to 10
(with 1 being easiest to keep)

SIZE
in the wild
in captivity

MELANOCHROMIS JOHANNI

FAMILY: *CICHLIDAE*
COMMON NAME: *JOHANNI*

FEEDING

COMPATIBILITY

EASE OF KEEPING
4

SIZE
4.7 in (12 cm) 4.7 in (12 cm)

This fish, formerly known as *"Pseudotropheus daviesi,"* has an elongated, slightly laterally-compressed body. Mature males have blue-black-brown bodies with a silvery-light blue line running across the forehead, over the top of the eyes, and along the body just above the center-line to end on the caudal peduncle. Another short light colored line appears below the first on the forehead, level with the eye. Approximately the same distance below the center-line is another silvery-blue-gray line. The long-based dorsal fin is dark blue with a lighter shade at its base, particularly toward the rear of the fin; the pelvic and anal fins are dark with light blue edges, the anal fin also carries a few egg spots. The dark caudal fin has light blue top, bottom, and rear edges. Females have a light brownish-yellow coloration with a faint dark brown band along the body. The fins are a lighter shade of the main body color with a dark margin in the dorsal fin. The coloration of fishes within the genus varies not only from species to species but also within the species themselves according to location on the lake.

SPECIAL CARE: This fish should be cared for in the same way as the other African lake cichlids (see *Melanochromis auratus*).

NANOCHROMIS NUDICEPS

FAMILY: *CICHLIDAE*
COMMON NAME:
CONGO DWARF CICHLID

FEEDING

COMPATIBILITY

EASE OF KEEPING
1

SIZE
3.2 in (8 cm) 3 in (7.5 cm)

This fish native to the waters of Zaire is a soft-looking gray-brown color with some bluish areas toward the head and purplish areas on the belly, particularly visible on the female. Male fish are generally larger and have more pointed dorsal and anal fins. Some experts suggest that the name *N. parilus* is more correct and that this fish is merely a color variant of that species.

SPECIAL CARE: When about to breed the female extends a breeding tube (ovipositor) from her vent and her belly takes on a reddish-purple hue. It often spawns in a cave or, in captivity, a flower-pot. This fish may be more content in a single-species aquarium.

NEOLAMPROLOGUS BRICHARDI

FAMILY: *CICHLIDAE*
COMMON NAME: *BRICHARD'S LAMPROLOGUS*

This fish is a schooling species that only pairs up in order to mate. Spawning occurs in caves (often the eggs are laid on the "ceiling") in the rocky shallows of Lake Tanganyika. It will raise several broods of young consecutively and will continue to care for the whole family even when a new group hatches. Its light brown body, with clearly defined scales, is elongated and its dorsal surface is slightly more arched than the ventral surface. On the rear of the gill cover is a gold-yellow spot followed by a black patch. Some blue facial markings below the mouth may be noticeable and the eyes are brilliant blue. All fins (with the exception of the pectoral) are edged in blue-white. Both the dorsal and anal fins are long-based with pointed extensions in the male, and rounded tips in the female. The caudal fin has well-produced extensions on each tip, making it lyre-shaped, again the prerogative of the male.
SPECIAL CARE: To successfully breed this fish in captivity the aquarium should be spacious and furnished with many rocky retreats. This peaceful fish does best in medium to hard water, reflecting the conditions found in its natural habitat.

FEEDING

COMPATIBILITY

EASE OF KEEPING

4

SIZE

3.5 in (9 cm) 3.5 in (9 cm)

NEOLAMPROLOGUS LELEUPI

FAMILY: *CICHLIDAE*
COMMON NAME: *LEMON CICHLID*

FEEDING

COMPATIBILITY

EASE OF KEEPING

4

SIZE

3.5 in (9 cm) 3.5 in (9 cm)

The elongated body of the Lemon Cichlid is not dissimilar to that of the genus *Julidochromis*, a lake-sharing species. Its body is bright yellow with well-defined scales. The mouth region may have some light brown coloring. The pupils of the eyes are dark and separated from the iris by a gold ring. All fins share the same color as the body with only a hint of a darker shading at their rear edges. The dorsal fin is very long-based and the caudal fin is broad. The pelvic and anal fins trail somewhat. Differentiating between the sexes is not easy, and observations of the shape of the head and its degree of "slope" have been suggested as a means of doing so. There are several color variations, often a shade or two nearer to orange than the popular name suggests, and these have become known as the subspecies *N. leleupi leleupi* and *N. leleupi longior*. When these fish mate in the waters of Lake Tanganyika they become a real parenting team. The female takes care of the fry while the male guards their territory.
SPECIAL CARE: This fish is generally peaceful, although it may become territorial during spawning. Keep in a spacious aquarium that has many rocky cave-like retreats.

PAPILIOCHROMIS RAMIREZI

FAMILY: *CICHLIDAE*
COMMON NAME: *RAM; DWARF BUTTERFLY CICHLID*

FEEDING

COMPATIBILITY

EASE OF KEEPING

1

SIZE

2.8 in (7 cm) 2.5 in (6.5 cm)

This attractive, peaceful species native to the waters of Venezuela and Colombia has had several changes in its generic name including *Apistogramma* and *Microgeophagus*. Now known as *Papiliochromis*, its body is elongated yet slightly oval with an arched dorsal profile, a convex belly, and a narrow caudal peduncle. The rear two-thirds of the golden brown body is covered with violet-blue iridescent scales with a dark blotch below the dorsal fin. The front part is more yellowish with a dark bar running through the bright red eye. The forehead is rounded and there are some blue-green facial markings. The dorsal, anal, and caudal fins are reddish and all carry iridescent blue specklings and the pelvic fins are red with a dark front edge. The second ray of the male's dorsal fin is black and much extended. Most aquarium stocks are captive-bred with aquarium-developed gold and long-finned strains available.
SPECIAL CARE: Usually preferring soft water, it can be acclimatized to domestic water supplies by regular partial replacements of harder water. The Ram will flourish in a well-planted aquarium with areas created in which the fish can hide.

PELVICACHROMIS PULCHER

FAMILY: *CICHLIDAE*
COMMON NAME: *KRIBENSIS*

This species, found in the Niger Delta, west Africa, is particularly interesting because of the distinct differences between the sexes. The body is elongated, with approximately equal dorsal and ventral contours although the latter may be fuller in the female. The lower-half of the body is silvery-pinkish-violet in the male with the belly area of the female taking on a deep purple, rich plum color. The female has gold areas above and below the eyes.

SPECIAL CARE: This prolific spawner often disappears for long periods into rocks and plants and then emerges with a huge family. Water pH values are said to have an effect on the proportion of the sexes within the brood.

FEEDING

COMPATIBILITY

EASE OF KEEPING
I

SIZE
4 in (10 cm) 4 in (10 cm)

SYMBOL KEY

FEEDING
Herbivore

Omnivore

Predator

COMPATIBILITY
single specimen

community fish

safe with small fish

safe with invertebrates

EASE OF KEEPING
scale of 1 to 10
(with 1 being easiest to keep)

SIZE
in the wild

in captivity

PARAPETENIA FESTAE

FAMILY: *CICHLIDAE*
COMMON NAME: *FESTAE CICHLID*

FEEDING

COMPATIBILITY

EASE OF KEEPING
6

SIZE
20 in (50 cm) 12 in (30 cm)

Recent re-classifications have moved this fish from *Cichlasoma* and *Heros* to its current resting place. Its elongated heavily-built body is golden yellow-red, although its dorsal surface is slightly darker. A number of bluish-green iridescent dark bands cross the flanks vertically between the rear of the gill covers and the caudal peduncle. A bright-ringed similarly-colored dark spot appears on the base of the caudal fin, slightly above the horizontal. Partial dark bars cross the top of the head, which itself is a plain color; the eyes are dark. The front part of the dorsal fin shares the same color as the body bands but its rear part is bright red, as is the caudal fin. The anal fin is red with some blue-black streaking on its front rays; the pelvic fins are also blue-black; the pectoral reddish. It seems that the more beautiful the fish is, the more aggressive and belligerent it becomes. Its coloring intensifies or fades according to its mood. The dorsal and anal fins of the male are more pointed than those of the female. This Amazonian species is very similar in appearance to the mid-American species *Cichlasoma urophthalmus*.

SPECIAL CARE: This fish spawns in the open water, laying its eggs on flat surfaces. Often aggressive, it should be kept in a spacious aquarium with plastic plants, and is suitable for a community collection of large fishes.

PSEUDOTROPHEUS ELONGATUS

FAMILY: *CICHLIDAE*
COMMON NAME: *SLENDER MBUNA*

As one would presume from its common name, the Slender Mbuna has an elongated body, much more so than other members of the genus. The body, including the head, is sooty-black/deep blue in color. From behind the gill covers a number of light blue bands cross the body vertically, stopping short of the ventral surface. The final blue band extends into the caudal fin, flaring out among the otherwise dark rays. The dorsal fin runs almost the entire length of the body and the anal fin about one-third. The pectoral and pelvic fins are dark; the other fins are similarly-colored but may have light blue edging and, of course, the male's anal fin features egg spots. This species, whose natural habitiat is Lake Malawi, can vary in color according to the mood of the fish.

SPECIAL CARE: Despite being relatively easy to care for, this species is not the best example of the typical cichlid happy family group as the male and female only stay together long enough for the purposes of mating, after which the mouthbrooding female is left on her own. This aggressive fish should be kept in a spacious aquarium with plenty of rocky furnishing and algal growth.

FEEDING

COMPATIBILITY

EASE OF KEEPING
4

SIZE
5 in (13 cm) 4 in (10 cm)

The male (left) and female (above) Kennyi have very different coloring.

PSEUDOTROPHEUS LOMBARDOI

FAMILY: *CICHLIDAE*
COMMON NAME: *KENNYI*

Unlike most of the other species in this genus, the dorsal contour is more highly arched with a flatter ventral surface. This species is one of the very few examples where the female has the more attractive patterning. The male is bright yellow with some brown bars partially crossing the body. The fins are plain yellow with egg spots on the anal fin. The eyes have dark centers surounded by silvery-yellow. The female has a pale white/blue body with a number of equally-spaced, tapering blue/black vertical bands almost crossing the body having originated midway across the width of the dorsal fin. A further pair of dark bands, connected at their lower end, cross the top of the head immediately in front of the dorsal fin and a small dark bar appears between the eyes. Her anal, pelvic, and pectoral fins are pale blue and the caudal fin is light blue with dark vertical bands or interconnected speckles.
SPECIAL CARE: This is another species native to the rocky shores of Lake Malawi. It should be kept in a spacious aquarium with rocky retreats and algal growth. This aggressive fish follows the typical mouthbrooding pattern and is suitable for a community collection or a single species aquarium.

FEEDING

COMPATIBILITY

EASE OF KEEPING

4

SIZE

5.5 in (14 cm) 4 in (10 cm)

PSEUDOTROPHEUS TROPHEOPS

FAMILY: *CICHLIDAE*
COMMON NAME: *TROPHEOPS*

This species has many varying color morphs. These differing color variations are found at different locations in their natural habitat of Lake Malawi. The body is usually brownish and crossed

vertically by numerous indistinct dark bars. These bars may show up more clearly when the fish is under stress. The head is blunt with a very steep forehead between the large, high-set eyes and mouth where the upper lip turns over the lower. The pelvic and anal fins have dark and light blue edges and the male's anal fin bears a few egg spots. Females often have a mottled coloration totally different to that of the males. This species follows the typical mouthbrooding pattern.
SPECIAL CARE: This middle- and lower-level swimmer is more suited to a single species aquarium with rocky retreats and algal growth.

FEEDING

COMPATIBILITY

EASE OF KEEPING
4

SIZE

5.5 in (14 cm) 5.5 in (14 cm)

PSEUDOTROPHEUS ZEBRA

FAMILY: *CICHLIDAE*
COMMON NAME: *ZEBRA MBUNA*

The Zebra Mbuna was instantly received with enthusiasm due to its coloration, especially by aquarists whose hard domestic tapwater often precluded them from keeping colorful fish that require soft water. It was not long before many numerous color morphs became available and these include blue or orange blotch forms, plain yellow or blue, or almost any variation in between. Its body is light blue with numerous, gradually fading, dark blue bands vertically crossing the body. The area below the eyes, together with the gill cover, mouth, throat, and forward part of the ventral region, is dark blue. The dorsal, anal, and caudal fins are, by contrast, light blue, with the typical family yellow egg spots occurring on the rear of the male's anal fin. Females may be the same color as the males or be of a plain but speckled appearance of quite a different color.
SPECIAL CARE: This fish requires a spacious aquarium with rocky retreats and algal growth to recreate its natural habitat of Lake Malawi. This fish can be territorial and aggressive and may be better suited to a single species aquarium.

FEEDING

COMPATIBILITY

EASE OF KEEPING
4

SIZE

6 in (15 cm) 5 in (13 cm)

Right: A red variant of the original Zebra Mbuna.

PTEROPHYLLUM ALTUM

FAMILY: *CICHLIDAE*
COMMON NAME: *DEEP ANGELFISH*

FEEDING

COMPATIBILITY

EASE OF KEEPING

SIZE

7 in (18 cm) 5 in (13 cm)

The Deep Angelfish's body shape is not immediately associated as being typically characteristic of the general cichlid family. It is disc-like and severely compressed laterally. The physical shape of this species makes it adept at moving in and out of reed stems, while its coloration camouflages it perfectly when at rest among plants in the Orinoco river system. Body coloration is silver with several dark bands crossing vertically and entering the dorsal and anal fins. There may be some dark speckling between the dark bands but the most distinguishing feature of the species is the distinct notch in the outline of the forehead above the snout. The dorsal and anal fins are long and in mature specimens filaments extend from their tips. The threadlike pelvic fins consist of a few bony rays and extend well below the anal fin. The caudal fin is fan-shaped with the top and bottom rays also extending as filaments. This species is not imported as often as *P. scalare*, which itself may come from non-natural sources.
SPECIAL CARE: Despite its modest body length, the high dorsal and long anal fins make the fish a very tall species, requiring a deep, well-planted tank to accommodate it comfortably. This fish spawns on slanting, often near vertical, firm surfaces.

PTEROPHYLLUM SCALARE

FAMILY: *CICHLIDAE*
COMMON NAME: *ANGELFISH*

FEEDING

COMPATIBILITY

EASE OF KEEPING

SIZE

6 in (15 cm) 5 in (13 cm)

The body shape of the Angelfish is similar to the previous *Pterophyllum* species. Since it became one of the most popular aquarium fishes, selective breeding programs have resulted in many different color strains and finnage patterns including varieties such as Black, Gold, Marbled, Half-black, Lace, and Veiltail. The body coloration of the original wild species is silver with several dark vertical bands crossing the body and entering the dorsal and anal fins with occasional dark speckling between the bands. Its fins are very similar in shape and formation to the Deep Angelfish—long dorsal and anal fins with filaments extending from their tips in mature specimens, threadlike pelvic fins with a few bony rays extending well below the anal fin, and a fan-shaped caudal fin with the top and bottom rays also extending as filaments. Sexual differences are hard to spot but generally there is a difference in the shape and dimensions of the ovipositor (breeding tube) which is best observed at spawning times. Other, often described differences (head contours, angle of fins to body, etc.) may apply only to certain specimens and are usually also founded in hindsight!
SPECIAL CARE: These fishes, native to the Amazon and *Rio Negro*, are not difficult to spawn and make excellent parents. This middle- and lower-level swimmer should be kept in a well-planted, deep aquarium.

SYMBOL KEY

FEEDING

Herbivore

Omnivore

Predator

COMPATIBILITY

single specimen

community fish

safe with small fish

safe with invertebrates

EASE OF KEEPING

scale of 1 to 10
(with 1 being easiest to keep)

SIZE

in the wild

in captivity

SATANOPERCA JURAPARI

FAMILY: *CICHLIDAE*
COMMON NAME: *EARTHEATER; DEMONFISH*

This cichlid was once known as "*Geophagus jurapari.*" It is found in Brazil and Guyana, where it inhabits neutral to slightly acidic waters over sandy substrates. The entire body is silvery, with colorless fins. The face and dorsal surface down to the lateral line are decorated with olive green lines that help to camouflage the fish in its natural habitat.

SPECIAL CARE: Commonly available from commercial hatcheries, this cichlid is easily spawned in a roomy tank, provided you have a mated pair in good condition. The eggs are first placed on a rock by the female, who subsequently takes them into her mouth for brooding after they are fertilized by the male. Both parents then share the duty of brooding the eggs in the mouth. For a time after the fry become free-swimming, they may return to the parent's mouth at night or at the approach of danger. Because of its habitual digging behavior, only the hardiest plants should be included in its tank.

FEEDING

COMPATIBILITY

EASE OF KEEPING
1

SIZE
10 in (25 cm) 6 in (15 cm)

SCIAENOCHROMIS AHLI

FAMILY: *CICHLIDAE*
COMMON NAME: *ELECTRIC BLUE "HAPLOCHROMIS"*

FEEDING

COMPATIBILITY

EASE OF KEEPING
3

SIZE
8 in (20 cm) 8 in (20 cm)

This fish was once known as "*Haplochromis serranoides,*" and the genus name has stuck within the aquarium trade, despite the taxonomic revisions that have taken place in the cichlid family. Although it is not one of the "Haps," this denizen of the rocky shallows of Lake Malawi is aptly described by its common name. The brilliant blue body is marked by indistinct, dark blue vertical bars, and the anal and dorsal fins are edged in paler blue. The eyes are golden, and thus appear larger than they actually are.

SPECIAL CARE: This is a good choice for a community of cichlids from Lake Malawi. Provide plenty of room and hard, alkaline water. In the lake, it feeds mostly on the fry of other fishes, so smaller species are obviously to be avoided as tankmates. It adapts readily to most available aquarium foods, live or frozen. Filtration for a tank of Lake Malawi cichlids must be adequate to compensate for their greedy appetites and messy behavior.

STEATOCRANUS TINANTI

FAMILY: *CICHLIDAE*
COMMON NAME: *BLOCKHEAD CICHLID*

Native to Zaire, this species has a cylindrical body with a flattened ventral surface. It is a bottom-dweller, inhabiting fast flowing waters, although its low profile prevents it from being swept away by the strong water currents. The head is quite large in proportion to the rest of the body and the swim bladder barely existent. The cryptic dark vertical bands on the cream-yellow body help to disguise its presence on the riverbed.

SPECIAL CARE: This cichlid is a cave brooder, and will accept a clay flowerpot turned on its side as a substitute. Water conditions need not be perfect, but best results are likely to be had in the moderately soft, slightly acidic water favored by many stream dwellers. Parental care extends to feeding of the fry by the mother. Broods are tended assiduously, and the fish are intolerant of any intrusion. Provide a roomy tank with rocks and driftwood instead of plants. Once mated, the pair become territorial and pugnacious, and are best given a tank to themselves. It greedily accepts all types of aquarium foods.

FEEDING

COMPATIBILITY

EASE OF KEEPING
1

SIZE
6 in (15 cm) 4 in (10 cm)

Symphysodon aequifasciata haraldi

FAMILY: *CICHLIDAE*
COMMON NAME: *BLUE DISCUS*

This splendid fish, native to *Amazonia*, has a round body that is laterally-compressed and, as the name suggests, disc-like. Its body is brown and crossed with dark vertical bars over which is laid a pattern of blue wavy lines that extend into the dorsal and anal fins.

The head has a steeply rising forehead and red eyes. The dorsal and anal fin are long-based, almost reaching the caudal fin. The dorsal fin may have a red edge, the anal a dark inner margin covering the blue markings. Sexing is difficult; some reports indicate the difference in shape of the breeding tube is a guide—that of the male is pointed, the female's rounded.

SPECIAL CARE: This species requires plenty of special treatment from exact water conditions to a secluded and separate aquarium. The aquarium should be spacious and either furnished with tall plants or should be quite stark with only terra-cotta spawning cones and perhaps an Amazon Sword Plant for decoration. Various aquarium-developed strains are available, confirming that not only can this fish be bred with a little determination, but also that there appears to be scope for further, even more exotic strains. The fry are best left with the parents for the first few weeks; they feed from the parents' skin secretions. Some aquarists have apparently perfected a feeding program which allows separate development to occur.

FEEDING

COMPATIBILITY

EASE OF KEEPING
7

SIZE
6 in (15 cm) 6 in (15 cm)

Thorichthys maronii

FAMILY: *CICHLIDAE*
COMMON NAME: *KEYHOLE CICHLID*

This fish has been known as "*Aequidens maronii*" and most recently as "*Cleithracara maronii*." It is pale gray in color, with a distinctive, keyhole-shaped pattern of dark blotches on the flanks. Juvenile specimens have a dark band that runs vertically through the eye, and a single dark blotch that later develops into the "keyhole" pattern. This fish has declined in popularity with fishkeepers in recent years, owing to the poor condition of most specimens. This problem is thought by some authorities to be due to excessive inbreeding by hatcheries.

SPECIAL CARE: It prospers in moderately hard, slightly acidic or neutral water. Provide ample filtration, and hiding places among rocks or driftwood. This cichlid is unusual in that it will not damage plants, and actually appreciates vegetation in the aquarium. Feeding is simple, with most aquarium foods readily accepted.

FEEDING

COMPATIBILITY

EASE OF KEEPING
3

SIZE
6 in (15 cm) 3.2 in (8 cm)

Thorichthys meeki

FAMILY: *CICHLIDAE*
COMMON NAME: *FIREMOUTH*

The Firemouth, recently re-classified from genus *Cichlasoma*, has a deep, elongated body shape. Its body is greenish-gray with clearly defined scales and there is a dark spot on the gill cover just behind the eyes. This is repeated at intervals along the flanks, although in some circumstances these extend upward and downward as dark stripes, according to the particular mood of the fish. The fiery red coloration of the lower mouth and chest region, the distinguishing feature of the species, is found particularly in adult males. The dorsal and anal fins are long-based with those of the male being very pointed. This fish's natural habitat is the waters of Guatemala and the Yucatan. Some experts now refer to this fish as *Cleithracara maronii*.

SPECIAL CARE: This fish is often quite happy to linger among the foliage in a well-planted tank. It spawns on flat surfaces and is a good parent although it may become aggressive toward other fish at this time.

FEEDING

COMPATIBILITY

EASE OF KEEPING
1

SIZE
6 in (15 cm) 5 in (13 cm)

SYMBOL KEY

FEEDING

Herbivore

Omnivore

Predator

COMPATIBILITY

single specimen

community fish

safe with small fish

safe with invertebrates

EASE OF KEEPING

scale of 1 to 10
(with 1 being easiest to keep)

SIZE

in the wild

in captivity

LABYRINTHFISHES

Strictly speaking the Anabantidae family only contains the Climbing Perch fishes, but the family name has become almost a blanket term for labyrinthfishes, to give them their popular name. A feature of the whole group is the extra breathing accessory—the labyrinth organ—which is located in the head just behind the gills. This organ consists of a mass of convoluted tissue into which moist air, gulped at the surface, is stored and from which oxygen can be extracted. This organ is of enormous benefit to the fish should the waters in which they live become depleted of oxygen through pollution. The group, whose members have their natural habitats in Southeast Asia and equatorial Africa, contains fishes of modest and giant size, of peaceful and predatory dispositions. The predatory genus, *Ctenopoma*, is found in equatorial Africa but, while some of these fishes are quite beautifully marked, careful consideration has to be given as to the fishes that they are kept with.

Trichogaster trichopterus
THREE SPOT GOURAMI

The popular and numerous species of gourami belong to the Belontidae family. These fishes have adapted pelvic fins that are mostly single filaments with taste buds at the end. Another family member is the Siamese Fighting Fish, *Betta splendens*. All the specimens found in the aquatic dealers are captive bred; wild specimens do not have the bright colors or the elaborate finnage. The "life and death" battles that the males of this species engage in form the basis of wagers in Thailand. The Kissing Gourami, *Helostoma temmincki*, belongs to the Helostomidae family and the very large Giant Gourami, *Osphronemus goramy*, is the sole species in the Osphronemidae family.

These fishes can be kept as part of a community collection with small fishes, as solitary specimens in their own spacious tank, or in a single species collection. The majority are bubble nest builders—the males construct a floating nest of bubbles and saliva, under which the female is coaxed and the eggs expelled and fertilized. Males usually undergo color intensification during breeding periods and also become territorial when guarding the eggs. It is best to remove the female after spawning to save her from unwarranted attacks by the male. An exception to this method of reproduction is the Chocolate Gourami, *Sphaerichthys osphromenoides*, which is a mouthbrooder.

Helostoma temmincki
KISSING GOURAMI

CROAKING GOURAMI
The Croaking Gourami is an ideal fish for the smaller aquarium, and it will often breed quite happily.

CTENOPOMA ACUTIROSTRE

FAMILY: *ANABANTIDAE*
COMMON NAME: *SPOTTED CLIMBING PERCH;*
LEOPARD BUSHFISH

The Spotted Climbing Perch, native to the streams of Zaire, has an oval-shaped body, a pointed snout, and a truncated rear. It is almost lacking a caudal peduncle entirely. Body coloration is golden brown with a covering of leopard-like spots, hence its other common name. A dark spot features immediately at the base of the caudal fin. The terminally-situated mouth appears normal but it can be extended outward very rapidly, forming a wide tube in which unsuspecting prey are instantly engulfed. Dorsal and anal fins are predominantly spiny only moderating to softer rays at their rear portions; both anal and dorsal fins are long-based reaching almost around to include the caudal fin itself. All of the fins are a golden brown color but some, including the short pelvic fins and caudal fin, have slightly darker speckling. Some reports now refer to this species as *C. ocellatum.*
SPECIAL CARE: This predatory fish cannot be kept with smaller fishes for obvious reasons, but makes a very attractive and spectacular specimen for the larger, well-planted aquarium. It should be fed mainly on meat-based foods with live foods, such as earthworms, forming a regular part of its diet.

FEEDING

COMPATIBILITY

EASE OF KEEPING

5

SIZE

8 in (20 cm) 6 in (15 cm)

CTENOPOMA MULTISPINIS

FAMILY: *ANABANTIDAE*
COMMON NAME: *MANY-SPINED CTENOPOMA*

FEEDING

COMPATIBILITY

EASE OF KEEPING

4

SIZE

6.3 in (16 cm) 6 in (15 cm)

From the rivers and lakes of southern Africa comes this interesting anabantid. The tan body is marked with a checkerboard pattern of dark scales. The colorless dorsal fin bears numerous spines, although it is the spines on the cheeks and gill covers that give this species its name. It grows rather large for an anabantid, and sheer size may account for much of its popularity.
SPECIAL CARE: This species is easily maintained, provided the aquarium is of sufficient size, at least 50 gallons (190 liters). Ample filtration should be provided to offset the waste produced by a large fish with a hearty appetite. Water chemistry is not important for a species with so wide a natural range as this, but it is important to prevent the accumulation of nitrogenous wastes. Regular partial water changes should be carried out. Feeding presents no problem, as it is greedy and aggressive. Live insects of all types are preferred, but many frozen and prepared aquarium foods will serve just as well, unless you plan to attempt spawning a pair.

MICROCTENOPOMA NANUM

FAMILY: *ANABANTIDAE*
COMMON NAME: *DWARF CLIMBING PERCH*

This, the smallest member of its African clan, is perhaps the best community fish of its family. Nevertheless, a pair may become quite aggressive at spawning time. The pale body is marked with a series of olive vertical bars beginning at the gill cover and ending at the caudal peduncle. The bars extend onto the dorsal and anal fins, which are otherwise pale, as are the paired fins. The tail fin is also colorless, with white along the spines.There are olive markings on the head and a dark spot on the gill cover.
SPECIAL CARE: This species does best in a planted tank, with soft, slightly acidic water and a temperature of about 75°F (24°C). Provide small live foods at first, gradually combining them with flake and frozen foods until the fish learn to eat whatever is offered. Spawning occurs after construction of a bubble nest among floating plants. Suitable for a community tank of large fishes.

FEEDING

COMPATIBILITY

EASE OF KEEPING

5

SIZE

3.2 in (8 cm) 3.2 in (8 cm)

BETTA SPLENDENS

FAMILY: *BELONTIIDAE*
COMMON NAME: *SIAMESE FIGHTING FISH*

This fish has a cylindrical body with only a moderate curvature of the dorsal and ventral surfaces. The gill covers can be held erect, away from the body, and used as a threat or courtship posture by the male. The male has a long and flowing dorsal fin that has a relatively small base; the anal fin is long-based but is equally flowing, as is the well-rounded caudal fin. The pelvic fins are very long with only a few rays. The female has much shorter fins. No exact details of coloration can be given, as all species kept in the aquarium (with the exception perhaps of some wild-caught females from the streams and stationary waters of Thailand) are obtained from captivity-bred specimens whose colors have been developed over many years of aquarium breeding. Males are much more highly-colored than the females. A variety where the body is cream-colored with differently colored fins is known as the Cambodia Fighter. Several associations specialize in these fishes worldwide and the various color patterns are internationally recognized.

SPECIAL CARE: Males are very aggressive toward each other so it is advisable to have only one per aquarium. This fish will live contentedly swimming in the upper and middle levels of a well-planted aquarium.

FEEDING

COMPATIBILITY

EASE OF KEEPING
1

SIZE
2.5 in (6.5 cm) 2.5 in (6.5 cm)

COLISA FASCIATA

FAMILY: *BELONTIIDAE*
COMMON NAME: *BANDED GOURAMI*

FEEDING

COMPATIBILITY

EASE OF KEEPING
4

SIZE

4 in (10 cm) 3.2 in (8 cm)

An "old-fashioned" species, this gourami is worth seeking out for a species tank. Both the pale body and colorless fins are marked in rust red and neon blue, forming a banded pattern on the flanks. The anal fin is electric blue, edged in red. In females, the coloration is similar, but not as bright. Males are larger with more flowing fins. It is native to India and nearby areas of Southeast Asia.

SPECIAL CARE: Soft, acidic water, a temperature near 80°F (27°C) and plenty of vegetation suit this species best. It can be included in a community aquarium with species having similar requirements, but shows off its beautiful coloration best if given a tank of its own. Aquarists who wish to spawn this species will also have better luck keeping it by itself. A 20-gallon (76-liter) tank is sufficient for a pair. Feeding seldom poses any problems.

COLISA LABIOSA

FAMILY:
BELONTIIDAE
COMMON NAME: *THICKLIPPED GOURAMI*

The *Colisa labiosa*, found in the waters of northern India and Burma, is a very prolific breeder. Its bubble nest may cover quite a large area but may not be as meticulously constructed as in other species. It has a long but fairly deep body that is golden brown in color, crossed diagonally with equally-spaced bands of turquoise on the rear two-thirds. At spawning time, the male turns dark brown. The coloring of the throat region is a good indication of sex—the male's is turquoise, the female's silver. The upturned mouth has, as the popular name suggests, well-formed lips. The male's dorsal fin is very pointed. The anal fin is brown, with turquoise speckling in the male, with lighter edging. In general the female is less colorful.

SPECIAL CARE: A large well-planted aquarium is ideal and a gentle flow of water is beneficial. For optimum breeding conditions the water should be soft.

FEEDING

COMPATIBILITY

EASE OF KEEPING
1

SIZE

3.2 in (8 cm) 3.2 in (8 cm)

SYMBOL KEY

FEEDING
Herbivore

Omnivore

Predator

COMPATIBILITY
single specimen

community fish

safe with small fish

safe with invertebrates

EASE OF KEEPING
scale of 1 to 10
(with 1 being easiest to keep)

SIZE
in the wild

in captivity

COLISA LALIA

FAMILY: *BELONTIIDAE*
COMMON NAME: *DWARF GOURAMI*

The body of this popular aquarium fish appears to be oblong at first glance due to the shape of the dorsal and anal fins, but in fact, it is oval with a slightly high-backed formation. Its body is silvery-gray with numerous bright red and blue stripes running vertically across it. The lower head and throat areas are turquoise blue, the mouth slightly upturned, and the eyes red. The long-based dorsal and anal fins are blue with red specklings; the orange pelvic fins are threadlike, can be moved in all directions, and carry taste cells at their tips. The caudal fin is also blue with red patterning. This brilliant male coloration becomes even more intense at spawning times. Females are less highly-colored and are often plumper in the body. A number of highly-colored strains are now available.

FEEDING

COMPATIBILITY

EASE OF KEEPING

SIZE

2.4 in (6 cm) 2 in (5 cm)

SPECIAL CARE: The Dwarf Gourami is hardy and willing to breed. Usually quite peaceful in the community aquarium, the male can become very pugnacious when breeding, both to the female (after spawning) and to other fishes venturing too near his carefully-built, and egg-filled, bubble nest. The subsequent fry are very small and require the smallest of foods to begin with.

COLISA LALIA 'RED FORM'

FAMILY: *BELONTIIDAE*
COMMON NAME: *RED SUNSET GOURAMI*

This color form of the wild-type Sunset or Dwarf Gourami is a peaceful and non-aggressive species. The body is a golden orange from the gill cover to the caudal fin, while the head is silvery. The dorsal fin is a lovely shade of blue, becoming golden posteriorly. The caudal fin rays and those of the posterior part of the anal fin are orange with colorless tissue in between. The anal fin becomes blue on its anterior edge. The whiskerlike pectoral fins are white.

FEEDING

COMPATIBILITY

EASE OF KEEPING

SIZE

2 in (5 cm) 2 in (5 cm)

SPECIAL CARE: Due to its very passive nature this fish is unlikely to thrive in a community tank Requires a roomy, well-planted tank with soft, slightly acidic water at a temperature of around 80°F (27°C). Frequent water changes should be carried out to maintain good conditions. Feed a variety of flakes and, especially, any types of small live foods that are available. Even with the best of care, this species seldom survives past two years of age.

MACROPODUS OPERCULARIS

FAMILY: *BELONTIIDAE*
COMMON NAME: *PARADISE FISH*

Pugnacious and aggressive, this inhabitant of eastern Asian rice paddies and other shallow, somewhat stagnant habitats has been a popular aquarium fish for over a century. The body is a pale, electric blue, darkening to nearly black on the long, flowing dorsal and anal fins. Vertical red bars begin as a diffuse patch behind the gill cover and continue to the caudal peduncle. The caudal fin is red with light blue markings. Males are generally larger and more brightly colored than females.

FEEDING

COMPATIBILITY

EASE OF KEEPING

SIZE

4 in (10 cm) 3.2 in (8 cm)

SPECIAL CARE: This fish enjoys somewhat cooler waters than many other members of its family, and can be maintained under conditions similar to those required by goldfish, with the exception that this species cannot tolerate water temperatures below 50°F (10°C). Spawning occurs after the male builds a large bubble nest under floating vegetation. Some aquarists report that the floating leaves of water lilies are preferred. Up to 500 eggs are deposited by the female, who is then driven away by the male. He subsequently guards the nest until the tiny fry hatch out.

TRICHOGASTER LEERI

FAMILY: *BELONTIIDAE*
COMMON NAME: *LACE, PEARL, OR MOSAIC GOURAMI*

FEEDING

COMPATIBILITY

EASE OF KEEPING

SIZE

4.7 in (12 cm)   4.3 in (11 cm)

The elongated oval body shape of this fish is made less apparent by the wide, long-based anal fin. Native to the waters of Borneo, Malaysia, and Sumatra, its silvery body is covered with a mosaic pattern of dark spots (accounting for one of its common names) and a dark line runs unevenly from the snout, through the eyes and along the flanks to the caudal peduncle. The head is shallow and the mouth upturned. The male's dorsal fin is short-based but is very long (hanging well over the caudal fin) with trailing filaments in the rear portion. The anal fin is also very long-based almost reaching the caudal fin and again, that of the male has trailing filaments. The female's dorsal fin is shorter and rounder than that of the male, so this characteristic makes the sexes easily distinguishable. The male develops a bright orange coloration to the throat and chest, the pelvic fins, and the front portion of the anal fin. The female has a silvery throat region.
SPECIAL CARE: This is a peaceful fish that is suitable to be kept with a community collection of mixed-size fishes and will cruise the middle- and upper-levels of the tank. Spawning is quite possible in the aquarium but this fish often does not reach sexual maturity until it reaches full adult size.

TRICHOGASTER MICROLEPIS

FAMILY: *BELONTIIDAE*
COMMON NAME: *MOONLIGHT GOURAMI*

The Moonlight Gourami, an inhabitant of the waters of Cambodia and Thailand, has a very similar body shape to that of the previous species but there is one obvious difference. It has a notch in the profile of the head just above the upturned mouth. The silver body is very polished in appearance—the even sheen being achieved by the smallness of the scales. This is the physical characteristic that gives the fish its name—*micro* meaning tiny and *lepis* meaning scales. The eyes have dark pupils with reddish-gold irises and are set level with the mouth. The anal fin is long-based, with some silver coloration spreading from the body, and runs from just behind the pelvic fins along the length of the body ending immediately before the caudal fin itself begins. The very long pelvic fins are orange and threadlike. Sexing is fairly straightforward—the male has a much longer dorsal fin and the pelvic fins of the female are less colored.

FEEDING

COMPATIBILITY

EASE OF KEEPING

SIZE

7 in (18 cm)   5.5 in (14 cm)

SPECIAL CARE: A peaceful species, the Moonlight Gourami often utilizes pieces of plants in the construction of its bubble nest. It should therefore be kept in a well-planted aquarium. It will deposit up to 1,000 fertilized eggs following the spawning embrace which occurs immediately below the floating nest. It is worth noting that this species breeds better in soft water.

TRICHOGASTER TRICHOPTERUS

FAMILY: *BELONTIIDAE*
COMMON NAME: *THREE SPOT GOURAMI*

FEEDING

COMPATIBILITY

EASE OF KEEPING

SIZE

4.7 in (12 cm) 4.3 in (11 cm)

This fish, found in the waters of Southeast Asia, has an elongated, oval body with dorsal and ventral contours that are approximately equal in their rounded curvature. The body is a delicate light powder blue with two dark spots on the flanks—one at the midway point, the other at the end of the caudal peduncle. For those querying the popular name, the eyes form the third "spot" and are set well forward on the small head. All the fins are reasonably clear with some blue specklings. Males can be distinguished by their longer dorsal fin and some orange coloring to the threadlike pelvic fins. The very similar species, Blue Gourami, has a plain blue body and no spots. It is regarded as the subspecies, *T. trichopterus trichopterus*. Other color strains such as the Cosby and Opaline (both blue and gold varieties) have been introduced. A further blue-colored sub-species *T. trichopterus sumatranus* has been suggested.

SPECIAL CARE: The Three Spot Gourami is a very hardy fish that usually has a long life. It will be content in a well-planted aquarium and live peaceably with a community collection of mixed-size fish. It is a prolific breeder, but females may need protection from vigorously chasing males after spawning.

TRICHOGASTER PECTORALIS

FAMILY: *BELONTIIDAE*
COMMON NAME: *SNAKESKIN GOURAMI*

With its pale green to silvery body and simple color pattern of dark blotches along the mid-line from the gill cover to the caudal peduncle, this gourami is not as popular with aquarists as some of its more colorful congenerics. It makes up for its lack of coloration with a non-aggressive disposition and a willingness to spawn in captivity. The anal fin is edged in bright yellow in the female and the male possesses orange-red pelvic fins. Thus, the fish has a certain elegant appeal. It inhabits rice paddies and other shallow waters in Southeast Asia.

FEEDING

COMPATIBILITY

EASE OF KEEPING

SIZE

8 in (20 cm) 6 in (15 cm)

SPECIAL CARE: Spawning is as for other members of the genus: a bubble nest is constructed by the male. Some texts recommend lowering the water level of the aquarium suddenly in order to induce gouramis to spawn. The trick is thought to mimic conditions at the onset of the dry season in the fish's natural habitat. Unlike some *Trichogaster* species, this one is peaceful toward tankmates even when it is spawning. Provide plants or other hiding places.

TRICHOPSIS VITTATUS

FAMILY: *BELONTIIDAE*
COMMON NAME: *CROAKING GOURAMI*

FEEDING

COMPATIBILITY

EASE OF KEEPING

SIZE

3.2 in (8 cm) 2.4 in (6 cm)

This species is distinctive because it makes a croaking sound, usually during spawning, hence its popular name. An inhabitant of the streams of Southeast Asia, particularly Vietnam, Thailand, and Malaysia, it has a relatively slim body, with a front-half deeper than the rear. The body coloration is golden brown with two or three longitudinal markings made up of reddish-brown dots or small blotches. Some reddish-brown streaking occurs on the small head, where the red-rimmed blue eyes are set well forward. The dorsal fin has a fairly short base and is set well back on the body. The anal fin is much longer-based with the rear section much wider than the front. All fins are speckled with red on a bluish background.

SPECIAL CARE: This fish swims at the middle and lower levels of the aquarium and likes to hide among plants.

HELOSTOMA TEMMINCKI

FAMILY: *HELOSTOMIDAE*
COMMON NAME: *KISSING GOURAMI*

The Kissing Gourami is an inhabitant of the streams and rivers of Borneo, Java, Sumatra, and Thailand. The habit of "kissing" that this species often demonstrates has never been thoroughly explained to anyone's total satisfaction. It may be a trial of strength between males or a preliminary to spawning; one thing is for sure, the lips are certainly expert at removing algae. Other fishes may come in for a flank-sucking experience too. Its body is oval in shape with dorsal and ventral profiles equally convex. The body can be either greenish-silver with rows of tiny darker dots or, as is more usual in aquarium fishes, a pale rose-pink. The head is pointed with a terminal, thick-lipped mouth. The dorsal and anal fins are both very long-based, with spines for about two-thirds of their length. The caudal fin has a straight rear edge. All fins are fairly colorless.
SPECIAL CARE: This peaceful fish is suitable for a community collection of larger fishes. It swims at the middle and lower levels of the aquarium and generally breeds more successfully in soft water.

FEEDING

COMPATIBILITY

EASE OF KEEPING
3

SIZE
10 in (25 cm) 8 in (20 cm)

OSPHRONEMUS GORAMY

FAMILY: *OSPHRONEMIDAE*
COMMON NAME: *GOURAMI*

A juvenile Gourami has an elongated, laterally-compressed body, similar to that of the Kissing Gourami (*H. temmincki*) but it becomes very much more heavily-built when adult and soon outgrows its original aquarium. Like the Oscar (*Astronotus ocellatus*), this species is far more attractive when juvenile. Young fish have silvery-bronze-gray bodies crossed by several vertical dark bars. The head is pointed and the eyes set well forward. The fins are bronze, the pelvic fins being filamentous and bronze-yellow. The adult fish is dull gray with well-defined scales. There is a light gray area on the head above the relatively small eyes and the large fleshy lips are upturned. The dorsal and caudal fins are dark gray, although the anal fin is a little lighter. A golden variety has been aquarium-developed. While both adult fish look similar, males may have more pointed fins and the female is more heavily-built. It is not uncommon for this fish to be found in ornamental ponds in tropical countries; their large size makes them easily visible.
SPECIAL CARE: Known as *Kalui* in its native home-waters of the Greater Sunda Islands in Southeast Asia, where it is a food fish, it needs plenty of vegetable matter and has a prodigious appetite for aquarium plants. Best kept on its own, or with large cichlids, in a suitably-sized, rockily-furnished aquarium. It is reported to build a submerged bubble nest in which to spawn and breeds better in soft water.

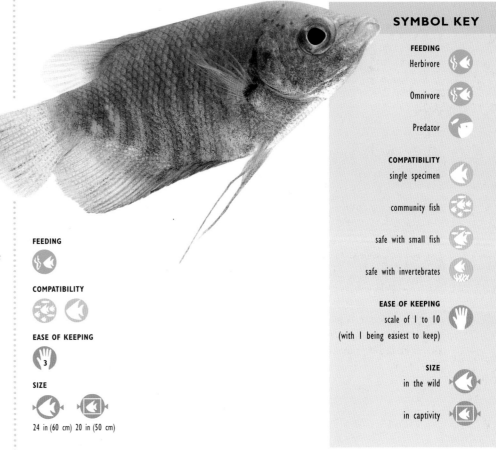

FEEDING

COMPATIBILITY

EASE OF KEEPING
3

SIZE
24 in (60 cm) 20 in (50 cm)

SYMBOL KEY

FEEDING
Herbivore

Omnivore

Predator

COMPATIBILITY
single specimen

community fish

safe with small fish

safe with invertebrates

EASE OF KEEPING
scale of 1 to 10
(with 1 being easiest to keep)

SIZE
in the wild

in captivity

CATFISHES

See-through fishes, fishes that swim upside down, fishes that walk on land, fishes that use electricity to kill, and fishes that emit sound are but a few of the piscine attractions to be found in this group of fishes from the Americas, Africa, and Asia. The variety in size is astonishing—from midgets of 1 inch (2.5 cm) right up to South American giants reaching 4.5 feet (120 cm).

Corydoras aeneus
BRONZE CORYDORAS

A common feature among the majority of catfish is their bottom-dwelling habit. Another characteristic, often missed by aquarists keeping just one as a cleaner, is that many species are quite gregarious and delight in being kept in numbers of their own kind. Many are nocturnal by nature, and so their "normal" activities often go unnoticed, unless they can be fooled into coming out earlier in the evening by altering the lighting times of their aquarium.

Catfishes' flat-bottomed bodies allow them to hug the bottom of the river or streambed without being swept away by water currents. They are excellent at locating food among the debris on the aquarium floor; taste cells in the barbels assist in this

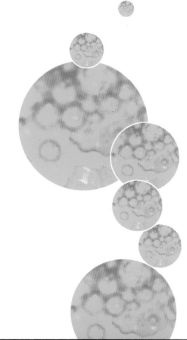

task, and are particularly useful in muddy water or at night, when visibility is impaired. Unlike the majority of other fishes, catfishes have no scales as such; their skin may be left naked or covered with overlapping bony plates called scutes. They often take in air from the surface, but, unlike anabantids, they have no auxiliary breathing organ in the head, and oxygen is extracted from gulped atmospheric air in the hind part of the gut.

Usually omnivorous (and with vigorous appetites), some species are more herbivorous and are sought after by hobbyists as a means of controlling algae. Such species have suckerlike mouths equipped with rasping teeth; in the absence of an algae-covered tank (having performed their algae-removing duties) they require extra green matter in their diet, which can be lettuce, spinach, or even canned peas.

Catfishes spawn in several ways: *Corydoras*, for instance, deposit eggs on any flat surface, the eggs being carried to the site by the female between her pelvic fins. The Armored Catfish, *Callichthys callichthys*, builds a bubble nest in which to place the eggs beneath a plant leaf. Others spawn on flat surfaces much in the manner of cichlids, in pits dug in the gravel, or inside plastic pipes, still others are mouthbrooders.

Agamyxis pectinifrons
WHITE-SPOTTED DORADID

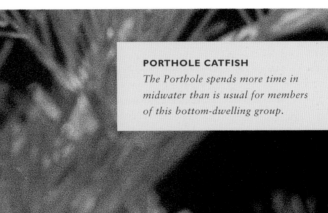

PORTHOLE CATFISH
The Porthole spends more time in midwater than is usual for members of this bottom-dwelling group.

FEATURED IN THIS SECTION

ARIUS SEEMANI

FAMILY: *ARIIDAE*
COMMON NAME: *AMERICAN SHARK CATFISH*

This is a riverine species that ranges from Colombia to as far north as California. The body is silvery with charcoal gray fins. The anal, pelvic, and pectoral fins are darker than the dorsal, adipose, and caudal fins, and are edged in white. It sometimes enters the Pacific Ocean, and thus adapts to brackish or fresh water.
SPECIAL CARE: Like most catfishes, this one feeds greedily. In nature it prefers insect larvae and can be fed mosquito larvae or frozen crustaceans, along with the usual flake foods and tablets. It needs water currents and oxygenation, both of which can be supplied with a properly designed filtration system. Usually only young specimens are imported for the aquarium. As they grow older, the color fades to a uniform dull gray, and the fish's appetite increases in proportion to its size. Since adults spend their lives in the sea, a marine tank will be required after this fish reaches maturity.

FEEDING

COMPATIBILITY

EASE OF KEEPING
5

SIZE
13.8 in (35 cm) 12 in (30 cm)

AUCHENIPTERICHTHYS THORACATUS

FAMILY: *AUCHENIPTERIDAE*
COMMON NAME: *MIDNIGHT CATFISH; ZAMORA WOODCAT*

FEEDING

COMPATIBILITY

EASE OF KEEPING
1

SIZE
4.7 in (12 cm) 4 in (10 cm)

From the upper Amazon region and its tributaries in Peru, this popular "oddball" catfish is frequently imported. The body is steel gray, with yellow dots concentrated in a pattern along the lateral line. The dorsal fin is colorless, except for its black tip. The gray coloration of the caudal peduncle extends onto the caudal fin, interrupted in the center by a band of yellow. The pectoral and pelvic fins are white, the anal and adipose fins colorless. The barbels are short, white, and closely clustered around the mouth.
SPECIAL CARE: As long as tank mates are too large to swallow, this is a good community fish. Mostly nocturnal in nature, it hides during the day and forages by night. Provide a well-planted, roomy aquarium with driftwood. Moderately soft, slightly acidic water suits them well, although this is a very tolerant species. Feeding poses no problems, although food should be offered in the early evening hours when the fish are searching for it.

CHRYSICHTHYS ORNATUS

FAMILY: *BAGRIDAE*
COMMON NAME: *ORNATE CATFISH*

This predatory fish is found in the upper and central regions of Zaire and central tropical Africa. The body shape of this heavily-built fish is elongated, with a slightly arched dorsal surface. The lower ventral profile is flattened. The body is golden brown in color with some areas of darker patterning, notably from the snout through the eyes and up to the base of the dorsal fin and from the midpoint of the body along the flanks and extending into the upper and lower lobes of the caudal fin. The lower ventral surface is silvery white. These patterns and colors disappear with age. The head is flattened and the eyes are set high above the general profile. There are two distinct barbels present on the upper snout with six other barbels around the wide mouth. The dorsal fin is held erect and, like most fins, including the small adipose fin, speckled with dark dots. The male fish has long spines in the pectoral fins.
SPECIAL CARE: While seemingly peaceful during the day, this fish becomes active at night when it goes about its predatory work in the lower-levels of the aquarium. It is best kept in a well-planted aquarium with plenty of hiding places with fishes that are larger than itself. This fish has not been bred in captivity.

FEEDING

COMPATIBILITY

EASE OF KEEPING
2

SIZE
10 in (25 cm) 8 in (20 cm)

BROCHIS SPLENDENS

FAMILY: *CALLICHTHYIDAE*
COMMON NAME: *GREEN CAT; SHORT-BODIED CATFISH*

This peaceful, shoaling species is a native of *Amazonia*, found on sandy streambeds in Brazil, Ecuador, and Peru. Though a bottom-dwelling species, this fish may make brief dashes to the surface to take in atmospheric air; the oxygen is then extracted in its hindgut. The stockily built body is proportionately shorter than the *Corydoras*, which looks similar, though the Green Cat's dorsal fin has a much longer base. A feature of the species in this genus is the replacement of scales by overlapping bony plates, known as scutes. Its body is covered with two rows of greenish-gray, metallic-looking bony scutes. The ventral surface is slightly pink. A dark blotch may appear on the rear of the gill cover. The head is also a metallic green; its eyes are very mobile and often move independently of one another. There are three pairs of barbels on the downturned mouth. The fins are mostly pinkish brown in color. An adipose fin is present and the dorsal fin has a long base.

SPECIAL CARE: *B. splendens* needs a well-planted aquarium that has open areas of soft, sandy substrate. The female carries the eggs between her fins and deposits them on a firm surface.

FEEDING

COMPATIBILITY

EASE OF KEEPING

SIZE

3 in (7.5 cm) 3 in (7.5 cm)

CALLICHTHYS CALLICHTHYS

FAMILY: *CALLICHTHYIDAE*
COMMON NAME: *HASSAR; SLENDER ARMORED CATFISH*

This peaceful, stocky fish from Brazil has a cylindrical shape. Two rows of scutes cover the entire length of the body from behind the gill cover rearward. A darkish line appears where the two rows of scutes overlap, but generally the body color is brownish-gray. The head is broad and shallow and covered in armor plating; the eyes are small. The underslung mouth indicates that it is a bottom-feeder. Two pairs of very long barbels are present. The adipose fin has a strong first spine, while those on the pectoral fins are exceptionally stout, especially on the male.

SPECIAL CARE: Nocturnal by nature, this fish needs to be fed at night. The best method is to add fast-sinking food after the aquarium lights have been switched off. Provide plenty of retreats for daytime use, with some floating plant cover. This fish spawns differently from the rest of the family. It builds a bubble nest below a broad-leaved plant or floating plants in which to deposit the eggs until hatching occurs; the male guards the nest and emits a grunting sound from time to time.

FEEDING

COMPATIBILITY

EASE OF KEEPING

SIZE

7 in (18 cm) 6 in (15 cm)

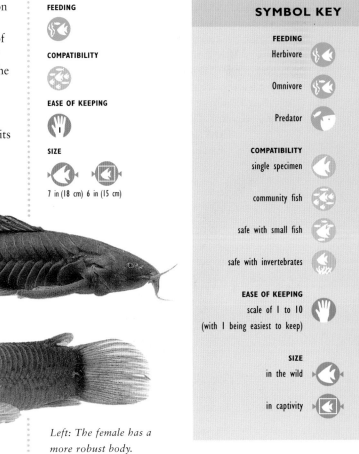

Above: The male Hassar has stout pectoral fins.

Left: The female has a more robust body.

SYMBOL KEY

FEEDING
Herbivore

Omnivore

Predator

COMPATIBILITY
single specimen

community fish

safe with small fish

safe with invertebrates

EASE OF KEEPING
scale of 1 to 10
(with 1 being easiest to keep)

SIZE
in the wild

in captivity

CORYDORAS AENEUS

FAMILY: *CALLICHTHYIDAE*
COMMON NAME: *BRONZE CORYDORAS*

This peaceful fish, widely distributed in South America from Trinidad to the Plate River, between Uruguay and Argentina, is the most common cory and the one most often bought as a scavenger. The stocky body has a bronze coloration and is covered with two rows of bony scutes, the top row giving a dark grayish-green, metallic sheen. A dark blotch may appear on the top of the head toward the front of the dorsal fin. The gill cover and cheeks below the eyes, which can move independently, are also a metallic green. There are three pairs of barbels on the downturned mouth. Fins are mostly pinkish-brown, and an adipose fin is present. The pelvic fins are short. Albino forms and, most recently (and regrettably), color-injected forms have been developed in captivity. Seen from above, the females are usually distinguished by their extra girth at the pectoral fins.

FEEDING

COMPATIBILITY

EASE OF KEEPING

SIZE

2.8 in (7 cm)   2.8 in (7 cm)

SPECIAL CARE: This cory, which prefers to be kept in a shoal, swims at the lower level of the aquarium, which should be well-planted and have open areas of soft, sandy substrate. The Bronze Corydoras breeds relatively easily in captivity. Often the addition of cooler water provides the necessary stimulus. The female carries the fertilized eggs to the selected hatching site using her pelvic fins.

CORYDORAS BARBATUS

FAMILY: *CALLICHTHYIDAE*
COMMON NAME: *BEARDED CORYDORAS; FILIGREE CORY*

Brazil, especially around Rio de Janeiro and São Paulo, is this shoaling fish's natural habitat. A relative newcomer to the hobby, it is more active after dark, like all members of the genus. Although quite similar to *C. macropterus*, whose waters it shares, it lacks the extra-long finnage. The body, which is noticeably more elongated than others in the genus, is covered with two rows of bony scutes; the creamy-white coloration has a dark reticulated patterning, especially from the snout to the rear of the dorsal fin. A dark band also runs along the flanks to the end of the caudal peduncle, and there may be further dark markings elsewhere on the body. The ventral surface is a plain creamy shade. The real distinguishing feature is the thin, creamy-white stripe on the dorsal ridge from the snout to the dorsal fin. The long, relatively shallow-sloping head, which has bristles in the mature male, has three pairs of barbels; the first looks like a dark, dapper mustache. The fins have both dark and light speckling. The dorsal fin is fairly tall, and there is an adipose fin.

FEEDING

COMPATIBILITY

EASE OF KEEPING

SIZE

3.3 in (8.5 cm)   3.3 in (8.5 cm)

SPECIAL CARE: This fish swims at the lower level of the aquarium, which needs to be well-planted and have open areas of soft, sandy substrate. The female carries the eggs between her fins and deposits them on a firm surface.

CORYDORAS ELEGANS

FAMILY: *CALLICHTHYIDAE*
COMMON NAME: *ELEGANT CORYDORAS*

FEEDING

COMPATIBILITY

EASE OF KEEPING

SIZE

2.5 in (6.5 cm)   2.5 in (6.5 cm)

This peaceful native of central *Amazonia* has a moderately arched dorsal contour and is slightly convex on the ventral surface. The stocky body is covered with two rows of bony scutes; the upper area of the upper row of scutes is dark, with another dark band running just above the meeting of the two rows. The patterning may vary between the sexes, with the male fish being more marked than the female. The ventral surface is a creamy grayish-pink. The head itself is fairly short and the eyes relatively large. There are three pairs of barbels. The dorsal fin is fairly high, with that of the male coming to a point. The fins may have dark specklings.

SPECIAL CARE: The aquarium should be well-planted. To prevent the barbels from wearing down due to foraging in the substrate, many hobbyists provide this low-swimming fish with open areas of soft sand instead of gravel.

CORYDORAS HARALDSHULTZI

FAMILY: *CALLICHTHYIDAE*
COMMON NAME: *HARALD SHULTZ'S CORY*

Found in the sandy-bottomed streams in *Amazonia*, this species looks similar to *C. sterbai*, though there are differences in the patterning on the sides of the body and *C. sterbai* has almost lemon-colored pectoral fins. The dorsal contour of this peaceful fish is only slightly more convex than the ventral, giving it a stocky, rounded-out appearance. Two rows of bony scutes cover the body, but this is well disguised by the overall body patterning. The background color is a silvery blue-gray; the ventral surface is slightly pink, and a dark reticulated pattern covers the whole body. Toward the rear some of the patterning along the flanks forms parallel lines. The moderately large head is also covered with numerous separate dark spots. The downturned mouth has three pairs of barbels. Most of the fins (with the exception of the pelvic fins, which are clear) carry the dark patterning of the body, and there is an adipose fin.

SPECIAL CARE: Provide a well-planted aquarium with open areas of soft, sandy substrate for this bottom-swimmer. The female carries the eggs between her fins and deposits them on a firm surface.

FEEDING

COMPATIBILITY

EASE OF KEEPING

SIZE

3 in (7.5 cm) 3 in (7.5 cm)

CORYDORAS LEUCOMELAS

FAMILY: *CALLICHTHYIDAE*
COMMON NAME: *BLACKFIN CORYDORAS; FALSE SPOTTED CATFISH*

This short and stocky fish is a native of the streambeds of Colombia and Peru. Smaller than the similar *C. ambiacus*, it is also sometimes mistaken for *C. punctatus*. Two rows of bony scutes cover its body, which is a silvery gray becoming a very pale yellowish-white on the ventral surface. Except for the ventral surface itself and the area around the base of the pectoral fins, the body is sprinkled with black spots. A vertical dark bar crosses the eyes and curves up toward the dorsal fin. The area immediately behind the eyes, although carrying dark spots, is a light gold color; the head in front of the eyes is also spotted. A dark blotch at the base of the dorsal fin extends into the fin to color its front part, while dotted patterning on the caudal fin forms vertical banding. An adipose fin is present, as are three pairs of fairly short barbels. The mouth is downturned, a characteristic of the family. The females are reported to be generally larger than the males.

SPECIAL CARE: These lower-level shoaling fish need a well-planted aquarium with open areas of soft, sandy substrate. The female carries the eggs between her fins and deposits them on a firm surface.

FEEDING

COMPATIBILITY

EASE OF KEEPING

SIZE

2.4 in (6 cm) 2.4 in (6 cm)

SYMBOL KEY	
FEEDING	
Herbivore	
Omnivore	
Predator	
COMPATIBILITY	
single specimen	
community fish	
safe with small fish	
safe with invertebrates	
EASE OF KEEPING	
scale of 1 to 10 (with 1 being easiest to keep)	
SIZE	
in the wild	
in captivity	

CORYDORAS PANDA

FAMILY: *CALLICHTHYIDAE*
COMMON NAME: *PANDA CORY*

FEEDING

COMPATIBILITY

EASE OF KEEPING

SIZE

2 in (5 cm) 2 in (5 cm)

The Ucuyali River system in Peru is the home of this relative newcomer, which was described to science only as recently as 1971. A peaceful fish that has rapidly become very popular among hobbyists, it appears at first glance to be a slim-bodied *C. aeneus*, with the normal two rows of scutes along the flanks clearly defined. However, four dark patches—one covering each eye, one on the dorsal fin, and one on the caudal peduncle—mark this fish out as a different species and explain why its popular name is Panda.

The overall body coloration is a pale golden brown.
SPECIAL CARE: The Panda Cory is best kept and seen in a small shoal. It likes a well-planted aquarium, where it will swim at the lower level, and open areas of soft, sandy substrate. The female carries the eggs between her fins and deposits them on a firm surface.

DIANEMA LONGIBARBIS

FAMILY: *CALLICHTHYIDAE*
COMMON NAME: *PORTHOLE CATFISH*

This long-lived, peaceful shoaling fish is found throughout the Amazonian region. Perhaps because of its less impressive tail markings, it is not as actively sought after by aquarists as the following species, *D. urostriata*. The dorsal contour is more noticeably curved than the ventral, and this gives the body an elongated, cylindrical appearance. Two rows of bony scutes cover the body rearward of the gill cover. The body color is a creamy gray with a pinkish ventral surface. Some dark speckling occurs over the body, but this is generally more concentrated on the upper row of scutes. The head is long and flattened, with a mouth that is more terminal than underslung. It carries two long pairs of barbels, which are usually held out in front of the fish as it swims. The fins are colorless; the anal fin is set very far back, opposite the small adipose fin. The caudal fin is reasonably forked.
SPECIAL CARE: This middle-level swimmer thrives in a well-planted aquarium that has some broad-leaved plants on which it may rest. This fish is reported to breed in a similar manner to *Callichthys callichthys*, in that it builds a bubble nest.

FEEDING

COMPATIBILITY

EASE OF KEEPING

SIZE

4 in (10 cm) 4 in (10 cm)

DIANEMA UROSTRIATA

FAMILY: *CALLICHTHYIDAE*
COMMON NAME: *STRIPE-TAILED CATFISH; FLAGTAIL PORTHOLE CATFISH*

Found throughout the Amazonian region of South America, this is an active shoaling fish that is mainly nocturnal. Although very popular, paradoxically it is not as readily available as the previous species,

FEEDING

COMPATIBILITY

EASE OF KEEPING

SIZE

5 in (13 cm) 5 in (13 cm)

D. longibarbis. The body shape of this fish is elongated and cylindrical, with the curve of the dorsal contour more pronounced than the flatter ventral surface. Two rows of bony scutes cover the body rearward of the gill cover. Some dark speckling occurs on the body, which is a creamy grayish-brown, shading down from the dorsal surface to a lighter color on the belly and silver below the head. The head is long and flattened, and the mouth is more terminal than underslung. There are two pairs of long barbels, which are usually held out in front of the fish as it swims. The most attractive feature is the reasonably forked caudal fin, which carries horizontal black and white stripes, giving this species its popular name. The anal fin is set very far back, opposite the small adipose fin.
SPECIAL CARE: Swimming at the middle level of the aquarium, the Stripe-Tailed Catfish prefers a well-planted aquarium that includes some broad-leaved plants on which it can rest. This fish probably follows a bubble-nesting pattern, but it has not been widely reported.

SYMBOL KEY

FEEDING

Herbivore

Omnivore

Predator

COMPATIBILITY

single specimen

community fish

safe with small fish

safe with invertebrates

EASE OF KEEPING

scale of 1 to 10
(with 1 being easiest to keep)

SIZE

in the wild

in captivity

HOPLOSTERNUM THORACATUM

FAMILY: *CALLICHTHYIDAE*
COMMON NAME: *PORT HOPLO; ATIPA*

A native of Panama and northern South America to Brazil, this stockily-built, cylindrical fish has two rows of bony scutes covering its body, instead of scales, extending rearward from the gill cover. The body color is variable, usually a mixture of red and brown or black and brown; this carries some darker speckling, although the speckling may fade with increased age. The compressed head forms a pointed snout, and two pairs of long barbels are present, usually pointing forward. The fins are rounded with some dark speckling over a bluish tinge. The anal fin is set well behind the caudal peduncle underneath the adipose fin. The rounded caudal fin has a light-colored area across its root, and it is the shape of this fin that distinguishes the Port Hoplo from the related *H. littorale*. The male is slightly smaller than the female and has the darker coloring. She is, however, more easily distinguished by the thicker reddish-brown first rays of the pectoral fins; also, females are usually white underneath.

SPECIAL CARE: This fish, which swims at the lower level, likes plenty of hideaways in a generally well-planted aquarium. It is a bubble nest spawner. The fertilized eggs are carried to the nest (often built among plants) by the female, using her pelvic fins. The male guards the nest and fry.

FEEDING

COMPATIBILITY

EASE OF KEEPING

SIZE

8 in (20 cm) 8 in (20 cm)

ACANTHODORAS SPINOSISSIMUS

FAMILY: *DORADIDAE*
COMMON NAME: *CHOCOLATE CATFISH; SPINY CATFISH; CHANNEL CATFISH; TALKING CATFISH*

Amazonia and the *Orinoco* regions of South America are the natural home of this species, which has several alternative names—Talking Catfish refers to the sounds the fish makes either by rotating its pectoral fins or by vibrating the swim bladder. Other talents include the ability to lock its dorsal and pectoral fins at a ninety-degree angle to prevent itself from being swallowed or captured by its predators. It can also expel a noxious fluid, if necessary, to spoil the meal of a successful predator. Although this fish is wide at the head, the maximum width is at the pectoral fins. The width tapers to the caudal peduncle, and it is slightly vertically compressed. The body color is a darkish-brown; a creamy white line, consisting of thorny spines, runs from the shoulder to the end of the caudal peduncle. There are other rows of spines on each side, but being the same color as the body they are not quite as obvious. Forward of the anal fin, the lower half of the body is marked with wavy cream-colored lines. All the fins are cream with some dark speckling; the adipose fin is dark with a cream surround; the pectoral fins have strong first rays. The three pairs of barbels are colored in alternate brown and white rings but are not very long. The mouth is large.

SPECIAL CARE: Swimming at the lower level, this fish appreciates plenty of retreats in a generously planted aquarium.

FEEDING

COMPATIBILITY

EASE OF KEEPING

SIZE

6 in (15 cm) 6 in (15 cm)

AGAMYXIS PECTINIFRONS

FAMILY: *DORADIDAE*
COMMON NAME: *WHITE-SPOTTED DORADID*

Found in Ecuador and Peru, this fish is generally nocturnal by nature, but is often seen around the aquarium in daylight too. The specific name *pectinifrons* refers to the comblike structure, or serration, on the front of the fins. This fish is often confused with the previous species, *Acanthodoras spinosissimus*. The body shape at the head is wide and tapers to the caudal peduncle; it is slightly vertically-compressed. The body, fins, and the three pairs of barbels are black with white spots, and the mouth is large. Several horizontal rows of spines run along the body between the dorsal surface and midway down the body; there is also a sharp serration on the leading edges of the dorsal and pectoral fins. A small adipose fin is present. The caudal fin is rounded.

SPECIAL CARE: The White-Spotted Doradid likes a well-planted aquarium, where it swims at the lower level, and plenty of retreats to feel safe in. No information is available on its breeding habits.

FEEDING

COMPATIBILITY

EASE OF KEEPING

SIZE

5.5 in (14 cm) 5.5 in (14 cm)

AMBLYDORAS HANCOCKI

FAMILY: *DORADIDAE*
COMMON NAME: *HANCOCK'S AMBLYDORAS*

In nature this peaceful fish is to be found in Brazil, Guyana, and Colombia. The elongated body shape has a relatively broad, deep forward section. The bony plates that cover its body have thorny spikes, and a wrinkling effect on the head reaches back to the dorsal fin. The mouth is terminal with three pairs of long, white and brown barbels. The body color can vary, but is usually a shade of dark brown with irregular blotches. A line of whitish "thorns" runs horizontally along the body from below the dorsal fin to the end of the caudal peduncle; beneath, a striking dark area quickly fades to a whitish ventral surface. The first ray or two of the tall dorsal fin are darkly pigmented, while the large pectoral fins have stouter first rays that are lighter in color than the remainder. The dark adipose fin has contrasting lighter edges at the front and rear. The speckled caudal fin is set off by a dark band across its base.

FEEDING

COMPATIBILITY

EASE OF KEEPING

SIZE

5 in (13 cm) 5 in (13 cm)

SPECIAL CARE: A well-planted aquarium with retreats formed from roots or rocks will suit this species, which keeps to the lower level. It has been reported to spawn following the addition of fresher water, using a bubble nest built from plant materials; in the wild this fish reportedly builds a bubble nest among surface plants.

ANCISTRUS TEMMINCKI

FAMILY: *LORICARIIDAE*
COMMON NAME: *TEMMINCK'S BRISTLENOSE*

This popular native of Guyana is a peaceful, algae-eating species whose former generic name was *Xenocara*. Its stocky build has a flat-bottomed airfoil shape, with a slightly arched dorsal contour and a lengthened caudal peduncle. Bony scutes take the place of scales as a body covering. The dark greenish-brown body color contrasts with a dense pattern of lighter small spots, which also extends into the fins. The snout's upper surface has growths of tentacle-like bristles—a single row for females, a double row for males. These bristles develop more at spawning time and revert to their normal size afterward. The lips of the underslung mouth form a suckerlike disk. The dorsal, pectoral, pelvic, and caudal fins are well-developed. The anal fin is small, about the same size as the adipose fin. Juveniles are bluish with white dots, and their dorsal and caudal fins have pale edges.

FEEDING

COMPATIBILITY

EASE OF KEEPING

SIZE

5.5 in (14 cm) 5.5 in (14 cm)

SPECIAL CARE: This low-level swimmer needs plenty of retreats formed from roots, rocks, plastic pipes, and so on. It often breeds spontaneously if it is contented.

FARLOWELLA GRACILIS

FAMILY: *LORICARIIDAE*
COMMON NAME: *MOTTLED TWIG CATFISH*

FEEDING

COMPATIBILITY

EASE OF KEEPING

SIZE

8 in (20 cm)   8 in (20 cm)

Hiding away during the day is quite a safe proposition for this Colombian species, as its presence is admirably disguised by its unusual body shape, which is long and sticklike; any appreciable body width terminates near the dorsal fin. Contrasting with the creamy brown body color is a darker brown line running from the tip of the snout, through the eyes, to the end of the caudal peduncle, where it turns up to continue along the top edge of the caudal fin itself. Some brown blotches may be present, and the fins have speckling on the rays. The underside of the body is pale, and the body is covered in bony scutes. The head is broad and very flattened, and in males the prominent snout develops bristles. The disklike mouth is located beneath the head. The dorsal fin is set about halfway back, immediately above the anal fin. The caudal fin is somewhat lyre-shaped, and outer rays may be extended in mature specimens.

SPECIAL CARE: Swimming at the middle and lower levels of the aquarium, this herbivore requires a well-planted, well-oxygenated environment with some algal growth; if not enough algae is available, it may need supplementary vegetable matter. The female lays her eggs on any firm, pre-cleaned surface, and the males guard the eggs.

HYPOSTOMUS PLECOSTOMUS

FAMILY: *LORICARIIDAE*
COMMON NAME: *SUCKERMOUTH CATFISH; COMMON PLEC; PLECO; PLECOSTOMUS*

FEEDING

COMPATIBILITY

EASE OF KEEPING

SIZE

17.5 in (45 cm)   12 in (30 cm)

Found in both northern and central South America, the peaceful Suckermouth is a favorite, mainly due to its reputation as an algae remover. It is usually active at the beginning and end of the day. Its generic name, formerly *Plecostomus*, has been reclassified as *Hypostomus*, but a number of its common names reflect the old classification. Its flat-bottomed body has an airfoil shape, a fairly arched dorsal contour, and a lengthened caudal peduncle. Bony scutes take the place of scales as a body covering. The body coloration is greenish-brown, covered with a patterning of dark brown spots that continues into the fins. The broad, slightly compressed head has high-set eyes with a light-controlling lobe of skin, which shades the eyes from bright light. The mouth is underslung with lips forming a suckerlike disk; this enables the fish both to maintain its position in fast-flowing waters and also to rasp off algae. The dorsal fin is very tall, triangular, and flaglike. The caudal fin is almost lyre-shaped, with the lower lobe usually longer than the upper. The pectoral and pelvic fins are well-developed, the anal fin is small, and an adipose fin is present.

SPECIAL CARE: Cruising the middle and lower levels, this species needs generous planting in a well-oxygenated aquarium, as well as some water currents and algal growth. Although an algae-free aquarium may well mean that the fish is doing its job, it still needs additional green foodstuffs as a matter of course, especially as an adult. No information is available on its breeding habits.

SYMBOL KEY

FEEDING
Herbivore

Omnivore

Predator

COMPATIBILITY
single specimen

community fish

safe with small fish

safe with invertebrates

EASE OF KEEPING
scale of 1 to 10
(with 1 being easiest to keep)

SIZE
in the wild

in captivity

PECKOLTIA PULCHER

FEEDING

FAMILY: *LORICARIIDAE*
COMMON NAME: *PRETTY PECKOLTIA*

COMPATIBILITY

This species native to the *Rio Negro* and *Amazonia* is, as its popular name suggests, a very attractive fish. It has a slightly compressed body shape with a flattened ventral surface. Bristle-covered bony scutes cover its blue-black body, with narrow bands of light gray vertically crossing the body; two light bands also run down the snout. The same coloration is continued into all the fins. The eyes are set well apart, are placed high on the head, and have a slightly upward-looking appearance. The underslung mouth forms a sucker disk. When erect, the dorsal fin is flaglike; its first ray coincides with the tallest part of the body, which then tapers down slowly to the long caudal peduncle. A small adipose fin is present, set opposite the rear edge of the anal fin. Pectoral and pelvic fins are winglike with a reasonable-sized span when viewed from above. The caudal fin is forked and well spread with sharp tips.

EASE OF KEEPING

SIZE

3.5 in (9 cm) 2.4 in (6 cm)

SPECIAL CARE: This fish has algae-eating talents but may not compete very well in the company of larger vegetarian fishes. It should be kept in a spacious, generously-planted tank containing algae growth. Its peaceful demeanor toward most other fishes makes it a suitable community aquarium fish, although unless given enough space, it may not tolerate its own kind at close quarters. No information on breeding is available.

RINELORICARIA LANCEOLATA

FAMILY: *LORICARIIDAE*
COMMON NAME: *LANCEOLATE WHIPTAIL CATFISH*

FEEDING

COMPATIBILITY

EASE OF KEEPING

SIZE

5 in (13 cm) 4 in (10 cm)

Bolivia, Brazil, Ecuador, and Peru are the natural habitats of this fish. Coloration, which is somewhat variable depending on the furnishings of its surroundings, is usually light brown with distinctive blotches; specimens with darker markings are the most sought-after. Bony scutes cover the body. The dorsal fin, although short-based, is usually held erect like a flag. The caudal fin is likely to have long, threadlike filaments on the tips of each lobe (hence the common name of Whiptail). Males appear slimmer than females when viewed from above, and their color patterning is often more clearly defined. In addition, males develop bristles on the head and pectoral fins when mature.

SPECIAL CARE: Provide plenty of broad-leaved plants to offer perching places. The female lays her eggs on firm surfaces; pieces of plastic pipe make good spawning sites as well as hiding places for this species. The male guards the eggs and the subsequent fry.

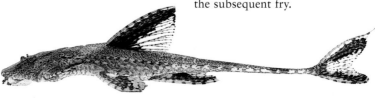

OTOCINCLUS AFFINIS

FAMILY: *LORICARIIDAE*
COMMON NAME: *DWARF SUCKER CATFISH*

This small and peaceful Brazilian species is sought by aquarists as an algae-eater. It spends a lot of its time working its way around the aquarium rasping algae off all surfaces, including the sides and front of the tank, where it is often seen resting, but it is likely to appear anywhere as it searches for algae. Its very elongated body has an almost kite-like shape; the dorsal contour is only slightly arched, and the ventral surface is flat. The caudal peduncle is rather long. It has two body colors, separated by a dark band running from the snout to the end of caudal peduncle; the upper-half is golden brown and the lower-half pale yellow. The head is flattened, the snout fairly long, and the eyes large. The disk-shaped mouth is underslung for sucking. In addition to enabling the easy removal of algae, the sucker mouth is also used to prevent the fish from being swept away in fast-flowing waters. The dorsal fin is set immediately above the pelvic fins, with the anal fin set farther back. Some speckling appears in the dorsal, anal, and the caudal fins, especially.

SPECIAL CARE: Plenty of algae growth in a well-planted aquarium is what this middle- and lower-level swimmer particularly requires. The fish deposits its eggs on firm surfaces.

FEEDING

COMPATIBILITY

EASE OF KEEPING

SIZE

2 in (5 cm) 2 in (5 cm)

SYNODONTIS BRICHARDI

FAMILY: *MOCHOKIDAE*
COMMON NAME: *BRICHARD'S SYNODONTIS*

An inhabitant of rapids along the lower stretches of the Zaire River, this beautiful catfish is regularly imported. Though it commands a high price in shops, its beautiful pattern of black markings overlaid on a snow-white body makes it among the most desirable and attractive members of its family. Even the fins are patterned attractively in black and white. During daylight hours, the fish seeks shelter among roots or rocks, emerging at twilight to begin its search for food.

FEEDING

COMPATIBILITY

EASE OF KEEPING
3

SIZE
6 in (15 cm) 6 in (15 cm)

SPECIAL CARE: Although a tolerant and durable species, Brichard's Synodontis should have clean, well-oxygenated water and a roomy tank. It is adapted to fast-flowing water, and can even hang onto glass surfaces against a surprisingly forceful current. Virtually any type of aquarium flake, frozen foods, or live foods such as small earthworms and mosquito larvae will be greedily accepted. It does not feed on plants, but may uproot delicate ones as it digs in the gravel. As with many members of the catfish clan, breeding behavior is a mystery.

SYNODONTIS MULTIPUNCTATUS

FAMILY: *MOCHOKIDAE*
COMMON NAME: *CUCKOO SYNODONTIS; MULTI-SPOTTED SYNODONTIS*

As might be assumed from the specific name (*multi* meaning many and *punctatus* meaning spots), the light colored body is covered with many dark spots; these range in size from the smaller ones distributed over the head and shoulder regions, to the largest ones rearward on the rest of the body. All the fins have black in their leading edges while the caudal fin lobes are both jet black edged in white. The barbels around the mouth are white. Breeding details are quite specialized, for this species (along with some other *Synodontis* species), has its eggs incubated by mouthbrooding cichlids sharing its habitat. Eggs are laid and fertilized opportunistically in an area that is being used by breeding cichlids and they are picked up by the mouthbrooding female cichlid along with her own eggs. This action is called "cuckoo spawning" and, like their avian counterparts, the newly-hatched *Synodontis* often take over from the cichlid fry during the time they share together.

SPECIAL CARE: Because the fish's natural habitat is Africa's Lake Tanganyika, it is quite happy in hard, alkaline water. Consequently, it makes a good aquarium tank mate for Rift Valley cichlids from the same location.

FEEDING

COMPATIBILITY

EASE OF KEEPING
1

SIZE
8 in (20 cm) 8 in (20 cm)

SYMBOL KEY

FEEDING
Herbivore
Omnivore
Predator

COMPATIBILITY
single specimen
community fish
safe with small fish
safe with invertebrates

EASE OF KEEPING
scale of 1 to 10
(with 1 being easiest to keep)

SIZE
in the wild
in captivity

SYNODONTIS NIGRIVENTRIS

FAMILY: *MOCHOKIDAE*
COMMON NAME: *BLACK-SPOTTED UPSIDE-DOWN CATFISH; CONGO BACKSWIMMER*

The tropics of the Congo region of central Africa are the natural home of this peaceful, stockily built species. The body coloration is light brown covered with numerous dark, leopard-like spots, some of which may merge to form bands. The nearly flat underside is often dark-colored—an unusual reversal of the normal shading progression of darker dorsal surface, lighter ventral. This is because the fish spends a lot of its time swimming upside-down, so a normally light-colored belly would easily be spotted by an above-water predator. (Adult fish, particularly those kept in a frequently fed aquarium, may lose the tendency—or the inclination—to continue this behavior.) The eyes are large and there are three pairs of barbels. The dorsal fin is quite large, and most fins carry some dark blotches.

SPECIAL CARE: Swimming at all levels of the aquarium, this species needs well-planted surroundings with root systems for hideaways, together with some floating plants. Its ability to swim inverted, coupled with a nearly flat underside, makes eating from the surface easy. No information is available on breeding.

FEEDING

COMPATIBILITY

EASE OF KEEPING

SIZE

3.5 in (9 cm) 3.5 in (9 cm)

SYNODONTIS SCHOUTEDENI

FAMILY: *MOCHOKIDAE*
COMMON NAME: *VERMICULATED SYNODONTIS*

FEEDING

COMPATIBILITY

EASE OF KEEPING

SIZE

4.7 in (12 cm) 4 in (10 cm)

Among the most attractive of the African catfishes of the central Zaire region, this largely nocturnal catfish is peaceful, hardy, and easy to feed. The body is white, overlaid with a bold pattern of black swirls and squiggles. The colorless fins are highlighted by black rays, and even the barbels are marked in black and white. Though it does not feed on smaller fishes, its rambunctious and sometimes aggressive behavior toward conspecifics makes it best suited to a species tank.

SPECIAL CARE: Provide plenty of plants and driftwood. Water conditions are not critical, but care should be taken to use aged water free of chlorine, to which this catfish seems particularly sensitive. It feeds greedily on a variety of easily available aquarium foods, including flakes, tablets, and frozen or live invertebrates. It characteristically swims upside down, a trait it shares with other members of its family.

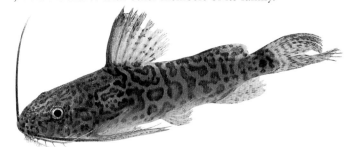

PANGASIUS HYPOPHTHALMUS

FAMILY: *PANGASIIDAE*
COMMON NAME: *IRIDESCENT SHARK*

This silvery blue fish with black fins and tail is misidentified as a shark because of its sleek, streamlined appearance and constant swimming. Found in the wild in Thailand, it has never been spawned in the aquarium, but Asian breeders raise the fish successfully in outdoor ponds. Despite the fact that it spends most of its time on the bottom, like some other catfishes it can breathe atmospheric oxygen and will dash to the surface to gulp air. It is also a good jumper, and may demonstrate this trait in response to a sudden movement or tapping on the glass.

FEEDING

COMPATIBILITY

EASE OF KEEPING

SIZE

39 in (1 m) 13.8 in (35 cm)

SPECIAL CARE: Because of this fish's tendency to jump the aquarium should be well-covered and located in an area where the fish is not likely to be disturbed by constant foot traffic. Because this species is capable of growing to a large size, only one or two specimens should be exhibited in a roomy, well-planted tank. Filtration should be adequate to counteract its greedy appetite. This fish becomes more vegetarian as it ages, although few hobbyists will maintain one long enough for it to reach this state. Most will find that the fish outgrows the accommodations they can provide.

PHRACTOCEPHALUS HEMILIOCEPHALUS

FAMILY: *PIMELODIDAE*
COMMON NAME: *RED-TAILED CATFISH*

Widespread throughout the Amazonian areas of Peru, Guyana, and Brazil, this very aggressive catfish has an extremely hefty body shape and a large, broad, flattened head. The upper body, including the top lip of the mouth, is gray-black with small darker specklings; the lower body, including the lower lip and the three pairs of very long barbels, is pure white. The eyes are set fairly near the front of the shallow head, and the mouth is very wide. The main physical feature is the bright orange/red caudal fin, not deeply cleft but with rounded tips. The dorsal and adipose fins are speckled, dark for most of their areas, shading to red with red edging. The large pectoral, pelvic, and anal fins are also dark, with some red and even white coloring at their edges. Juvenile fish are often the more highly colored.

FEEDING

COMPATIBILITY

EASE OF KEEPING
8

SIZE
29.5 in (75 cm) 29.5 in (75 cm)

SPECIAL CARE: Definitely not a subject for the domestic aquarium, this species has a very hearty appetite but thankfully does not feed regularly (i.e., daily) when adult. This fish is likely to eat smaller fishes and will try to do the same to larger species, so is only suitably to be kept with other large fish. It is also capable of breaking equipment inside the tank. It needs an extremely spacious aquarium, where it swims at the lower levels. This species has never been bred in an aquarium.

PIMELODUS ALBOFASCIATUS

FAMILY: *PIMELODIDAE*
COMMON NAME: *WHITE-STRIPED PIMELODUS*

Like its more commonly seen cousin, *P. pictus*, this one is easily maintained in a roomy aquarium. The body is pale and silvery, with darker blotches forming horizontal bands along its entire length. The blotches, though paler, extend onto the dorsal, adipose, caudal, and anal fins. The pelvic and pectoral fins are colorless, and the latter bear venom glands at the base of the first spine, with which the fish can inflict a painful sting. Use caution when handling this species. It is collected along the northern coast of South America in Guyana and Surinam.

SPECIAL CARE: This species will swallow anything that will fit into its mouth, and can be fed a wide variety of common aquarium foods. Earthworms and feeder fish can be offered as a treat. They are territorial, but usually not aggressive toward tank mates that cannot be eaten. Sexual differences and spawning behavior are unknown.

FEEDING

COMPATIBILITY

EASE OF KEEPING
1

SIZE
10 in (25 cm) 6 in (15 cm)

SYMBOL KEY

FEEDING
Herbivore

Omnivore

Predator

COMPATIBILITY
single specimen

community fish

safe with small fish

safe with invertebrates

EASE OF KEEPING
scale of 1 to 10
(with 1 being easiest to keep)

SIZE
in the wild

in captivity

PSEUDOPIMELODUS RANINUS RANINUS

FAMILY: *PIMELODIDAE*
COMMON NAME: *BUMBLEBEE CATFISH*

This nocturnal species from the Amazonian areas of Peru and Brazil is predatory and not to be trusted in the company of small fishes. It has, over many years, been confused with the smaller lookalike, but different, species *Microglanis parahybae*. The body shape of this fish is stocky and tubular. Its coloration ranges from dark blue/black to brown with irregular blotches and narrow bands of lighter brown. A narrow light band runs across the body following the rear outline of the gill cover, an ill-defined, broadening band crosses the caudal peduncle, and there is an even less sharply outlined blotch on the lower-half of the body between the pelvic and anal fins. The ventral surface itself is pinkish. The blunt, flattened head has small eyes, a wide mouth, and three pairs of barbels, with those on the snout darker and longer than the others. The dorsal fin is the same color as the body and has a whitish area near its base. The adipose fin has lighter front and rear sections, and the pectoral fins are also dark-colored with white first rays. The pelvic and anal fins are whitish. The attractive caudal fin has a dark rear edge, with the front part a lighter gray with small dark speckles.

FEEDING

COMPATIBILITY

EASE OF KEEPING

1

SIZE

4.7 in (12 cm)   4.7 in (12 cm)

SPECIAL CARE: A well-planted aquarium provided with plenty of hideaways and retreats is required by the Bumblebee Catfish, which prefers the lower levels. There is no information available on its breeding habits.

PSEUDOPLATYSTOMA FASCIATA

FAMILY: *PIMELODIDAE*
COMMON NAME: *TIGER SHOVELNOSE CATFISH*

This nocturnal predatory fish from Venezuela and Peru is only suitable for large public-display aquariums. A number of subspecies exist, all sharing the same antisocial and physical characteristics, which include a very elongated and streamlined shape. Its dark-gray coloration shades to silvery-white on the belly. A number of equally-spaced dark bands cross the body vertically but do not quite encircle it; some dark dots may appear between the rearmost bands at their bottom ends. The head is very large and broad with a very shallow-sloping forehead; the eyes are set high. There are three long pairs of barbels. For such a large fish the fins are surprisingly small; the dorsal fin is positioned at the highest part of the body, while the adipose and anal fins are well to the rear. The caudal fin is crescent-shaped. All fins have dark specklings.

SPECIAL CARE: Only a very large aquarium can provide enough space for this low-level swimmer. This species has not been bred in captivity.

FEEDING

COMPATIBILITY

EASE OF KEEPING

8

SIZE

35.4 in (90 cm)   35.4 in (90 cm)

SORUBIM LIMA

FAMILY: *PIMELODIDAE*
COMMON NAME: *SHOVELNOSE CATFISH*

This species hails from the Amazon region, where it is widespread. The somewhat flattened body is white underneath, dark brown or black above. Below the dorsal fin lies a longitudinal stripe of light brown to white. A dark mid-body stripe runs through the eyes, continuing anteriorly until it makes a sharp downward turn at the caudal peduncle and ends at the tip of the lower element of the caudal fin. The longest pair of barbels is black, the others are white. Thin black stripes define the edges of the dorsal and pectoral fins.

SPECIAL CARE: It tolerates a wide range of water conditions, but should have plenty of hiding places. During the day the fish spends its time in hiding. As darkness approaches, it lies motionless at some convenient spot, alert for the passage of small fish or invertebrates upon which it feeds. Harmless to plants, it will often select a clump of tall stems for its hiding place, where it remains, partially head down.

FEEDING

COMPATIBILITY

EASE OF KEEPING

1

SIZE

8 in (20 cm)   6 in (15 cm)

EUTROPIELLUS DEBAUWI

FAMILY: *SCHILBEIDAE*
COMMON NAME: *AFRICAN GLASS CATFISH; THREE-STRIPED GLASS CATFISH*

Coming from the Congo region of central Africa, this very sociable species prefers to be with its own kind and other nonboisterous fishes. Its correct scientific name has been the subject of discussion; many feel that the physical description of *E. debauwi* is better suited to *E. vanderweyeri*. It is usually constantly on the move with its caudal fin sloping downward, but when stationary it waves its tail from side to side. The body shape is very elongated and streamlined, almost identical to that of a female *Brachydanio*. The body color is a translucent, creamy blue-gold with three black stripes running horizontally. The upper stripe covers the dorsal surface; the middle one extends along the whole length of the fish from its snout to the rear edge of the caudal fin; and the third runs from behind the gill cover to the lower end of the caudal peduncle. The head is small with relatively large eyes; the mouth is terminal with three pairs of barbels. A narrow dorsal fin is set well forward, and the adipose fin well back on the caudal peduncle. The anal fin is narrow and long-based, but not as long-based as that of the subsequent species, *Kryptopterus bicirrhis*.

SPECIAL CARE: This middle-level swimmer needs a well-planted aquarium with some water currents and floating plants. The species has not been bred in the aquarium.

FEEDING

COMPATIBILITY

EASE OF KEEPING

SIZE

3 in (7.5 cm) 3 in (7.5 cm)

KRYPTOPTERUS BICIRRHIS

FAMILY: *SILURIDAE*
COMMON NAME: *GLASS CATFISH*

Borneo, Java, Sumatra, and Thailand are home to this species, which thrives in a shoal and is suitable for a collection of nonboisterous fishes. Active during daylight hours, this fish may float among plants keeping its caudal peduncle region constantly waving to and fro—it appears incapable of remaining motionless—which presumes a need to keep balanced in its native flowing waters. The elongated body shape is laterally compressed, its general appearance like that of an airfoil section. In this scaleless species, body color is almost completely missing, the skin having only the slightest hint of blue. The backbone and internal organ sac are clearly visible. An indistinct black-violet shoulder blotch is present just behind the gill cover. The head is small with large eyes; one pair of very long barbels, trailing back past the pectoral fins, can be maneuvered in all directions. The dorsal fin is very rudimentary, just a single ray; the anal fin runs the length of the body but is not joined to the caudal fin. The lower lobe of the deeply cleft caudal fin is slightly larger than the upper lobe, and the pelvic fins are very small.

SPECIAL CARE: For this middle- and lower-level swimmer, the aquarium should be well-planted and include floating plants, with some strong currents supplied by an efficient filtration system. No information is available on breeding.

FEEDING

COMPATIBILITY

EASE OF KEEPING

SIZE

4 in (10 cm) 3.5 in (9 cm)

SYMBOL KEY

FEEDING
Herbivore
Omnivore
Predator

COMPATIBILITY
single specimen
community fish
safe with small fish
safe with invertebrates

EASE OF KEEPING
scale of 1 to 10
(with 1 being easiest to keep)

SIZE
in the wild
in captivity

OTHER EGG-LAYERS

There are many egg-laying fishes that cannot be neatly classified. Some are monotypic (a single species within a genus), other families have very few representative species, and there are those that just won't fit into recognized groups. Although diverse in natural habitats and in body shapes and sizes, all make excellent aquarium subjects. Some, because of their size, behavioral characteristics, or needs for special conditions, would be better suited in a single species collection. Some may come from brackish waters, as well as freshwater, and are almost a convenient interim choice on the way to keeping fully fledged marine fishes. Faced with the problems of describing such fishes we have arranged them quite straightforwardly in scientific alphabetical family order.

In the aquarium trade, fishes come from a wide variety of habitats. Local

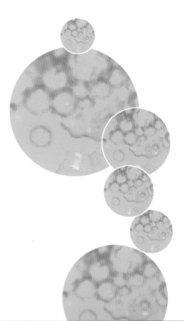

Monodactylus argenteus
MONO

conditions, including military coups and political upheavals, can influence the availability of wild-caught fishes, as can the weather, season, or even an interruption in air cargo service.

Furthermore, fishes may come from a variety of water conditions, but a dealer can usually only provide a single set of conditions for his inventory (aside from maintaining freshwater, coldwater, and marine species in separate holding systems.) Thus, the actual availability of species varies widely from place to place and dealer to dealer. When considering any species that is not commonly available in your area, consult references to determine if you can provide for its needs.

In this chapter we can only hope that the following collection of varying shapes, sizes, and colors will at least give some indication of the vast range of interesting fishes from around the tropical waters of the world that can delight, even in the most modest aquarium.

Brachygobius doriae
BUMBLEBEE FISH

SCAT
A brackish water species with a propensity to eat almost anything—including some aquarium plants.

APTERONOTUS SP.

FAMILY: *APTERONOTIDAE*

COMMON NAME: *UNIDENTIFIED SPECKLED KNIFEFISH*

FEEDING

COMPATIBILITY

EASE OF KEEPING

6

SIZE

20 in (50 cm) 12 in (30 cm)

This fish belongs to a South American family that is poorly studied. Generally nocturnal, all species are drably colored in black, dark brown, or mottled shades of tan. Timid in the aquarium, especially until they become accustomed to life in captivity, knifefishes nevertheless can develop into pets, owing to their unusual level of intelligence. They are capable of swimming equally well backward or forward.

SPECIAL CARE: Provide a hiding place roomy enough for the fish to retire into during the daylight hours. Exhibiting a single specimen in a tank devoted to its needs is the best approach. Although not fussy about water conditions, the fish will adapt best to slightly acidic, moderately soft water. The tank should be heavily planted. Feeding poses few problems once the fish has adjusted to its quarters. Expect any knifefish to live a long life and reach more than 1 foot (30 cm) in length if cared for properly.

BEDOTIA GEAYI

FAMILY: *ATHERINIDAE*

COMMON NAME: *MADAGASCAR RAINBOWFISH*

This pencillike fish can be found in the wild in the streams of Madagascar. Its elongated body has a slight degree of curvature in both the dorsal and ventral contours. Body coloration is light greenish-yellow with a bluish-violet sheen apparent under sidelighting conditions. Its scales are well-defined and a dark line runs from the snout right through to the rear edge of the caudal fin. This fish has two dorsal fins, the first of which is hardly noticeable as it is folded down most of the time. The long-based second dorsal and anal fins are set well back: those of the male are dark with yellowish-orange streaks and a black-red margin; the female's only have a dark edge. The caudal fin is slightly spade-shaped and has a yellowish center (crossed by the dark body stripe) with black and red outer margins in the male, and black and white edging in the female.

SPECIAL CARE: An active, peaceful shoaling species, these fishes need plenty of swimming space and generous plantings. It lays its eggs among plants or artificial spawning mops. It will accept hard water.

FEEDING

COMPATIBILITY

EASE OF KEEPING

3

SIZE

4.3 in (11 cm) 4 in (10 cm)

TELMATHERINA LADIGESI

FAMILY: *ATHERINIDAE*

COMMON NAME: *CELEBES RAINBOWFISH*

Found in the running streams and estuarine waters of Sulawesi, Indonesia, this fish has an elongated body with equally-curved dorsal and ventral contours. Its coloration varies according to lighting conditions: a light yellow-gold body shading down to an apparently silver belly. This silvery effect is caused by the transparency of the skin which allows the internal organs to be seen. An iridescent light blue line runs from midway along the flanks to the end of the caudal peduncle. The large, dark-centered eyes have a silvery-blue rim. The Celebes Rainbowfish has two dorsal fins—the first is small, the second has well-developed black and yellow filaments, particularly in the male. The anal fin is almost divided into two parts, again the male has filamentous extensions to this fin. The top and bottom edges of the caudal fin are yellow with black edging inside. A general guideline to follow for spotting the difference between the sexes is that the female is generally less robust and is less brightly colored. This fish has recently been reclassified as *Marosatherina ladigesi* after the town of Maros, near where it is found.

FEEDING

COMPATIBILITY

EASE OF KEEPING

2

SIZE

2.8 in (7 cm) 3 in (7.5 cm)

SPECIAL CARE: Unlike many Asian fishes, this species adapts to hard water very well and some additions of sea salt to the water are beneficial. It needs a well-planted aquarium as it lays its eggs among plants. If artificial nylon mops are used as spawning receptacles these can be removed to a separate tank for hatching as the adults may eat the eggs. Spawning takes place over a lengthy period.

The male Badis (left) is more brightly colored than the female (right).

BADIS BADIS

FAMILY: *BADIDAE*
COMMON NAME: *BADIS*

The classification of this fish is interesting as it was formerly classified in the Family Nandidae and now some experts are including this fish within the Labyrinth family. It is stocky and appears to be slightly bowed as the ventral contour is often slightly concave while the dorsal surface is often arched. The overall shape of this species is not dissimilar to *Apistogramma spp.* The Badis is also sometimes called the Dwarf Chameleon Fish as it appears to change color to suit its surroundings of the standing waters in India. Generally its body is reddish-brown in color but in prime specimens this will change to a red and blue speckled pattern with clearly-defined scales. The dorsal fin is long-based with spiny and soft-rayed parts and has bluish markings. Females are less brightly colored even at breeding times when the colors of the male intensify dramatically.

SPECIAL CARE: This fish appreciates a well-planted aquarium with plenty of rocky retreats, caves, or flowerpots as it spends most of its time in the lower levels of the tank. It is a secretive spawner and after some trials of strength (jaw wrestling, etc.) the spawning embrace produces adhesive eggs which stick to the cave ceiling. Generally shy and peaceful, it may become territorial when spawning. It has a particular preference for worm foods.

FEEDING

COMPATIBILITY

EASE OF KEEPING
3

SIZE

2.5 in (6.5 cm)   2.5 in (6.5 cm)

DORMITATOR MACULATUS

FAMILY: *ELEOTRIDAE = GOBIIDAE*
COMMON NAME: *SPOTTED SLEEPER GOBY; STRIPED SLEEPER GOBY*

Gobies are characterized by fusion of the pectoral fins to create an attachment organ that the fish uses to hang onto solid substrates. This species is no exception. It is found in brackish water around the coast of Southeast Asia, sometimes making its way upriver to completely fresh water. The body is silvery to olive green in color with numerous dark spots. A blue to blue-green patch of pigment often lies just anterior to the gill cover. Like all gobies, it has paired dorsal fins. Both are marked with spots, and each is lighter in color along its upper margin. Males usually have larger, more colorful dorsal fins than females.

SPECIAL CARE: The need for brackish water limits the selection of plants that can be included with this interesting species. Fortunately, Java Fern, *Microsorum*, is a suitable choice that has the added advantage of being found in the same region as this goby. Lowering the salinity of the water is said to aid in inducing spawning.

FEEDING

COMPATIBILITY

EASE OF KEEPING
5

SIZE
10 in (25 cm)   6 in (15 cm)

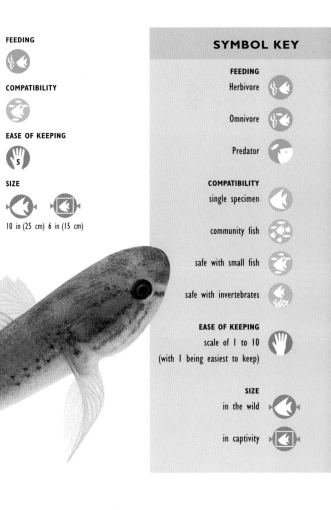

SYMBOL KEY

FEEDING
Herbivore
Omnivore
Predator

COMPATIBILITY
single specimen
community fish
safe with small fish
safe with invertebrates

EASE OF KEEPING
scale of 1 to 10
(with 1 being easiest to keep)

SIZE
in the wild
in captivity

HYPSELEOTRIS COMPRESSUS

FAMILY: *ELEOTRIDAE = GOBIIDAE*
COMMON NAME: *AUSTRALIAN FIRE GOBY; CARP GUDGEON; EMPIRE FISH*

FEEDING

COMPATIBILITY

EASE OF KEEPING
3

SIZE
6 in (15 cm) 6 in (15 cm)

Despite being a member of the Sleepy Goby group, this species does not have the usual goby characteristic of fused pelvic fins that form a suction disk. Its stocky, cylindrical body has some curvature to both the dorsal and ventral profiles. This fish has well-defined scales on its golden brown body which has a darker dorsal surface. There is a dark spot just above the base of the pectoral fin. The male has the most coloration, especially when breeding. The chest and ventral areas are suffused with red, a color which appears at the base of both of the dorsal fins and the anal fin; these fins are further adorned with black borders and blue outer-edgings. The pelvic fins are also edged in light blue but the caudal fin is plain. The female is plain golden brown in color with a dark band along the flanks and has uncolored fins. The Australian Fire Goby is, not surprisingly, found in the fresh, brackish waters of Australia (apart from the southern coasts) and southern Papua New Guinea.
SPECIAL CARE: This fish will lay its eggs on practically any surface. It spends most of its time at the lower level of the aquarium and appreciates generous planting and some hideaways.

BRACHYGOBIUS DORIAE

FAMILY: *GOBIIDAE*
COMMON NAME: *BUMBLEBEE FISH; BUMBLEBEE GOBY*

FEEDING

COMPATIBILITY

EASE OF KEEPING
5

SIZE
2 in (5 cm) 1.5 in (4 cm)

The sooty black-blue body of this fish is encircled with some pale yellow bands of differing widths. Its head is broad and blunt with a large mouth and high-set eyes. Both of the dorsal fins and anal fin have dark bases and yellowish outer margins. The pelvic fins are a distinguishing feature of all gobies in that they are fused together to form a suction cup. This helps to anchor the fish to a rock (or any other chosen resting place) and becomes especially useful in running waters. The swim bladder is also missing which assists in keeping the fish "on the bottom" by making it less buoyant. It is found in the brackish waters of Borneo, Malaysia, Java, and Thailand. Similar species are *B. aggregatus*, *B. nunus,* and *B. xanthozona*.
SPECIAL CARE: This species needs plenty of retreats, in which it can deposit its eggs, in a well-planted tank and the company of its own kind or that of non-boisterous, fishes; the addition of some sea salt to the water is acceptable. This fish will thrive in a species tank.

GYRINOCHEILUS AYMONIERI

FAMILY: *GYRINOCHEILIDAE*
COMMON NAME: *CHINESE SUCKING LOACH; CHINESE ALGAE EATER*

FEEDING

COMPATIBILITY

EASE OF KEEPING
1

SIZE
10 in (25 cm) 8 in (20 cm)

The popular name for this fish is misleading as it doesn't come from China—it is found in Thailand and Laos—and neither is it a member of the loach family. Its elongated body has a slightly-arched dorsal profile and a flat ventral contour. The yellow-gold coloration is complemented by dark-edged scales. A dark band runs from the snout to the caudal peduncle and is crossed at regular intervals by dark bars. The fins are generally clear of patterning although the caudal fin may have some small dark dots. The mouth is underslung and forms a sucking disk by which the fish rasps algae from firm surfaces. It breathes through special slits in its head while sucking onto surfaces such as the front glass of the aquarium.
SPECIAL CARE: Another appropriate common name for this fish would be "algae eater" although it often loses this tendency with age when it may also get very territorially minded. It should be kept in a well-planted aquarium with some algal growth, as this omnivore requires a lot of green matter in its diet.
No information is available on captive breeding.

MASTACEMBELUS ARMATUS

FAMILY: *MASTACEMBELIDAE*
COMMON NAME: *SPINY EEL*

This fish's natural habitat is the muddy, weedy streams of India, Sri Lanka, Thailand, and Sumatra. The upper part of its body is golden yellow-brown, gradually darkening on the lower parts. A dark brown band, with attached blotches to its upper edge, runs from the pointed snout to the end of the caudal peduncle. Two rows of oval blotches appear on the lower-half of the body; these are more elongated particularly toward the head and below the jaw. The alternative popular name, Tire-track Spiny Eel, is quite apt as the markings do resemble the tread pattern of a tire. The snout has a distinctly moveable portion at its tip and the eyes appear small as they are hidden within the dark stripe. The dorsal, anal, and caudal fins form one complete unit encircling the rear-half of the body; the dorsal fin is preceded by a row of tiny spines or finlets. The pelvic fins are absent.

SPECIAL CARE: This fish is often nocturnal and requires many hiding places. The aquarium should be well-planted and contain soft substrate that it can burrow in, as it spends much of its time at the lower levels of the tank. As its natural habitats may include partially brackish water, a small addition of salt to the water will not harm this fish. It should not be kept with small fishes and is probably better suited to a single species aquarium. It has a preference for worm-type foods. No breeding information is available.

FEEDING

COMPATIBILITY

EASE OF KEEPING

SIZE

29.5 in (75 cm) 29.5 in (75 cm)

DATNIOIDES MICROLEPIS

FAMILY: *LOBOTIDAE*
COMMON NAME: *SIAMESE TIGER FISH*

FEEDING

COMPATIBILITY

EASE OF KEEPING

5

SIZE

16 in (40 cm) 12 in (30 cm)

This powerful, predatory species is found in Borneo, Thailand, and Sumatra. Its golden brown, oblong body has a pointed snout and a narrow caudal peduncle. Several vertical dark bars cross the body and a dark-edged pale stripe runs from the tip of the snout, along the forehead, to the dorsal fin. This long-based fin carries continuations of the dark body and has a black edge to its spiny front section; the rear part is clear and soft-rayed. The large, dark pelvic fins have creamy front edges; the anal fin is crossed by a body bar. The otherwise clear yellow caudal fin has a dark bar across its base.

SPECIAL CARE: The Siamese Tiger Fish is often found in brackish waters, so the addition of some sea salt to the water is acceptable. It requires a spacious, heavily planted tank, which is not always easy to maintain in salt-enriched water, with plenty of retreats. Feed with meaty foods. This aggressive fish is best kept in a single species aquarium, it is certainly not safe to be kept with smaller fishes. No information is available on captive breeding.

SYMBOL KEY

FEEDING
Herbivore
Omnivore
Predator

COMPATIBILITY
single specimen
community fish
safe with small fish
safe with invertebrates

EASE OF KEEPING
scale of 1 to 10
(with 1 being easiest to keep)

SIZE
in the wild
in captivity

MASTACEMBELUS ERYTHROTAENIA

FAMILY: *MASTACEMBELIDAE*
COMMON NAME: *FIRE EEL*

A very attractive species which is often kept as a prize specimen in its own aquarium. The act of transferring it from its transportation plastic container into its show tank at the beginning and end of exhibitions usually attracts a crowd! Native to Southeast Asia, Borneo, Burma, Sumatra, and Thailand, it has a deep brown or even black body that is marked with a number of fiery red lines that run from the pointed snout to the end of the caudal peduncle. The pectoral fins are similarly marked and the caudal fin is red. The continuity of these lines may break up into dots once the level of the dorsal and anal fins is reached. The head is small and the red facial markings may contain some yellow coloring.
SPECIAL CARE: This fish should be kept in an aquarium that is furnished with plenty of hiding places as it is a bottom-dweller. No breeding information is available. Similarly to the related species *M. armatus*, it prefers worm-type foods and is best kept in a single species aquarium.

FEEDING

COMPATIBILITY

EASE OF KEEPING
4

SIZE
3.3 ft (1 m) 26 in (66 cm)

IRIATHERINA WERNERI

FAMILY: *MELANOTAENIIDAE*
COMMON NAME: *THREADFIN RAINBOWFISH*

This distinctive fish is endemic to the swamps and rivers in Papua New Guinea and northern Australia. Its elongated body has equally-curved dorsal and ventral contours and is golden brown-silver with a bluish shine to the dorsal ridge. Some fine, reddish-brown vertical lines cross the body and its scales are well-defined. It has a small head with dark-centered golden eyes. The main feature of this species is the fins: the first dorsal fin is held high and has a rounded tip; the second dorsal has some separated rays which are sooty-black and extremely filamentous or threadlike. Pelvic fins are also black and threadlike and the anal fin is long-based and also carries long black extensions. The caudal fin is lyre-shaped and has extended rays from the top and bottom tips.
SPECIAL CARE: This shoaling species likes to be kept in small groups with other non-boisterous fishes in a well-planted aquarium. The water should not have too much movement in it. To achieve successful breeding, slightly acidic, fairly soft water is preferable. The eggs are laid in bushy plants or artificial nylon mops over a period of days. Remove to a separate tank for hatching to occur as the adults may eat the eggs.

FEEDING

COMPATIBILITY

EASE OF KEEPING
3

SIZE
2 in (5 cm) 1.5 in (4 cm)

GLOSSOLEPIS INCISUS

FAMILY: *MELANOTAENIIDAE*
COMMON NAME: *RED RAINBOWFISH*

This brilliantly colored species is unique to Lake Sentani in northern Papua New Guinea. Its body is elongated and deep with a pointed snout and a drawn-out caudal peduncle. Its predominantly red coloration is formed by chromium-silver scales with bright red edges, but not with an entirely uniform distribution. The lower-half of the body is often a more dense shade of red and there is a silver-white area behind and below the gill cover. The head is small with the dorsal surface rising very steeply just behind the eyes. There are two dorsal fins, the second of which is the larger; the anal fin is long-based. All of the fins are red. Male fish have a more highly-arched back, females tend to be slimmer with a more yellowish coloration to the body and fins.
SPECIAL CARE: This shy shoaling fish will lose some of its timidity when kept with companions of its own kind. It needs plenty of swimming space and bushy plants or artificial nylon mops in which to spawn. It will tolerate hard water.

FEEDING

COMPATIBILITY

EASE OF KEEPING
1

SIZE
6 in (15 cm) 4.7 in (12 cm)

MELANOTAENIA HERBERTAXELRODI

FAMILY: *MELANOTAENIIDAE*
COMMON NAME: *AXELROD'S RAINBOWFISH*

Found only in the Lake Terbera basin of Papua New Guinea, it is pale golden yellow all over, with a bright blue horizontal stripe running from the eyes to the caudal peduncle. The paired fins and the caudal fin are colorless, but the dorsal and anal fins shimmer with golden yellow highlights. Its brightly metallic scales give it a striking, vivid appearance. Juveniles tend to be pale blue-gray in color. Because it forms schools, several should be kept together. This popular species is named after Dr. Herbert Axelrod, an American fish-collector and publisher.

SPECIAL CARE: A community of different species from this family can be chosen, but in the case of this species, a school should be given a tank of its own. Leave a swimming area near the center, but plant the tank heavily with *Vallisneria*, Java ferns, and Java moss, all of which tolerate the water chemistry that this fish prefers. Provide hard, slightly alkaline water, and a temperature of about 80°F (27°C). It is a good jumper, so the tank should be adequately covered.

FEEDING

COMPATIBILITY

EASE OF KEEPING
7

SIZE
3.2 in (8 cm)   3.2 in (8 cm)

MELANOTAENIA BOESMANI

FAMILY: *MELANOTAENIIDAE*
COMMON NAME: *BOSEMAN'S RAINBOWFISH*

Found only in Papua New Guinea, this fish has blue on the anterior portion of the body and golden yellow posteriorly, with the division, at about the point where the anterior and posterior dorsal fins are separated, being formed by alternating vertical bars of the two colors. The paired fins are colorless, while the dorsal, caudal, and anal fins mimic the golden yellow of the body. The dorsal fin is edged in white, while the anal is edged in sky blue.

SPECIAL CARE: Rainbowfishes are best exhibited in a tank devoted to their needs. A community of different species from this family can be chosen, but other community fish, such as tetras or barbs, should probably be avoided. Provide moderately hard, alkaline water, and rather warm temperatures, for this species in particular, up to about 85°F (29°C). It is a good jumper. Plants should be included in the tank—Java ferns and Java moss are found in its natural habitat.

FEEDING

COMPATIBILITY

EASE OF KEEPING
5

SIZE
4 in (10 cm)   3.2 in (8 cm)

SYMBOL KEY

FEEDING
Herbivore
Omnivore
Predator

COMPATIBILITY
single specimen
community fish
safe with small fish
safe with invertebrates

EASE OF KEEPING
scale of 1 to 10
(with 1 being easiest to keep)

SIZE
in the wild
in captivity

MELANOTAENIA MACCULLOCHI

FAMILY: *MELANOTAENIIDAE*
COMMON NAME: *DWARF RAINBOWFISH*

FEEDING

This rainbowfish is found in Australia, from the tropical regions of the north, as far south as Sydney. The silvery body is highlighted with horizontal lines made up of fine, rust colored dots. The dorsal and anal fins are edged in bright scarlet and a scarlet blotch lies in the center of the caudal fin. Females are less colorful than males.

COMPATIBILITY

SPECIAL CARE: This is a schooling species that should be given a tank to itself. Provide moderately hard, alkaline water, and a temperature of 77°F (25°C) or slightly lower. Like all members of its genus, it is a good jumper. Plants should be included in the tank, but leave ample swimming room. Good filtration is essential, and regular partial water changes should be carried out. Feeding poses few problems, although start with various live foods and gradually increase the proportion of prepared flake foods offered until the fish become accustomed to them.

EASE OF KEEPING

SIZE

4.7 in (12 cm) 4 in (10 cm)

MELANOTAENIA LACUSTRIS

FAMILY: *MELANOTAENIIDAE*
COMMON NAME: *LAKE KUTUBU RAINBOWFISH*

Found only in Lake Kutubu of the southern mountains of Papua New Guinea, it is electric blue on the upper-half of the body, with a dark blue horizontal band along the lateral line. The lower portion of the body is silvery. The paired fins are colorless, while the dorsal, caudal, and anal fins are tinged with blue. Often the blue area of the back shimmers with a greenish iridescence. The head is silvery. Females are less colorful than males.

SPECIAL CARE: A community of different species from this family can be chosen, but other community fish, such as tetras or barbs, should probably be avoided. Provide moderately hard, alkaline water, and a temperature of 80°F (27°C) or slightly lower. Like all members of its genus, it is a good jumper. Plants should be included in the tank, and although this species needs a significant proportion of vegetable matter in its diet, it obtains this from algae and small floating plants, such as duckweed.

FEEDING

COMPATIBILITY

EASE OF KEEPING
5

SIZE
4.7 in (12 cm) 4 in (10 cm)

MELANOTAENIA PRAECOX

FAMILY: *MELANOTAENIIDAE*
COMMON NAME: *DIAMOND RAINBOWFISH*

FEEDING

Although this fish was known to scientists as long ago as the 1920s, it was not until the early 1990s that numbers began to be imported regularly from New Guinea and Irian Jaya. This fish, with its metallic, electric blue body coloration, offset by bright red edging to its fins, caused wonderment wherever it was seen. Females, when young, have blue edgings to the yellowish fins with the red coloration being more intense in the males.

COMPATIBILITY

EASE OF KEEPING
4

SIZE
2.4 in (6 cm) 2.4 in (6 cm)

SPECIAL CARE: Of modest proportions, it does not need a spacious aquarium in which to thrive, although like its relatives, it does appreciate adequate swimming space combined with planted thickets to provide security. To get the best "visual effect" from these fishes, the aquarium should receive some sunshine through the front glass; this "lights up" the fishes quite spectacularly, especially if they are kept as a shoal. Breeding occurs, often as a shoal, among bushy plants or in spawning mops provided by the aquarist. Brood numbers produced may be small.

MONODACTYLUS ARGENTEUS

FAMILY: *MONODACTYLIDAE*
COMMON NAME: *MONO; MALAYSIAN OR SINGAPORE ANGEL; FINGERFISH*

The Mono has a tall and apparently diamond-shaped body due to the positioning of the dorsal and anal fin at the top and bottom apexes.
In actuality it is disc-shaped; laterally-compressed similar to the Freshwater Angelfish (*Pterophyllum sp*). Its body is silver with small scales; a dark bar passes down the head and through the large eyes and another, slightly thinner line runs down from the front of the dorsal fin, through the base of the pectoral fin to the pelvic fins. The highly-arched lateral line is clearly visible in this species. The dorsal and anal fins are yellowish-orange having black front edges. The very small pelvic fins and caudal fin are plain yellow. Its natural habitats are the tropical coastal waters from India to Tahiti, including the Philippines and coastal Australia.

SPECIAL CARE: Similar in habits and requirements to the Scat (*Scatophagus sp.*). It tolerates brackish water and can be acclimatized to sea-strength water. This fish is omnivorous, but it particularly has an appetite for plants. It is best kept in shoals in a spacious aquarium which allows it plenty of swimming space.
No breeding information is available.

FEEDING

COMPATIBILITY

EASE OF KEEPING
2

SIZE
9 in (23 cm)   6 in (15 cm)

MONODACTYLUS SEBAE

FAMILY: *MONODACTYLIDAE*
COMMON NAME: *SEBA MONO*

This is a species sometimes found in the brackish water of estuaries along the west African coast from Senegal south to Zaire. It is best suited to a marine aquarium, as its occurrence in fresh or brackish waters is probably only accidental. Nevertheless, specimens are available in stores that do not have a marine department. The flattened body is silver in color, with the most noticeable features being the elongated dorsal and anal fins that give the fish an almost diamond shape. Dark vertical bands run through the eyes, just anterior to the gill cover, down the middle of the body from the tip of the dorsal fin to the tip of the anal fin, and along the rear margins of the body where the upper and lower bands join at the caudal peduncle.

SPECIAL CARE: Provide full-strength sea water in a roomy tank and a variety of foods. It will prey on smaller fishes and crustaceans or other invertebrates it can swallow. Not demanding as marine fish go, it can be kept peacefully in a small school if the tank is sufficiently roomy.

FEEDING

COMPATIBILITY

EASE OF KEEPING
6

SIZE
8 in (20 cm)   6 in (15 cm)

SYMBOL KEY

FEEDING
Herbivore

Omnivore

Predator

COMPATIBILITY
single specimen

community fish

safe with small fish

safe with invertebrates

EASE OF KEEPING
scale of 1 to 10
(with 1 being easiest to keep)

SIZE
in the wild

in captivity

GNATHONEMUS PETERSI

FAMILY: *MORMYRIDAE*
COMMON NAME: *LONG-NOSED ELEPHANT FISH; PETER'S ELEPHANT-NOSE; UBANGI MORMYRID*

This fish is native to the streams and rivers of Nigeria, Cameroon, and Zaire. This often nocturnal species emits electrical impulses by which it navigates in the dark or in muddy waters. It is sensitive to water quality changes and has been used to monitor water quality in industrial contexts. Its elongated body is deep and laterally-compressed. As its popular name suggests, it has a long snout that is balanced by an equally-long and narrow caudal peduncle. Body coloration is very dark gray with two pinkish-white bracket-shaped marks on the flanks linking the beginning of the dorsal and anal fins. The head forms about a quarter of the main body length and the extended lower jaw is fingerlike. The dorsal and anal fins are set very far back on the body and the narrow, but deeply-forked, caudal fin is set at the end of the very thin caudal peduncle. The pectoral fins are flipperlike, the pelvic fins fairly small.

SPECIAL CARE: This peaceful fish spends most of its time at the bottom of the aquarium and likes a thickly-planted habitat with plenty of hideaways to which it can retreat. Generally, it is better suited to a single-species aquarium. It is omnivorous but prefers live foods. No breeding information is available.

FEEDING

COMPATIBILITY

EASE OF KEEPING

SIZE

10 in (25 cm) 9 in (23 cm)

MONOCIRRHUS POLYACANTHUS

FAMILY: *NANDIDAE*
COMMON NAME: *SOUTH AMERICAN LEAF FISH*

This species uses its similarity to a floating leaf to drift up to unsuspecting prey and then engulf them with its large protrusive mouth. It lives in the waters of the Amazon region and Guyana, South America. The oval body has a concave forehead and the dorsal surface is more arched than the gently-curving ventral profile. The coloration varies according to the fish's needs for camouflage in prevailing conditions, but generally it is a golden brown with darker irregular blotches very much like a decaying leaf in fall. There is a thin dark horizontal line along the flanks from about midway to the caudal peduncle and there are two similar dark lines on the head making a "V" shape with the eye at their forward meeting point. The mouth is very large and can be opened out into a funnel-shape for taking in food. The caudal fin is often held in a closed position when the fish is swimming in its characteristic head-down fashion.

SPECIAL CARE: This fish swims at all levels of the aquarium. It requires plenty of plants in which it can lurk and plenty of live foods (even young livebearers) on which it can prey. It will lay its eggs on any flat surface, cichlid-style.

FEEDING

COMPATIBILITY

EASE OF KEEPING

SIZE

4 in (10 cm) 3.5 in (9 cm)

NOTOPTERUS CHITALA

FAMILY: *NOTOPTERIDAE*
COMMON NAME: *CLOWN KNIFEFISH; FEATHERBACK*

Known in its native countries of Burma, India, Sumatra, and Thailand as *Ikan Belida*, this species can swim effortlessly in either direction using an undulating wave-movement of its long anal fin. Nocturnal by nature, it navigates in total darkness using a self-generated electro-magnetic force field. By detecting changes in the reflected strength of this field (caused by obstacles and other fishes), the Clown Knifefish instinctively knows where it is and what direction to take. It is highly regarded as a food fish and is encouraged to spawn on stakes specially inserted in the riverbed—a convenient way of increasing stocks. Its body is similar in shape to an aerofoil section and is flattened ventrally with a highly arched dorsal surface. It is silvery gray-brown with irregular-sized, white-rimmed black spots occurring on the flanks below the lateral line. The pelvic fins are either very rudimentary, are hardly visible, or are absent completely.

SPECIAL CARE: The Clown Knifefish is aggressive and predatory to smaller fishes so it should be kept with much larger species or given it its own

FEEDING

COMPATIBILITY

EASE OF KEEPING

4

SIZE

35.4 in (90 cm) 28 in (71 cm)

spacious living quarters with plenty of hiding places. Experts have suggested that this fish lays its eggs on firm surfaces.

SCLEROPAGES JARDINI

FAMILY: *OSTEOGLOSSIDAE*
COMMON NAME: *GULF SARATOGA; NORTHERN SPOTTED BARRAMUNDI*

FEEDING

COMPATIBILITY

EASE OF KEEPING

5

SIZE

35.4 in (90 cm) 35.4 in (90 cm)

It is often thought that this fish was named after one of its natural locations—the Jardine River in northern Australia—but it is, in fact, named after the collector F. Jardine. Its elongated body is heavily-built and is dullish gray in color. This somewhat drab coloration is much relieved by the gold-yellow rear edges to the scales and the facial markings on the head and gill covers. It has a large upturned mouth, a bony tongue, and chin barbels are present. The dorsal and anal fins are set well back on the body; the pectoral fins are pointed, the caudal fin rounded. Little is know about sex difference in this species. Any differences that do develop are not likely to be discernible until adult maturity is reached at around five years of age. It is a protected species which prohibits its exportation but some accredited breeders are allowed to trade with captive bred (and duly certificated) offspring.

SPECIAL CARE: This fish will swim at all levels of the aquarium—basically anywhere that food can be found. It breeds by the mouthbrooding method. It requires a very spacious aquarium with a very secure lid.

SYMBOL KEY

FEEDING

Herbivore

Omnivore

Predator

COMPATIBILITY

single specimen

community fish

safe with small fish

safe with invertebrates

EASE OF KEEPING

scale of 1 to 10
(with 1 being easiest to keep)

SIZE

in the wild

in captivity

PANTODON BUCHHOLZI

FAMILY: *PANTODONTIDAE*
COMMON NAME: *BUTTERFLYFISH*

The boat-shaped body of the Butterflyfish is a blotchy dark brown color with a hint of a horizontal line along the flanks. A dark bar passes diagonally through the eyes. The caudal fin has several extended central rays; the pelvic fins are extremely long with the amount of inter-ray tissue decreasing with distance from the body. The darkly-patterned pectoral fins are very large and resemble butterfly wings when viewed from above. It inhabits the still waters of tropical west Africa—Nigeria, Cameroon, and Zaire.

SPECIAL CARE: The only species in the genus, the Butterflyfish can be intolerant of other fishes, especially those invading its surface-dwelling areas, so it is best to keep it with middle- and bottom-dwelling species. It can also be predatory toward smaller fishes. Make sure that the aquarium hood is kept firmly in place as it is an excellent jumper. Up to 200 eggs may be laid at one time; they float so they can be collected for hatching in a separate aquarium.

FEEDING

COMPATIBILITY

EASE OF KEEPING

1

SIZE

4 in (10 cm) 4 in (10 cm)

POLYPTERUS SENEGALUS

FAMILY: *POLYPTERIDAE*
COMMON NAME: *SENEGAL BICHIR; ROPE FISH*

Africa, including Senegal, Gambia and Niger, is home to this member of the family known as "lobe-finned pikes." Uniformly brown with colorless fins, the multiple elements of the dorsal fin are characteristic. Medium-hard water of neutral pH is characteristic of the natural habitat, but this species will adapt to any reasonable aquarium conditions. It is generally peaceful toward fishes too large to eat, but commonly will not tolerate another member of its own kind in the same aquarium.

SPECIAL CARE: Nothing is known about sexual dimorphism or breeding behavior in this species; however in other bichirs, eggs are released over a gravel substrate after a long and elaborate courtship ritual. Among fishes that are intolerant of conspecifics, courtship is a commonplace way of reducing aggressive behavior to a level consistent with successful spawning. The aquarium should have good filtration and a secure hood. Since this species grows large, it needs a roomy tank. Provide lots of plants and driftwood.

FEEDING

COMPATIBILITY

EASE OF KEEPING

7

SIZE

12 in (30 cm) 10 in (25 cm)

The difference in patterning of these two Scats shows just how varied their markings can be.

SCATOPHAGUS ARGUS

FAMILY: *SCATOPHAGIDAE*
COMMON NAME: *SCAT; ARGUS FISH*

The Scat has a tall, laterally-compressed body. The fins are set at the "corners" of the body. Its coloration is a mixture of streaky brown and gold with numerous round dark spots. The head has two dark lines running up the steep forehead and there is a distinct golden streak running vertically behind the gill cover. Some red markings appear toward the top of the dorsal surface. The long-based dorsal fin has a spiny front section and a clear, soft rear portion. The pelvic, pectoral, and anal fins have reddish-brown coloring, the anal fin has spines at the front. It is endemic to coastal waters from India to Tahiti, including the Philippines and Australia.
SPECIAL CARE: This fish has similar needs to *Mondactylus sp.*; it is particularly important to ensure it has plenty of room to swim, as it is very active. The Scat is a true scavenger and seems to eat anything—including aquarium plants. The addition of some sea salt in its aquarium water can be recommended. No breeding information is available. This shoaling species is suitable for a community collection of mixed-size fishes, but it will also do well in a single species aquarium.

FEEDING

COMPATIBILITY

EASE OF KEEPING

SIZE

12 in (30 cm) 10 in (25 cm)

TOXOTES JACULATOR

FAMILY: *TOXOTIDAE*
COMMON NAME: *ARCHERFISH*

Although a very smart-looking fish in its own right, the fascination of this species is its ability to shoot down perching insects with well-aimed spit; its pursed mouth acts as a form of primitive gun-barrel. The fish's real gift is being able to judge the correct amount of offset in its aim to allow for the displaced view of the target caused by refraction at the water's surface. It can be found in estuarine rivers from East Africa to Australia. It has an elongated body but it appears to be a lot shorter than it actually is because of the well set back dorsal and anal fins. Its body is silver with a number of dark blotches on the flanks, the largest of these occuring immediately below the start of the dorsal fin. The anal fin has a dark band along its outer edge, the dorsal fin is also marked with black, and the caudal fin is clear. The head is long and tapered with the lower lip protruding beyond the upper; the eyes are set well forward.
SPECIAL CARE: This fish requires ample swimming space with perhaps some "above-water" plant roots hanging in the water to simulate mangrove roots. Ideally, the aquarium could form part of a paludarium. No breeding information is available.

FEEDING

COMPATIBILITY

EASE OF KEEPING

SIZE

10 in (25 cm) 6.7 in (17 cm)

SYMBOL KEY

FEEDING
Herbivore

Omnivore

Predator

COMPATIBILITY
single specimen

community fish

safe with small fish

safe with invertebrates

EASE OF KEEPING
scale of 1 to 10
(with 1 being easiest to keep)

SIZE
in the wild

in captivity

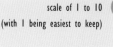

LIVEBEARERS

The main attraction of livebearers for hobbyists,

Xiphophorus variatus
VARIATUS PLATY

particularly the aquarium-developed strains such as guppies, mollies, platies, and swordtails, is their sheer willingness to breed. Another plus point is that the young fish are ready to swim immediately after birth, saving the fishkeeper from a long wait for externally-fertilized eggs to hatch (or be eaten) and the worry of finding the appropriate food.

These "cultivated" varieties of livebearers are generally peaceful and bring vibrant color to the aquarium. In order to maintain the quality of the strain, careful control must be exercised over specimen selection, the number of varieties kept, and how the sexes are distributed as these fishes will interbreed without hesitation, often introducing unwanted physical characteristics.

Specialist societies have been established that are dedicated to the breeding of the lesser-known "wild" genera for conservation purposes. These fishes may lack some of the coloration of the cultivated strains, but they have other points of interest. These "wild" species may be more aggressive in captivity than the cultivated strains.

Males have a modified anal fin although this may be more difficult to judge clearly in the "wild" species. Male guppies, swordtails, platies, and mollies all have an easily visible, rod-like anal fin whereas the anal fins of other male species are merely "notched" a few rays from the front of the fin. In all species the female has a normal fan-shaped anal fin and is generally larger than the male.

The secret to breeding these fish successfully is recognizing when to take the gravid (pregnant) female from the main aquarium and put her into a nursery tank. Too soon is far better than too late. At normal aquarium temperatures the gestation period is around 30 days. Although floating breeding traps are effective in isolating the female from her newly-born fry (and from other fishes in the same tank), these also introduce unnecessary stress at a most critical time, often causing premature births. A heavily-planted, separate nursery tank is preferable, in which the female can give birth more naturally, and where the young can find refuge.

Females of the cultivated species of livebearers can also continue producing further broods of young without needing to re-mate with a male fish by virtue of being able to store sperm within her body. Among "wild" species, re-mating is necessary.

Xiphophorus nezahuacoyotl
DWARF LIVEBEARER

FEATURED IN THIS SECTION

RED SWORDTAIL
A fine pair of Red Swordtails. Sexing is easy as the male has the extension to the caudal fin.

ALFARO CULTRATUS

FAMILY: *POECILIIDAE*
COMMON NAME: *KNIFE LIVEBEARER*

The Knife Livebearer's body is elongated and has a flat dorsal profile. The ventral contour is keel-like, formed from modified scales, and is not to be confused with the anal fin. It is silvery yellowish-brown (some metallic blue is visible under sidelighting) with a darker dorsal surface. The body is semitransparent and the spine visible. Its head is small and the eyes are set well forward. The dorsal fin is rounded and set halfway along the body. All the fins are yellowish, but the caudal fin may have a dark edge. As with other members of the family, the anal fins differ between sexes; the female's fin is fan-shaped, the slightly smaller male has a modified anal fin that is called the *gonopodium*, which acts as a means of internally fertilizing the female. This fish originates from Costa Rica, Guatemala, Panama, and Nicaragua.
SPECIAL CARE: This rather aggressive fish appreciates well-filtered water that can be given some movement by using a power filter. Make sure that the aquarium is well-planted as the plants are necessary to provide refuge for the fry from their hungry parents.

FEEDING

COMPATIBILITY

EASE OF KEEPING
5

SIZE

4 in (10 cm) 3 in (7.5 cm)

CHARACODON AUDAX

FAMILY: *GOODEIDAE*
COMMON NAME: *BLACK PRINCE; BOLD CHARACODON*

Characterized by an elongated body shape, this species is stocky but with rounded contours; the caudal peduncle is somewhat narrow and lengthened. The body coloration is sooty-gray on the dorsal surface with lighter gray-brown colored flanks beneath; there may be a hint of pink around the throat and belly region. Its scales are slightly iridescent but its coloration depends upon lighting conditions. The dorsal fin is set well back on the body opposite the anal fin; all the fins are rounded and, as the popular name suggests, are jet black. The alternative common name may reflect the species' slight aggressiveness between often territorially-minded males. In general females tend to be slightly bigger.
SPECIAL CARE: This generally peaceful, shy fish requires a well-planted aquarium to mimic its natural habitat of the waters of Mexico. Provide some floating plants to which young fish can retreat. This species will produce a small number of fry approximately every two months, but occasionally a larger brood will occur. It prefers a tank with little water movement, so the waterflow return from any power filter used must be directed into the tank so that minimum disturbance is caused.

FEEDING

COMPATIBILITY

EASE OF KEEPING
5

SIZE
2.2 in (5.5 cm) 2.2 in (5.5 cm)

DERMOGENYS PUSILLUS

FAMILY: *HEMIRHAMPHIDAE*
COMMON NAME: *WRESTLING HALFBEAK; MALAYAN HALFBEAK*

This fish has a spindly body shape with a very flat dorsal surface. It is greenish-yellow-gold with some blue colors apparent under sidelighting conditions and there may be a semblance of a gold line along the flanks. The special identifying physical characteristic of this species is the formation of the jaw. The lower jaw is extended to about twice the length of the short upper jaw, making feeding from anywhere but the surface quite difficult. The small dorsal fin and anal fin are set very far back. The male's anal fin appears semi-folded rather than rodlike, the female's is fan shaped. This very distinctive fish is found in the wild in Indonesia, Java, Sumatra, Malaysia, and Thailand.
SPECIAL CARE: Keep a male with a "harem" of two or three females. Males tend to fight, interlocking their jaws for several minutes at a time. The species tolerates both fresh and brackish waters, but keep the aquarium firmly covered as these fish are excellent jumpers. If startled, they may also dash into the side walls of the tank injuring their "beaks" so make sure the perimeter of the tank is well-planted to act as a deceleration zone. Some floating plants are also beneficial to young fish seeking a place to hide.

FEEDING

COMPATIBILITY

EASE OF KEEPING
5

SIZE

3.2 in (8 cm) 3.2 in (8 cm)

POECILIA (LEBISTES) RETICULATA

FAMILY: *POECILIIDAE*
COMMON NAME: *GUPPY; MILLIONSFISH*

The wild species of Guppy is an inhabitant of the waters of Central America, Trinidad, and northern South America. It is dark olive green in color, shading down to light silver on the ventral surface. Its fins are short, but those of aquarium-cultivated species vary to conform to recognized standards and may be of a delta-tail, fantail, double swordtail, top-swordtail, bottom-swordtail, pintail, roundtail, veiltail, or other configuration. Similarly, body coloration can vary from fish to fish within a strain and, of course, vary enormously from strain to strain as the breeder so decrees. Females are larger than males; they lack their coloration and extravagant finnage, although some females now have color in their fins. Females take on extra body depth when gravid (pregnant) and a dark spot appears around the vent to signify this condition. The male's rodlike anal fin is known as the *gonopodium*; the female's anal fin is fan-shaped. The alternative name is a good indication of this species' willingness to breed. Females can store sperm internally and so produce successive broods of young without re-mating. All guppies offered for sale are commercially-bred.

SPECIAL CARE: To maintain any particular color strain great care has to be exercised to prevent unwanted spawnings occurring between "wrong-colored" fishes, as the fish will interbreed without hesitation. This fish is content in a well-planted aquarium with a collection of similar-size fishes.

FEEDING

COMPATIBILITY

EASE OF KEEPING

SIZE

N/A in wild   2.5 in (6.5 cm)

POECILIA SPHENOPS

FAMILY: *POECILIIDAE*
COMMON NAME: *LYRETAIL BLACK MOLLY*

The Black Molly is a long-established aquarium favorite, as its jet black coloration contrasts sharply with the silver, red, and yellow coloring of other fish. As with many of the livebearing fishes, sexing is unproblematic; the male has a modified rod-like anal fin by which internal fertilization of the female is achieved. The female's anal fin, as can be seen in the illustration below, is the normal fan shape. In this aquarium cultivated variety, the caudal fin is in the shape of a lyre. The blackness on the belly is showing a little silver, an effect of the stretching of the skin as the fish's "pregnancy" develops.

SPECIAL CARE: This fish requires a regular supply of green matter in its diet and plenty of space for optimum development. The addition of some natural salt in the water also helps as many fishes encounter brackish conditions in nature. When the female is carrying young, it is very stressful to move her near the end of her gestation period (around 30 days), as premature births may occur. A separate, well-planted aquarium is an ideal place in which she can give birth undisturbed by other fishes.

FEEDING

COMPATIBILITY

EASE OF KEEPING

SIZE

N/A   2.4 in (6 cm)

SYMBOL KEY

FEEDING

Herbivore

Omnivore

Predator

COMPATIBILITY

single specimen

community fish

safe with small fish

safe with invertebrates

EASE OF KEEPING

scale of 1 to 10
(with 1 being easiest to keep)

SIZE

in the wild

in captivity

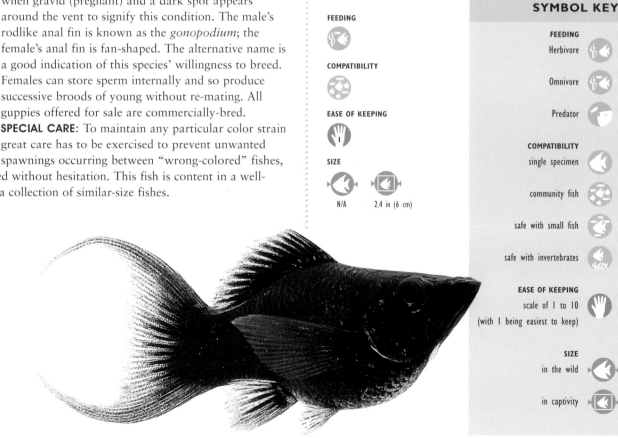

Many different color strains of the Platy are commercially available.

XIPHOPHORUS HELLERI

FAMILY: *POECILIIDAE*
COMMON NAME: *SWORDTAIL*

The body shape of this fish is elongated, with a slightly arched dorsal contour and a fairly deep caudal peduncle. Original wild forms found in Central America are greenish-yellow with clearly defined brown-edged scales. A dark line runs from the snout, along the flanks, and continues along the top edge of the swordlike extension of the caudal fin. The lower edge of the "sword" is also black and the area between the two edges may be yellow, green, or orange. In the male the anal fin is rodlike while the female's anal fin is fan-shaped. Females carry no "sword" and are slightly larger. Occasionally sex-reversal appears to occur—with females turning, usually late in life, into males. Like the Guppy, the Swordtail has been selectively bred to produce many varying color strains, including several finnage variants. Strains with very exaggerated finnage may suffer from *gonopodium* abnormalities and as a consequence of this may not be able to reproduce.

SPECIAL CARE: This fish swims at all levels of the aquarium and will thrive in a well-planted tank with some algal growth. Although generally peaceful, males may quarrel between themselves.

FEEDING

COMPATIBILITY

EASE OF KEEPING

SIZE

4 in (10 cm) 4 in (10 cm)

XIPHOPHORUS MACULATUS

FAMILY: *POECILIIDAE*
COMMON NAME: *PLATY*

Wild forms of this fish are found in Mexico, Guatemala, and Honduras but it is now predominantly captive-bred for the commercial aquarium market. This species is stocky and, in the best specimens, deep with a short caudal peduncle. Body coloration of wild forms is grayish-brown with some dark speckling and clear fins, with possibly some red in the dorsal fin. The male's anal fin is modified to a *gonopodium*; the female is usually larger than the male, has a fan-shaped anal fin, and becomes noticeably fatter when gravid. The Platy is now represented in the aquarium by a wide variety of color strains, all of which are internationally recognized by fishkeepers. The popular Wagtail strains feature black fins and mouth combined with red or yellow body colors; the Moon strain has a dark crescent shape on the caudal peduncle, and the Comet has a dark line on the top and bottom edges of the caudal fin. Many of the color strains have also been developed in aquarium varieties of the Swordtail, *X. helleri*.

SPECIAL CARE: This fish will thrive in an aquarium that is well-planted and that has some algal growth as this forms an important part of its diet. The colors of the young will degenerate unless strict quality of selection and segregation of color strains and sexes is exercised, as interbreeding occurs freely with absolutely no regard for color or strain.

FEEDING

COMPATIBILITY

EASE OF KEEPING

SIZE

2.4 in (6 cm) 2.5 in (6.5 cm)

XIPHOPHORUS NEZAHUACOYOTL

FAMILY: *POECILIIDAE*
COMMON NAME: *NORTHERN MOUNTAIN SWORDTAIL; DWARF LIVEBEARER; DWARF TOPMINNOW*

This fish is one example of many species of *Xiphophorus* that are becoming popular and being successfully maintained by aquarists specializing in these non-cultivated swordtails. It has an elongated body, the dorsal and ventral profiles having equal curvature. The caudal peduncle is fairly deep and relatively long. Its creamy-yellow body has some violet iridescences when viewed under sidelighting. The flanks are marked with erratic dark specklings; the dark edges present on some scales join up to form small lengths of zigzag lines. Its fins are almost clear with a hint of yellow; only the dorsal fin shows signs of speckling. The male carries a short "sword" which is edged in black and the anal fin is rodlike. Females do not carry a sword and have fan-shaped anal fins.

SPECIAL CARE: Native to Mexico, this species is best kept in a well-planted, single-species aquarium where it will inhabit the middle and upper levels.

FEEDING

COMPATIBILITY

EASE OF KEEPING
5

SIZE
2.4 in (6 cm) 2.4 in (6 cm)

XIPHOPHORUS VARIATUS

FAMILY: *POECILIIDAE*
COMMON NAME: *VARIATUS PLATY*

The body shape of this fish is more elongated than the previous *Xiphophorus* species, particularly in the caudal peduncle region, and the body is not quite as deep. The original wild form, found in the streams of southern Mexico, is greenish-yellow with clearly defined, dark-edged scales (and maybe some dark flecking) on the flanks. Sexual differences are easily confirmed by observation of the anal fins as described for other species in this genus. The female is also generally a longer fish. Selective breeding has resulted in many color strains being produced. The Green Variatus Platy is probably nearest in color to the wild form.

SPECIAL CARE: This omnivorous fish needs green matter in its diet so some algal growth in the tank is important. The aquarium should be generally well-planted and be sure to include some floating plants for young fish to seek refuge in. It is suitable to keep in a collection of mixed-size fishes.

FEEDING

COMPATIBILITY

EASE OF KEEPING
1

SIZE
2.75 in (7 cm) 2.5 in (6.5 cm)

MARINE FISH

Marine fishes demand the same attention as to the keeping (and collection) of endangered species or those whose aquarium acclimation is known to be problematical as with freshwater fish. A typical case is that of the seahorse. For every fishkeeper who strives (usually unsuccessfully) to keep it there is also a huge demand for it in the curio souvenir trade and also in the oriental medical trade where it is thought to be endowed with special properties. Throughout this book it has been the intention to keep some conformity so that you become familiar with the pattern of knowledge presented. However, one cannot find a common set of parameters to fit all species under all circumstances, especially when there is the difference between freshwater and saltwater fishes to be considered, so some of the symbols take on a slightly different meaning in this section.

EXPLANATORY NOTES FOR CARE SYMBOLS

FEEDING
HERBIVORE prefers mainly vegetable matter in diet.

OMNIVORE all foods taken, any preferences are noted in the text.

PREDATOR mainly a carnivorous diet, which often includes other fish.

COMPATIBILITY
SINGLE SPECIMEN this usually means only one representative of any such species within a community collection. Some fishes won't tolerate a different species if it is of a similar shape or color.

COMMUNITY FISH may be kept in a mixed collection with due regard to any extremes of physical size between species being kept together.

SAFE WITH SMALL FISH large fish with a peaceful disposition toward smaller tank mates.

SAFE WITH INVERTEBRATES while this means that the fish isn't likely to eat the invertebrates, note that keeping fish and invertebrates together presents an additional problem; the copper-based remedies used to treat fish diseases successfully is lethal to invertebrates.

✋ EASE OF KEEPING
Indicated on a scale of 1 to 10, with 1 being the easiest.
1 to 3—the easiest species to care for.
5 to 8—extra care needed.
9 to 10—most difficult.

5 to 8—intermediate numbers indicate that the species requires special care (diet, water conditions, temperature adjustments, incompatibility, etc.) beyond those required for normal community collections.
9 to 10—you should carefully consider your reasons for wanting to keep any species with this high rating. Some species cannot be easily acclimated to aquarium life and some may be endangered through over-collection.

SIZE
The sizes given are for mature fish, but for very sound commercial reasons, the majority of aquarium-suitable species are caught (and transported) as juveniles. Increasingly more and more species are being captive-bred, but are still marketed as juveniles. The size attained in captivity is dependent upon the fishkeeper's skills and, of course, the conditions under which the species are kept. Therefore, definite figures on size in captivity are not possible and the information provided is for guidance only so that you can estimate the total number of species your aquarium may support

IN THE WILD indicates adult size (in inches and centimeters), of species in nature.

IN CAPTIVITY indicates size species may attain in captivity under ideal conditions, i.e., plenty of room, correct feeding, and optimum water conditions.

NOTE
Within each aquarium group the fish species are ordered alphabetically, first according to their biological family affiliation, then by species within each family.

ANEMONEFISHES AND DAMSELFISHES

The modestly proportioned members of this family are, without doubt, where every marine aquarist begins his or her collection. The fishes have several factors in their favor which set them apart from the rest.

First, they are hardy, readily available, and relatively inexpensive. Second, being of modest sizes you can accommodate more of them (providing some caution is exercised) in the aquarium and so your collection appears to build up quite quickly. Third, and this applies primarily to the anemonefishes, there is the fascination of watching a symbiotic (some say commensal) relationship exist before your very eyes as the anemonefish conforms to its description and enters into a joint existence with a sea

Pomacentrus caeruleus
BLUE DEVIL

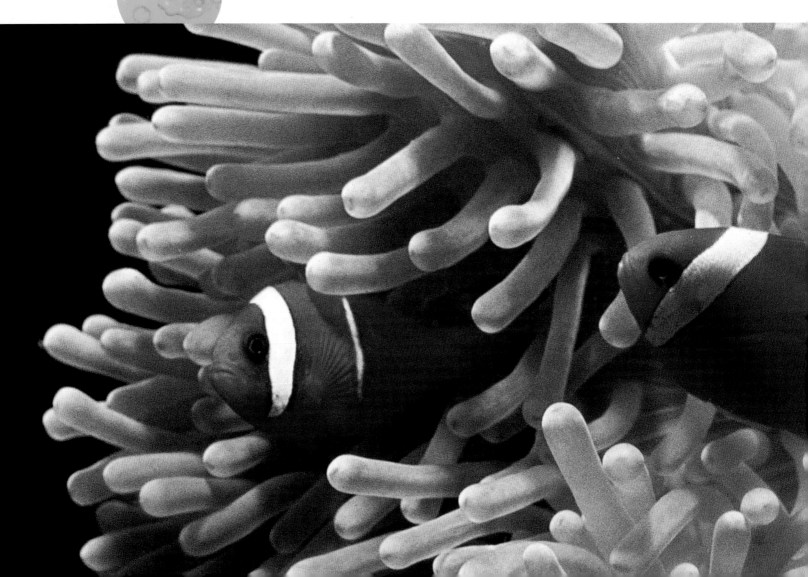

anemone. In recent years, clownfish, as anemonefishes are sometimes known, have been commercially-bred in increasing numbers. To be sure of getting damselfish off to a good start in your aquarium, it is recommended that you do not buy either the smallest or largest specimens, as the smallest often die off quickly while the largest can be the most difficult to acclimatize to captivity.

Being "nitrite-tolerant" fishes, they can be introduced into the newly set up aquarium earlier than most other genera and their waste products will supply "food" which biological filtration's nitrifying bacteria can utilize and so build up the filter's effectiveness that much faster.

Throughout the group you will find herbivores, omnivores, and planktivores. In nature these fish will be found at different levels of water depth, and near to the pertinent type of reef that supplies their needs most readily. Hence, planktivores are found near the surface to catch the drifting microscopic foods while the herbivores hang around algae encrusted outcrops in slightly deeper water. In both clownfishes and damselfishes breeding takes the form of egg depositing on hard surfaces and the subsequent guarding and fry care is very reminiscent of that of freshwater cichlids.

Dascyllus aruanus
HUMBUG

FEATURED IN THIS SECTION

TOMATO CLOWNFISH
Some Tomato Clownfishes "at home" in the reassuring safety of their sea anemone.

ANEMONEFISHES

Anemonefish are also known as "clownfish" because of their characteristic waddling swimming action. They have intimate contact with sea anemones within whose tentacles they frolic, seek refuge, and generally feel at home. The fish develops a mucus covering to its skin which appears to prevent the stinging cells of the sea anemone from "firing" due to the presence of something within its tentacles. This picture of symbiotic happiness is not common to all clownfish, as some do not seem to depend on a sea anemone as much as others. All anemonefishes begin life as males and remain so as long as a female is present in the host anemone. If the female is lost, the dominant male changes to a female and undergoes a spurt of growth. This adaptation assures that a female will always be present in an occupied anemone, the anemones being essential to the survival of the fish in the wild. A natural host anemone has been suggested for most species within this family, but keeping them can be extremely challenging and is not required for success with the fish.

AMPHIPRION AKALLOPISOS

FAMILY: *POMACENTRIDAE*
COMMON NAME: *SKUNK ANEMONEFISH*

Found in East Africa, Bali, India, and western Thailand, this fish has a slim body that is golden brown in color. The white line along the dorsal surface places this species within the "Skunk" group of clownfishes. The dorsal and caudal fins are white, while the pectoral, pelvic, and anal fins are the same color as the fish's body. An egg depositor, this species prefers the middle and lower levels of the aquarium.

SPECIAL CARE: This species requires high-quality water conditions with low levels of nitrogenous wastes (ammonia, nitrite, nitrate). Some coral retreats are needed and *Heteractis magnifica* or *Stichodactyla mertensii* sea anemones would be appropriate.

FEEDING

COMPATIBILITY

EASE OF KEEPING

3

SIZE

4.3 in (11 cm) 2.4 in (6 cm)

AMPHIPRION CLARKII

FAMILY: *POMACENTRIDAE*
COMMON NAME: *CLARK'S ANEMONEFISH*

This fish can be found in the Arabian Gulf, Fiji, Japan, Western Australia, the Great Barrier Reef, and New Caledonia. Its body coloration is dark brown, with the portion of the head in front of the eyes a bright yellow. It has three vertical white stripes: one between the eyes and the pectoral fins, another midway along the flanks, and one at the end of the caudal peduncle across the body. The caudal and pectoral fins are yellow, while the others are the same color as the body. The dorsal fin may have a yellow area at its rear. The fish can typically be found swimming in the middle and lower levels of the aquarium. It is an egg depositor, similar to freshwater cichlids.

SPECIAL CARE: High-quality water conditions with low levels of nitrogenous wastes (ammonia, nitrite, nitrate) are necessary. This fish also needs a number of coral retreats and its natural host anemones are *Cryptodendrum*, *Heteractis magnifica*, and *Stichodactyla mertensii*.

FEEDING

COMPATIBILITY

EASE OF KEEPING

3

SIZE

5 in (13 cm) 3 in (7.5 cm)

AMPHIPRION FRENATUS

FAMILY: *POMACENTRIDAE*
COMMON NAME: *TOMATO CLOWNFISH; BRIDLED CLOWNFISH; FIRE CLOWN*

This colorful fish is found in coral reefs around the Philippines and also in the western Pacific up to Japan. Omnivorous and peaceful, the fish has an oval body shape and a blunt-shaped head that tapers gently at the caudal peduncle; the dorsal and ventral contours are equally curved. Its body is a rich tomato red-brown, with a darker suffusion of color toward the rear end of the gill cover. A dark-edged white vertical bar runs behind the eyes and across the gill covers. It is not uncommon for juveniles to have two bars. The fins are rounded, and are the same color as the body. The dorsal fin is long and spiny. Females tend to be slightly larger than males. An egg depositor that is similar to freshwater cichlids, this fish tends to swim in the middle and lower levels of the aquarium.

SPECIAL CARE: High-quality water conditions with low levels of nitrogenous wastes (ammonia, nitrite, nitrate) are required. Some coral retreats are needed as well. It will eagerly eat live, frozen, vegetable, and flake foods. This species of clownfish is not as dependent upon the presence of a sea anemone as other member of this genus.

FEEDING

COMPATIBILITY

EASE OF KEEPING

3

SIZE

5.5 in (14 cm) 3 in (7.5 cm)

AMPHIPRION NIGRIPES

FAMILY: *POMACENTRIDAE*
COMMON NAME: *MALDIVES ANEMONEFISH*

Found in the Maldive Islands and Sri Lanka, this fish is yellow, with a vertical white band across its head. The Maldives Anemonefish is grouped by aquarists with the other "Skunk" anemonefishes, with whom it shares a vertical facial stripe. However, the dorsal surface lacks either a longitudinal stripe and any other white markings found in many of its near relatives. The pelvic and anal fins are dark brown-black. It prefers the middle and lower levels of the aquarium, and is an egg-depositor, similar to freshwater cichlids.

SPECIAL CARE: The species requires high-quality water conditions, with low levels of nitrogenous wastes (ammonia, nitrite, nitrate). It is also in need of some coral retreats and, if desired, a *Heteractis* sea anemone.

FEEDING

COMPATIBILITY

EASE OF KEEPING

3

SIZE

4.3 in (11 cm) 2.4 in (6 cm)

SYMBOL KEY
FEEDING
Herbivore
Omnivore
Predator
COMPATIBILITY
single specimen
community fish
safe with small fish
safe with invertebrates
EASE OF KEEPING
scale of 1 to 10 (with 1 being easiest to keep)
SIZE
in the wild
in captivity

AMPHIPRION OCELLARIS

FAMILY: *POMACENTRIDAE*
COMMON NAME: *COMMON CLOWNFISH*

FEEDING

COMPATIBILITY

EASE OF KEEPING
3

SIZE
4.3 in (11 cm) 2.4 in (6 cm)

Found widely throughout the Indian and Pacific oceans, from Sri Lanka to the Philippines and northern Australia, this omnivorous species is often confused with the similar-looking *Amphiprion percula*. It is perhaps the most widely available and inexpensive member of its genus. Its body shape is elongated and its head is blunt, with the dorsal and ventral contours equally curved. The fish is bright orange, with three black-edged white bands traversing its body: the first band follows the outline of the gill cover; the central band, with its forward-projecting point, runs from below the narrowest part of the dorsal fin, finishing between the pelvic and anal fins; the last band passes across the rear of the caudal peduncle. All of the fins are rounded, and are the same color as the body, with black outlines. The center of the eye is black.
SPECIAL CARE: A peaceful species, this fish prefers the middle and lower levels of the aquarium. It is an egg depositor, similar to freshwater cichlids.

AMPHIPRION PERCULA

FAMILY: *POMACENTRIDAE*
COMMON NAME: *PERCULA CLOWN*

Originating from Papua New Guinea, the Solomon Islands, and the Great Barrier Reef, this fish is often mistaken for the *Amphiprion ocellaris* (or the other way around), as the two species are remarkable similar. The best way to differentiate between them is to note the thickness of the black edges of the white areas—those of *Amphiprion percula* are much more defined. Typically found swimming at the middle and lower levels of the aquarium, this fish is an egg depositor, similar to freshwater cichlids.
SPECIAL CARE: High-quality water conditions with low levels of nitrogenous wastes (ammonia, nitrite, nitrate) are required for this fish. It prefers to have some coral retreats, as well as a number of *Heteractis magnifica* or *Stichodactyla gigantea* sea anemones.

FEEDING

COMPATIBILITY

EASE OF KEEPING
3

SIZE
4.3 in (11 cm) 2.4 in (6 cm)

PREMNAS BIACULEATUS

FAMILY: *POMACENTRIDAE*
COMMON NAME: *MAROON CLOWNFISH; SPINE-CHEEKED CLOWNFISH*

This species is the only one in the genus *Premnas*. Its classification has an interesting history. It had been re-classified back into *Amphiprion* at one time but currently it still retains its taxonomic exclusivity. It is found in the waters between Madagascar in the Indian Ocean to the Solomon Islands in the mid-Pacific by way of the Philippines and Queensland, Australia. The Maroon Clownfish is much more heavily-built than other species of clownfish. It has an oval body and rather a blunt head that tapers more gently at the caudal peduncle, with equally curved dorsal and ventral contours. The rich, dark, brown-red body is crossed vertically by three thin white stripes positioned similarly to those of *A. ocellaris*. A distinguishing feature of this species is the pair of large spines below the eyes (*Amphiprion* Clownfishes lack these but do have numerous tiny spines at the rear of the gill cover and more scales on the head). Although predominantly body-colored, the rounded fins may have some blacker areas inside their orange edges.
SPECIAL CARE: It may become aggressive if kept as a solitary species; keeping a number of differently-sized specimens may help to establish a more peaceful community. Its dependence on the sea anemone is not so strong as others in this family.

FEEDING

COMPATIBILITY

EASE OF KEEPING
3

SIZE
6.7 in (17 cm) 4.5 in (11.5 cm)

DAMSELFISHES

Damselfishes have a characteristic way of swimming, constantly bobbing up and down as though influenced by variations in water height above their heads, as they move between coral branches. Although gregarious, damselfish have a habit of being argumentative but this can be reduced by providing enough hiding places and retreats within the aquarium. Bullies ought to be removed and the introduction of one or two larger fish (of other genera) sometimes brings an overall peace to the aquarium. However, don't use very large fish that might look upon your damselfish as a potential meal.

SYMBOL KEY

FEEDING
Herbivore
Omnivore
Predator

COMPATIBILITY
single specimen
community fish
safe with small fish
safe with invertebrates

EASE OF KEEPING
scale of 1 to 10
(with 1 being easiest to keep)

SIZE
in the wild
in captivity

ABUDEFDUF SAXATILIS

FAMILY: *POMACENTRIDAE*
COMMON NAME: *SERGEANT MAJOR*

This fish is found in the tropical waters of the Caribbean and western Atlantic. It is interesting to note that a corresponding, almost identical species (*A. troschelii*) lives in the Pacific. Its body is deep with a highly-arched dorsal profile matched by the ventral contour. Its yellowish-blue body has well-defined scales and is crossed vertically with five complete dark bands; a sixth band may just be visible at the top and bottom of the caudal peduncle. The anal, pelvic, and pectoral fins are white and the dorsal and caudal fins have some darkish coloration. Generally this fish is not as brightly colored as some of its neighbors.

FEEDING

COMPATIBILITY

EASE OF KEEPING

SIZE

6 in (15 cm)   4 in (10 cm)

SPECIAL CARE: This is a shoaling species that is peaceful when juvenile but becomes increasingly territorial with age and when spawning. If a number are to be kept together they will need a large aquarium in which they will swim at the middle and upper levels. It is important that high-quality water conditions are maintained with low levels of nitrogenous wastes (ammonia, nitrite, nitrate). Create some coral retreats and ensure that there is a little algal growth

CHROMIS CYANEA

FAMILY: *POMACENTRIDAE*
COMMON NAME: *BLUE CHROMIS; BLUE REEF FISH*

Found in shoals in clear, open waters near coral reefs, where it snatches plankton from the water, it is the most commonly imported member of its family from the Atlantic–Caribbean region. Adults and juveniles are bright blue, with jet black on the dorsal surface. The outer margins of the caudal fin are edged in black. The dorsal, anal, and pelvic fins are electric blue, while the pectoral fins are colorless.
SPECIAL CARE: Provide this fish with a roomy tank with perfect water conditions, and keep a group of at least three specimens together. Feed live brine shrimp, frozen brine shrimp, brine shrimp *nauplii*, and as wide a variety of other plankton substitutes as the fish will accept. An inability to provide a continuous supply of suitable foods has led to unnecessary failures with this species. It is as hardy as any solitary damselfish, provided its special needs are met.

FEEDING

COMPATIBILITY

EASE OF KEEPING

SIZE

4.7 in (12 cm)   3.2 in (8 cm)

CHROMIS IOMELAS

FAMILY: *POMACENTRIDAE*
COMMON NAME: *BICOLOR CHROMIS*

Endemic to the Red Sea, this lovely chromis should be kept in a school of five or more. It looks for all the world as if a pale yellow fish has been dipped head first into black paint. The first dorsal and the paired fins are black, while the second dorsal, anal, and caudal fins match the body color. It is nonaggressive, feeding on plankton in mid-water from the safety of a vast shoal of its own kind.

FEEDING

COMPATIBILITY

EASE OF KEEPING

SIZE

3.2 in (8 cm) 3.2 in (8 cm)

SPECIAL CARE: A large tank with ample filtration is best. Reef conditions suit most *Chromis* species, and this one is no exception. Feed any plankton substitute available, always remembering to vary the diet to ensure adequate nutrition. Invertebrates are ignored. Avoid keeping it with aggressive species, such as triggers or lionfish, which might regard the *Chromis* as dinner. It is perhaps exhibited to best advantage in a species tank. Brilliant illumination, as is required for living corals, shows off its coloration to perfection.

CHROMIS SCOTTI

FAMILY: *POMACENTRIDAE*
COMMON NAME: *PURPLE REEF FISH*

Although the bright electric blue juveniles are most commonly imported, adults are colorful, too, an eye-catching cerulean blue all over. Juveniles have a brilliant blue "V" on the snout, and a similarly gaudy crescent above each eye. Both of these features disappear as the fish matures. This is an uncommonly seen species, because it spends its time in waters as deep as 100 ft (30 m) huddled near the bottom in small shoals.

SPECIAL CARE: Damselfishes are hardy and tolerant of suboptimal conditions, but nevertheless should be given clean, high-quality water with ample filtration. Keeping a small group together will mimic the social situation to which these fishes are accustomed, and enhance success in maintaining them. Many members of the damselfish family have been successfully spawned and reared by aquarists. Mixing damselfish species in the same aquarium is likely to result in territorial squabbles, unless the tank is very large.

FEEDING

COMPATIBILITY

EASE OF KEEPING

SIZE

4 in (10 cm) 3.2 in (8 cm)

CHRYSIPTERA PARASEMA

FAMILY: *POMACENTRIDAE*
COMMON NAME: *YELLOW-TAILED DAMSELFISH*

This attractive fish is widespread throughout the Indo-Pacific and the Red Sea where it congregates around coral heads, feeding on drifting plankton and algae. It has an elongated body with a slightly-arched dorsal profile matching that of the ventral contour. It is brilliant blue in color with dark-centered scales. A few dark lines cover the head and cross the large eyes. The caudal peduncle, together with the majority of the caudal fin itself, is bright yellow and this color encroaches a short distance on the body above the anal fin. The rear portions of the dorsal, anal, and caudal fins are uncolored. This fish is also referred to as *Glyphidodontops hemicyaneus*.

SPECIAL CARE: This fish will be content in an aquarium where the water conditions are carefully maintained—they should be high-quality with low levels of nitrogenous wastes. Create some coral retreats and ensure there is a little algal growth so as to mimic its natural environment. At times this fish can display territorial behavior.

FEEDING

COMPATIBILITY

EASE OF KEEPING
3

SIZE
2.8 in (7 cm) 2 in (5 cm)

DASCYLLUS ARUANUS

FAMILY: *POMACENTRIDAE*
COMMON NAME: *HUMBUG; WHITE-TAILED DAMSELFISH; THREE-STRIPED DAMSELFISH*

The Humbug is a hardy species and is an ideal choice for the beginner aquarist. It originates from the Indo-Pacific oceans, including the Red Sea, but it is worth noting that it is not found in Hawaii. Its body form is stocky with the forehead rising relatively steeply. Basically it is a black and white fish, with each color almost equally represented. The first black stripe runs from the mouth over the forehead into the first rays of the dorsal fin, continuing along both the dorsal fin and the top of the body. The next stripe begins level with (and including) the pelvic fins and crosses the body at a slight angle to reach the dorsal fin. The final band includes the rear part of the anal fin, the front-half of the caudal peduncle, and the rear of the dorsal fin.

SPECIAL CARE: Although it can be quarrelsome with its own species and somewhat territorially-minded in the aquarium, a roomy aquarium with many retreats should help to keep the number of skirmishes to a minimum. As with other species in this family, it requires high-quality water conditions.

FEEDING

COMPATIBILITY

EASE OF KEEPING
3

SIZE
3.2 in (8 cm) 2 in (5 cm)

SYMBOL KEY

FEEDING
Herbivore
Omnivore
Predator

COMPATIBILITY
single specimen
community fish
safe with small fish
safe with invertebrates

EASE OF KEEPING
scale of 1 to 10
(with 1 being easiest to keep)

SIZE
in the wild
in captivity

DASCYLLUS CARNEUS

FAMILY: *POMACENTRIDAE*
COMMON NAME: *CLOUDY DAMSEL*

This fish has a stocky, rather deep body, with a steeply-rising forehead typical of the family. Although its body coloration is quite recognizable in pattern, it is not so contrasting in colors as other members. The body varies from cream to velvety black-brown, spotted with blue, with an ill-defined white blotch on the upper part, just beneath the dorsal fin. An indistinct black stripe separates the creamy brown head area (again spotted with blue) from the main body. All of the fins are black, with the rear edge of the dorsal fin slightly clear with a blue edge, with the exception of the caudal fin which is white. Some literature shows this fish with a vertical dark stripe connecting the dorsal and anal fins on the rear part of the body. It is this coloration which has led to some confusion with another similar-patterned species, *D. reticulatus* that has less black in the dorsal and anal fins. This fish is native to the stretch of water from East Africa to the Maldives, the Andaman Sea, and the waters surrounding Java.

FEEDING

COMPATIBILITY

EASE OF KEEPING

SIZE

2.4 in (6 cm) 2 in (5 cm)

SPECIAL CARE: Like many of the genus, the Cloudy Damsel may quarrel with its own kind but it is generally peaceful toward nonrelated species and is therefore suitable for a community collection.

DASCYLLUS MELANURUS

FAMILY: *POMACENTRIDAE*
COMMON NAME: *BLACK-TAILED HUMBUG*

The Black-Tailed Humbug is very similar in appearance to the previously-described Humbug (*D. aruanus*), with its white body covered by three equally-spaced black stripes. The positive identifying feature, as the common name suggests, is that this species has a black area on the caudal fin, almost making up a fourth "stripe," in comparison with the plain white caudal fin of the Humbug.

SPECIAL CARE: Like most of the genus, in its natural habitat of the western Pacific Ocean (again, this does not include Hawaii) this fish is never far away from coral heads and any other handy hiding places. The aquarium should be furnished to mimic its natural environment. It is suitable to be kept with a community collection of fishes.

FEEDING

COMPATIBILITY

EASE OF KEEPING

SIZE

3.2 in (8 cm) 2.4 in (6 cm)

SYMBOL KEY

FEEDING

Herbivore

Omnivore

Predator

COMPATIBILITY

single specimen

community fish

safe with small fish

safe with invertebrates

EASE OF KEEPING

scale of 1 to 10

(with 1 being easiest to keep)

SIZE

in the wild ▶

in captivity ▶

DASCYLLUS TRIMACULATUS

FAMILY: *POMACENTRIDAE*
COMMON NAME: *DOMINO DAMSELFISH*

The only parts of this fish that aren't black are the rearmost part of the dorsal fin and the outer edges of the anal and caudal fins. What gives this fish its popular name are the three white spots on its body—one on each side, halfway along the base of the dorsal fin and one centrally-placed on the forehead. Two things affect the coloration—discontentment with its conditions may make the blackness fade and old age may have the same effect upon the white spots. A small consolation is that should the colors fade the scales are dark-edged and so become more visible, giving the fish a net-covered appearance. It is found throughout the Indo-Pacific oceans and the Red Sea.

FEEDING

COMPATIBILITY

EASE OF KEEPING

SIZE

5.5 in (14 cm) 4 in (10 cm)

SPECIAL CARE: Although this fish can sometimes be boisterous, it is easy to keep. It usually leads the rush for food, even to the extent of snatching it away from others in the process. Maintain high-quality water conditions in the aquarium with low levels of nitrogenous wastes. Furnish the tank to resemble its natural environment.

HYPSYPOPS RUBICUNDUS

FAMILY: *POMACENTRIDAE*
COMMON NAME: *GARIBALDI DAMSELFISH*

Although this fish turns up all the time in the company of tropical species from both the Indo-Pacific and Atlantic-Caribbean regions, it is actually from the cold waters of the Pacific coast of California, where it inhabits kelp forests. The large size, bright orange coloration and apparent adaptability to captive conditions have combined to result in a constant low level of importation despite its protected status in many areas. Aquarists report that the fish does not survive beyond a few months in a tropical tank.

SPECIAL CARE: Because this fish is not a resident of coral reefs, it is a totally inappropriate choice for combining with the other marine species mentioned in this book. Aquarists unable to resist the temptation to purchase one of these animals should provide a tank of at least 100 gallons (378 liters), a maximum temperature of 70°F (21°C), and décor appropriate to the kelp forest. This is definitely not a species for beginners.

FEEDING

COMPATIBILITY

EASE OF KEEPING

SIZE

10 in (25 cm) 6 in (15 cm)

MICROSPATHODON CHRYSURUS

FAMILY: *POMACENTRIDAE*
COMMON NAME: *JEWEL FISH; YELLOWTAILED DAMSEL*

The deep, stocky shape of this fish is typical of the Pomacentridae family. Its body color changes as the fish ages from juvenile to adult. Juveniles are dark blue-black with a covering of bright blue spots; the caudal fin is colorless. The dorsal, anal, and pelvic fins are dark blue with light blue edging. The adult fish loses the body spots but makes up for it by developing a vivid yellow caudal fin. During spawning, the adult male may lose color while that of the female deepens. This fish is native to the Caribbean and the tropical waters of the western Atlantic.

SPECIAL CARE: This fish cruises the middle and upper levels of the aquarium and enjoys retreating to shady coral areas. Provide some algal growth.

FEEDING

COMPATIBILITY

EASE OF KEEPING
3

SIZE
8.3 in (21 cm) 6 in (15 cm)

POMACENTRUS CAERULEUS

FAMILY: *POMACENTRIDAE*
COMMON NAME: *BLUE DEVIL*

Positive identification of this fish, which is widespread throughout the Indo-Pacific region, is often problematic. Fishes with more (or less) darker spots, for instance, may be no more than local variants of a single species; some may develop more yellow coloring in later life. Other generic names offered include *Eupomacentrus* and *Glyphidodontops*, while the alternative specific names of *cyaneus* and *coelestis* only add more confusion to the debate. Its elongated body has only a shallow curvature to the dorsal and ventral contours. The brilliant blue of the body is divided with a black line from the snout crossing the eyes and each scale has a central mark. A small black blotch appears at the base of the soft portion of the long-based dorsal fin. The caudal fin and the rearmost areas of the dorsal and anal fins are clear.

SPECIAL CARE: Observe the same guidelines for keeping this fish as for other members of this family. Note that this species can often be territorial.

FEEDING

COMPATIBILITY

EASE OF KEEPING
3

SIZE
3.2 in (8 cm) 2.4 in (6 cm)

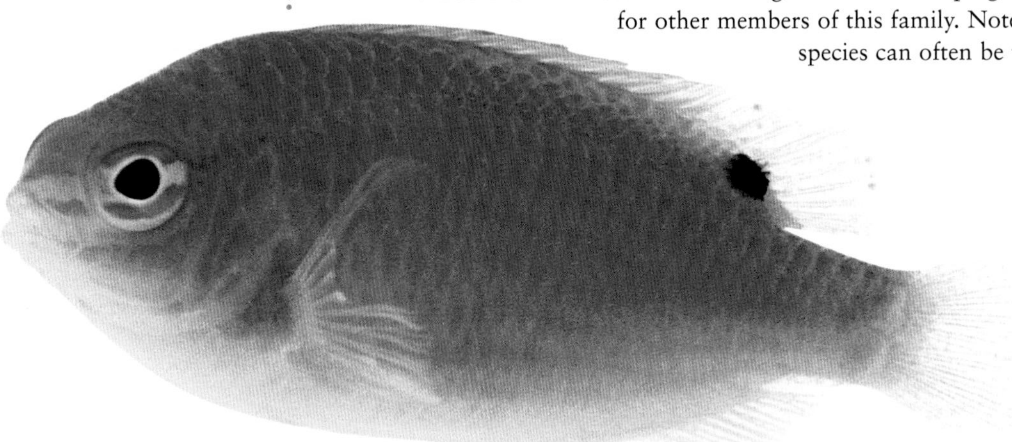

STEGASTES PLANIFRONS

FAMILY: *POMACENTRIDAE*
COMMON NAME: *ORANGE DAMSELFISH; THREESPOT DAMSELFISH*

Formerly scientifically-known as *"Eupomacentrus planifrons,"* this fish's body shape is slightly more elongated than most damsels. Its yellow body is marked with three spots; one appears just below the dorsal fin, one on the top of the caudal peduncle, and one at the base of the pectoral fin. The body spots may vary in size with age, getting larger in the adult. The young fish is very similar to the Honey Gregory (*E. mellis*) but lacks the blue facial lines of that species. The eyes have a black center and all of the fins are plain yellow. It is endemic to the Caribbean and the western Atlantic Ocean.

SPECIAL CARE: Set up the aquarium as described for all of the fishes in this family. This species is rather aggressive (especially when adult) toward others venturing into its territory. Juveniles tend to be more passive.

FEEDING

COMPATIBILITY

EASE OF KEEPING
3

SIZE

4.9 in (12.5 cm) 3 in (7.5 cm)

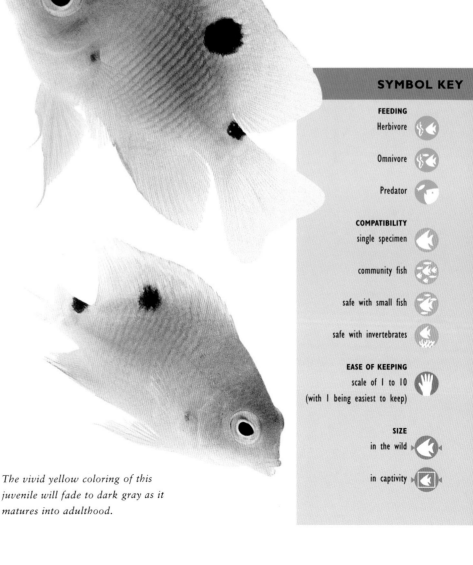

The vivid yellow coloring of this juvenile will fade to dark gray as it matures into adulthood.

STEGASTES LEUCOSTICTUS

FAMILY: *POMACENTRIDAE*
COMMON NAME: *BEAU GREGORY*

Common in Florida and the Caribbean, this damselfish ranges from Maine to Brazil. As a juvenile it has a dark blue crown marked with bright blue dots extending to about the level of the eye, as far back as the middle of the dorsal fin. Below this, the crown breaks into blue dots scattered on the otherwise sulfur yellow body. The fins are also yellow. By the time the fish reaches adulthood, the bright colors are lost and it is olive brown with a few specks of yellow here and there on the body and fins.

SPECIAL CARE: Among the hardiest and most durable of marine fishes, adults can become so aggressive as to require a small tank to themselves. Apart from typical marine tank conditions, provide it with a rock, coral head, or other structure around which it will establish and defend a territory. Invertebrates are not suitable as food, as they are ignored. This would be a good choice for a tank depicting the inshore environment of the Florida Keys, with only invertebrates as its tank mates. Feed any marine food of suitable size. Algae will also be cropped from the tank decorations.

FEEDING

COMPATIBILITY

EASE OF KEEPING
3

SIZE
4.2 in (10 cm) 3.2 in (8 cm)

SYMBOL KEY

FEEDING
Herbivore

Omnivore

Predator

COMPATIBILITY
single specimen

community fish

safe with small fish

safe with invertebrates

EASE OF KEEPING
scale of 1 to 10
(with 1 being easiest to keep)

SIZE
in the wild

in captivity

ANGELFISHES

Recognizing a member of this family is relatively easy due to the characteristic stout, sharp spine that extends backward from the rear of the gill cover. While distributed worldwide throughout tropical seas, the allocation is disproportionate.

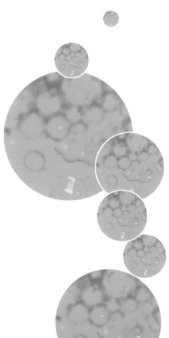

Centropyge eibli
EIBL'S ANGELFISH

The majority of species are found in the western Pacific Ocean, with fewer in the Atlantic, and even fewer in the eastern Pacific. Their physical size varies from the small, ideally-suited-to-aquarium-life fishes, to those whose bulk may mean they are considered as food fishes.

In nature, angelfish tend to be quite independent usually cruising around alone. Sometimes a pair will be seen together, but you will never see a school of angelfish. This leads the fish to feel very confident about its role in life and this often translates into aggressiveness toward other fish. In the aquarium it likes to be boss, a position it may adopt if it is one of the first species introduced into a brand new tank. Putting an angelfish into an already well-established aquarium where the pecking order has already been decided may lessen its antisocial behavior, but it really depends upon the

circumstances it finds itself in, for example the size of the aquarium and the number of retreats.

As angelfish feed on benthic invertebrates and seaweeds, living corals and sponges will not survive in their presence. Feeding the more exotic species may be problematic because of the lack of availability of appropriate foods, however manufacturers have now started producing them. A proportion of green matter is important too, so algae should not be discouraged in the aquarium. Should a fish refuse to eat at first, offer it a wide variety of seafood (shellfish, shrimp, etc.) to get it feeding as quickly as possible.

Despite their sturdy proportions, which are reminiscent of freshwater cichlids, angelfish do not share their breeding habits. They are egg scatterers. The eggs are expelled and fertilized at the water's surface—after a spiraling, rising chase up through the water—to drift away on the currents. No parental care is exercised and the spawning pair soon part and go their separate ways. Egg scattering is unlikely to occur in the average size aquarium because the fishes may not have reached full maturity or because there is not enough space.

Pomacanthus paru
FRENCH ANGELFISH

FEATURED IN THIS SECTION

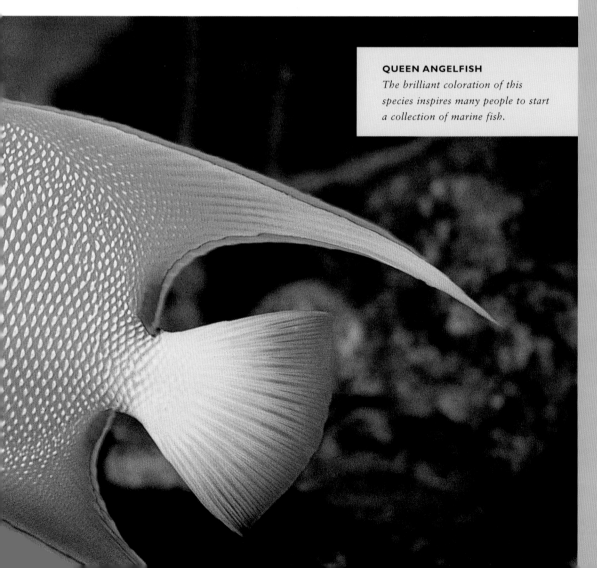

QUEEN ANGELFISH
The brilliant coloration of this species inspires many people to start a collection of marine fish.

CENTROPYGE ARGI

FAMILY: *POMACANTHIDAE*
COMMON NAME: *CHERUBFISH; PURPLE FIREBALL; PYGMY ANGELFISH*

It is not surprising that several commercial names have been coined for this fish as it can vary dramatically in color. Generally the body color is a deep rich blue over which are sprinkled dark dots. The long-based dorsal and anal fins share the basic coloration and have black streaks radiating outward until a dark margin is reached just before an electric blue edging. The pelvic fins are similarly marked. The caudal fin has lighter-blue top and bottom edges but the rearmost edge lacks the paler shade. The coloring of the head and throat region will include shades from yellow to golden purple. The yellow-gold eyes are ringed with the deep blue of the body and the spine on the operculum is also blue. Sexual differences are unknown but it is not unusual for the fish to choose their own partners by a process of natural pairing. In the western Atlantic Ocean these fish live at depths of 95 feet (29 m) or more, in regions where there is plenty of rubble and debris in which it can hide It is also found in the tropical waters of the Caribbean, and in contrast, here it can be found in shallower waters swimming in and out of corals. When purchasing look for two that appear to be inseparable in the tank.

SPECIAL CARE: This fish is hardy, requiring a modest-sized aquarium with plenty of algae-covered retreats. The water should be well-oxygenated with a moderate water current. This species is an egg scatterer but this is unlikely to occur in the average-sized aquarium.

FEEDING

COMPATIBILITY

EASE OF KEEPING

4

SIZE

3.2 in (8 cm) 3.2 in (8 cm)

CENTROPYGE AURANTOPS

FAMILY: *POMACANTHIDAE*
COMMON NAME: *FLAMEBACK DWARF ANGELFISH*

Like its cousin the Pygmy Angelfish, *C. argi*, this species is hardy, undemanding, and easily maintained in a small marine tank. It is much less common, however, being only seen occasionally around the southeastern islands of the Caribbean. It therefore commands a higher price in aquarium shops. The body is dark iridescent blue. The bright yellow to orange coloration of the face and nape continues along the dorsal surface to just anterior to the caudal peduncle.

SPECIAL CARE: This splendid Dwarf Angel should be given a tank to itself, ideally with two or three individuals of the same size. The fish will form a natural harem, and the aquarist may be treated to the almost daily spawning activity, provided they are in prime condition. This can be achieved by maintaining perfect water conditions, and by feeding a varied diet. This species consumes a large amount of filamentous algae, which can be encouraged to grow in the tank.

FEEDING

COMPATIBILITY

EASE OF KEEPING

3

SIZE

3.2 in (8 cm) 2 in (5 cm)

CENTROPYGE BISPINOSUS

FAMILY: *POMACANTHIDAE*
COMMON NAME: *CORAL BEAUTY; DUSKY ANGELFISH; RED AND BLUE ANGELFISH*

This fish has variable coloration patterns which are usually determined by the geographical area in which it is found. Generally, it is a deep blue-purple over which a red-gold oval shape has been laid, and both are then further covered by a number of vertical dark bars and speckles. The long-based dorsal, anal, and caudal fins are dark, patterned with blue, with light blue edgings. The pectoral fins are plain yellow, the pelvic fins bright yellow-orange. The head is blue-purple with dark-ringed eyes, the throat region beneath the gills is the red-gold color which then merges into the main background on the vertically striped flanks. The spine on the operculum is blue. Young fish have more blue-purple coloration than gold, but as the fish becomes older these dark areas fade giving a much brighter color. Specimens have even been seen that lack the vertical stripes. This fish can be found in places as far apart as east Africa to the East Indies, Australasia to the mid-Pacific. One interesting difference to note, that appears to be related to geography, is that specimens from the Philippines have more red in their coloring than those from the Great Barrier Reef.

SPECIAL CARE: This species does tend to be a little shy and spends much of its time in the lower levels of the aquarium where it will appreciate lots of retreats. For general care and breeding information see *C. argi* on page 152.

FEEDING

COMPATIBILITY

EASE OF KEEPING

4

SIZE

4 in (10 cm)   4 in (10 cm)

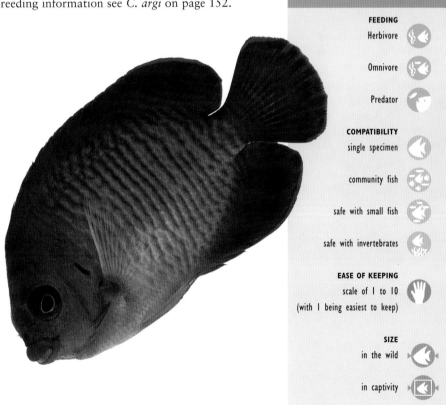

CENTROPYGE BICOLOR

FAMILY: *POMACANTHIDAE*
COMMON NAME: *BICOLOR CHERUB; BLUE AND GOLD ANGEL; ORIOLE ANGEL*

This striking fish is endemic to coral reefs from the East Indies to Samoa and it is also widespread in the western Pacific Ocean. The deep blue rear portion of the body appears to have a pattern superimposed on it; this is due to the scales having lighter-colored rear edges. This dark area is separated from the bright yellow forward portion of the fish (and the similarly-colored caudal fin) by narrow bands of white which vertically cross the body, one at the end of the caudal peduncle and one from within the dorsal fin down to a point midway between the anal and pelvic fins. A small band of blue crosses the forehead and ends at the eyes on either side of the head. The dorsal fin is dark and flecked blue for most of its length, but the first few rays, together with its outer edge, are the same bright yellow as the head. A thin strip of pale blue runs along the edge of the dark-flecked deep blue anal fin.

SPECIAL CARE: For general care and breeding information see *C. argi* on page 152. However, this species is less hardy and is especially susceptible to any remedial treatments containing copper, which should be used with care. In a group containing a male and several females, a female will change sex to replace the male if he dies or is otherwise removed.

FEEDING

COMPATIBILITY

EASE OF KEEPING

6

SIZE

6 in (15 cm)   6 in (15 cm)

SYMBOL KEY

FEEDING
Herbivore
Omnivore
Predator

COMPATIBILITY
single specimen
community fish
safe with small fish
safe with invertebrates

EASE OF KEEPING
scale of 1 to 10
(with 1 being easiest to keep)

SIZE
in the wild
in captivity

CENTROPYGE EIBLI

FAMILY: *POMACANTHIDAE*
COMMON NAME: *EIBL'S ANGELFISH*

This fish is found in deep water from the Maldive Islands, Australia, Indonesia, and the mid-Pacific Ocean. The majority of the body area is colored gray-gold and covered vertically with evenly-spaced wavy lines. These lines are red-gold at the front of the body but gradually change to gold-black toward the rear where they match the black rear portion of the long-based dorsal fin, caudal peduncle, and caudal fin. Depending upon where the fish is found, the dorsal, anal, and caudal fins may have gold or pale blue edgings. The pectoral and pelvic fins are yellow. Some gold flecks appear on the blue-green anal fin and also in the dorsal fin where they too change to a darker color nearer to the rear of the fin. The eyes are ringed with three concentric circles, first gold, then blue then gold again. The juvenile form of *Acanthurus pyroferus*, the Orange-Gilled Surgeonfish, mimics the appearance and behavior of this species.

SPECIAL CARE: For general care and breeding information see *C. argi* on page 152.

FEEDING

COMPATIBILITY

EASE OF KEEPING

4

SIZE

6 in (15 cm) 4 in (10 cm)

HOLACANTHUS CILIARIS

FAMILY: *POMACANTHIDAE*
COMMON NAME: *QUEEN ANGELFISH*

The simplest color characteristic and one that is common to both juveniles and adults is that the whole body is outlined in bright blue with the exception of the plain yellow caudal fin. This overall ground color can be changeable depending upon lighting conditions (and also to unknown hybridization between similar species). The rear edge of the gills and the base of the pectoral fins are bright blue; a small dark circular patch on the forehead is also ringed with bright blue. The opercular spine is blue and there are several extra small spines on the gill cover itself. The body coloration extends into both the anal and dorsal fins; these two fins are extremely well-produced and sweep back well past the edge of the caudal fin. Juvenile specimens have dark blue bodies crossed by vertical light blue lines; the snout, pectoral fin area, and caudal fin are yellow-orange. The juveniles often act as cleanerfishes to larger species. These fish, often found in pairs, live among the coral reefs of the Caribbean and the western Atlantic.

SPECIAL CARE: Caribbean fishes are native to waters of slightly higher specific gravity than Indo-Pacific fishes and may need careful acclimatization to aquarium water conditions. This species is usually hardy and will respond to copper-based remedial treatments well. It requires plenty of swimming space in well-oxygenated water with a strong current, as well as many retreats.

FEEDING

COMPATIBILITY

EASE OF KEEPING

4

SIZE

17.5 in (45 cm) 12 in (30 cm)

HOLACANTHUS TRICOLOR

FAMILY: *POMACANTHIDAE*
COMMON NAME: *ROCK BEAUTY*

Frequently exhibited by large public aquariums, this species is nevertheless challenging for the home hobbyist. It is rather common in the Caribbean; despite being found from Brazil as far north as Georgia, it is not abundant outside the center of its range. Juveniles are yellow-orange with a black spot on the flank. In the youngest specimens, the spot is ringed in bright blue. As the fish matures, the spot enlarges to encompass the entire posterior two-thirds of the body, and most of the dorsal and anal fins. The latter remains edged in yellow and the caudal fin completely yellow. The lips, in some individuals, are blue.

SPECIAL CARE: Perfect marine tank water quality, a regular routine of maintenance, and a varied, appropriate diet are essential for success. This species cannot be recommended to any but the most experienced and dedicated aquarists who can provide for its demanding requirements. Juveniles eat a large proportion of algae, mixed with benthic invertebrates. Adults feed mostly upon benthic invertebrates, especially sponges. It is possible that dietary specialization limits the ability of this species to adapt readily to aquarium life.

FEEDING

COMPATIBILITY

EASE OF KEEPING
10

SIZE
12 in (30 cm) 6 in (15 cm)

POMACANTHUS ANNULARIS

FAMILY: *POMACANTHIDAE*
COMMON NAME: *BLUE RING ANGELFISH*

Juveniles of this species have the basic patterning of dark blue with white markings, a characteristic shared with juveniles of other angelfish species. In this fish the markings take the form of alternate thin and thick, equally-spaced white lines running vertically downward across the body, and slanting backward into the blue dorsal and anal fins, whose outlines are pale blue. The caudal fin is barely colored but may have a few pale spots. Identification of juveniles may be confusing as this species is very similar to the juvenile *P. chrysurus*. The differentiating factor however, is the color of the caudal fin which is yellow, in that species. The adult fish is golden brown with royal blue lines running diagonally across the body from behind the gill cover; two more blue lines run backward horizontally above the mouth, the upper one passing through the eyes, to terminate at the base of the pectoral fin. The lower lip and the lower half of the gill cover are gray, the gill spine is blue. The caudal fin is white with a thin yellow rear edging. The common name is derived from the blue ring marking on the shoulder just above and to the rear of the gill cover. This fish is found in the stretch of water from Sri Lanka in the Indian Ocean to the Solomon Islands in the western edges of the Pacific.

SPECIAL CARE: Keep this angelfish in a spacious aquarium furnished with plenty of algae-covered retreats. The water should be well-oxygenated and have a strong current. The fish grazes on algae but will accept live and prepared foods once recognized. This fish can be territorial. This species is an egg scatterer, but this is unlikey to occur in an average size aquarium.

FEEDING

COMPATIBILITY

EASE OF KEEPING
4

SIZE
17.5 in (45 cm) 12 in (30 cm)

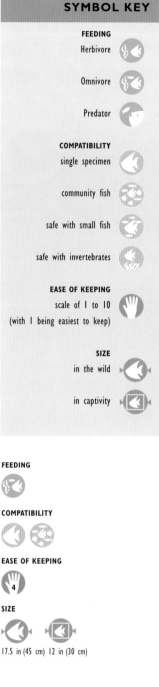

SYMBOL KEY

FEEDING
Herbivore

Omnivore

Predator

COMPATIBILITY
single specimen

community fish

safe with small fish

safe with invertebrates

EASE OF KEEPING
scale of 1 to 10
(with 1 being easiest to keep)

SIZE
in the wild

in captivity

A juvenile Emperor Angelfish.

POMACANTHUS IMPERATOR

FAMILY: *POMACANTHIDAE*
COMMON NAME: *EMPEROR ANGELFISH*

The young fish is dark blue with concentric, slightly oval-patterned white markings on the body rearward of the gill cover. Forward of this point, the lines are almost vertical with only a slight sweep-back in their pattern. The anal, dorsal, and caudal fins are marked with dark flecking, the outer edge of the dorsal fin is white while that of the caudal is colorless. The adult form has a plain yellow caudal fin and the yellow body is crossed diagonally by many light blue lines extending into the dorsal fin, which becomes pointed in mature fishes. The anal fin retains the dark blue of the juvenile and is marked with lighter blue lines. A dark patch spreads upward from beneath the pectoral fins to separate the main body pattern from a blue-edged plain yellow forehead and cheeks. The eyes are hidden within another dark band but the mouth area is blue-gray, again edged with light blue, a color repeated in the opercular spine. The pelvic fins carry some red color among their basic blue. The natural habitat of this fish is the Indo-Pacific region from the East African coast (including the Red Sea) to Hawaii, via Australia however, it is not found in abundant numbers anywhere.

SPECIAL CARE: To keep this species from juvenile to adult, the aquarium's swimming space and furnishings must be adequate to accommodate the needs of a fish that grows to a large size. Ensure there are plenty of algae-covered retreats and that the water is well-oxygenated and has a strong current.

FEEDING

COMPATIBILITY

EASE OF KEEPING

4

SIZE

16 in (40 cm) 12 in (30 cm)

POMACANTHUS MACULOSUS

FAMILY: *POMACANTHIDAE*
COMMON NAME: *HALF MOON ANGELFISH; PURPLE MOON ANGELFISH; RED SEA HALF-MOON ANGELFISH; SEABRIDE; YELLOWBAR ANGELFISH*

FEEDING

COMPATIBILITY

EASE OF KEEPING

6

SIZE

20 in (50 cm) 16 in (40 cm)

Juveniles have the standard angelfish coloration—a dark blue body with transverse white lines, but take on the "new moon" crescent-shape yellow marking of the adult before the white lines fade away with approaching maturity. The adult fish is a purple-gray with some darker speckling, particularly around the rear of the head and forehead above the gill covers.

A curved yellow arc appears across the mid-point of the body, extending upward and rearward into the dorsal fin but stopping short of the anal fin. The pectoral, pelvic, anal, and dorsal fins are the same color as the body but the caudal fin is yellow. The dorsal and anal fins sweep back more with increasing age and often have extended filaments at their extremities. This fish is found naturally in the Red Sea and the east African coast of the Indian Ocean. Blessed with several alternative popular names, this species is similar in coloration to *Arusetta asfur*, but in this fish the yellow marking is shorter, more vertical, and ends ahead of the anal fin.

SPECIAL CARE: This territorial fish will swim at all levels of the aquarium. For care information see *P. imperator*.

Left: This fish still has the white markings of juvenility.

POMACANTHUS PARU

FAMILY: *POMACANTHIDAE*
COMMON NAME: *FRENCH ANGELFISH*

This fish is endemic to Florida, the Caribbean, and the tropical western Atlantic Ocean as far south as Brazil. Young fish, which tend to inhabit shallower waters, are plain black with four or five thin yellow vertical stripes, their caudal fin may also be outlined in yellow. As adulthood approaches, the yellow bands fade and the fish takes on an overall dark gray color although the majority of the body to the rear of the gill covers is speckled thanks to the yellow-white edges of the scales. Limited speckling extends into the anal fin but much more appears in the dorsal fin, which often has a light colored tip to the extension found in mature adults. The eyes have a yellow surround while the forehead, cheeks, and mouth are light gray. The throat and pelvic regions, including the pelvic fins themselves, are black. The adult fish looks very similar to the Gray Angelfish, *P. arcuatus*, but has more "sparkle," a distinct yellow patch at the base of the pectoral fins, and generally frequents deeper water.

SPECIAL CARE: Young specimens may quarrel among themselves in the aquarium, but generally this fish is suitable to keep as part of a community. It should be kept in a spacious aquarium, with well-oxygenated water that has a strong current and some algal growth.

FEEDING

COMPATIBILITY

EASE OF KEEPING

6

SIZE

12 in (30 cm) 10 in (25 cm)

POMACANTHUS SEMICIRCULATUS

FAMILY: *POMACANTHIDAE*
COMMON NAME: *KORAN ANGELFISH*

The young fish has a dark blue-brown body covered by thin white lines; these lines are based on a semicircular pattern that radiates from a center on the rear end of the caudal peduncle. Closer to the head, the lines gradually become straighter and veer more toward the vertical. Lighter blue wavy lines appear on the rear parts of the dorsal and anal fins; some white lines appear on the caudal fin. During the juvenile-adult transitional phase the white lines gradually fade and the caudal fin attains a patterning of blue lines that are said to approximate Arabic writing characters, especially those found in the Koran, hence the fish's popular name. Adult fishes are more drab with the one-color background (a green-brown-blue color) being covered with dark spots. From the front edge of the dorsal fin, right around to the beginning of the anal fin, the rear outline of the fish is outlined in light blue, as are the pelvic fins. The gill cover is also outlined similarly, as is the opercular spine. The mouth, nostrils, and front-half of the eyes are yellow. This fish is widespread, although often solitary, in the Indo-Pacific oceans from east Africa, including the Red Sea, to Samoa, even as far as Japan. Semi-adult and adult fishes are not often imported.

SPECIAL CARE: The Koran Angelfish is a good aquarium subject but like all angelfishes of this size, it needs swimming space and algae-covered retreats. The water should be well-oxygenated with a strong water current.

FEEDING

COMPATIBILITY

EASE OF KEEPING

6

SIZE

15 in (38 cm) 12 in (30 cm)

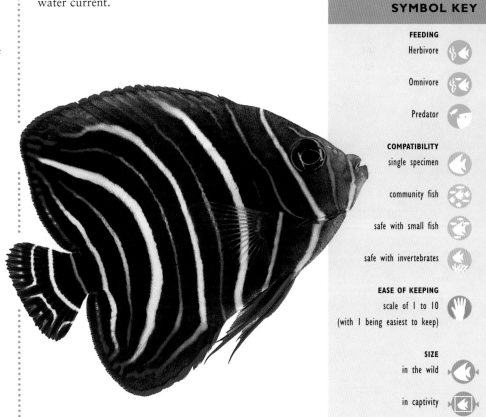

SYMBOL KEY

FEEDING

Herbivore

Omnivore

Predator

COMPATIBILITY

single specimen

community fish

safe with small fish

safe with invertebrates

EASE OF KEEPING

scale of 1 to 10
(with 1 being easiest to keep)

SIZE

in the wild

in captivity

BUTTERFLYFISHES

This stunning family of fishes is probably more responsible for the attraction of marine fishkeeping than any other. However, butterflyfishes can be both a source of delight and despair to the aquarist. Some are suited to the aquarium, others are not; some are easy to feed, others are exasperatingly difficult. As a general guideline, the more exotically colored species are usually the hardest to keep and the most expensive to buy. The most important thing to bear in mind when considering any species, is to know what type of care it requires and the food it will need before you buy it.

Butterflyfishes are found worldwide in tropical waters on coral reefs and near the shore. They can be found in the Indo-Pacific region (including the Red Sea) as well as the Atlantic. Their size ranges from 3 inches (7.5 cm) to 12 inches (30 cm). All have laterally-compressed, oval-shaped bodies

Chaetodon vagabundus
VAGABOND BUTTERFLYFISH

with a pointed snout, ideally suited for flitting in and out of the crevices of coral stands in the search for food.

Taking into account the considerations of providing ample space and numerous retreats, the butterflyfish (if a correct, aquarium-suitable species is chosen) will thrive in captivity. They require clean, fairly agitated, well-oxygenated water in an aquarium that is well lit. Many are intolerant of their own kind and, perhaps more importantly, should not be included in a reef system as they will devour the invertebrate life.

Most of the hardy species will accept foods (fresh or frozen) but those species that feed on coral life in the wild may prove impossible to acclimate to the aquarium. Similarly to angelfish, butterflyfish may refuse to eat and again, the answer is to offer a wide variety of foods until they regain their appetite.

Butterflyfishes are often seen traveling in pairs on the reef, although gender differences are not usually apparent. Many, however, must select their own partners, and may not tolerate a choice made by the aquarist. Spawning follows the pattern of the angelfish, with the eggs being released and fertilized at the water's surface, usually at dusk. The young often take several months to develop into miniature fishes.

Heniochus acuminatus
WIMPLEFISH

FEATURED IN THIS SECTION

COPPERBAND BUTTERFLYFISH
This fish uses its long snout to find food among crevices in the coral.

CHAETODON ACULEATUS

FAMILY: *CHAETODONTIDAE*
COMMON NAME: *ATLANTIC LONGNOSED BUTTERFLYFISH*

Do not confuse this species with the similar and more commonly imported *Forcipiger longirostris* from the Indo-Pacific. The dorsal fin is dark, with some streaks of yellow that continue onto the upper-half of the body. The lower-half is blue-white. The anal and pectoral fins are yellow with light blue edging. The face is pale, streaked with yellow. Common in Florida and the Caribbean region, it is usually solitary.
SPECIAL CARE: Provide a roomy tank and maintain high-quality water conditions with a stable pH level, and moderate currents. These are the basic requirements for the care of all butterflyfishes. Specimens about 3 inches (8 cm) in diameter offer the best chance for acclimation to aquarium life. Feed small, live invertebrates until the fish are thoroughly accepting of aquarium foods. Experimentation may be necessary to determine the best diet. Because the fish uses its long snout to probe for invertebrates in recesses of the reef, try pressing various food items into the rough surface of a rock or piece of coral.

FEEDING

COMPATIBILITY

EASE OF KEEPING

9

SIZE

2.8 in (7 cm) 2 in (5 cm)

CHAETODON AURIGA

FAMILY: *CHAETODONTIDAE*
COMMON NAME: *THREADFIN BUTTERFLYFISH*

Widespread throughout the Indo-Pacific regions, this widely available fish is a good subject for the beginner. Three-quarters of its body is white, with two overlaid areas of diagonal dark lines, one group rising up from behind the head into the dorsal fin, the other running down at right angles to the first set of lines toward the anal fin. The rear uppermost part of the body is darkish as the diagonal bands almost merge together. A vertical dark bar crosses the head passing through the eyes and there are yellow lines across the snout. The dorsal fin is spiky and changes from a white background to yellow about halfway back; the rear portion is plain yellow with a false eye spot in the upper rear corner. The caudal peduncle and the majority of the caudal fin are yellow. The anal fin is yellow with a blue edge; the pectoral fins white. A threadlike extension is carried on the dorsal fin in more mature fishes. Juveniles tend to have paler bodies.

SPECIAL CARE: Provide a roomy tank with lots of decorations among which the fish can feel secure. It will occupy the middle and lower levels. Maintain high-quality water conditions with a stable pH level and moderate currents. No information is available on breeding in captivity.

FEEDING

COMPATIBILITY

EASE OF KEEPING
5

SIZE

9 in (23 cm) 4.9 in (12.5 cm)

CHAETODON CAPISTRATUS

FAMILY: *CHAETODONTIDAE*
COMMON NAME: *FOUREYE BUTTERFLYFISH*

Arguably the most beautiful butterflyfish of the Atlantic-Caribbean region, it is among the most difficult to acclimate to the home aquarium. The black spot ringed in white, near the upper part of the caudal peduncle, is characteristic. The pure white body is marked with a trace of dark lines, running diagonally in opposite directions above and below the lateral line. The snout and the pelvic and pectoral fins are yellow, with this color continuing on the belly and to the lower edge of the anal fin. The dorsal, caudal, and anal fins bear a pale line flanked on each side by a dark one, in a smooth continuous arc outlining the rear edge of the fish.

SPECIAL CARE: This attractive species adapts with difficulty to a small home aquarium, despite being exhibited successfully in large public aquariums. Best results can be expected with specimens about 3 inches (8 cm) in diameter, maintained in a species tank with perfect water conditions (see *C. auriga* on page 160). This fish is usually seen in pairs and may benefit from a companion in the aquarium.

FEEDING

COMPATIBILITY

EASE OF KEEPING

10

SIZE
6 in (15 cm) 3.2 in (8 cm)

CHAETODON DECUSSATUS

FAMILY: *CHAETODONTIDAE*
COMMON NAME: *DECUSSATE BUTTERFLYFISH*

The pale cream body of this fish is patterned in two areas with dark diagonal lines; the first patch rises up from behind the head to the dorsal region, the other runs down from the first set of lines toward the rear of the anal fin. A vertical dark bar crosses the head passing through the eyes. The rear part of the body is black, the color shared with the long-based anal and dorsal fins. The caudal fin is yellow with a black vertical bar at its mid-point and has a white outer edge. The dark anal fin has two longitudinal yellow lines. The Decussate Butterflyfish is very similar to the more commonly found *C. vagabundus*. They can be distinguished by the fact that the latter fish is marked with a dark vertical line, rather than a dark area, across the rear of the body.

SPECIAL CARE: See *C. auriga* on page 160 for care and breeding information.

FEEDING

COMPATIBILITY

EASE OF KEEPING
5

SIZE
8 in (20 cm) 4.9 in (12.5 cm)

SYMBOL KEY

FEEDING
Herbivore
Omnivore
Predator

COMPATIBILITY
single specimen
community fish
safe with small fish
safe with invertebrates

EASE OF KEEPING
scale of 1 to 10
(with 1 being easiest to keep)

SIZE
in the wild
in captivity

CHAETODON LUNULA

FAMILY: *CHAETODONTIDAE*
COMMON NAME: *RACOON BUTTERFLYFISH*

FEEDING

COMPATIBILITY

EASE OF KEEPING
6

SIZE
8 in (20 cm)   4.9 in (12.5 cm)

This fish is endemic to the shallow waters of East Africa, New Guinea, Australia, and the Pacific Ocean. Dark diagonal lines cross the body upward from the pectoral fins becoming less distinct as they reach the dark brown upper flanks toward the dorsal surface. A dark saddle, bordered in front by a thin white line and backed by a broad white band, crosses the forehead to mask each eye. A tapering yellow-edged black or dark brown area runs from the white coloration up into the dorsal fin where it splits into two, to run forward down the forehead, not quite as far as the white band, and rearward to end at the rear of the caudal peduncle. There are noticeable hard, spiky rays at the front of both the dorsal and anal fins. Juveniles are much paler in color ahead of the eye bar and have an eye spot on the rear of the dorsal fin. Both of these characteristics alter with adulthood—the eye spot fades while the pale area deepens into yellow. A lookalike species from the Red Sea, *C. fasciatus*, lacks the dark area on the caudal peduncle.

SPECIAL CARE: See *C. auriga* on page 160 for care and breeding information. This is the only nocturnal butterflyfish imported for the aquarium. It should be offered food at first after the lights are out, and will eventually learn to eat during the daylight hours if it is otherwise comfortable.

CHAETODON QUADRIMACULATUS

FAMILY: *CHAETODONTIDAE*
COMMON NAME: *HAWAIIAN TEARDROP BUTTERFLYFISH*

FEEDING

COMPATIBILITY

EASE OF KEEPING
10

SIZE
6.3 in (16 cm)   4 in (10 cm)

The Hawaiian Teardrop Butterflyfish has a deep body with a sharply-rising forehead. Its coloration is divided into two distinct areas: the dorsal area is dark brown shading to a deep golden yellow midway down the body. Two white patches appear within the brown area just below the base of the dorsal fin. The fins are golden reddish-yellow; the dorsal and anal fins have a blue line along their midsections, the dorsal fin having a brown base while that of the anal fin is yellow. The base of the caudal fin is red. This fish is mostly concentrated around Hawaii, although it is also found in Japanese, Micronesian, and Polynesian waters.

SPECIAL CARE: Very often, a limitation in geographical range indicates a specialized feeder (it is an omnivorous fish, that especially likes coral polyps, sponges, etc.) which generally means the fish may have problems acclimating in the aquarium. *C. quadrimaculatus* may well be one of those species which, until suitable foods can be mass-produced commercially, is best left where it really belongs, on the coral reef. For other general care and breeding information see *C. auriga* on page 160.

CHAETODON SEDENTARIUS

FAMILY: *CHAETODONTIDAE*
COMMON NAME: *REEF BUTTERFLYFISH*

FEEDING

COMPATIBILITY

EASE OF KEEPING
9

SIZE
5.5 in (14 cm)   4 in (10 cm)

Often seen in pairs on reef tops in Florida and the Caribbean, this is among the more aquarium-adaptable of the Atlantic butterflyfish species. Easily recognized by the broad, dark bar edged in light blue that extends from the rear portion of the dorsal fin, across the caudal peduncle and onto the upper portion of the anal fin.

SPECIAL CARE: Provide a roomy tank with perfect water conditions (see *C. auriga* on page 160). These fish are found only near coral reefs, and are intolerant of suboptimal conditions. Many individuals will refuse to eat in captivity, and for this reason it is suggested that juveniles be obtained. Specimens about 3 inches (8 cm) in diameter offer the best chance for acclimation to aquarium life.

CHAETODON STRIATUS

FAMILY: *CHAETODONTIDAE*
COMMON NAME: *BANDED BUTTERFLYFISH*

Common in Florida and the Caribbean, it ranges from New Jersey (during warmer weather) south to Brazil. The body is white to silver, with a dark band through the eyes. Two more vertical bands across the mid-body region—a band from the dorsal fin to the anal, and a band on the outer portion of the caudal fin—are complete with blue and pale yellow lines on each side, at the tips of the dorsal and anal fins.

FEEDING

COMPATIBILITY

EASE OF KEEPING

10

SIZE

5.5 in (14 cm) 4 in (10 cm)

SPECIAL CARE: Provide a roomy tank with perfect water conditions for all butterflyfishes (see *C. auriga* on page 160). These fish are found only near coral reefs, and are intolerant of suboptimal conditions. Most individuals of this species will refuse to eat in captivity, and for this reason it is suggested that only specimens that eat well in the dealer's tank be obtained. Specimens about 3 inches (8 cm) in diameter offer the best chance for acclimation to aquarium life. Feed small, live invertebrates until the fish are thoroughly accepting of aquarium foods. Experimentation may be necessary to determine the best diet.

CHAETODON UNIMACULATUS

FAMILY: *CHAETODONTIDAE*
COMMON NAME: *TEARDROP BUTTERFLYFISH*

The Teardrop's body coloration is yellow with a slightly paler patch between the eyes and the center of the flanks. Obtuse-angled yellow chevron patterning crosses the pale area. Midway along the body, there is a large dark teardrop marking; very often in adult fishes all that is left of this mark is a circular blob, the rest of the "tear" being smudged (as though running down the face) or missing altogether. A dark vertical bar passes down across the head passing through the eyes and another passes across the caudal peduncle and is picked up again, this time bordered on each side by a narrow white margin, in the rear edges of the yellow dorsal and anal fins. Juveniles are paler in color with a well-marked teardrop. This fish is found throughout a wide geographical area—from the Red Sea, to Sri Lanka in the Indian Ocean, to Hawaii in the mid-Pacific.
SPECIAL CARE: This butterflyfish responds well to captivity and will spend most of its time at the middle and lower levels of the aquarium. For care and breeding information see *C. auriga* on page 160.

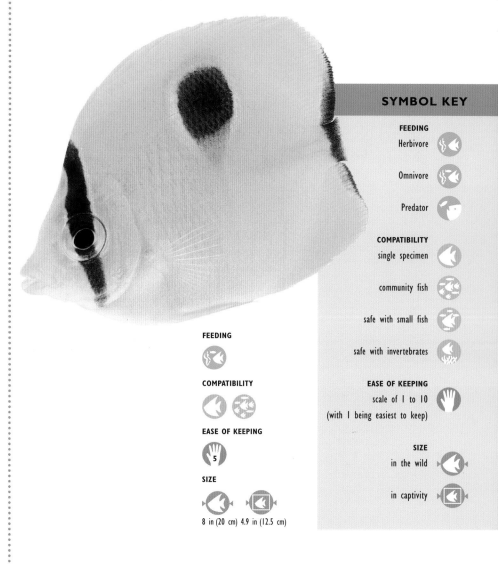

FEEDING

COMPATIBILITY

EASE OF KEEPING

5

SIZE

8 in (20 cm) 4.9 in (12.5 cm)

SYMBOL KEY

FEEDING

Herbivore

Omnivore

Predator

COMPATIBILITY

single specimen

community fish

safe with small fish

safe with invertebrates

EASE OF KEEPING

scale of 1 to 10
(with 1 being easiest to keep)

SIZE

in the wild

in captivity

CHAETODON VAGABUNDUS

FAMILY: *CHAETODONTIDAE*
COMMON NAME: *VAGABOND BUTTERFLYFISH*

The Vagabond Butterflyfish is widespread throughout the Indo-Pacific regions and is a good fish for an inexperienced aquarist to keep. The pale cream body is overlaid with two areas of diagonal dark lines, one group rising up from behind the head to the dorsal region, the other running down from the first set of lines toward the rear of the anal fin. A vertical dark bar crosses the head passing through the eyes; another passes across the caudal peduncle and carries on through both the dorsal and anal fins. Similarly colored lines to those on the body cross the forehead in front of the dark eye bar. The caudal fin is yellow with a black vertical bar midway along with another dark outer margin. The dorsal and anal fins have yellow rear portions—the dorsal is blue-edged and the anal white-edged. Juveniles of this species have pale bodies—the yellow coloration is limited to the body areas behind the rearmost black bar and carry a dark eye spot in the rear of the dorsal fin but this fades with maturity.

SPECIAL CARE: For care and breeding information see *C. auriga* on page 160.

FEEDING

COMPATIBILITY

EASE OF KEEPING

5

SIZE

9 in (23 cm)   4.9 in (12.5 cm)

CHELMON ROSTRATUS

FAMILY: *CHAETODONTIDAE*
COMMON NAME: *COPPERBAND BUTTERFLYFISH*

This species bears an unusual background body color for the butterflyfish family: it is plain silver. However, this lack of dense coloration is more than compensated for by the four black-edged deep orange bands which vertically cross the body. The first band covers the eyes, the fourth carries a white-ringed dark eye spot (a decoy eye found in the patterning of many marine fish that is used to present any attacker with a false target). A fifth band crosses the rear parts of the dorsal and anal fins and caudal peduncle where it precedes a white-edged black vertical band. A further orange stripe runs down the forehead and along the top of the long snout. Pelvic fins are marked with orange and white, the pectoral fins are clear. Juveniles generally have more intense orange coloring, while the adults pale toward yellow in the bands. In its natural habitats of the Red Sea and the Indo-Pacific oceans, it uses its long snout to good effect, picking its food from between crevices in the corals, where most other fish cannot reach.

SPECIAL CARE: This species may be delicate and short-lived in captivity, it also has a tendency to quarrel with its own kind. For care and breeding information see *C. auriga* on page 160.

FEEDING

COMPATIBILITY

EASE OF KEEPING
7

SIZE

8 in (20 cm) 4.9 in (12.5 cm)

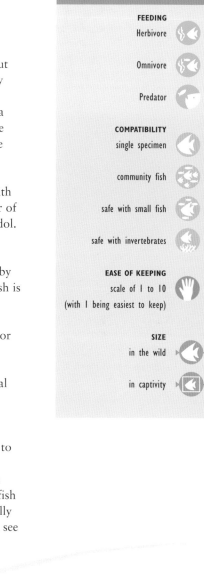

FORCIPIGER LONGIROSTRIS

FAMILY: *CHAETODONTIDAE*
COMMON NAME: *LONGNOSED BUTTERFLYFISH; FORCEPSFISH*

This very distinctive fish has a plain bright yellow body but the top-half of its head, including the top jaw, from the gill cover forward is jet black. The lower-half of the head, lower jaw, and throat region, is silver. The rear edge of the dorsal is light blue (as is the same part of the anal fin and extreme edge of the caudal peduncle) and the anal fin is also marked with a black eye spot in the upper corner nearest to the body. The front few rays of the dorsal and anal fins are distinctly spiky. Seen from a distance, the striking color pattern camouflages the fish's actual outline very well and, of the course, the eye spot also distracts any attacker's attention from the real eye hidden in its black patch. The slightly smaller *F. flavissimus* is similarly marked, with "snout dimensions" distinguishing the two species, together with a difference in the number of dorsal fin spines. This fish can be found in the shallow waters from the Red Sea and the Indo-Pacific oceans right across to Central America and southern California **SPECIAL CARE:** For information on care see *C. auriga* on page 160.

FEEDING

COMPATIBILITY

EASE OF KEEPING

5

SIZE

8.7 in (22 cm) 4.9 in (12.5 cm)

HENIOCHUS ACUMINATUS

FAMILY: *CHAETODONTIDAE*
COMMON NAME: *WIMPLEFISH*

This fish, found in the Red Sea and throughout the Indo-Pacific oceans, may have small horny protuberances just above the eyes, a physical feature which caused ichthyologists to create a separate genus from other members within the Butterflyfish group. Despite its very distinctive forward-sloping color patterning and bright yellow tail, this species (also known as the Pennant Fish) always seems to be confused with *Zanclus canescens* which may explain another of its popular names, the Poor Man's Moorish Idol. The appellation of Wimplefish refers to the resemblance of the flowing dorsal fin to the medieval headwear or to the headdress worn by nuns. Although very distinctive, the Wimplefish is not a solitary species within the genus; sadly, hardly any of the others (*H. chrysostomus*, *H. diphreutes*, *H. monoceros*, *H. singularius*, or *H. varius*) are ever imported. Its body form is reminiscent of the Freshwater Angelfish, *Pterophyllum scalare*, particularly as the dorsal and anal fins make it a "high" rather than an elongated fish as is more the case with other members of the family. Juveniles are similarly colored to adults, but lack the long extension to the dorsal fin which develops with age.
SPECIAL CARE: A large aquarium is needed to keep several of these fishes, however a single fish which considers itself to be the leader may bully the others. For care and breeding information see *C. auriga* on page 160.

FEEDING

COMPATIBILITY

EASE OF KEEPING

5

SIZE

10 in (25 cm) 6 in (15 cm)

SURGEONFISHES AND TANGS

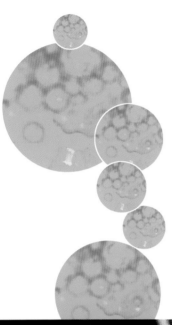

Fishes in this family have oval-shaped bodies, steep sloping foreheads, and some extremely bizarre facial decoration. Another physical characteristic that most share is the presence of one, or sometimes two, sharp spines on each side of the caudal peduncle. It takes little imagination to appreciate what damage these "scalpels" can do to anything that they come into contact with (including the aquarist's hand or net) when held erect from the side of the fish and moved like a razor-sharp scythe as the fish flexes its body.

A further common feature of these fishes is that they are mostly herbivores, content to graze endlessly over lush macro-algae. A hungry school can lay bare any green outcrop in a very short space of time. A notable exception among the members of this family is the popular

Paracanthurus hepatus
HIPPO TANG

Hippo Tang, that lacks the scalpel at the base of the tail, and feeds mostly on plankton rather than plant matter. These fish are safe with invertebrates. Most species are found in all tropical seas around reefs where the light encourages green growth. Breeding occurs at the water's surface, with the fertilized eggs being swept away to develop naturally.

These active, constantly-browsing fish require well-oxygenated water and an efficient filtration system to deal with the constantly-produced waste. Although these fish may school in the wild, they do like to find less crowded areas in which to seek refuge every now and then. In the aquarium this isn't really possible and very often they will resent fellow surgeons intruding into their swimming space. However, given a large enough aquarium and with the presence of some other non-surgeonfish species to distract their attention, small numbers can successfully be kept together.

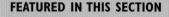

Zebrasoma flavescens
YELLOW TANG

POWDER BLUE SURGEON
This fish is readily available, but it does have a reputation for quarrelling with its own kind.

ACANTHURUS CAERULEUS

FAMILY: *ACANTHURIDAE*
COMMON NAME: *ATLANTIC BLUE TANG; BLUE SURGEONFISH*

Aquarists always get confused about this fish, especially if the dealer has more than one specimen of different sizes in the shop. Juveniles are bright yellow, with slightly darker, wavy yellow lines running along the rear-half of the body. The dorsal and anal fins are edged in bright blue. As the fish ages, the blue on the fins expands, moving from the outer edges toward the center of the body. Eventually, only the tail remains yellow. In the final phase, the entire body is dark blue, marked with wavy lines of electric blue that undoubtedly provide camouflage against a background of rippling water. They are most common around Florida, the Bahamas, and in the Caribbean.

SPECIAL CARE: All surgeonfish can deliver a nasty cut with the scalpel-like modified scale that lies in a groove on the caudal peduncle. Exercise caution when handling, especially with large specimens. When young, these fish can be domineering, but this does lessen with maturity. Given a roomy tank, this is a hardy and adaptable species. Color changes do not depend upon size, adding to the confusion surrounding the identification of this fish. Its diet is largely vegetarian.

FEEDING

COMPATIBILITY

EASE OF KEEPING

3

SIZE

15 in (38 cm) 8 in (20 cm)

ACANTHURUS GLAUCOPAREIUS

FAMILY: *ACANTHURIDAE*
COMMON NAME: *GOLD-RIM TANG*

This fish is characteristic of the *Acanthuridae* family with its oval body and steeply-sloping forehead. The mouth is placed at the extreme of the snout enabling the fish to browse easily upon algal growths. Body coloration is rich brown at the front shading to bright yellow on the caudal peduncle. Immediately behind the mouth a white area runs upward to surround the eye. There is a small yellow area at the base of the pectoral fin. Both dorsal and anal fins have a yellow line along their long bases, and run right around to the start of the caudal peduncle. The scalpels (one on each side of the body) are yellow and almost invisible on the similarly-colored caudal peduncle. The white marking on the cheek may vary in size and has also given the fish another popular name—White-cheeked Surgeon. This fish is widespread in the Pacific Ocean (East Indies to the west coast of America) but some reports cite Indian Ocean habitation as well.

FEEDING

COMPATIBILITY

EASE OF KEEPING

5

SIZE

8 in (20 cm) 4 in (10 cm)

SPECIAL CARE: The Gold-rim Tang should be kept in a spacious aquarium, as this fish swims at all levels, with plenty of macroalgal growth. In captivity it can be quarrelsome with its own kind, even though they are more sociable in the wild. No information on breeding in captivity is available.

ACANTHURUS LEUCOSTERNON

FAMILY: *ACANTHURIDAE*
COMMON NAME: *POWDER BLUE SURGEON*

This is one of the most popular surgeonfish with home aquarists and is found throughout the Indo-Pacific oceans. Its outstanding coloration must be a major contributory factor in its ability to attract the attention of fishkeepers. The head and gills are dark blue-black relieved by a white line running beneath the lower lip. The throat region is white and shades into the light blue body. The center of the high-set eyes is dark with a pale surround. The dorsal fin is bright yellow, the anal fin is white, and both of these long-based fins have a light edging. The bright yellow scalpel bridges the blue and yellow areas at the front of the caudal peduncle.

FEEDING

COMPATIBILITY

EASE OF KEEPING
5

SIZE
9 in (23 cm)   4.9 in (12.5 cm)

SPECIAL CARE: Young fishes quarrel among themselves, so it is better to have only one specimen in the aquarium. It is an active fish that needs plenty of swimming room and luxuriant algal growth on which to browse.

NASO LITERATUS

FAMILY: *ACANTHURIDAE*
COMMON NAME: *LIPSTICK TANG; SMOOTHHEAD UNICORNFISH; JAPANESE TANG*

The Lipstick Tang's body is very sleekly streamlined, a characteristic enhanced by its pale gray-brown coloration. The mouth is strikingly accentuated by a combination of red-orange lips set against a yellow-edged dark brown area which runs up the forehead to enclose the eyes. A combination of blue-brown lines on the gill covers gives the area a folded-skin effect. A yellow patch separates the eyes from another dark brown band coloring the base of the long dorsal fin that is separated from the body by a light blue line. The anal fin retains some of the body color together with yellow and has a light blue outer edge. This species carries two scalpels on each side and these are "hidden" in two bright yellow patches on the caudal peduncle. The crescent-shaped caudal fin is light-colored with dark top, bottom, and rear edges. The top and bottom few rays of the caudal fin are produced into long filaments. The collective name of Unicornfish for this genus refers to the protuberance that some species grow on the forehead; this species does not conform to this. This fish is found in the Red Sea, the Indian Ocean, and Hawaii in the mid-Pacific Ocean.

SPECIAL CARE: This species needs a spacious aquarium. It feeds largely on brown algae (kelp) and some plankton in the wild. The captive diet must not include only green algae, or the fish will not thrive. No information on breeding in captivity is available.

FEEDING

COMPATIBILITY

EASE OF KEEPING
8

SIZE
12 in (30 cm)   6.9 in (17.5 cm)

SYMBOL KEY

FEEDING
Herbivore

Omnivore

Predator

COMPATIBILITY
single specimen

community fish

safe with small fish

safe with invertebrates

EASE OF KEEPING
scale of 1 to 10
(with 1 being easiest to keep)

SIZE
in the wild

in captivity

PARACANTHURUS HEPATUS

FAMILY: *ACANTHURIDAE*
COMMON NAME: *HIPPO TANG; YELLOW-TAIL BLUE TANG; REGAL TANG*

This striking fish is found throughout the waters of the Indo-Pacific, East Africa, and the mid-Pacific. The deep royal blue body of this fish, with its distinctive black markings and bright yellow triangular area in the center of the tail, makes species recognition easy. The Regal Tang carries scalpels on the caudal peduncle, but these are not obvious as they are hidden in the apex of the yellow area on the caudal peduncle.

SPECIAL CARE: This species spends its time around specific types of branching corals and should be provided with several in its aquarium habitat. Unlike other surgeons, its diet consists largely of plankton and other animal matter, with roughly one third consisting of microalgae. More than one specimen can be kept if the tank is roomy and there are numerous retreats.

FEEDING

COMPATIBILITY

EASE OF KEEPING

5

SIZE

12.2 in (31 cm) 6 in (15 cm)

ZEBRASOMA FLAVESCENS

FAMILY: *ACANTHURIDAE*
COMMON NAME: *YELLOW TANG*

The actual body shape of this fish is oval but this is exaggerated by the surrounding fins to give a disc-shape appearance. It has a relatively long snout with a steeply-sloping forehead and high-set eyes. The overall body color is a bright yellow; only the lighter coloration around the eyes and the white scalpels on the caudal peduncle bring any contrasting relief. The dorsal fin is very long-based, running from the top of the forehead to the beginning of the short caudal peduncle; the anal fin runs from midway around the lower circumference to end opposite the terminating point of the dorsal fin. All fins share the same yellow body coloration. This coloration is maintained throughout the fish's life span. Its very small scales give the body a velvety look. The Yellow Tang is very similar in appearance to the juvenile form of *Acanthurus caeruleus* from which it can be distinguished by the deeper body shape and the absence of blue coloring around the eyes and dorsal and anal fins. This fish is found in the tropical waters surrounding the Hawaiian islands.

SPECIAL CARE: This herbivorous fish will spend most of its time at the middle and lower levels of the aquarium. It requires adequate swimming space and plenty of macroalgal growth on which to feed. It can be territorial. No captive breeding information is available.

FEEDING

COMPATIBILITY

EASE OF KEEPING

5

SIZE

8 in (20 cm) 3 in (7.5 cm)

ZEBRASOMA XANTHURUM

FAMILY: *ACANTHURIDAE*
COMMON NAME: *PURPLE SAILFIN TANG*

The specific name, *xanthurum*, comes from the words "*xantho*" meaning yellow, and "*urus*" meaning tail, presumably due to the brilliant color of the caudal fin. Similarly to *Z. flavescens*, its body profile is oval but appears disc-shaped by the stiffly-held surrounding fins. Its deep blue-purple body is marked with darker, purple-red dots and lines concentrated mainly on the head and front portion of the body, petering out gradually at the dorsal fin. The edge of the gill cover is clearly demarcated by a dark line. The snout is fairly well-produced with a steep forehead and the high-set eyes have a red ring around the iris. The retractable scalpel on the caudal peduncle is scarcely visible as it is the same color as the body. This fish is found in the stretch of water from the Red Sea, throughout the Indian Ocean to the mid-Pacific.
SPECIAL CARE: Although territorially-minded and probably best kept as a single specimen, some reports suggest keeping a shoal might be possible. It requires plenty of green foods—algae-coated aquarium decorations provide an ideal grazing ground. No information is available on breeding in captivity.

FEEDING

COMPATIBILITY

EASE OF KEEPING
5

SIZE

8.7 in (22 cm) 6 in (15 cm)

SYMBOL KEY

FEEDING
Herbivore

Omnivore

Predator

COMPATIBILITY
single specimen

community fish

safe with small fish

safe with invertebrates

EASE OF KEEPING
scale of 1 to 10
(with 1 being easiest to keep)

SIZE
in the wild

in captivity

TRIGGERFISHES AND FILEFISHES

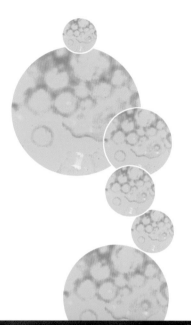

Oblong, or lozenge-shaped bodies, very sharp teeth, and bizarre markings are among the physical features of members of this family. However, the most distinctive characteristic that these fishes have is what gives it its common name. The name triggerfish is very descriptive—the "trigger" is part of the mechanism that locks the dorsal fin into an upright position—either to prevent the fish from being swallowed by a predator, or sometimes, to help wedge it in a crevice from which it cannot be moved, until it releases the "trigger" to lower the fin once more. When purchasing a triggerfish don't refuse to buy it on the grounds that its pelvic fins look stumpy, or that they've broken off, as it doesn't have any.

Xanthichthys ringens
SARGASSUM TRIGGERFISH

Found in shallow tropical waters of the Indo-Pacific and Atlantic Oceans, triggerfishes are both solitary and territorial which, in terms of aquarium culture, means that they need space if quarrels are to be avoided between similar species. As well as needing space, they also require retreats and places to rummage in. Make sure the aquarium decorations are fixed firmly in place as these fish will attempt (and usually succeed) in rearranging the substrate and other "fixtures and fittings" if they get a chance. They will assume that anything is good to eat and will attempt to chew at it, so their inclusion in a mixed fish and invertebrate collection is not a good idea. Because triggerfishes are not fussy feeders this makes feeding unproblematic, but take care their sharp teeth don't have a chance to get a taste of you when maintaining their aquarium.

Their relations, filefishes, differ in that they are unable to lock the first dorsal spine into an upright position. They have extremely rough skin and are known by the alternative popular name of "leather-jackets."

Monacanthus ciliaris
FRINGED FILEFISH

CLOWN TRIGGER
The first dorsal fin of the Clown Trigger is normally carried folded flat in its dark groove.

BALISTOIDES CONSPICILLUM

FAMILY: *BALISTIDAE*
COMMON NAME: *CLOWN TRIGGER*

The Clown Trigger has an unsymmetrical contour—the dorsal surface is slightly curved, the ventral surface more pointed. The general body background color is dark brown-black mostly covered with white round spots of varying sizes. A shallow yellow saddle area surrounds the base of the generally folded, flat first dorsal fin; a small similarly-colored saddle marks the top of the small caudal peduncle. A black patch crosses the forehead to include the eyes and is separated from the snout by a white band. The eyes have a dark black ring around their circumference. The mouth is small, armed with sharp teeth, and surrounded by a wide yellow "lipstick" band that has a light blue/white rear edging. The disruptive coloration may be variable depending upon the fish's age. Adults may have some white in the dorsal and anal fins and the caudal fin often appears to be black with a white central area. In its natural habitat from East Africa, throughout the Indian Ocean to the mid-Pacific, this fish deposits its eggs in nests on the seabed. No information is available on breeding in captivity.

SPECIAL CARE: This highly popular fish can be difficult to acclimate to aquarium life; this is particularly the case with juveniles, that although "affordable" can be easily stressed. It has a tendency to become aggressive and requires plenty of well-anchored retreats and protected "hardware."

FEEDING

COMPATIBILITY

EASE OF KEEPING
5

SIZE
20 in (50 cm)   4.9 in (12.5 cm)

XANTHICHTHYS RINGENS

FAMILY: *BALISTIDAE*
COMMON NAME: *SARGASSUM TRIGGERFISH*

This elegant species is found in western Atlantic waters, off the shores of North Carolina—Bermuda down to Brazil. The gray-blue body is flecked with red-brown dots, arranged in parallel, horizontal rows from the rear of the head to the caudal peduncle. The bases of the dorsal and anal fins and the foldable first dorsal fin are reddish-brown. The margins of the caudal fin are red-orange. Three blue streaks appear across the cheeks. As with all triggerfishes, the pelvic fins are reduced to rudimentary stumps. It spawns in deep waters and has an elaborate courtship ritual involving horizontal and spiraling swimming patterns before spawning actually occurs. The common name refers to the fact that juveniles (mottled green in color) are found in floating *Sargassum* seaweed. It is interesting to note that three other species, *X. auromarginatus*, *X. lineopunctatus*, and *X. mento* are found in Indo-Pacific waters.

SPECIAL CARE: This modest-sized triggerfish is reported to be an excellent subject for the marine aquarium and, because of its relatively small size, may well provide excellent prospects for captive breeding. Once established in an aquarium it may not take too kindly to new introductions.

FEEDING

COMPATIBILITY

EASE OF KEEPING
5

SIZE
8 in (20 cm)   6 in (15 cm)

MONACANTHUS CILIARIS

FAMILY: *MONACANTHIDAE*
COMMON NAME: *FRINGED FILEFISH*

The first spines of the dorsal and anal fins of filefishes can be erected to permit the fish to lodge itself tightly in a crevice when danger threatens. Never forcibly remove a fish from such a position. The body of this fish varies in color from tan to green, with lighter spots and blotches arranged to provide camouflage as the fish hides in sea grass, seaweed, or among floating clumps of algae. Swimming slowly, it uses its tiny mouth to grab benthic invertebrates. There is a noticeable hump at the anterior base of the dorsal fin, a reliable identification characteristic for a species highly variable in coloration.

SPECIAL CARE: Provide perfect water conditions and plenty of rocks with algae and invertebrates. Feed small, live invertebrates until the fish learns to accept a wider variety of aquarium foods. A habitat tank featuring sea grasses and a sandy bottom would make this species feel more at home than a traditional reef tank.

FEEDING

COMPATIBILITY

EASE OF KEEPING
5

SIZE

8 in (20 cm)   6 in (15 cm)

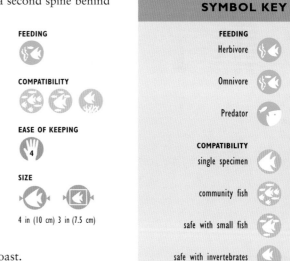

MONACANTHUS SETIFER

FAMILY: *MONACANTHIDAE*
COMMON NAME: *PYGMY FILEFISH*

Filefishes are flattened like a cracker. The first spines of the dorsal and anal fins can be erected to permit the fish to lodge itself tightly in a crevice when danger threatens. Never forcibly remove a fish from such a position. The body of this fish is pale yellow to cream in coloration, with a pattern of dashes and blotches arranged to give the impression of stripes. The color pattern provides nearly perfect camouflage as it hides in masses of floating seaweed, or hovers just above rocks encrusted with algae and invertebrates. Swimming slowly, it uses its tiny mouth to pluck food from recesses in its surroundings.

SPECIAL CARE: Provide perfect water conditions and plenty of rocks with algae and invertebrates. Feed small, live invertebrates until the fish is acclimated to aquarium foods. Since it remains small, it is a good candidate for a species tank. Corals and other reef invertebrates capable of stinging are usually left alone.

FEEDING

COMPATIBILITY

EASE OF KEEPING

5

SIZE

4 in (10 cm)   3.2 in (8 cm)

PERVAGOR MELANOCEPHALUS

FAMILY: *MONACANTHIDAE*
COMMON NAME: *RED-TAILED FILEFISH; LACE-FINNED LEATHERJACKET*

This shy, peaceful fish has an elongated body with a long snout and a short caudal peduncle. Its body is divided into two halves by coloration; the front-half of the fish is purple, but this shades through brown to a bright yellow at the caudal fin. The scales are very tiny and have small spines. The forehead rises steeply above the red-rimmed eyes to the first of the two dorsal fins. There is a single spine that can be locked into the upright position by means of a second spine behind it (much in the same fashion as triggerfishes.) The second dorsal fin is long-based and set behind the midway position, immediately above the equally long-based anal fin. The pelvic fins are very rudimentary but it has a moveable pelvic spine. The yellow fan-shaped caudal fin is streaked with brown-red radial stripes and has a blue edge. This fish is found in the Indo-Pacific region including the waters of Hawaii and the Queensland coast.

SPECIAL CARE: The aquarium must be furnished with numerous retreats—caves, outcrops, sea fans, and coral heads—almost anything that will offer the fish sanctuary.

FEEDING

COMPATIBILITY

EASE OF KEEPING

4

SIZE

4 in (10 cm)   3 in (7.5 cm)

SYMBOL KEY

FEEDING
Herbivore

Omnivore

Predator

COMPATIBILITY
single specimen

community fish

safe with small fish

safe with invertebrates

EASE OF KEEPING
scale of 1 to 10
(with 1 being easiest to keep)

SIZE
in the wild

in captivity

WRASSES

If asked to put a name to a member of the Labridae family, a fishkeeper would probably answer, "Cleaner Wrasse" but there are other fish that are included in this family, that at first glance, seem to be "outsiders." This is not surprising given that the family contains over 50 genera, represented by over 500 species, so some of them must, by the law of averages, be different. Factor in the physical differences between juveniles and adults, males and females, and, just to add further confusion the fact that the fishes often change sex, and you have an indication as to what an interesting family of fishes this is.

Lienardella fasciata
HARLEQUIN TUSKFISH

Wrasses are found worldwide in shallow waters and vary greatly in size. They are inveterate eaters and forage around coral rubble for food, darting in and out of caves. The Cleaner Wrasse offers a cleaning service to all fish that visit its "service station" usually a definite area on the coral reef. It picks off parasites from the visiting fishes' skin, even from inside the mouth and gills of larger specimens. While very welcome, this service has important ramifications for members of this genus; Labroides aren't

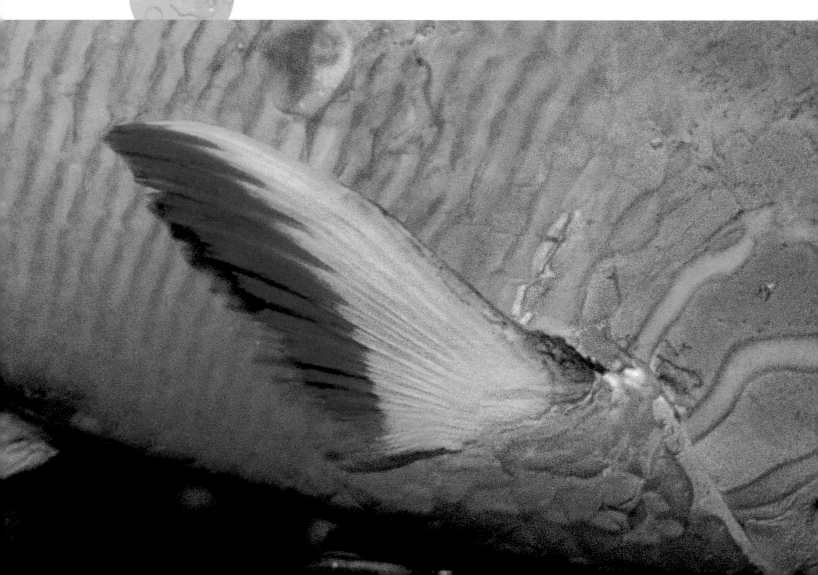

doing this job for fun, they do it in order to get food and are dependent on other fish bringing it to them. Removing Cleaner Fish from the reef results in other species of fish ceasing to visit, as they know that its services will no longer be available. This dependency between species is a vital part of coral reef life and denuding the reef of Cleaner Fish is to be discouraged. One also has to consider what the Cleaner Wrasse might feed on once the parasites have been cleaned from its aquarium tank mates.

Some wrasses burrow into the substrate at night. To ensure that you provide suitable "sleeping accommodation" for these species, the substrate should be sandy and be some inches deep. Wrasses are territorial which means that considerable thought has to be given as to their tank mates, but, on the other hand, they are quite hardy. Don't always assume that the sight of a wrasse "flashing" off the substrate as a sign of skin irritation—they sometimes adopt this tactic to uncover food. Look carefully at how your wrasses swim—they hardly use their caudal fin at all, all of the movement is generated with the pectoral fins which allows the fish to glide through the water.

Thalassoma bifasciatum
BLUEHEAD WRASSE

FEATURED IN THIS SECTION

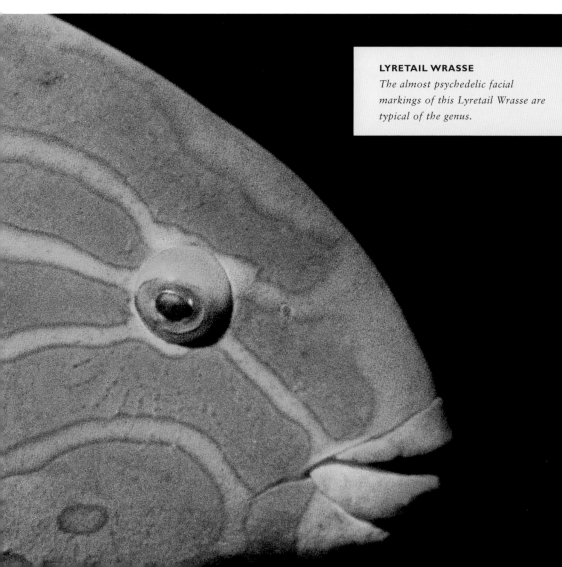

LYRETAIL WRASSE
The almost psychedelic facial markings of this Lyretail Wrasse are typical of the genus.

BODIANUS PULCHELLUS

FAMILY: *LABRIDAE*
COMMON NAME: *CUBAN HOGFISH; SPOTFIN*

Adults are found in deeper waters around coral heads and underwater cliffs in the Caribbean, although young fishes may frequent more shallow waters. The juvenile coloration is similar to that of the juvenile form of the Bluehead Wrasse, *Thalassoma bifasciatum*, which shares the same waters. Both perform cleaning services on other fishes when young. Like all members of the Labridae family, the fish is, at first, female, changing into a functional male when dominating a "harem" of other females. Its spawning pattern features fast pursuit of the female by the "male," which creates a circling rise in the water and culminates in pelagic eggs being released at the surface. A dark spot appears on the tip of the pectoral fins which accounts for the fish's alternative name. Juveniles are yellow with a dark mark on the front of the dorsal fin and red lines running through the eyes.
SPECIAL CARE: An efficient filtration system is required to deal with the detritus that is stirred up by the actions of these fishes. Provide some hiding places for them to explore and lurk in and a suitably soft substrate in which they can burrow at night. No information is available on breeding in captivity.

FEEDING

COMPATIBILITY

EASE OF KEEPING
4

SIZE
8 in (20 cm) 5 in (12.5 cm)

BODIANUS RUFUS

FAMILY: *LABRIDAE*
COMMON NAME: *SPANISH HOGFISH*

This fish has an elongated, yet stockily-built body with a tapering snout and a fairly long caudal peduncle. The basic overall body coloration is bright yellow but the upper section from the eyes back almost to the rear of the dorsal fin (including the fin itself) is blue-brown in juveniles and red in adults. The coloration may vary however, depending upon the depth at which the fish swims: shallow water specimens retain the blue shade while deep-water fishes display red and yellow coloring. All of the fins are yellow, with the exception of the dorsal fin. Filamentous extensions are found on the dorsal and anal fins of adult fishes. The Spanish Hogfish is endemic to rocky and coral outcrops in the Caribbean.
SPECIAL CARE: Young specimens make good aquarium subjects and may act as "cleaners" to other fishes. Locomotion is usually provided by the pectoral fins alone, as is the case with other Labridae species. For care and breeding information see *B. pulchellus* above.

FEEDING

COMPATIBILITY

EASE OF KEEPING
4

SIZE
16 in (40 cm) 8 in (20 cm)

CIRRHILABRUS LEUTEOVITTATUS

FAMILY: *LABRIDAE*
COMMON NAME: *YELLOWBAR FAIRY WRASSE*

Fairy Wrasses, as this genus is known, are becoming more and more popular with reef tank enthusiasts, despite the difficulties associated with successfully keeping certain species. Males are uniformly burgundy red, with a bright yellow streak from the caudal peduncle almost to the gill cover. The dorsal and anal fins are edged in yellow and decorated with blue lines. Females, less frequently seen in the aquarium trade, are greenish and purple, with a double row of red spots where the male wears his yellow stripe.
SPECIAL CARE: Although this fish will not harm reef invertebrates, it does best in dim light, which is incompatible with most corals. A 50-gallon (189-liter) species tank, decorated with fanworms, colorful shrimps, and other invertebrates that do not require light would suit it best. Feed these energetic wrasses at least three small feedings daily, consisting of meaty seafoods of appropriate size for its small mouth. Variation in the diet, and the addition of vitamin supplements to the food, seem to be essential for long survival in captivity. Keep only one male and several females in the same tank.

FEEDING

COMPATIBILITY

EASE OF KEEPING
7

SIZE
4.7 in (12 cm) 4.7 in (12 cm)

GOMPHOSUS COERULEUS

FAMILY: *LABRIDAE*
COMMON NAME: *BIRDMOUTH WRASSE*

This fish has an elongated body with a fairly deep mid-section, and a much extended snout. Body coloration varies considerably from juvenile to adult and also between the sexes. Juveniles and adult females are brown with red speckles and occasionally red snouts. Adult males are a plain dark blue-green. Its head is almost triangular in shape with the eyes high-set; the jaws are produced into a birdlike beak. It is a grazer and uses its beak to extract food from crevices in the coral in the reefs throughout the Indo-Pacific region. The long-based dorsal and anal fins are green, the pectoral fins are purple. The caudal fin is green with darker outer rays and may become lyre-shaped with age. It has several common names (as is usual with any widely distributed species) and it is suspected that scientific names such as G. *varius* and G. *tricolor* may have been erroneously applied to juveniles or females.
SPECIAL CARE: This very active species mainly uses its pectoral fins for propulsion. No information is available on breeding in captivity. It is important that the aquarium has an efficient filtration system and that it is furnished with some rubble and soft substrate.

FEEDING

COMPATIBILITY

EASE OF KEEPING
4

SIZE
11 in (28 cm) 4.9 in (12.5 cm)

HALICHOERES BIVITTATUS

FAMILY: *LABRIDAE*
COMMON NAME: *SLIPPERY DICK*

Possibly the most commonly seen wrasse in south Florida, this fish ranges all the way from North Carolina to Brazil. It swims in all major reef habitats, from back reef margins to grass flats and sandy lagoons. Juveniles have been popular with collectors and hobbyists for many years. Most juveniles are collected when they bear longitudinal stripes in tan, red-brown, white, gold, and white, in that order, from the dorsal to the ventral side. Adults are a gaudy mix of sea foam green, yellow, purple, and turquoise. The intermediate stages are complex in coloration also, making identification confusing.
SPECIAL CARE: Provide good water conditions and feed a variety of live or frozen invertebrates and any of the usual aquarium foods. Corals and other reef invertebrates capable of stinging are usually left alone, but its constant swimming may be disruptive to less active fish. Don't trust this or any other wrasse with any fish or crustacean small enough to eat. Even comparatively large crustaceans may be seized, bashed to pieces on the rocks, and dined upon by the wrasse.

FEEDING

COMPATIBILITY

EASE OF KEEPING
1

SIZE
8.7 in (22 cm) 6 in (15 cm)

SYMBOL KEY	
FEEDING	
Herbivore	
Omnivore	
Predator	
COMPATIBILITY	
single specimen	
community fish	
safe with small fish	
safe with invertebrates	
EASE OF KEEPING	
scale of 1 to 10 (with 1 being easiest to keep)	
SIZE	
in the wild	
in captivity	

HALICHOERES GARNOTI

FAMILY: *LABRIDAE*
COMMON NAME: *YELLOWHEAD WRASSE*

All members of the wrasse family go through several color phases, and this common Florida-Caribbean species is no exception. Most individuals collected for the aquarium trade are juveniles, bright yellow-orange in color with a striking electric blue line down the midline of each side of the body. A thin black edging separates the blue from a ruddy orange that extends a short distance toward the back and belly like ink spreading on absorbent paper. Intermediate-phase adults are dark turquoise, with a stunning bright yellow band replacing the blue band of the juvenile. Terminal phase adults are even gaudier, with a bright yellow head and anterior body, black body posteriorly highlighted in fluorescent green, and an outrageous purple stripe along the anal fin.

FEEDING

COMPATIBILITY

EASE OF KEEPING
2

SIZE
8 in (20 cm) 6 in (15 cm)

SPECIAL CARE:
Accommodating a large, active wrasse requires a roomy tank, but otherwise this is an easily maintained species. Feedings should be frequent and consist of a variety of seafoods, primarily of animal origin. Filtration must be adequate to maintain reef tank water conditions.

HALICHOERES MACULIPINNA

FAMILY: *LABRIDAE*
COMMON NAME: *CLOWN WRASSE*

FEEDING

COMPATIBILITY

EASE OF KEEPING
3

SIZE

6 in (15 cm) 4 in (10 cm)

The juvenile color form of the Clown Wrasse has a dark brown upper body and pearly white belly. A bright yellow band begins as a "V" on the snout and extends posteriorly along the dorsal surface to the caudal peduncle. The dorsal fin and the tip of the snout are brick red. This color form matures to a bright blue phase with a broad yellow stripe running from just beneath the eye to the tail. The dorsal fin is marked with a dark eye spot, with a similar spot on the side above the belly and just anterior to the anal fin.

SPECIAL CARE: Provide perfect water conditions and plenty of rocks with algae and invertebrates. Feed small, live invertebrates, feeder fish, or chopped seafoods. Corals and other reef invertebrates capable of stinging are usually left alone. This is another species that may bury itself in the substrate, and should be provided with a layer of sand several inches deep on the bottom of the aquarium.

HALICHOERES RADIATUS

FAMILY: *LABRIDAE*
COMMON NAME: *PUDDINGWIFE*

Its charming name and the brilliant coloration of juveniles have made it a favorite with collectors for years. The yellow-orange body is marked with a ladder pattern of electric blue from the lateral line to the dorsal fin. A dark eye spot, lighter in the center and outlined in pale blue, lies in the middle of the dorsal fin and extends down the back. Only juveniles have this color pattern, with adults becoming progressively more blue-green in color. Intermediate specimens are golden, and develop blue lines on the face, paired fins, and caudal fin. The juvenile eye spot expands to form a dark area flanked by white blotches on the dorsal fin and back.

SPECIAL CARE: Like most labrids, this one feeds on a wide variety of organisms, from shrimp to small fishes. It swims constantly, but may become lazy in the aquarium and spend time resting in a favored spot. Feed a broad selection of aquarium foods, and provide ample filtration.

FEEDING

COMPATIBILITY

EASE OF KEEPING
1

SIZE

17.7 in (45 cm) 10 in (25 cm)

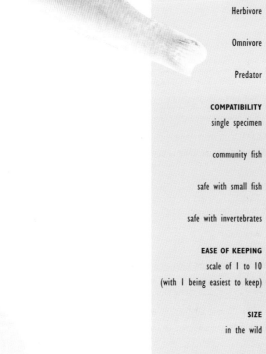

HEMIPTERONOTUS MARTINICENSIS

FAMILY: *LABRIDAE*
COMMON NAME: *ROSY RAZORFISH*

The cheeks and gill covers are pale greenish-yellow with a blue line. An area of deep blue surrounds the eye, which is perpetually coral red. The body color is a mixture of pastels, blue, yellow, and green. It is widespread in the Atlantic-Caribbean region, usually found near sea grass beds over a sandy bottom. It has the ability to dive into the sand to escape danger, tunneling some distance under the surface before emerging at a safe haven.

SPECIAL CARE: Provide a sandy substrate several inches deep or the fish may injure itself trying to escape perceived harm. Easily fed and harmless to anything it cannot eat, it can be accommodated in a long, shallow tank decorated to mimic the sea grass habitat. Water conditions should be as for other tropical marine species, although this one is not too fussy. It can be maintained with stinging invertebrates, such as the *Condylactis* anemone that shares its sea grass habitat.

FEEDING

COMPATIBILITY

EASE OF KEEPING

3

SIZE

6 in (15 cm) 4 in (10 cm)

SYMBOL KEY

FEEDING

Herbivore

Omnivore

Predator

COMPATIBILITY

single specimen

community fish

safe with small fish

safe with invertebrates

EASE OF KEEPING

scale of 1 to 10
(with 1 being easiest to keep)

SIZE

in the wild

in captivity

LIENARDELLA FASCIATA

FAMILY: *LABRIDAE*
COMMON NAME: *HARLEQUIN TUSKFISH*

FEEDING

COMPATIBILITY

EASE OF KEEPING

4

SIZE

12 in (30 cm) 7 in (18 cm)

This spectacular species has a heavily-built body with a steeply-rising forehead and arched dorsal surface, very similar to large freshwater mid-America cichlids. Its gray body is crossed by vertical, bright red blue-edged bands. The dorsal and anal fins are bright red, the pelvic and caudal fins have red edges, and the pectoral fins are yellow with a red base. The eyes are small and are high-set, but the main feature of the head is the mouth, filled with bright blue teeth. It is found in coral reefs in the western Pacific, including Australia's Great Barrier Reef, the New Hebrides, and Taiwan.

SPECIAL CARE: The Harlequin Tuskfish requires plenty of room and also appreciates a soft substrate on the aquarium floor as, like many of its relatives, it likes to burrow at night. Ensure that the aquarium has an efficient filtration system.

PSEUDOCHEILINUS HEXATAENIA

FAMILY: *LABRIDAE*
COMMON NAME: *NEON WRASSE; SIXLINE WRASSE*

Specimens are regularly imported in excellent condition from Hawaii, although the species ranges throughout the Indo-Pacific region. The body is mauve, marked on the flanks with alternating horizontal bars of golden yellow and blue.

SPECIAL CARE: Although it might eat small shrimps, this is nearly an ideal species for the reef aquarium. It feeds on a wide variety of readily available foods, including certain snails that parasitize giant clams, and certain flatworms that feed on living corals. It thus earns its place in the tank not only because of its extraordinary beauty, but also due to its usefulness in controling these pests. Provide numerous hiding places into which it can retire if it feels threatened.

FEEDING

COMPATIBILITY

EASE OF KEEPING

4

SIZE

2.8 in (7 cm) 2 in (5 cm)

PSEUDOCHEILINUS OCTOTAENIA

FAMILY: *LABRIDAE*
COMMON NAME: *EIGHT-LINED WRASSE*

FEEDING

COMPATIBILITY

EASE OF KEEPING

SIZE

5 in (13 cm) 5 in (13 cm)

Aggressive and likely to feed on some types of invertebrates, this is a hardy and adaptable wrasse that can be recommended even to beginners. It is pale orange in color with red horizontal stripes. The dorsal, caudal, and anal fins are translucent orange; the paired fins are colorless. It is an excitable species, and a jumper, so special attention must be taken to keep the tank covered and to avoid stressing it unnecessarily.
SPECIAL CARE: A large tank with ample filtration is best. Reef conditions suit most smaller wrasse species, and this one is no exception. Feed meaty seafoods in small pieces. It does best when the tank is stocked with more aggressive examples of community species, such as larger surgeonfishes, or if it is maintained alone. It has a tendency to attack more docile tank mates, and is capable of injuring them severely with its sharp canine teeth.

THALASSOMA BIFASCIATUM

FAMILY: *LABRIDAE*
COMMON NAME: *BLUEHEAD WRASSE*

FEEDING

COMPATIBILITY

EASE OF KEEPING

SIZE

6 in (15 cm) 4 in (10 cm)

This wrasse is among the most popular species imported from the Atlantic-Caribbean region. Terminal males are most commonly available. The head is bright blue, with a collar of alternating black and white bands immediately behind. The streamlined body is green, with black marks accenting the fins and tail. Juveniles are bright yellow, with a black spot on the anterior portion of the dorsal fin. They are often collected and sold under the name "banana wrasse."
SPECIAL CARE: Like most other *Thalassoma*, this one is easy to keep. It needs reef tank water quality, plenty of swimming room, and regular feedings with a variety of chopped seafoods, guppies, small shrimp, and similar fare. It will not harm corals, anemones, or other invertebrates that do not form part of its diet. This species has been successfully propagated in captivity, but commercial specimens are all collected from the sea.

THALASSOMA KLUNZINGERI

FAMILY: *LABRIDAE*
COMMON NAME: *KLUNZINGER'S WRASSE*

Like others of its genus, this Red Sea species is quite hardy, adapting greedily to the aquarium and seldom refusing typical foods. The torpedo-shaped body is pale turquoise, with a white stripe, outlined in orange, on each flank. The face bears lines in orange and blue. The fins are largely colorless. This genus of wrasses does not bury in the substrate at night, as many others do, preferring instead to sleep among rocks. Appropriate attention to this need in the arrangement of tank decorations is essential.
SPECIAL CARE: Wrasses by and large are carnivorous and predatory, although they usually eat a variety of things. This species easily reaches its natural size in a roomy tank with typical marine water quality parameters and a regular maintenance schedule. Do not keep it with any smaller, mobile organisms that it might consider as food.

FEEDING

COMPATIBILITY

EASE OF KEEPING

3

SIZE

6 in (15 cm) 6 in (15 cm)

THALASSOMA LUNARE

FAMILY: *LABRIDAE*
COMMON NAME: *MOON WRASSE; GREEN PARROT WRASSE; LYRETAIL WRASSE*

This very distinctive, attractive fish has an elongated, cylindrical body. Adult body coloration is green with purple-dotted scales making a reticulated pattern. The smoothly contoured head is marked with purple and green streaks. The long-based dorsal and anal fins are relatively narrow and have red, yellow, and blue lines along their margins. The center of the pectoral fins is purple; the center of the caudal fin is bright yellow with red and blue top and bottom edges. Juvenile fishes have dark blotches on their dorsal and caudal fins. This fish can be found in coral reefs from east Africa in the Indian Ocean, to the Solomon Islands in the mid-Pacific by way of the Philippines and Queensland, Australia.

SPECIAL CARE: This is an active species. It requires a spacious aquarium as it is constantly on the move throughout the day; however, it rests at night. It may be prudent to choose tank mates that will not be disturbed by its increasing activity. The tank should have ample filtration. No information is available on breeding in captivity.

FEEDING

COMPATIBILITY

EASE OF KEEPING
4

SIZE
10 in (25 cm) 4.9 in (12.5 cm)

THALASSOMA LUCASANUM

FAMILY: *LABRIDAE*
COMMON NAME: *RAINBOW WRASSE; PADDLEFIN WRASSE*

The male of this species is most commonly called "paddlefin" while the female is usually known as "rainbow," owing to the striking color difference. The male has a turquoise head, with a bright yellow collar, pink body, and blue tail. The female is dark brown, with white on the head, yellow on the back, a yellow stripe running from the mouth to the caudal peduncle, and a red stripe on the posterior flank that extends to the lower element of the caudal fin. Both swim with a rowing motion of the pectoral fins.

FEEDING

COMPATIBILITY

EASE OF KEEPING
3

SIZE
6 in (15 cm) 6 in (15 cm)

SPECIAL CARE: This is an easily maintained wrasse that can be recommended for the hobbyist with a community of larger, more aggressive fishes rather than a reef tank. Provide the usual care and a varied diet, and this fish should thrive for just about anyone. Feed frozen or fresh seafoods, chopped into pieces appropriate for the size of the fish's mouth.

THALASSOMA QUINQUEVITTATUM

FAMILY: *LABRIDAE*
COMMON NAME: *RED AND GREEN WRASSE*

Often imported from Hawaii, this is an excellent aquarium fish for a beginning aquarist who wants a larger tank of moderately aggressive species that are easy to keep. The body is olive green in color, fading to white on the belly. A coral red line runs along the base of the dorsal fin, and another, broken into dashes by a series of white patches, decorates the midline of the body.

SPECIAL CARE: Do not keep this wrasse with any smaller, mobile organisms that it might consider as food, and select moderately aggressive, larger tank mates. Normal marine water quality and regular maintenance are all that is necessary. Feed a varied diet of meaty seafoods.

FEEDING

COMPATIBILITY

EASE OF KEEPING
3

SIZE
6 in (15 cm) 6 in (15 cm)

SYMBOL KEY	
FEEDING	
Herbivore	
Omnivore	
Predator	
COMPATIBILITY	
single specimen	
community fish	
safe with small fish	
safe with invertebrates	
EASE OF KEEPING	
scale of 1 to 10 (with 1 being easiest to keep)	
SIZE	
in the wild	
in captivity	

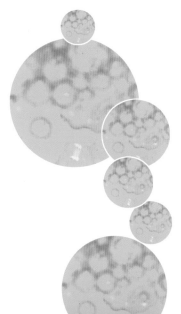

BLENNIES AND GOBIES

Because these species are often confused with each other—an understandable occurrence given that they both inhabit the same part of the aquarium and have similarly shaped bodies and swimming actions—it seems equally understandable to group them together in this encyclopedia, while pointing out the differences where they exist. These fishes are bottom-dwelling species and, to a certain extent, share a similar cylindrical body shape, with the eyes set up fairly high toward the front of a steeply-rising forehead.

These fishes often make efficient use of the substrate by making burrows and generally hiding themselves among the rubble. At times they do become territorial and decide that certain areas of the aquarium belong to them and skirmishes with tank mates can occur. Paradoxically, for bottom-

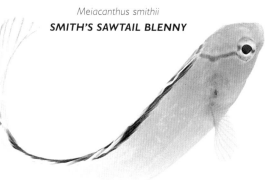

Meiacanthus smithii
SMITH'S SAWTAIL BLENNY

dwelling species, these fishes are excellent jumpers, so keep the aquarium cover firmly in place. However, maintaining blennies and gobies successfully in the aquarium is fairly easy for the aquarist, particularly as feeding presents few problems. They have an appetite for almost anything small enough to swallow.

Despite their diminutive forms, these two families have much to offer. Because these fish are of modest size, they can be accommodated in a medium-sized aquarium provided there are hideaways for territories to be set up and defended. They do not need a great deal of swimming space as they confine their activities to the substrate level, with only one or two gobies venturing into midwater.

Despite the fact that they do not strictly belong to either the Blenniidae or Gobiidae families, for convenience, fishes such as Fire Gobies (Microdesmidae) have been included in this chapter as they are often spoken of within these groups as far as aquarium-keeping is concerned.

Nemateleotris decora
PURPLE FIREFISH

CATALINA GOBY
It is quite surprising that a fish so brilliantly colored spends so much time beneath rubble on the seabed.

BLENNIES

In spite of their limited area of activity, blennies soon become the characters of the aquarium, with their constant bustling ways as they scurry to and fro among the rocky rubble, with the sudden dash for cover as something passes overhead. Blennies can be recognized quite easily from their bottom-sharing neighbors the gobies—blennies have a single, long-based, dorsal fin and separated pelvic fins that, unlike other fishes, emerge on the body ahead of the pectoral fins. They often sport curly eyebrow-like growths, called "cirri," on their heads. Body coloration is cryptic, making for excellent camouflage among their surroundings while one species—the Saber-tooth Blenny (*Aspidontus taeniatus*), not only has identical body shape and coloration to the Cleanerfish (*Labroides dimidiatus*) but mimics its actions so successfully that it can get close enough to unsuspecting fish to tear chunks of flesh from them. Blennies are egg depositors (usually in hiding places such as pipes or caves) and exercise parental care of their young.

ACANTHEMBLEMARIA ASPERA

FAMILY: *BLENNIIDAE*
COMMON NAME: *ROUGHHEAD BLENNY*

The common name for this fish comes from the collection of spines and densely branched cirri on its head. Coloration varies from yellow to tan and various combinations of brown and gray that allow the blenny to blend into its surroundings. It lives on coral reefs, where it seeks out a hole in the coral rock made by a burrowing worm or mollusk. From this secure haven it peers out, darting to snatch food and returning instantly to the hole.
SPECIAL CARE: Provide perfect water conditions and rocks with suitable holes. Feed small, live invertebrates, such as brine, shrimp, *nauplii*, blackworms, or other plankton substitutes. Eventually, the fish learns to accept finely chopped seafoods. Since this fish remains small, it is a good candidate for a species tank. Corals and other reef invertebrates capable of stinging are usually left alone.

FEEDING

COMPATIBILITY

EASE OF KEEPING
3

SIZE
1.5 in (4 cm) 1.5 in (4 cm)

ECSENIUS BICOLOR

FAMILY: *BLENNIIDAE*
COMMON NAME: *TWO-COLORED BLENNY*

The Two-Colored Blenny, found throughout the Indo-Pacific region, has a laterally-compressed, elongated body with a blunt head and a tapering rear section. The front two-thirds of the body is brown-purple shading to yellow-orange at the rear, which reaches into the center of the caudal fin. When spawning the coloration changes—the male changes to red with white bars, the female is light brown and orange-yellow. After spawning the male is often dark blue with pale blotches on the flanks. The head has an almost vertical forehead with the eyes set up high. The long-based dorsal fin nearly joins up with the spade-shaped caudal fin; the anal fin runs along the bottom of the yellow rear part of the body and shares its color at its base. The dorsal fin is the same color as the front of the body, the caudal and anal fins have body-colored edges.
SPECIAL CARE: This fish requires a modest-sized aquarium with a rubble-type substrate with some open areas of sand. It appreciates plenty of retreats, so you may not always be able to see its full coloration. It is an egg depositor that displays considerable parental care. It is best kept in a species aquarium.

FEEDING

COMPATIBILITY

EASE OF KEEPING
3

SIZE
4 in (10 cm) 2.5 in (6.5 cm)

MEIACANTHUS SMITHII

FAMILY: *BLENNIIDAE*
COMMON NAME: *SMITH'S SAWTAIL BLENNY*

FEEDING

COMPATIBILITY

EASE OF KEEPING
3

SIZE
3.2 in (8 cm) 2 in (5 cm)

The sawtooth effect on the rear ends of the rays on its caudal fin accounts for this fish's popular name. Body coloration is a delicate gray, shading down to a paler hue on the ventral surface. A dark stripe runs from the eyes diagonally upward to the front of the dorsal fin. The head is rather blunt but the forehead is not quite as steep as in other species within the family. The eyes are set well forward, almost at the corner of the slightly downturned mouth. The long-based dorsal fin has a broad black stripe along its length bordered by light blue and white on the outside edge; the anal fin and rounded caudal fin are blue. This fish is endemic to both the Indian and Pacific oceans. This species has a lookalike, *Plagiotremus sp*. The differences are that it lacks the diagonal stripe from the eyes to the dorsal fin and it has a white edge on both sides of the dark stripe on the dorsal fin.

SPECIAL CARE: This species is best kept in a modest-sized aquarium that is furnished with rubble-type substrate with some open, sandy areas. It likes to hide, so include some rocks in the tank set-up. It will be most content in a species aquarium.

OPHIOBLENNIUS ATLANTICUS

FAMILY: *BLENNIIDAE*
COMMON NAME: *REDLIP BLENNY*

FEEDING

COMPATIBILITY

EASE OF KEEPING
3

SIZE
4.7 in (12 cm) 3 in (7.5 cm)

Found in the waters of the west Atlantic from North Carolina, north to Bermuda, and south to Brazil, the high-set eyes on the almost vertical forehead give this comb tooth blenny a commanding view of its surroundings. Its red-lipped terminal mouth is wide and businesslike too, making this territorially obsessed species a force to be reckoned with. The front-half of the thickset but tapering body is black-brown, fading to a delicate blue-gray. However, coloration is varied with some species being dark all over or others predominantly pale. The dorsal fin runs the entire length of the dorsal surface but the anal fin is only half-length. The small caudal fin has a dark center section fanning out from the caudal peduncle.

SPECIAL CARE: This fish requires a modest-sized aquarium with a rubble-type substrate and some open areas of sand. Rocks and caves are needed to provide retreats in which it can hide. This species prefers lower levels of the aquarium and is an egg-depositor that provides parental care for its young.

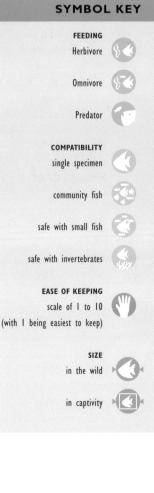

SYMBOL KEY

FEEDING
Herbivore

Omnivore

Predator

COMPATIBILITY
single specimen

community fish

safe with small fish

safe with invertebrates

EASE OF KEEPING
scale of 1 to 10
(with 1 being easiest to keep)

SIZE
in the wild

in captivity

GOBIES

Gobies and their related species total over 2,000. Species are found in all manner of waters—salt, brackish, and freshwater. Gobies have two separate dorsal fins and their pelvic fins are fused together to form a suction disc, by means of which the fish can anchor itself in position. There are no lateral line system openings along the flanks but such a sensory system is present with the opening pores appearing on the head. It is the arrangement of these pores that may be the main distinguishing feature among the various species in this large family. Vertebrae counts and adult coloration patterns are also often used to sort out the lookalikes. Gobies deposit their eggs under a stone or a similar hiding place, and they are guarded by the male.

GOBIOSOMA MULTIFASCIATUM

FAMILY: *GOBIIDAE*
COMMON NAME: *GREEN-BANDED GOBY*

FEEDING

COMPATIBILITY

EASE OF KEEPING
3

SIZE
1.5 in (4 cm) 1.2 in (3 cm)

Should you care to count them, there are no less than 19 light green bands encircling this fish's dark green body. Two red stripes run from the snout rearward, each crossing an eye to end just above the pectoral fins. The underside of the head is white. All fins, including the two dorsal fins, are pale green. There is a lookalike species, *Ginsburgellus novemlineatus*, that has a bluish-black body marked with blue rings. Found in the Bahamas, Cuba, Venzuela, and the western Atlantic, this shy species prefers the lower levels of the aquarium.
SPECIAL CARE: Provide a modest-sized aquarium with a rubble-type substrate and some open areas of sand. Rocks and caves will provide retreats.

AMBLYELEOTRIS GUTTATA

FEEDING

COMPATIBILITY

EASE OF KEEPING
3

SIZE
3.5 in (9 cm) 2.5 in (6.5 cm)

FAMILY: *GOBIIDAE*
COMMON NAME: *SPOTTED PRAWN GOBY*

Originating in the Philippines, Samoa, northwest Australia, and the Great Barrier Reef, this fish has a body and fins covered with a sprinkling of bright red spots. Two dark triangular areas spread upward from the ventral surface, one on either side of the pelvic fins. The eyes are set high on the head and are marked with four dark quadrants. The caudal fin is spear-shaped.
SPECIAL CARE: This species prefers the middle and lower levels of a modest-sized aquarium. Provide rubble-type substrate and some open areas of sand; rocky caves and pieces of plastic pipe will supply retreats.

GOBIOSOMA OCEANOPS

FAMILY: *GOBIIDAE*
COMMON NAME: *NEON GOBY; CLEANER GOBY*

FEEDING

COMPATIBILITY

EASE OF KEEPING
3

SIZE
1.5 in (4 cm) 1.2 in (3 cm)

The outstanding feature of this species, endemic to the western Atlantic, is its coloration. The dark body is trimmed with two parallel electric blue lines running along the dorsal surface from snout to caudal fin. It is the position and variance in pattern in these lines, particularly over the head, that helps distinguish this fish from other species of *Gobiosoma*. While the sexes can be recognized at breeding time—the genital papilla of the male is pointed, the female's blunter—generally there are no other visual differences.
SPECIAL CARE: This longstanding favorite is a hardy fish that has been bred in captivity for many years. It should be kept in a modest-sized aquarium with plenty of rubble, as it spends most of its time at the bottom of the tank. As its alternative name implies, it offers some degree of "cleaning service" to other fish. Although peaceful, the Neon Goby may be more interesting in an aquarium of its own.

VALENCIENNEA STRIGATA

FAMILY: *GOBIIDAE*
COMMON NAME: *BLUE-STREAK GOBY; BLUE CHEEK GOBY*

Native to East Africa and the Marquesas Islands, the Ryuku Islands, and Lord Howe Island in the Pacific Ocean. The basic body color of this species is steely-blue. The most striking feature, however, is the bright yellow area of the snout, lower face, and gill cover that is topped by an electric blue line. There is a faint covering of red lines on the body and fins. Its eggs are laid freshwater cichlid-fashion and are guarded by the male.

SPECIAL CARE: This species prefers the lower levels of the tank. Provide a modest-sized aquarium with a rubble-type substrate and some open areas of sand; rocks and caves will supply retreats.

FEEDING

COMPATIBILITY

EASE OF KEEPING

5

SIZE

7 in (18 cm) 3 in (7.5 cm)

NEMATELEOTRIS DECORA

FEEDING

COMPATIBILITY

EASE OF KEEPING
3

SIZE

3.5 in (9 cm) 2.4 in (6 cm)

FAMILY: *MICRODESMIDAE*
COMMON NAME: *PURPLE FIREFISH*

This striking fish is found in the region of the central Indian Ocean to the central Pacific Ocean. It has an elongated, slightly cylindrical body with a blunt head and a tapering rear section. Body coloration is divided into two distinct areas: the front-half of the body is silvery-cream with a violet area to the top of the head and along the dorsal surface; the rear-half of the body is brownish-gray. The small head has large eyes that are set well forward. The first few rays of the first dorsal fin are extended and are black, violet, and red just like the long-based second dorsal fin, anal fin, and lyre-patterned caudal fin. Even the small pelvic fins are similarly-patterned. A feature of this species, together with other members within the genus, is that the pelvic fins are not fused together but are split into two as is more normal in other fishes.

SPECIAL CARE: Keep in a modest-sized aquarium with a rubble-type substrate. A number of these fishes can share an aquarium provided that enough retreats are available and that there are some open areas in which to swim. When shoaling together they make a spectacular display.

NEMATELEOTRIS MAGNIFICA

FAMILY: *MICRODESMIDAE*
COMMON NAME: *FIREFISH; MAGNIFICENT HOVER-GOBY*

The body shape of this fish is very similar to that of *N. decora*. As with the previous species, its body coloring is divided into two distinct areas. The front-half of the body is silvery-cream with a yellow area to the top of the head and along the dorsal surface; the rear-half is brownish-gray shading first to red and finally to very dark crimson. The small head has large bluish eyes that are set well forward. The first few rays of the first dorsal fin are extended and are yellow with a red front edge; the long-based second dorsal and anal fins have a yellow base with a dark red outer margin marked with a dark blue or brown line. The pelvic fins are elongated and whitish-yellow. It is endemic to the stretch of water from the central Indian Ocean to the central Pacific Ocean.

SPECIAL CARE: See *N. decora* for care information. Both of these species are equally interesting aquarium subjects.

FEEDING

COMPATIBILITY

EASE OF KEEPING
3

SIZE

2.8 in (7 cm) 2 in (5 cm)

SYMBOL KEY

FEEDING

Herbivore

Omnivore

Predator

COMPATIBILITY

single specimen

community fish

safe with small fish

safe with invertebrates

EASE OF KEEPING

scale of 1 to 10
(with 1 being easiest to keep)

SIZE

in the wild

in captivity

BOXFISHES, COWFISHES, AND PUFFERFISHES

Few other species of fishes have more sophisticated means of defense than those in this group, for they use almost every trick in the book to stay safe from harm. Bony plates (effectively an outside skeleton), cryptic camouflage, sharp spines, means of at least doubling their size, and the ability to exude toxins are all put to good use. Members of this group are found in most tropical areas of the Atlantic, Indian, and Pacific Oceans.

Boxfishes are the "armored tanks" of the fish world, with fins sited at almost all the corners of their oblong bodies. Cowfishes have "horns" on the head. Coloration is sometimes brilliant and bizarre, causing some

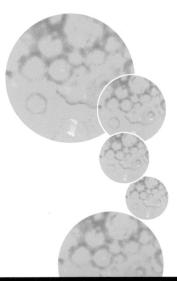

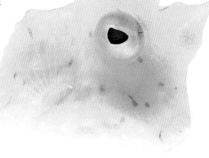

Lactoria cornuta
LONGHORNED COWFISH

confusion over species identification—this was eventually resolved when it was discovered that the color patterning was different between the sexes of the same species. Many attractive juveniles grow up to be large, less-appealing, and dull colored adults. Handle these fish with extreme care, as any kind of stress will trigger the release of a toxin which kills everything, including the originator.

Pufferfish use inflation tactics to thwart would-be predators; inflating their bodies not only makes the attacker question the practicability of swallowing the pufferfish, but also the presence of erectile spines over the body is another most effective deterrent. Should these deterrents not prove sufficient, the puffer's toxic flesh may kill the predator. Pufferfish have sharp teeth which are simply two bony plates on each jaw; these can sever equipment cables and crush heaters just as effortlessly as shelled invertebrates.

Because of their toxin-producing reaction in the face of possible adversity, these fishes should not be kept in a "busy" aquarium of active fishes which might stress them, and certainly not in a reef tank or with invertebrates.

Canthigaster valentini
BLACK-SADDLED PUFFER

SHARP-NOSED PUFFERFISH
This fish has a false eye spot near its dorsal fin to divert an attacker's attention from the real eye.

CHILOMYCTERUS SCHOEPFI

FAMILY: *DIODONTIDAE*
COMMON NAME: *SPINY BOXFISH; STRIPED BURRFISH*

The ground color of the body is yellow, marked with undulating dark lines and occasional yellow-ringed dark spots, the underside is white. Its body is covered in short spines that are held erect. The teeth on each jaw are fused together to form two large teeth (*diodon* meaning two teeth). Most species in this family have the ability to inflate themselves when threatened, making it difficult for a predator to swallow them. Their natural habitat is the coral reefs of the Caribbean.

SPECIAL CARE: This fish requires a well-furnished aquarium with excellent water quality maintained by frequent water changes and efficient filtration. Provide plenty of retreats. It is assumed to be more active at night since little information on daytime activities has been reported. This fish is best kept in a separate species aquarium, it should certainly not be kept with small fishes on whom it would prey. Males tend to quarrel among themselves.

FEEDING

COMPATIBILITY

EASE OF KEEPING
5

SIZE
12 in (30 cm) 6 in (15 cm)

DIODON HOLOCANTHUS

FAMILY: *DIODONTIDAE*
COMMON NAME: *LONGSPINED PORCUPINEFISH*

The body is patchy golden brown in color with a paler underside. Several widely-spaced dark dots appear all over the body. The pectoral fins are large; the dorsal and anal fins are set well back on the body, the caudal fin is rounded, and the pelvic fins are absent. Its spines are usually carried folded back against the body. Its mouth is terminally-placed and, as is characteristic of this species, its teeth are fused on each jaw. It is found among rocks and seaweeds in all warm seas.

SPECIAL CARE: The strong teeth of this predator can make short work of crustaceans, shellfish, and any other invertebrate life, so this fish should not be kept in an aquarium with them. It reaches a large size in nature but remains fairly small (6 in/15 cm) in the average aquarium. The tank should be well-furnished and excellent water quality maintained.

FEEDING

COMPATIBILITY

EASE OF KEEPING
5

SIZE
20 in (50 cm) 6 in (15 cm)

LACTORIA CORNUTA

FAMILY: *OSTRACIIDAE*
COMMON NAME: *LONGHORNED COWFISH*

Its body is a tapering box shape with the highest point almost perpendicularly-situated above the mouth. The skin is covered by a series of bony plates instead of scales with the result that the body is almost completely inflexible with the exception of the caudal peduncle which emerges from the back of the "box." Its body coloration is yellow with some blue dotting and facial lines. At each forward "top corner" of the head are two horn-like growths that have provided the species with its apt, popular name.

Two similar projections are found at the bottom rear corners too. The forehead is almost vertical with the eyes set high up, the mouth is downturned. The dorsal fin is set well back on the downward-sloping back, while the small anal fin is located between the two rear "horns." The caudal peduncle increases in length with age and supports a small caudal fin. Pelvic fins are absent. Propulsion is provided by combined movements of the dorsal, anal, and pectoral fins. It dwells on the seabed around coral reefs throughout the Indo-Pacific region with the exception of Hawaii.

SPECIAL CARE: A popular aquarium subject due to its unusual appearance; it rarely reaches its full size in captivity, even in public aquariums. Like all members of the cowfish family, it releases poison into the water when frightened. It is advisable to transport them separately. The tank should be well-furnished with excellent water quality maintained by frequent water changes and efficient filtration No information is available on breeding in captivity.

FEEDING

COMPATIBILITY

EASE OF KEEPING
5

SIZE
20 in (50 cm) 3 in (7.5 cm)

OSTRACION MELEAGRIS

FAMILY: *OSTRACIIDAE*
COMMON NAME: *BLUE-SPOTTED BOXFISH*

This fish has an elongated body shape but it retains the tapering box construction of other species in the Ostraciidae family. The sexes can be easily distinguished as their coloration is very different. Males have a black dorsal surface covered with white spots; this area is separated from the lower part of the body by a thin yellow line. The lower flanks are a violet color with yellow dots. The dorsal and anal fins are yellowish, the caudal fin is violet with black spots, and has a yellow rear edge. Females are generally black all over with a covering of white dots. The dorsal and anal fins are darkish, the caudal fin continues the body coloration. In both sexes the forehead is almost vertical and the mouth downturned. The male's eyes are dark surrounded by yellow, those of the female are dark with a white-spotted dark surround. The difference in coloration between the sexes resulted in incorrect classification for many years, *O. lentiginosum* being the erroneous name given to the male fish. The Blue-Spotted Boxfish can be found in coral reefs throughout the Indo-Pacific region.
SPECIAL CARE: Boxfishes need a peaceful aquarium with non-boisterous tankmates. A sandy substrate will help them to pick up food more easily. Ensure that water quality is maintained.

FEEDING

COMPATIBILITY

EASE OF KEEPING
7

SIZE
8 in (20 cm) 4.9 in (12.5 cm)

Coloration differs between male (below) and female (right) Blue-Spotted Boxfishes.

AROTHRON NIGROPUNCTATUS

FAMILY: *TETRAODONTIDAE*
COMMON NAME: *BLACK SPOTTED PUFFER; DOG FACE PUFFER*

Perhaps the favorite member of its family, this is a good choice for a community of moderately aggressive species, such as surgeonfishes and larger angels. It is highly variable in coloration, with overall pigmentation usually blue-gray or brownish, but in some individuals the entire body is black, gold, or orange. There are varying numbers of black and yellow spots. The face is commonly darker, with white below the eyes and on the snout, and the tip of the snout is black. The resemblance, in some specimens, to a dog's face is quite remarkable.
SPECIAL CARE: This species may be shy and refuse to eat at first, but once accustomed to the aquarium most become family pets. Feed a varied diet of meaty seafoods chopped into small pieces, and keep this fish in a community tank. Most invertebrates will be nibbled on, so do not keep it in a reef aquarium. More than one specimen can be housed in the same tank, unlike some members of the genus. Good news for those who find it irresistibly cute.

FEEDING

COMPATIBILITY

EASE OF KEEPING
3

SIZE
13 in (33 cm) 10 in (25 cm)

SYMBOL KEY

FEEDING
Herbivore

Omnivore

Predator

COMPATIBILITY
single specimen

community fish

safe with small fish

safe with invertebrates

EASE OF KEEPING
scale of 1 to 10
(with 1 being easiest to keep)

SIZE
in the wild

in captivity

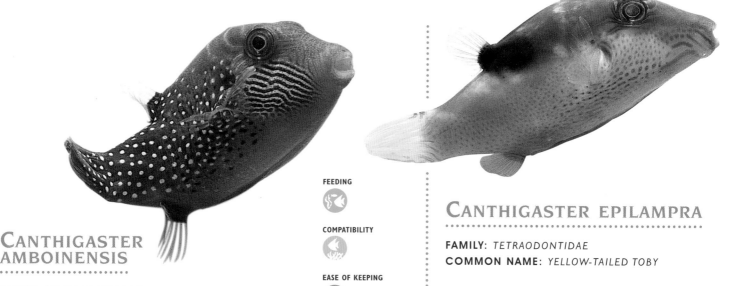

CANTHIGASTER AMBOINENSIS

FAMILY: *TETRAODONTIDAE*
COMMON NAME: *AMBON TOBY*

FEEDING

COMPATIBILITY

EASE OF KEEPING
3

SIZE
6 in (15 cm) 6 in (15 cm)

Puffers never fail to delight, despite a tendency to occasionally nip the fins of other fishes. This Indo-Pacific species is gray to brownish, overlaid with bluish-white dots on the flank and caudal peduncle, and darker dots and scrawls on the face and gill covers. Paired fins are colorless, while the dorsal, caudal, and anal fins are dark, often trimmed in a pale blue.
SPECIAL CARE: A large tank with ample filtration is the best environment for this fish. Reef conditions suit most puffer species, and this one is no exception. Feed any sort of meaty seafood products available, always remembering to vary the diet to ensure adequate nutrition. Chop foods into suitable-size pieces for the puffer's tiny mouth. Sessile invertebrates are ignored. Avoid keeping the Ambon Toby with aggressive species.

CANTHIGASTER CORONATA

FAMILY: *TETRAODONTIDAE*
COMMON NAME: *CROWNED TOBY; THREE-BARRED TOBY*

FEEDING

COMPATIBILITY

EASE OF KEEPING
3

SIZE
5 in (13 cm) 5 in (13 cm)

White with three dark brown saddles, each outlined in yellow-orange dots, this Indo-Pacific species is an ideal aquarium fish. Yellow and blue lines radiate from each eye, above which is the dark brown "crown" that gives the fish its common name. Blue-green and yellow spots on the tail and caudal peduncle and a yellow stripe on the cheek make it most appealing.
SPECIAL CARE: Feed any small, meaty seafoods available, always remembering to vary the diet to ensure adequate nutrition, and to provide pieces sufficiently small for the fish's mouth. Avoid keeping it with aggressive species, such as triggers or lionfish who might regard the puffer as dinner. Puffers are toxic, and the predator might also be lost as a result of such an incident. Brilliant illumination, as is required for living corals, shows off its coloration to perfection, and the fish tends to ignore invertebrates it cannot eat.

CANTHIGASTER EPILAMPRA

FAMILY: *TETRAODONTIDAE*
COMMON NAME: *YELLOW-TAILED TOBY*

FEEDING

COMPATIBILITY

EASE OF KEEPING
3

SIZE
4 in (10 cm) 4 in (10 cm)

Somewhat less common than the other members of its family, this sharp-nosed puffer, or toby, is mottled in gray, black, and white, with a distinctive, bright yellow caudal fin. The paired fins are colorless, while the dorsal and anal fins sometimes continue the coloration of the body. It is found in deeper waters on the outer reef in much of the Indo-Pacific.

SPECIAL CARE: Provide a roomy tank, and feed a varied diet of meaty seafoods, chopped into small pieces. Living as it does in deeper water, dim lighting is appreciated, and this species should not be kept in a typical reef tank with brilliant illumination, despite the fact that it, like most of its genus, is unlikely to harm sessile invertebrates, or anything else that it cannot eat. Because it has toxic flesh, it achieves a measure of protection from predators in its natural habitat, although in the aquarium an encounter may lead to the death of both the puffer and the predator. Choose instead surgeonfishes or larger angelfishes as tankmates for this fish.

CANTHIGASTER VALENTINI

FAMILY: *TETRAODONTIDAE*
COMMON NAME: *BLACK-SADDLED PUFFER*

The body coloration is white with two black wedged-shaped markings that extend down from the dorsal surface. A saddle marking extends across the eyes and another covers the top of the caudal peduncle; the areas between these dark patches are often yellowish. The pale areas of the body are covered with yellow-brown spots, the ventral surface is plain white. Its blue-lined forehead has a pronounced bulge to accommodate the gold-rimmed eyes and the small mouth is terminally-situated. All of the fins are yellowish—the caudal fin has black top and bottom edges at the section nearest to the body. Pelvic fins are absent. Its natural habitat is the coral reefs throughout the Indo-Pacific region, excluding Hawaii and the Queensland coast. A similar species is *C. cinctus*, although many authorities consider this to be a synonym for this species. Another totally different species, the Saddled Filefish, *Paraluteres prionurus*, mimics this fish.

SPECIAL CARE: While generally peaceful, some pufferfishes resent their own kind as tank companions and can be territorial. Snails (from a freshwater aquarium) are appreciated as food—the strong jaws soon crack open the shells. It requires a well-furnished aquarium with excellent water quality maintained by frequent water changes and efficient filtration.

FEEDING

COMPATIBILITY

EASE OF KEEPING
3

SIZE

1.2 in (3 cm) 3.2 in (8 cm)

CANTHIGASTER MARGARITATUS

FAMILY: *TETRAODONTIDAE*
COMMON NAME: *SHARP-NOSED PUFFER; OCELLATED PUFFERFISH; PEACOCK-EYED PUFFERFISH; DIAMOND-FLECKED PUFFERFISH*

FEEDING

COMPATIBILITY

EASE OF KEEPING
3

SIZE

4 in (10 cm) 3.2 in (8 cm)

The Sharp-Nosed Puffer is widespread throughout the Indo-Pacific region excluding Hawaii and the Queensland coast. This fish has an elongated body shape, that is relatively deep in the mid-section with equally convex dorsal and ventral contours. Body coloration is golden brown with a paler ventral surface. The upper surface is covered with dark-edged bluish-white lines (especially on the forehead and around the eyes), the lower flanks are covered with dark-edged white spots, patterning that extends into the caudal fin. A large, white-edged dark spot is situated at the base of the set-back dorsal fin. The forehead has a pronounced bulge to accommodate the eyes and the small mouth is terminally-situated. Pelvic fins are absent. The mouth is equipped with a divided bone on each jaw to give four "teeth," a characteristic noted in the family name, *tetra* meaning four and *odon* meaning toothed. The species' distinctive color pattern is an indication that its flesh is poisonous. Despite being a member of the pufferfish group, this species only partially inflates when stressed or threatened. The names *C. solandri* and *C. papus* have also been ascribed to this species due, no doubt, to its widespread distribution and subsequent "discovery" by various collectors.

SPECIAL CARE: This fish requires a well-furnished aquarium with excellent water quality. The cleanliness of the water should be maintained by frequent water changes and efficient filtration. It can be territorial, but it is generally peaceful. No information on breeding in captivity is available.

SYMBOL KEY

FEEDING
Herbivore

Omnivore

Predator

COMPATIBILITY
single specimen

community fish

safe with small fish

safe with invertebrates

EASE OF KEEPING
scale of 1 to 10
(with 1 being easiest to keep)

SIZE
in the wild

in captivity

EELS

An eel of generous (if not terrifying) proportions holds a certain morbid fascination. At once, they can be both very attractive and intimidating, but many are not practical for the average size home aquarium. Found in all tropical seas there are around 200 species belonging to the family Muraenidae, with sizes ranging from a few inches to around 10 feet (3 m), although most recognized aquarium specimens are a manageable 2 to 3 feet (61 to 91 cm).

Gymnothorax milliaris
GOLDENTAIL MORAY

As a cursory acquaintance with eels will show, most of their time is spent in rocky retreats with just their head protruding, usually with a regularly-gaping mouth to betray their presence. A large spacious but rockily-landscaped aquarium is therefore mandatory, with plentiful filtration and well-oxygenated water—the gaping mouth is a respiratory action not necessarily an invitation for food.

Moray eels are carnivores and a distinction between their preferred foods can be gauged by their teeth: sharp, needle-like teeth are handy for tearing off pieces of fish,

while larger teeth are more likely to be used for crushing invertebrates. Because of their appetites, regular partial water changes are necessary.

The cryptic patterning on many species makes them hard to spot in the constantly changing light patterns on the coral reef. Most have poor eyesight but possess an exceptional sense of smell which is extremely helpful to them, as many Morays are more active at night than during the day. Similarly to other marine fishes, some Moray eels are not suited to aquarium care, either because of their eventual adult size, death through self-imposed starvation, or simply because they climb out of the aquarium. Handling Moray eels is difficult and not without danger. A bite from their often bacteria-infected teeth can bring illness, so always wear strong gloves.

Snake eels, Family Opichthidae, so resemble a reptile that they have been mistaken for sea snakes.

Echidna polyzona
GIRDLED MORAY

MORAY EEL
All eels spend most of their time in among crevices in rocks, with only their heads protruding.

ECHIDNA CATENATA

FAMILY: *MURAENIDAE*
COMMON NAME: *CHAIN MORAY*

All Morays have elongated, snakelike bodies, lacking pectoral and pelvic fins. The dorsal, caudal, and anal fins are fused to form a continuous ribbon around the posterior portion of the body. Morays are nocturnal predators, and this one is no exception. It lives among rocks in shallow, clear waters, often coming inshore to feed on crab, its favorite food. The dark brown body is attractively patterned in scrawls of pale cream to bright yellow that bear a slight resemblance to chains, hence the common name. Found in western Atlantic waters from Florida to Brazil, including the Ascension Islands. The Chain Moray appears threatening but only actually bites if provoked.

SPECIAL CARE: Provide good water conditions and plenty of rocks with hiding places. Feed small, live crabs, shrimp, feeder fish, or pieces of fish or shellfish meat. Corals and other sessile invertebrates are ignored, but never trust a large Moray with any mobile creature large enough for it to swallow. The constant opening and closing of the fish's mouth is an aid to its breathing, and is not a threat display, as is often incorrectly assumed.

FEEDING

COMPATIBILITY

EASE OF KEEPING
5

SIZE
30 in (78 cm)   23.6 in (60 cm)

ECHIDNA POLYZONA

FAMILY: *MURAENIDAE*
COMMON NAME: *GIRDLED MORAY*

This fish's body shape is typical of the family. It has a blunt snout with a relatively small head when compared with the total length of its body. Its body is covered with tough skin and decorated with alternate bands of black and white, the former being the more predominant color. The dorsal and anal fins both extend around the rear end of the fish to include the caudal fin. The dorsal fin runs almost the complete length of the body, the anal fin for about one-third. This species is an egg-scatterer by nature but no information is available on captive breeding. It is widespread throughout the Red Sea, and Indian and Pacific oceans.

SPECIAL CARE: Like other members of the family, the Girdled Moray only presents its head for continuous viewing, the remainder being hidden behind rocks or in suitably-sized pots or pipes thoughtfully supplied by its owner. It is generally peaceful unless disturbed or threatened. Nocturnal by nature, this species is not suitable for a community collection of anything but very large fishes. It should be housed in a large aquarium and the hood must be very securely fixed for these fishes can easily escape.

FEEDING

COMPATIBILITY

EASE OF KEEPING
8

SIZE
23.6 in (60 cm)   23.6 in (60 cm)

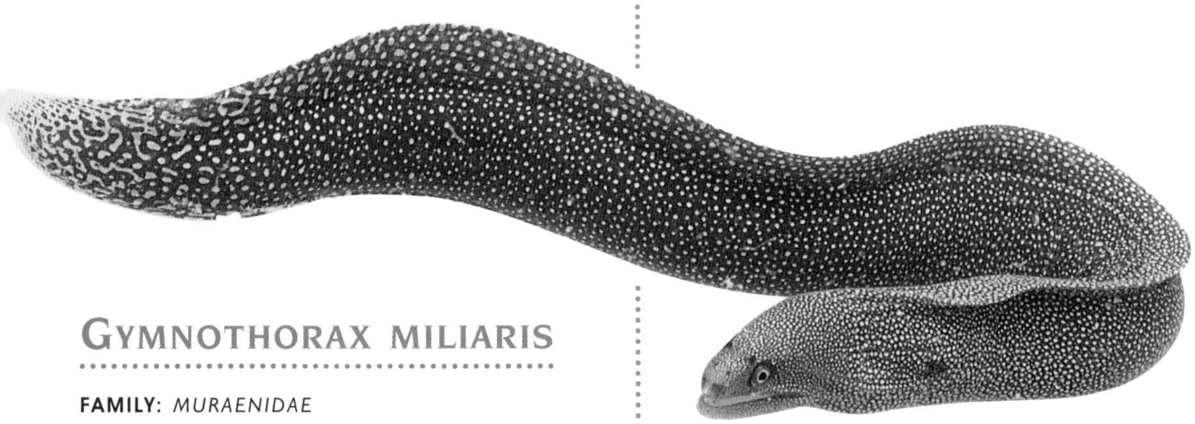

GYMNOTHORAX MILIARIS

FAMILY: *MURAENIDAE*
COMMON NAME: *GOLDENTAIL MORAY*

All Morays are nocturnal predators and this one is no exception. It lives among rocks on the reef, ranging down to deeper waters, and emerges from its lair at night to forage. This species is common in the Caribbean islands, less so in Florida. The dark brown body is covered with yellow spots that vary in size, depending upon the individual. The tip of the tail is bright golden yellow, and there is a golden ring encircling the eyes. This Moray has little fear of humans and may bite if provoked. Some authorities have suggested that it should be classified in the genus *Siderea*—a name derived from a Latin word meaning "star constellations"—possibly referring to the starry decorations on its flanks.

SPECIAL CARE: Provide good water conditions and plenty of rocks with hiding places. Feed small, live crabs, shrimp, feeder fish, or pieces of fish or shellfish meat. Corals and other sessile invertebrates are ignored, but never trust a large Moray with any mobile creature large enough for it to swallow. The constant opening and closing of the fish's mouth is an aid to its breathing, and is not a threat display, as is often incorrectly assumed.

FEEDING

COMPATIBILITY

EASE OF KEEPING
5

SIZE
23.6 in (60 cm) 17.7 in (45 cm)

MYRICHTHYS OCELLATUS

FAMILY: *OPHICHTHYIDAE*
COMMON NAME: *GOLD SPOTTED SNAKE EEL*

These eels lack paired fins and the dorsal, anal, and caudal fins combine to form a continuous band around the elongated body. The downward pointing snout often extends over the mouth, a characteristic that is typical of the genus. This species is tan, sometimes yellowish-green, with bright golden yellow spots surrounded by a diffuse area of dark pigment. They so strongly resemble snakes that even experienced aquarists may be fooled. Preferring a sandy bottom, the fish hides by day and forages at night for small invertebrates and fishes.

SPECIAL CARE: Provide good marine tank water conditions and plenty of rocks with hiding places. Feed live shrimp or pieces of shellfish, or fish meat. Placing the food on the end of a small, pointed stick and wiggling it enticingly near the eel may help train it to accept aquarium foods more quickly. Corals and other sessile invertebrates are ignored. Keep the tank tightly covered. Eels have a reputation for being able to squeeze through the smallest opening to escape.

FEEDING

COMPATIBILITY

EASE OF KEEPING
5

SIZE
45.2 in (115 cm) 35.4 in (90 cm)

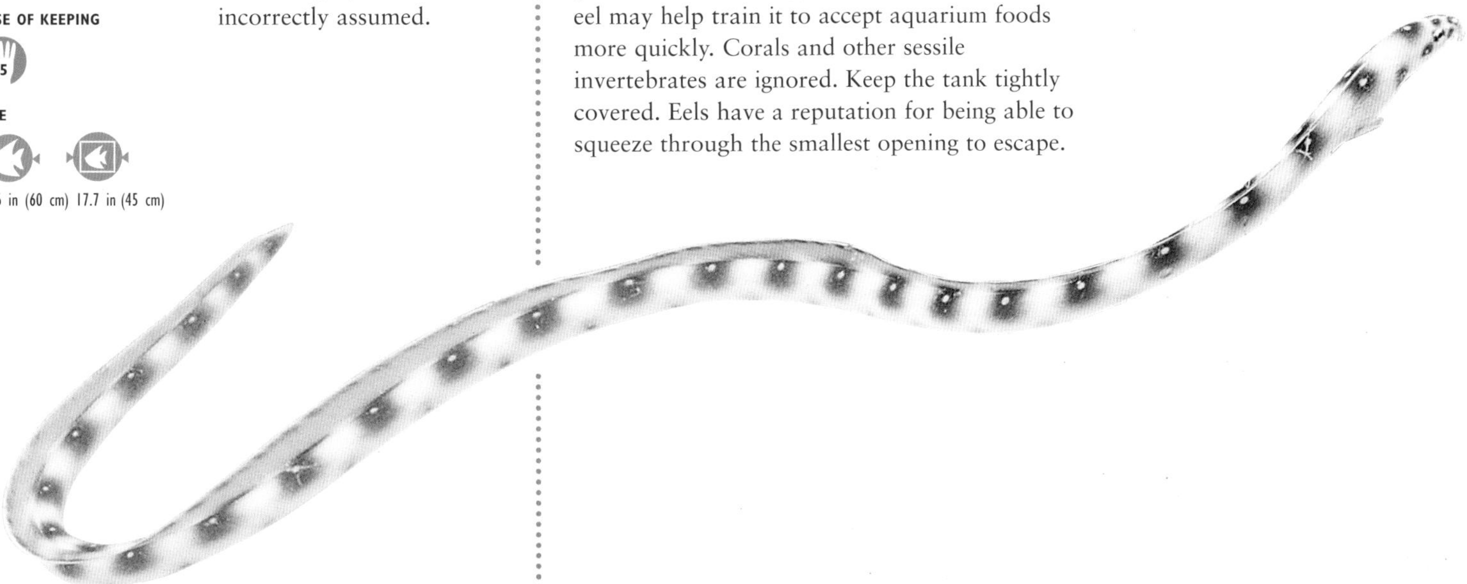

GROUPERS AND BASSLETS

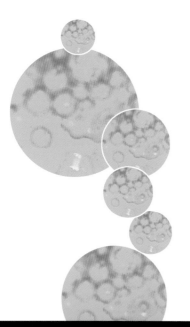

While the larger members of the Serranidae and Grammidae families might be regarded as "status symbols" for the larger aquarium, there are modest-sized species that are quite charming and suitable for most home aquariums.

Groupers are wide-ranging in their distribution as they can be found worldwide in all tropical seas. While they give the appearance of the "bully on the block," they are more likely to be found resting undercover and prowling around the bottom of coral stands. Therefore, the aquarium should be suitably furnished to accommodate this particular habit.

It is not unexpected that such fishes don't get on well together within the close confines of the aquarium and it is usual to keep a single

Gamma melacara
BLACK-CAP GRAMMA

specimen in each aquarium. However, there are exceptions, and while the smaller basslets may not be taxonomically tied to the same family tree, they could be regarded as miniature, or scaled down counterparts of their larger relative.

These brilliantly colored fishes include the rather delicate *Anthias*, the almost impossibly-colored dottybacks (*Pseudochromis*) and grammas. Many are very territorial and benefit from being kept in a one species collection in a separate aquarium. A further bonus of these particular fishes is that many advances have been made in captive breeding. Members of both of these families of fishes require the very best of conditions; the larger, hearty-eating species need good filtration while the smaller fishes are suitable for reef systems.

Variola louti
LYRETAIL GROUPER

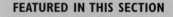
STRIATED GROUPER
Groupers like to hide in a lair, waiting to ambush any potential food that might pass by.

GRAMMA LORETO

FAMILY: *GRAMMIDAE*
COMMON NAME: *ROYAL GRAMMA*

This spectacular fish lives in the shallow waters and caves of the Caribbean. The Royal Gramma's body is two distinct colors; the front-half is a brilliant cerise, pink-violet; the rear-half is an equally brilliant yellow. The junction between the two colors, although quite distinct, is further decorated by some yellow speckles entering into the forward-half. A dark bar, bordered below by gold, slants down through the eyes to the mouth. A dark spot appears in the front rays of the long-based dorsal fin. The pectoral and the long and trailing pelvic fins are the same color as the front of the body. The majority of the dorsal fin is similarly colored, although the rear is yellow. Some of its physical characteristics are not dissimilar to those of the Yellow-Headed Jawfish (*Opisthognathus aurifrons*) and there has been some speculation as to how close, scientifically speaking, these two genera might be. The Two-Colour Dottyback, *Pseudochromis paccagnellae*, is a lookalike species but it has a faint white line between the two colored halves of the body and lacks the dark spot in the dorsal fin.

FEEDING

COMPATIBILITY

EASE OF KEEPING

4

SIZE

3.2 in (8 cm) 2 in (5 cm)

SPECIAL CARE: The aquarium or reef tank should be furnished with many rocky retreats, as this fish usually feels confident when a safe refuge is not too far away. This fish is generally peaceful but it may guard its chosen bolt-hole against other fishes. It is a nest builder and the male guards the eggs.

GRAMMA MELACARA

FAMILY: *GRAMMIDAE*
COMMON NAME: *BLACK-CAP GRAMMA*

The striking coloration comprises a beautiful violet-purple that covers the whole body and is topped off by a black "cap" that runs through the eyes, over the head, and into the top edge of the dorsal fin. Its natural habitat is the shallow waters and caves of the Caribbean.
SPECIAL CARE: Like its relative, the Royal Gramma, this fish is very much at home among crannies, crevices, and caves and can be found swimming at almost any angle, even inverted, as it goes about its aquatic business. The genus as a whole makes an excellent subject for reef tanks, where invertebrates will not be bothered by them. This fish is generally peaceful, but it may be a little territorial to members of its own kind. This fish is a nest builder and the male is responsible for guarding the eggs.

FEEDING

COMPATIBILITY

EASE OF KEEPING

4

SIZE

4 in (10 cm) 3 in (7.5 cm)

PSEUDOCHROMIS ALDEBARENSIS

FEEDING

COMPATIBILITY

EASE OF KEEPING

3

SIZE

2.8 in (7 cm) 2 in (5 cm)

FAMILY: *PSEUDOCHROMIDAE*
COMMON NAME: *NEON DOTTYBACK; PERSIAN DOTTYBACK*

This species is native to the Persian Gulf. Golden brown-yellow provides the basic body color but it emerges from the greenish-brown of the head area around the position of the yellow pectoral fins. The coloring then turns to orange on the caudal peduncle to continue into the caudal fin itself. To complete the fabulous colors of this species, electric blue lines decorate the outside edges of the major single fins. These also run along the sides of the head and the base of the dorsal fin. Throughout much aquarium literature, this species is often described under the name *P. dutoiti*. It prefers the middle and lower levels of the aquarium and, when breeding, the male guards a ball of fertilized eggs.
SPECIAL CARE: The aquarium (or reef tank) should be furnished with plenty of hiding places for this cave-loving species.

CHROMILEPTIS ALTIVELIS

FAMILY: *SERRANIDAE*
COMMON NAME: *POLKA-DOT GROUPER;*
HUMPED ROCK-COD; BARRAMUNDI COD;
KERAPU SONOH; PANTHERFISH

FEEDING

COMPATIBILITY

EASE OF KEEPING

SIZE

20 in (50 cm)   12 in (30 cm)

Basic body coloration is white, covered with numerous black spots; these spots become even more numerous but reduce in individual size with increasing age. The lateral line is arched, keeping clear of any water turbulence created by the pectoral fins. All of the fins are white and are marked with dark spots. The long-based dorsal fin has an obvious "step" halfway along at the beginning of the softer-rayed rear section. The anal fin is rounded, the caudal fin paddle-shaped, and the pectoral fins are large. It is found in the Indian Ocean around the East Indies, the Philippines, and the Queensland coast.
SPECIAL CARE: This species has a stealthy swimming style—head down and slightly sinuous, as it prowls around the aquarium. There should be plenty of hiding places and it will need as much space as you can give it. The water should be well-oxygenated and have efficient filtration and strong water currents. Young specimens usually take to aquarium culture very well. This species is an egg scatterer in the wild but no information on breeding in captivity is available.

EPINEPHALUS SP.

FAMILY: *SERRANIDAE*
COMMON NAME: *GROUPER*

Because Groupers can rapidly and dramatically change both their coloration and color pattern, they can be enormously confusing and difficult for the aquarist to identify. Fortunately, all require essentially the same care and will usually lie in ambush in a preferred spot, dashing out to grab food the moment it hits the water. They are not fussy eaters, and quickly learn to accept all kinds of aquarium foods. Within reason, they are not particularly sensitive to water conditions. The eventual large size and greedy appetite of any Grouper should be considered when planning the aquarium.
SPECIAL CARE: Provide good water conditions and a suitable lair among rocks. Feed with live marine fish of such size and in such quantity as is determined by the size of the specimen. Groupers usually require a species tank, as they may feed on any other fish or mobile invertebrate that is small enough to swallow. Many aquarists have underestimated the Grouper's abilities in this regard and wound up losing a prized fish. Groupers are intelligent and learn to recognize the aquarist.

FEEDING

COMPATIBILITY

EASE OF KEEPING

SIZE

3.3 ft (1 m)   23.6 in (60 cm)

SYMBOL KEY

FEEDING
Herbivore

Omnivore

Predator

COMPATIBILITY
single specimen

community fish

safe with small fish

safe with invertebrates

EASE OF KEEPING
scale of 1 to 10
(with 1 being easiest to keep)

SIZE
in the wild

in captivity

EPINEPHALUS MORIO

FAMILY: *SERRANIDAE*
COMMON NAME: *RED GROUPER*

Sought after by game fishermen as well as aquarium collectors, this is a typical member of the large grouper clan. The body is a uniform golden to tan color with a scattering of white spots. The fins are usually dark gray. Like all groupers, its coloration is variable, and can be altered by the fish at will. It lies in ambush, swallowing small fishes and similar mobile prey whole. It is found, usually near the margins of sea grass beds, from Massachusetts to Brazil.
SPECIAL CARE: This is not really a suitable fish for any but the largest marine tank. Given its rather drab coloration, prodigious appetite, and retiring habits, it is more likely to be exhibited by large public aquariums rather than home hobbyists. On the other hand, if one wants a long-lived pet that needs only a large tank, regular care, and daily feeding to thrive, this may be the species.

FEEDING

COMPATIBILITY

EASE OF KEEPING
1

SIZE
36.2 in (92 cm) 23.6 in (60 cm)

EPINEPHALUS UNDULATOSTRIATUS

FAMILY *SERRANIDAE*
COMMON NAME: *MAORI GROUPER*

This fish has a rather inappropriate name, considering that its natural range is confined to the Great Barrier Reef and the New South Wales areas of Australia, when apparently it ought to have a stronger affinity with New Zealand. The reddish-brown markings that cover the entire body and fins often line up to give an undulating, striated patterning, hence the accurate specific name. The fins have yellow outer margins.
SPECIAL CARE: This large grouper is obviously more suited to public aquariums where it can roam the spacious tanks to its heart's content, but can be kept in a home aquarium as long as it is given the space and proper care that it requires.

FEEDING

COMPATIBILITY

EASE OF KEEPING
4

SIZE
24 in (61 cm) 12 in (30 cm)

HYPOPLECTRUS INDIGO

FAMILY: *SERRANIDAE*
COMMON NAME: *INDIGO HAMLET*

This beautiful sea bass is blue, with a series of vertical white bars that begin behind the eyes. The dorsal, caudal, and anal fins are light blue, the pelvic fins are dark blue, and the pectoral fins are white or colorless. This fish is sparsely distributed through the western Caribbean region, but remains popular with collectors.
SPECIAL CARE: Provide perfect water conditions and plenty of rocks. Hamlets usually accept a wide range of aquarium foods. Since the fish remains small, it is a good candidate for a species tank. Corals and other reef invertebrates, not sought by the fish for food, are usually left alone. Some authorities regard all hamlets as color variants of a single species, *Hypoplectrus unicolor*. Some of the color variants resemble damselfishes, enabling the hamlet to hide within a school of the latter. This permits the hamlet to approach its prey undetected, among the harmless damsels.

FEEDING

COMPATIBILITY

EASE OF KEEPING
3

SIZE
4 in (10 cm) 3.2 in (8 cm)

RYPTICUS MACULATUS

FAMILY: *SERRANIDAE*
COMMON NAME: *WHITESPOTTED SOAPFISH*

Found from Rhode Island to Palm Beach, this is not a truly tropical marine fish. The common name comes from its ability to secrete a toxic substance resembling soapsuds when threatened. The body is a medium brown color, often with a pale area on the snout and pale stripes on the cheeks. White spots, often outlined in black, appear on the body. The fins are lighter brown in color.
SPECIAL CARE: Provide typical marine water conditions and plenty of rocks. Feed small fish, live shrimp, or other seafoods. It is a good candidate for a species tank, and usually adapts quickly to aquarium life. Corals and other sessile invertebrates are usually left alone, but the fish may eat any mobile tank mate small enough to swallow. Expect it to spend most of its time in hiding. This fish is normally inactive and will not be seen constantly swimming around the aquarium.

FEEDING

COMPATIBILITY

EASE OF KEEPING
3

SIZE

8 in (20 cm) 6 in (15 cm)

VARIOLA LOUTI

FAMILY: *SERRANIDAE*
COMMON NAME: *LYRETAIL GROUPER; CORONATION GROUPER*

This colorful Indo-Pacific grouper is a superb choice for a community of larger, more aggressive marine fishes. It selects a suitable hiding place among rocks, where it lies in ambush for small fish or crustaceans that just happen to pass by. The body is pale yellow on the belly, dark brown to black along the midline, and orange on top. Blue polka dots overlay most of the upper three-quarters of the body. The tail fin and dorsal fin carry some blue and reddish pigments, while the remaining fins are colorless.
SPECIAL CARE: This fish is hardy and long-lived, and will eventually need a tank of close to 200 gallons (750 liters) to accommodate it. It is easily fed on shrimp, fish meat, whole marine fish (never goldfish), clams, and so forth. It will also feed on any other fish it can swallow. Provide plenty of filtration to counter its prodigious appetite. As with most groupers, younger individuals are female and mature ones are male.

FEEDING

COMPATIBILITY

EASE OF KEEPING
1

SIZE

35 in (89 cm) 29.5 in (75 cm)

SYMBOL KEY

FEEDING
Herbivore
Omnivore
Predator

COMPATIBILITY
single specimen
community fish
safe with small fish
safe with invertebrates

EASE OF KEEPING
scale of 1 to 10
(with 1 being easiest to keep)

SIZE
in the wild
in captivity

OTHER MARINE SPECIES

Not all marine fishes fit conveniently into the major groups previously described. This has nothing to do with their popularity (or otherwise), but simply that some families do not contain so many individual genera or species. Compared to the previous genera, who, by their very orderliness, may appear quite conventional, each species in this section brings its own particular attraction.

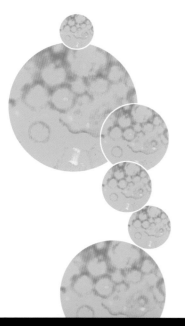

The disparity of body shapes, color patterns, exaggerated finnage, and even living styles all contribute something extra to the marine fishkeeper's enjoyment. From highly-colored sedentary species to

Pterosynchiropus splendidus
MANDARIN FISH

exotically-finned drifters, you will surely find your own particular favorite here. One problem area for those interested in keeping marine fish is breeding, because so little is known for certain of their reproductive behavior, either in captivity or in the wild. Details have been included where possible.

Pterois volitans
LIONFISH

REDSPOTTED HAWKFISH
This fish spends most of its time perching on a rocky outcrop looking out for a passing meal.

APOGON MACULATUS

FAMILY: *APOGONIDAE*
COMMON NAME: *FLAMEFISH*

FEEDING

COMPATIBILITY

EASE OF KEEPING

SIZE

4.3 in (11 cm) 3.2 in (8 cm)

This is one of the more popular imports from Florida and the Caribbean, where it is common in shallow waters. It is nocturnal, spending most of the daylight hours hiding under or among rocks, and coming out into open water at night to feed on small invertebrates and fish fry. It is bright scarlet, with a single dark spot at the base of the second dorsal fin. The eyes which are black, have two white horizontal lines running through them.

SPECIAL CARE: This fish does well in a reef tank, where it can find a suitable hiding place among the decorations. Remember to feed it after the tank lights go out. Good water conditions, nonaggressive tank mates, and a diet of meaty seafoods of appropriate size suit it best. Do not trust it with small fish or shrimps that it can swallow, as it will almost certainly do so. Corals, however, are ignored.

PTERAPOGON KAUDERNI

FAMILY: *APOGONIDAE*
COMMON NAME: *BANGGAI CARDINALFISH; BORNEO OR HIGHFIN CARDINAL*

FEEDING

COMPATIBILITY

EASE OF KEEPING

SIZE

4.9 in (12.5 cm) 2.5 in (6.5 cm)

This very recent introduction to the marine aquarium is quite spectacularly marked. The oval body is creamy-white and crossed vertically by three white-edged, black bands; the first crosses the large eyes, the second and third respectively connect the first dorsal with the pelvic fins, and the second dorsal with the anal fin. This perky species swims with its dorsal fins permanently erect and is an extraordinary sight as it moves around in numbers between the branched coral heads of the western Pacific. This species is a mouthbrooder, with the young growing large enough to feed on brine shrimp, *nauplii*, while in the parent's mouth.

SPECIAL CARE: Because of its enormous popularity and restricted distribution, this fish is now considered of special concern in its native habitat. Aquarists should obtain only hatchery produced specimens, which are becoming more widely available.

SPHAERAMIA NEMATOPTERA

FAMILY: *APOGONIDAE*
COMMON NAME: *PAJAMA CARDINALFISH*

FEEDING

COMPATIBILITY

EASE OF KEEPING

SIZE

3.2 in (8 cm) 2.5 in (6.5 cm)

The Pajama Cardinalfish has a stocky body with a relatively long caudal peduncle. Its body coloration and patterning appears haphazard, as though it belongs to several different species. The basic ground color is purplish-gray; rearward of a dividing line between the two separate dorsal fins, the body is covered with equally-spaced large red-brown spots. From beneath the first dorsal fin a dark band runs vertically down to the pelvic fins; ahead of this band the large yellowish head is unpatterned but the large red eyes have a dark center. The caudal fin has rounded lobes. It is found in sheltered lagoons among corals and mangrove roots in the Indo-Pacific region.

SPECIAL CARE: This shy species hides during the day among corals or mangrove roots, emerging at dusk to feed, assisted by their large information-gathering eyes. It is reported to be a mouthbrooder, with the male taking on the responsibility for incubating the eggs. May be best kept in a separate species aquarium.

PTEROSYNCHIROPUS SPLENDIDUS

FAMILY: *CALLIONYMIDAE*
COMMON NAME: *MANDARIN FISH*

This stunningly-colored fish has a chunky body with the head outline slightly above the dorsal surface due to the highly-set, slightly protuberant eyes. The background body color is bluish-green-gold with what appears to be a random pattern of wide, scribbled, dark-edged blue-colored lines, bars, and dots that extend into the fins. The eyes are gold and there are some black and light blue lines marking the head and face. The area immediately beneath the eyes is pale and separated from the rest of the body coloration by a horizontal dark line that runs back to the gill cover, which is covered with prominent gold spots. There are two dorsal fins—the first has an elongated first spine (probably an indication of the male) the rearmost being longer-based with a sprinkling of gold dots on its outer rear margin. All fins are dark-edged; the pelvic fins are broad and rounded having some blue markings as does the anal fin. The caudal fin has gold-yellow colored rays. A similar species, *P. picturatus*, is marked with a more blotchy pattern. It is likely to be found in hideaways at the bottom of reefs (or even piers and wharves) in the Indo-Pacific region, including Australia.

SPECIAL CARE: The Mandarin fish should be treated considerately by keeping it in a quiet tank, with plenty of hiding places, away from more boisterous or larger fishes. This species should only be placed in a well-established reef tank with a population of benthic copepods, barely visible as white specks moving about the rocks and coral, as these are its only food. Starvation, resulting from a lack of understanding of its needs, has claimed the lives of too many of these fishes needlessly.

FEEDING

COMPATIBILITY

EASE OF KEEPING
6

SIZE
2.4 in (6 cm) 2 in (5 cm)

CENTRISCUS SP.

FAMILY: *CENTRISCIDAE*
COMMON NAME: *SHRIMPFISH*

Shrimpfishes occur throughout the world. All are elongated and covered with bony plates rather than scales. The soft dorsal, caudal, and anal fins are located underneath and anterior to the spinous dorsal fin. Most specimens are pale, with a single dark horizontal stripe. All Shrimpfishes swim in a head down position, usually among the spines of a sea urchin or the branches of an Acroporid coral. The tiny, terminal mouth is used to pluck planktonic invertebrates from the water column.

SPECIAL CARE: Provide perfect water conditions and plenty of rocks, together with the appropriate host (urchin or coral) with which the fish associates. Feed small, live invertebrates such as cultured brine shrimp, *nauplii*, or a similar plankton substitute. Since the fish remains small, it is a good candidate for a species tank. Corals and other reef invertebrates capable of stinging are left alone. Don't keep with boisterous fish. A group of Shrimpfishes will usually stay together around a single coral head or large urchin.

FEEDING

COMPATIBILITY

EASE OF KEEPING
8

SIZE
6 in (15 cm) 4 in (10 cm)

SYMBOL KEY

FEEDING
Herbivore

Omnivore

Predator

COMPATIBILITY
single specimen

community fish

safe with small fish

safe with invertebrates

EASE OF KEEPING
scale of 1 to 10
(with 1 being easiest to keep)

SIZE
in the wild

in captivity

AMBLYCIRRHITES PINOS

FEEDING

COMPATIBILITY

EASE OF KEEPING

2

SIZE

4 in (10 cm) 3.2 in (8 cm)

FAMILY: *CIRRHITIDAE*
COMMON NAME: *REDSPOTTED HAWKFISH*

Hawkfishes have the amusing habit of perching on a rock as if surveying the passing scene. From the perch, the fish darts out to snatch small invertebrates that form the basis of its diet. This species is pale, with dark vertical bars, alternately narrow and wide, along the body, ending at the caudal peduncle. The entire body is overlain with tiny red dots The fins are white to colorless, and the dorsal fin spines are tipped with "tassels." It lives on coral reefs throughout Florida, the Caribbean, and the Gulf of Mexico.
SPECIAL CARE: Provide typical marine tank water conditions and plenty of rocks with algae and invertebrates. Feed any of the typical aquarium foods, such as frozen brine shrimp. Since the fish remains small, it is a good candidate for a reef tank. Corals and other reef invertebrates are left alone; only small shrimps or worms are at risk.

CIRRHITES FASCIATUS

FAMILY: *CIRRHITIDAE*
COMMON NAME: *RED BARRED HAWKFISH*

The body of this Hawaiian species is white, with a pattern of red lines on the face. Beginning at the gill cover, five vertical red bars mark the body, ending on the caudal peduncle. The paired fins are pale to colorless, with red rays on the dorsal fin and the characteristic "fringe" at the tips of the first dorsal spines, found in all members of this family, also in red. There is some red on the pectorals and the caudal fin, as well.
SPECIAL CARE: Hawkfishes like to perch atop a prominence, surveying all below, and snatching small organisms from the water. Therefore they are easy to feed, and adapt to the commonly available, meaty seafoods that all marine shops stock. Typical marine water quality parameters are acceptable, and hawkfishes thrive in reef tanks. While these hawkfishes pose no threat to corals or other sessile invertebrates, they cannot be trusted with small shrimps or fish small enough for them to eat.

FEEDING

COMPATIBILITY

EASE OF KEEPING

3

SIZE

4 in (10 cm) 4 in (10 cm)

NEOCIRRHITES ARMATUS

FAMILY: *CIRRHITIDAE*
COMMON NAME: *FLAME HAWKFISH*

The highly arched body of this fish is bright scarlet with only a dark margin appearing along the base of the long-based dorsal fin. The dark eyes are set high up on the steeply-sloping forehead. All of the fins are scarlet in color. Flame Hawkfish can be found in the Pacific Ocean, from the Philippines to Samoa, and the Ryuku Islands to New Caledonia. It is thought that this fish is an egg scatterer, spawning after dusk.
SPECIAL CARE: Hawkfish require plenty of perching places as they act out a rather sedentary lifestyle, only dashing out to grab food as it passes by. It requires a well-oxygenated aquarium furnished with rock and coral outcrops. Although it has a generally peaceful demeanor, the inclusion of other hawkfish species in the same aquarium may lead to quarrels; small fish and small invertebrates may be at risk.

FEEDING

COMPATIBILITY

EASE OF KEEPING

4

SIZE

3.5 in (9 cm) 2.5 in (6.5 cm)

OXYCIRRHITES TYPUS

FAMILY: *CIRRHITIDAE*
COMMON NAME: *LONGNOSED HAWKFISH*

This fish is native to the relatively deep waters of the Indo-Pacific region including the coastal waters of California. It has an elongated body with a relatively deep mid-section with the dorsal surface contour rising fairly sharply past the eye. The ventral surface has a definite convex curve but not to the same extent. It is marked with a bright red square pattern over a white background. The deep section of the body is balanced by a narrow caudal peduncle and a very long snout. The dorsal fin is spiky and usually held erect. All of its fins are whitish speckled with red.

SPECIAL CARE: Not an accomplished swimmer, this species sits on a convenient piece of coral or rock on the seabed waiting for food to pass by, so its natural habitat should be recreated in the aquarium. It appreciates small forms of food, living brine shrimp, etc., but may take manufactured foods provided they come within its reach. Although generally peaceful, it is not wise to keep this hawkfish with small fishes. Confusion exists as to whether wild fishes are egg scatterers or egg depositors. No information is available on captive breeding.

FEEDING

COMPATIBILITY

EASE OF KEEPING

4

SIZE

4.9 in (12.5 cm) 4 in (10 cm)

CHAETODIPTERUS FABER

FAMILY: *EPHIPPIDAE*
COMMON NAME: *ATLANTIC SPADEFISH*

The silvery body is marked by a series of five or six vertical bars, one of which extends to the leading edges of the dorsal and anal fins. The shape of its body is almost like an elongated disc. It can be found from Massachusetts to Brazil and in the Caribbean region. It is considered a desirable sport fish.

SPECIAL CARE: Provide good water conditions and a large tank. The fish hunts its food in open water, and has a voracious appetite. Several specimens can be kept together, as it is usually found in small aggregations. Small fish, live shrimps, and various other foods should be offered. Although it is seldom exhibited by home aquarists, owing to its need for plenty of space and a tank relatively bare of decoration, it is easily maintained, according to professional aquarists.

FEEDING

COMPATIBILITY

EASE OF KEEPING

5

SIZE

3.3 ft (1 m) 27.5 in (70 cm)

HOLOCENTRUS CORUSCUS

FAMILY: *HOLOCENTRIDAE*
COMMON NAME: *REEF SQUIRRELFISH*

Like other members of its family, it is reddish in color, bearing distinct white lines running lengthwise from the gill cover to the caudal peduncle. There is a black blotch on the first three or four dorsal fin spines, and each spine of the otherwise bright red dorsal fin is tipped in pure white. The paired fins are colorless. The large eyes are also characteristic, and indicate that the fish is a nocturnal predator. Although uncommon, the Reef Squirrelfish inhabits the waters throughout Florida and the Caribbean.

SPECIAL CARE: Provide typical marine water conditions and a suitable place for the fish to spend the day. Squirrelfish usually adapt readily to common aquarium foods, such as frozen brine shrimp or chopped shellfish. Corals and other reef invertebrates capable of stinging are usually left alone, but never trust a squirrelfish with any mobile creature it might swallow.

FEEDING

COMPATIBILITY

EASE OF KEEPING
2

SIZE

5 in (13 cm) 4 in (10 cm)

ANISOTREMUS VIRGINICUS

FAMILY: *HAEMULIDAE*
COMMON NAME: *PORKFISH*

Aquarists will most often see juveniles of this grunt, which is quite common in the Florida Keys. The body is white, with lemon yellow coloring on the head and back. The dorsal fin is yellow, as are the pelvics. The anal, caudal, pectoral, and soft dorsal fins are colorless. There is a single black dot on the caudal peduncle, and a pair of horizontal black lines run from the eyes to the tail. In adults, the fins are all yellow, a black bar runs vertically through the eyes, and another bar marks the rear margin of the gill cover.

SPECIAL CARE: This fish is sometimes found in large schools over reefs. It adapts well to the aquarium, but can become too large for some home tanks. Provide typical marine water quality, and a varied diet of meaty seafoods. Small fish, shrimps, and worms are likely to be eaten, but corals will be ignored.

FEEDING

COMPATIBILITY

EASE OF KEEPING
3

SIZE

14 in (36 cm) 8 in (20 cm)

HOLOCENTRUS RUFUS

FAMILY: *HOLOCENTRIDAE*
COMMON NAME: *LONGSPINE SQUIRRELFISH*

Squirrelfishes are nocturnal, spending the daylight hours resting under a rock ledge or in a crevice. Most are reddish in color, with vague white lines running lengthwise from the gill cover to the caudal peduncle. This species can be recognized by the particularly elongated dorsal fin spines, each tipped with a pure white triangle. The pectoral fins are edged in white, as well. Its large eyes aid in capturing prey at night. It is common in Florida, the Bahamas, and the Caribbean.

SPECIAL CARE: Provide typical marine water conditions and a suitable place for the fish to spend the day. Squirrelfish usually adapt readily to common aquarium foods, such as frozen brine shrimp or chopped shellfish. Corals and other reef invertebrates capable of stinging are usually left alone, but never trust a squirrelfish with any mobile creature it might swallow.

FEEDING

COMPATIBILITY

EASE OF KEEPING
2

SIZE

10 in (25 cm) 6 in (15 cm)

OGOCEPHALUS NASUTUS

FAMILY: *OGOCEPHALIDAE*
COMMON NAME: *SHORTNOSE BATFISH*

Sometimes called the "walking" batfish because of the stout paired fins that elevate the fish above the bottom, these fishes are for the hobbyist with a taste for the unusual. Relying on camouflage coloration, which is usually a blotched mixture of gray and chalk, it lies in wait, ready to lunge forward when a small fish or shrimp approaches, swallowing its prey whole. The elongated snout distinguishes this species from its relatives in waters from the Gulf of Mexico to Brazil. It is not particularly common. **SPECIAL CARE:** Provide typical marine tank water conditions. Feed small, live invertebrates until the fish are thoroughly accepting of aquarium foods. Corals and other sessile invertebrates are left alone. Feed small, live marine fish or crustaceans only. The fish sometimes learns to accept nonliving foods, if offered by a patient aquarist. This species is best exhibited by itself in a tank chosen to accommodate its large size and specialized lifestyle.

FEEDING

COMPATIBILITY

EASE OF KEEPING
5

SIZE
12 in (30 cm) 8 in (20 cm)

MYRIPRISTIS BARBONICUS

FAMILY: *HOLOCENTRIDAE*
COMMON NAME: *SQUIRRELFISH*

This fish has an elongated body with equally-curved dorsal and ventral surfaces. It is pale pink in color with red markings along the dorsal and ventral surfaces. The scales are dark edged and show up clearly. A dark vertical area appears behind the rear edge of the gill cover. There are two dorsal fins; the first is long-based and spiny, the second is triangular in shape and consists of softer tissues. The anal fin is small and set well back on the body. The pelvic fins are red and white and the caudal fin is pinkish with red markings at the top and bottom edges. The squirrelfishes' large eyes inspired the alternative popular names of Big-eye or Blotch-eye. This genus lacks the spines on the gill covers found in *Holocentrus*. The Squirrelfish is commonly found around reefs from East Africa to Tahiti, in both the Indian and Pacific Oceans.

SPECIAL CARE: This fish swims at all levels of the aquarium. The tank should have plenty of retreats and coral outcrops. This fish is active at night and will eat small fishes and crustaceans.

FEEDING

COMPATIBILITY

EASE OF KEEPING
4

SIZE
12 in (30 cm) 4 in (10 cm)

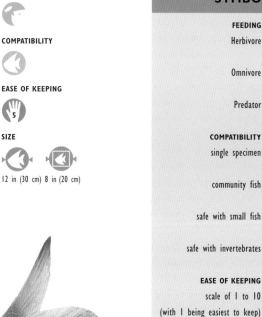

SYMBOL KEY

FEEDING
Herbivore

Omnivore

Predator

COMPATIBILITY
single specimen

community fish

safe with small fish

safe with invertebrates

EASE OF KEEPING
scale of 1 to 10
(with 1 being easiest to keep)

SIZE
in the wild

in captivity

OPISTHOGNATHUS AURIFRONS

FAMILY: *OPISTHOGNATHIDAE*
COMMON NAME: *YELLOW-FACED JAWFISH*

FEEDING

COMPATIBILITY

EASE OF KEEPING
4

SIZE
4 in (10 cm) 3 in (7.5 cm)

The Yellow-faced Jawfish is a mouthbrooder that can be found in the western tropical Atlantic. It has a very elongated body with a prominent, broad head. Its body is pale creamy-gray in color with the front part of the head a bright yellow; toward the rear of the body a bluish overcast occurs. Its large eyes are set well forward; the eye has a tear shaped pupil giving the fish a permanently sad expression. The mouth is relatively large and the gill opening is set quite a distance back. All of the single fins are rounded and are bright pastel blue. The pelvic fins are blue, although the first few rays are white. The pectoral fins are almost colorless. This fish has a rather ungainly swimming action, often hovering vertically just above the substrate. There are no perceivable differences between the sexes.
SPECIAL CARE: A rather shy species that generally resides in a burrow built in the substrate (which should be deep enough to accommodate the burrow) with only its yellow head protruding. This fish will dash out for food and re-enter the burrow, tail first, just as quickly. It may jump when frightened, especially when newly introduced, so ensure that the hood is secure. It is generally peaceful and may be evicted from its burrow by other cave dwelling types such as *Gramma loreto*. It is most suited to a reef tank or a species aquarium.

PLATAX ORBICULARIS

FAMILY: *PLATACIDAE*
COMMON NAME: *BATFISH*

FEEDING

COMPATIBILITY

EASE OF KEEPING
7

SIZE
22.4 in (57 cm) 4 in (10 cm)

As a juvenile this fish has a very tall body that fills out to form a disc shape with adulthood. The body color is usually reddish-brown in young specimens, with a darker stripe toward the head, but the stripe may fade with increasing age. Its forehead rises very steeply from the snout and the dark-centered red eyes are high set. The dark dorsal and anal fins are very long-based and tall, almost encircling the body. The pelvic fins are also long. This fish will scavenge around pilings and piers in the wild, especially after dusk. This fish is found among the seaweeds and corals of the shallow, coastal waters throughout the Indo-Pacific region but not as far as Hawaii or the eastern Pacific. Due to its wide distribution and varying colors from juvenile to adult, some confusion creeps into its exact taxonomic classification.
SPECIAL CARE: A constantly hungry species, the Batfish grows quickly in the aquarium and so needs ample space and deep water.

EQUETUS ACUMINATUS

FEEDING

COMPATIBILITY

EASE OF KEEPING
8

SIZE
10 in (25 cm) 6 in (15 cm)

FAMILY: *SCIAENIDAE*
COMMON NAME: *HIGH HAT*

Reef drums are most often collected as juveniles, when the body is white with three longitudinal black stripes, and a remarkably long, white dorsal fin with a black spot about halfway along its outer edge. The stripes extend to the caudal fin, and the paired fins are also striped in black and white. As the fish matures, the dorsal fin becomes shorter, and the body and fins gradually become a dark gray color, retaining the stripes only on the sides. Despite their amusing behavior and attractive coloration, this fish is often a challenging aquarium subject.
SPECIAL CARE: Provide perfect water conditions and hiding places for this shy, secretive species. Feed small, live invertebrates, as the fish are often difficult to acclimate to typical aquarium foods. Because of its specialized needs, it is a good candidate for a species tank.

EQUETUS LANCEOLATUS

FAMILY: *SCIANEIDAE*
COMMON NAME: *JACKNIFE FISH*

The reef drums retain popularity, despite being a challenge to keep. This one is pure white, with a black bar through the eye, another across the posterior edge of the gill cover, and a dramatic, sickle shaped one that extends from the lower element of the caudal fin to the tip of the dorsal. The elongated tip of the dorsal fin, and the black sickle produce the effect of an open jacknife. Juveniles are yellow, rather than white, but never lack the black bars.
SPECIAL CARE: Provide plenty of live foods at first, as this species is timid and difficult to acclimate to aquarium conditions. It is best given a tank to itself, with good water quality, ample filtration, and plenty of hiding places. It is a secretive species that lives hidden in secluded parts of the reef, emerging only at night to feed. Respecting this behavior in the aquarium is the most likely route to keeping it successfully.

FEEDING

COMPATIBILITY

EASE OF KEEPING

8

SIZE

9 in (23 cm) 6 in (15 cm)

PTEROIS RADIATA

FAMILY: *SCORPAENIDAE*
COMMON NAME: *WHITE-FIN LIONFISH*

This fish has a very stockily-built body, a fact that is often hidden by the surrounding array of fins. Its body coloration is deep reddish-brown with the exception of the head region, forward and below the eyes, which is whitish-pink. The body is crossed by a number of narrow white lines that branch out at their uppermost and extend into the extended front spiny rays of the two-part dorsal fin and into horny extensions above the eyes; the lower ends extend into the pelvic and pectoral fins. The decorated pectoral fins are very well-produced with the first white-edged few rays lacking tissue between them. The softer rear section of the dorsal fin, the anal, and caudal fin are slightly colored with a few lighter colored speckles. The White-fin Lionfish is found in the wild in the Red Sea and the Indo-Pacific region.
SPECIAL CARE: Like all members of the genus, this species lies in wait for its prey which is easily engulfed in the large mouth. The spines are venomous and this fish should be handled extemely carefully. It should be kept in a spacious aquarium with plenty of retreats.

FEEDING

COMPATIBILITY

EASE OF KEEPING

6

SIZE

9.4 in (24 cm) 4.9 in (12.5 cm)

SYMBOL KEY

FEEDING
Herbivore

Omnivore

Predator

COMPATIBILITY
single specimen

community fish

safe with small fish

safe with invertebrates

EASE OF KEEPING
scale of 1 to 10
(with 1 being easiest to keep)

SIZE
in the wild

in captivity

PTEROIS VOLITANS

FAMILY: *SCORPAENIDAE*
COMMON NAME: *LIONFISH*

Everything about this fish is threatening from its deep-set body with menacing fins to the expression on its face. The white body is crossed vertically by a succession of alternating narrow and thick deep brown-red bars. The similarly colored eyes are well hidden within this patterning. There is a pair of "horns" on the head. Its mouth is very large and may have extra barbel-like growths. The fin structure is a combination of single rays and very fine tissues: the first few rays of the dorsal fin are colored alternate white and brown-red, are spiny, well separated, and are very poisonous. The rear part is more conventional in structure and carries dark spots. The pelvic fins are similarly structured and colored. The rounded caudal and anal fins carry a pattern of dots. For the majority of the time it swims in a very languid manner, but it is capable of very swift movements when a suitable meal happens to pass by. The Lionfish is very common among the coral reefs of the Red Sea and the Indian and Pacific Oceans.

SPECIAL CARE: The attraction of this species is immediate, but it should only be kept by an experienced aquarist, as it must be handled with extreme caution. The venom in the fin-rays is just short of being lethal (providing instant medical assistance is on hand). It is long-lived and makes a superb aquarium subject but it must be provided with the right environment—a spacious aquarium with plenty of retreats and suitable amounts of living or dead meaty foods.

FEEDING

COMPATIBILITY

EASE OF KEEPING
6

SIZE
15 in (38 cm) 8 in (20 cm)

SPHYRAENA BARRACUDA

FAMILY: *SPHYRAENIDAE*
COMMON NAME: *BARRACUDA*

Famous for its supposed danger to humans, an actual unprovoked attack by this fish has never been recorded. Suitable only for the aquarist able to provide for its demands, it is a large silvery fish with a torpedo-like shape, great agility, and long, sharp teeth. The body is usually, but not always, marked with black blotches. It is found in almost all tropical waters, and ranges, in the Atlantic region, from Massachusetts to Brazil.

SPECIAL CARE: Requires an aquarium of at least 10 feet (3 meters) in length to accommodate its eventual size of around 6 feet (1.8 meters). It feeds exclusively on other fish, which it attacks in open water, depending upon its superior speed and agility to effect a kill. The powerful jaws and canine teeth of a large specimen are capable of severing a human hand at the wrist. This fish is definitely not a suitable choice for any but the most specialized aquarium tended by an expert aquarist.

FEEDING

COMPATIBILITY

EASE OF KEEPING
9

SIZE
6.6 ft (2 m) 6.6 ft (2 m)

HIPPOCAMPUS ERECTUS

FAMILY: *SYNGNATHIDAE*
COMMON NAME: *GIANT ATLANTIC SEAHORSE*

Seahorses never fail to attract attention, but unfortunately they are often challenging to maintain in a home aquarium. This tropical Atlantic representative is one of some 30 worldwide species, all of which live among sea grasses and feed on small crustaceans and fish larvae. This one reaches an enormous size; most other seahorses are only half as large. Its coloring is quite variable, but usually consists of mottled brown or dark gray. Male seahorses become pregnant after an elaborate courtship ritual, and mate for life. All species of seahorses are considered of special concern because of threats to their survival in the wild.

SPECIAL CARE: Apart from appropriate water conditions and suitable décor that mimics its sea grass habitat, the primary requirement in keeping seahorses is providing abundant supplies of the correct types of living foods. Complicating matters is the observation that the dietary requirements may change as the fish matures. So far, a complete protocol for maintaining captive seahorses through an entire life cycle has yet to be published in scientific literature.

FEEDING

COMPATIBILITY

EASE OF KEEPING
9

SIZE

6 in (15 cm) 6 in (15 cm)

PRIONOTUS OPHYRAS

FAMILY: *TRIGILIDAE*
COMMON NAME: *SEA ROBIN*

This remarkable fish actually "walks" on the elongated spines of its ventral fins. Divers have also observed them using its fin spines to overturn rubble in search of food. Generally mottled gray or reddish-brown, to match the bottom over which it forages, these fish are uncommon, but are found wherever sea grass occurs, from North Carolina to the Caribbean. They move slowly and deliberately through the vegetation, feeding on small invertebrates.

SPECIAL CARE: Provide typical marine water conditions and décor that mimics the sea grass habitat, either with artificial or living plants and a bottom of sand, shell fragments, and coral pieces. Feed with small live shrimps, clamworms, and bait fish. Offer chopped shellfish, shrimp, or fish meat when the fish becomes accustomed to captivity. This is a poorly understood family, owing largely to their secretive behavior and the fact that they live hidden among sea grasses.

FEEDING

COMPATIBILITY

EASE OF KEEPING
5

SIZE

6 in (15 cm) 4 in (10 cm)

SYMBOL KEY

FEEDING

Herbivore

Omnivore

Predator

COMPATIBILITY

single specimen

community fish

safe with small fish

safe with invertebrates

EASE OF KEEPING

scale of 1 to 10
(with 1 being easiest to keep)

SIZE

in the wild

in captivity

GLOSSARY

ACIDIC Referring to a solution with a pH less than 7.

ADIPOSE FIN Small extra fin between the main dorsal and caudal fins of some fishes.

AERATION Process of adding extra air into the aquarium water.

AEROBIC Requiring oxygen.

AIRPUMP A small electrically-driven vibrating diaphragm device used to pump air into the aquarium.

AIRSTONE Device for splitting the air flow from the airpump into small bubbles.

ALGAE Tiny, unicellular plants that may coat aquatic plants or cause a green cloudiness in the water.

ALKALINE Referring to a solution with a pH greater than 7.

ANAL FIN Single vertical fin beneath the rear of the body.

ANABANTID Family of fishes with an auxiliary breathing organ that enables them to utilize atmospheric air.

ANAEROBIC Not requiring oxygen.

BARBELS Elongate "whiskers" around the mouth of some fishes, having a sensory function.

BIOLOGICAL FILTRATION Water purifying method that uses bacteria to remove dissolved toxic substances.

BRACKISH Mixture of fresh and salt water; estuarine conditions.

BRINE SHRIMP *Artemia salina*, shrimp whose eggs can be hatched to make excellent first food for fry.

CARBON Filtration medium that adsorbs dissolved material from the water.

CAUDAL FIN Fin at the rear of the body.

CAUDAL PEDUNCLE Rear part of the body, just in front of the caudal fin.

CHROMATOPHORES Color cells.

COLDWATER Generally refers to fishes kept under ambient temperatures, without additional heating, i.e., goldfish.

CONDITIONING Separating the sexes and feeding with high quality foods prior to spawning.

COVER GLASS Sheet of plastic or glass on top of the tank to protect lighting equipment from spray damage and to prevent fishes from jumping out.

DEMERSAL Heavier than water.

DIFFUSER See *airstone*.

DORSAL (fin) Usually a single fin (some species have two), on the top surface of the fish.

EGG LAYER Fish whose eggs are fertilized and hatched externally.

FAMILY Group containing several genera. See *genus*.

FANCY GOLDFISH Aquarium-developed strains or varieties from *Carassius auratus*.

FILTER Device for removing suspended or dissolved wastes from aquarium water.

FILTER MEDIUM Any material used as a trapping, straining, absorptive, or bacterial-colonizing device in a filter system.

FINS External paddle-shaped growths, either single or paired, extending from the body of a fish.

FOAM FRACTIONATION Definition of protein skimming process. See *protein skimmer*.

FRY Recently hatched fish that have not absorbed the yolk sac.

GENUS A group of related species within a family.

GILLS Organ by which fish extract dissolved oxygen from the water.

GONOPODIUM Modified anal fin of male livebearing fishes.

GRAVEL NET Plastic netting buried horizontally in the substrate to prevent fishes from digging.

GRAVID Describing female livebearer when carrying young, i.e. pregnant.

GUANIN Crystals of urea deposited beneath the skin providing an iridescent sheen.

HAND-STRIPPING The manual removal of eggs from a female, and milt from a male fish. Practiced in the breeding of Fancy Goldfish and certain marine species.

HARDNESS Condition of water due to dissolved salts.

HOOD Lid of aquarium containing lighting equipment.

LATERAL LINE Row of pierced scales along flanks giving access to nervous system that detects vibrations in the surrounding water.

LENGTH Measured from the snout to end of caudal peduncle, excluding caudal fin.

LIVEBEARER Fishes whose eggs are fertilized and developed internally within the body of the parent, either with or without nourishment from parent.

MARINE Pertaining to the sea; saltwater.

MEDIUM Any material used to filter or treat water.

MILT Fertilizing fluid of male fish.

MOUTHBROODER Incubation of externally fertilized eggs occurs within one parent's throat cavity.

NITROBACTER Nitrifying bacteria turning nitrite into nitrate.

NITROSOMONAS Nitrifying bacteria turning ammonia-based compounds into nitrite.

OPERCULUM Gill cover.

OSMOREGULATION Method by which a fish regulates, or balances, its internal salt content against that of the surrounding water.

OVIPAROUS See *egg layer*.

OVIPOSITOR Tube for depositing eggs, extended at breeding times by the female of egg depositing fishes.

OVOVIVIPAROUS Livebearing with no nourishment gained from parent. See *livebearer*.

OZONE Triatomic oxygen used in water purification.

PECTORALS Paired fins, one on each side of the body, posterior to the gills.

PELAGIC Lighter than water; used in reference to drifting fertilized eggs after spawning.

PELVIC Paired fins, just ahead of the anal fin.

PH Measure, on a logarithmic scale, of acidity or alkalinity of a solution.

PHARYNGEAL TEETH Teeth in the throat of cyprinid species.

PHOTOSYNTHESIS Process by which, under illumination, green plants utilize carbon dioxide and nutrients to build sugars and starches, and give off surplus oxygen.

POWER FILTER Filtration equipment powered by electric impeller.

POWERHEAD Electric impeller fitted to top of return tube from undergravel filtration systems.

PROTEIN SKIMMER Device to remove dissolved organic substances from the water in marine aquariums.

QUARANTINE Period of isolation for new fish to prevent the introduction of disease into the aquarium.

RAYS Tissue-supporting bones in fins.

REFLECTOR See *hood*.

SALT Sodium chloride or, in marine systems, synthetic salt mix used to make artificial seawater.

SCALES Small platelets covering the fish's skin.

SCUTES Bony plates (in the place of scales) covering the fish's skin, especially in some catfishes.

SHOAL Large number of a single species of fish swimming together.

SINGLE-TAILS Goldfish that have only a single anal and caudal fin.

SOFT Condition of water due to lack of dissolved salts.

SPAWNING The reproductive action of fish.

SPAWNING TANK A separate aquarium for housing a breeding pair (or shoal) of adult fishes.

SPECIES Groups of actually (or potentially) interbreeding individuals, that do not interbreed with members of other, similar groups.

SPECIFIC GRAVITY (S.G.) Ratio of densities between salt and fresh water. Used to determine the strength of synthetic seawater in marine systems.

STRAIN Aquarium-developed variant, e.g., longer-finned than, or differently colored from, a natural species.

SUBSTRATE Material covering the aquarium tank floor.

SWIM BLADDER Internal organ that provides neutral buoyancy.

TUBERCLES Small white pimples seen on the head and/or gill covers of many male coldwater cyprinids when spawning.

TWIN-TAILS Goldfish that have divided anal and caudal fins.

ULTRA-VIOLET (UV) LAMPS Special lamps for disinfecting water.

UNDERGRAVEL FILTRATION See *biological filtration*.

VENTRAL Pertaining to the underside of the body; may be used in the plural form to refer to ventral fins.

VIVIPAROUS Livebearing with nourishment gained from parent. See *livebearer*.

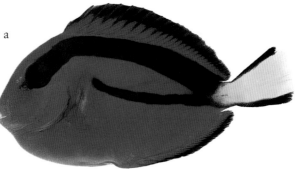

INDEX
OF SCIENTIFIC NAMES

INDEX OF COMMON NAMES

CREDITS

Quarto would like to thank and
acknowledge the following for supplying
pictures reproduced in this book:

Key: l left, r right, c center, t top,
b bottom

Heather Angel: p10br; p12tr (Photo: Ian Took);
p13c (Photo: Ian Took); p21tc&c p24b; p50b;
p70b; p92b; p100b; p116b; p130b; p138b;
p190b
The Art Archive: p8br
Biofotos: p150b (Photo: Ian Took); p158b
(Photo: Keith Sagar); p166b (Photo: Ian Took);
p176b (Photo: Soames Summerhavs); p200b
(Photo: Soames Summerhavs); p206b (Photo:
Ian Took)
Dick Mills: p12bl,tr&cr; p59br; p172b; p184b;
p196b
Pictor: p6; p9br

All other photographs and illustrations are
the copyright of Quarto Publishing plc.
While every effort has been made to credit
contributors, Quarto would like to apologize
should there have been any omissions or
errors.

ACKNOWLEDGMENTS

The publisher would like to thank the following
aquariums for allowing us to photograph their
fish:

Miami Aquatics
6830 Simms Street
Hollywood
Florida 33024
USA

Ornamental Fish Distributors Inc.
3802 NW 32nd Avenue
Miami
Florida 33142
USA

Z-Fish International Inc
7405 41st, Number 2
Miami
Florida 33166

USA

Thanks also go to Linda Bowling for her help
and assistance.

AUTHOR'S ACKNOWLEDGMENTS

I am particularly indebted to two important
people for their major contribution in bringing
this work to fruition:

Paul Forrester, our photographer, rose to the
almost impossible challenge of capturing the
fish as completely solo subjects; simply
tracking down the species might be
considered difficult enough but to ensure that
most of them presented their best colors and
poses took time and endless patience.

John Tullock must take a bow for his
constructive suggestions of species more
pertinent to American hobbyists and for his
direct contribution of many species
descriptions. John has a deserved reputation
for being a very knowledgeable and
conscientious fishkeeper, well-versed in
modern attitudes. Without him, this
encyclopedia would not truly reflect
international practices and I thank him most
sincerely for his forbearance and
supportiveness.

Consultant Editor's Acknowledgments

Having used and enjoyed Dick Mills'
aquarium books for years, I leapt at the
opportunity to work on this project. This
encyclopedia with its comprehensive
coverge of the most popular, hardy, and
readily-available species, each one depicted
in full-color, amply satisfies the need for a
convenient reference. It will remain a
standard for many years to come.

It is hard to imagine a better group of people
to work with than Dick, photographer Paul
Forrester, and the editors at Quarto. I can only
hope hobbyists who use this book have as
much fun with their aquariums as I have
enjoyed through my small part in its creation.